REACH FOR THE SKY

REACH FOR THE SKY

PAUL BRICKHILL

CASSELL

Cassell Military Paperbacks

Cassell
Wellington House, 125 Strand
London WC2R 0BB

First published in Great Britain by William Collins &
Sons 1954
This Paperback edition published in 2004

5 7 9 10 8 6 4

A CIP catalogue record for this book is available
from the British Library

ISBN-13 : 978-0-3043-5674-4
ISBN-10: 0-3043-5674-3

Printed and bound in Great Britain by Cox & Wyman Ltd.,
Reading, Berks.

The Orion Publishing group's policy is to use papers that are
natural, renewable and recyclable products and made from wood
grown in sustainable forests. The logging and manufacturing
processes are expected to conform to the environmental regulations
of the country of origin.

www.orionbooks.co.uk

To Thelma

ILLUSTRATIONS

1

IN 1909 the doctor warned Jessie Bader during her second pregnancy that the baby might not be born alive and that it would be risky for her to go ahead with it, but, rather imperiously, she resisted any interference. A tall and strikingly attractive girl of twenty with a cloud of black hair piled in thick Edwardian waves, Mrs. Bader was sometimes emotional and generally wilful.

Frederick Bader[1] brought his young wife and the other baby, Frederick, or 'Derick, home to England from India on furlough for the birth and they took a house at St. John's Wood. The doctor and midwife arrived on 21st February, 1910, and Frederick Bader walked restlessly round the house. Jessie's sister, Hazel, and the German nursemaid waited hours outside the bedroom door until a thin but persistent cry broke the quiet; a little later the door opened and the doctor came out with the pleased look of a family G.P. who has seen his friends through a crisis.

" The little trouble-maker has arrived," he said benignly. " It's a boy." The squalling kept sounding through the door and the doctor observed that the " little trouble-maker " seemed to have a talent for expressing himself forcibly. (The doctor is not alive now to marvel at the unwitting accuracy of his foresight.)

They christened the baby Douglas Robert Steuart; and the " Steuart," from his maternal great-grandfather, was not all that the baby inherited from the intractable John Steuart Amos, who drove to the Liverpool docks in the family carriage one day in the 1840's, got out pulling a kitbag after him, and told the coachman, " You may tell the family I will not be returning." He walked on board a windjammer, talked himself into a job as ship's carpenter (though he knew nothing

[1] Pronounced Bahder.

9

about either ships or carpentry) and worked his passage to India.

Ambition fortified his unruly spirit and in a few years John Amos was an officer in the Indian Naval Service. A photograph shows his character: within a fringe of crisp, black beard, large eyes with a bold dominating stare, and thin, straight lips clamped together. Not the face of a compromiser. He married, and later appalled his family of daughters by telling them how he watched the ringleaders of the Mutiny lashed across the cannon's mouth and blown out of this world. A detached hand flying through the air slapped him across the face and (he told the shuddering girls) dropped into his pocket.

His eldest daughter, Jessie, was least appalled by the story. She had her father's bold eyes and tight mouth and was impervious to fear. In the eighties she married a gentle engineer in India called McKenzie, and they had two daughters, Jessie and Hazel. Mr. McKenzie died then, and his wife brought up the two girls with a resourceful hand. They lived at Kotri, in the troublesome north-west (now Pakistan), but having no man in the house did not daunt the formidable Mrs. McKenzie. One night she and the two little girls were woken by a sound downstairs. She handed each terrified child a golf club, shepherded each into a strategic point behind a door and said, " Stand there and if anyone comes past . . . hit him." Then she strode through the house brandishing a niblick and shouting in a menacing voice, " Where are you? Come out at once."

No one came out. The thief, if it was a thief, vanished into the night.

Another time a face appeared at a window in the middle of the night. Mrs. McKenzie swung out of bed and ran, not away, but at the window. The owner of the face ran the other way.

Hazel was not fond of the dark but her mother brushed such fears aside, saying boldly, " I'd walk through a graveyard at midnight." Hazel shuddered. " Have no fear, God is near," said her mother. Hazel wanted to say that that would be all very well if she could see God, but prudently left it unsaid. She was a pretty girl who had inherited her father's gentleness, but it was becoming clear that her sister, Jessie, had inherited the mettle of John Steuart Amos and her mother. She had the large bold eyes, but this time long-lashed, darker and wide-set under arching brows. Her lips were full but had the same compressed look, and the jaw was substantial.

She was seventeen when she met Frederick Roberts Bader at the club which was the usual social centre for the district, and she was eighteen when she married him. He was twenty years older, a gruff, heavily moustached, almost confirmed bachelor captivated by the vital girl. Where Jessie was tall and slim, Frederick Bader was heavy-set, a civil engineer of note with thinning hair and a capacity for expressing himself forcefully (he and his temperamental bride had that in common.) They lived comfortably in the hot, dry plains around Sukkur and Kotri, and a year later the first baby was born. They christened him Frederick and called him 'Derick to distinguish him from his father. Both of them doted on 'Derick and within a year all three were on their way back to England for Jessie to have the second baby.

Three days after Douglas was born in St. John's Wood, both mother and baby caught measles, and as soon as both were better Jessie had to have a major operation. From the start baby and mother were virtually separated. Jessie recovered, though she had no more children, and then the family was due back in India. Douglas was only a few months old; a little young, they thought, for India's climate, so they left him with relatives on the Isle of Man.

He was almost two by the time he was taken out to join the family in Sukkur and that may have been the beginning of the loneliness that has been deep within him ever since. He was a stranger in India, like an affectionate puppy before he has been smacked for wetting the floor. 'Derick had been receiving the attention lavished on an only child and the new boy did not fit in. Their Aunt Hazel, visiting the Sukkur bungalow from Kotri one day, saw Douglas's face covered in little sores. Jessie said 'Derick had been pinching bits of skin off his face. 'Derick at four had vitality from both parents. Douglas, two and a half, was sweet-tempered but subdued.

Six months later, servants were constantly on duty to keep them apart—Douglas had begun fighting back like a tiger. It seemed that he, too, had inherited a bold vigour. From then on he always fought his own battles and never cried if he lost. The only times he cried were when his father and mother and 'Derick went visiting in the car and left him behind, which they often did.

In 1913 his father resigned his job in India to study law, and the family left for England and took a house in Kew, breaking three generations of residence in India. In that twilight year before war came to write an ending and a new beginning to England's ways, the Bader household was adjusting to a life where servants were not so plentiful. Jessie and Frederick still had their matrimonial differences which they aired with vigour, and the two boys, together in the care of one nanny instead of separated by servants, were a handful. Douglas could usually hold his own in scuffles, but when crises had to be resolved by parental judgment 'Derick had an advantage: in Jessie's indulgent eyes he could do little wrong.

Then the war came and Frederick Bader was commissioned in the Royal Engineers and went to France. Douglas, now a spirited five-year-old, was ever ready to show his mother and 'Derick that he was no minor underling, and 'Derick, finding he would leap at any challenge, used to dare him to carry out hazardous or punishable exploits. Never refusing a dare, Douglas came to be considered as much the naughtier of the two. Soon he regarded punishment as an inevitable part of life and so was able to endure it stoically.

One hurtful incident was when a ball bounced over tall, spiked railings into a locked churchyard near Kew Bridge. Dared by 'Derick to climb over the railings, Douglas ran at them and pulled himself to the top, where his foot slipped and his behind was impaled on one of the sharp spikes. White-faced, he hung on with his hands, unable to move. At last the nanny arrived and prised him clear and he walked silently half a mile to the house, gripping her hand with pain. The doctor put eight stitches in his rump without the patient letting out a murmur.

Soon Douglas joined 'Derick at Colet Court, a nearby

prep. school. Their Aunt Hazel was back from India and usually escorted them to and from school in the bus, a series of nightmare journeys which she still remembers vividly as they seldom stopped fighting in their struggle for supremacy. Though 'Derick was spirited, Douglas was even more so, and as he had never enjoyed the same attention, felt he had to assert himself. Yet he only became combative when affairs threatened his *amour propre*. Otherwise he bubbled with life, warm-hearted, impulsive, and insulated against rebuffs.

At Colet Court he had his first fights and they were always with bigger boys. Always the same story: bigger boys expect smaller boys to know their place and Douglas would not be forcibly put there. After a while there were not so many fights because he never lost one, though he fought several bloodstained draws: then the generosity showed because he had a tendency to stop fighting when he had hurt someone.

'Derick went on to prep. school at Temple Grove, near Eastbourne, and there was a little more peace in the house, except during the holidays when 'Derick was home and Douglas was relegated again to second place.

The boys seldom saw their father, who was in the thick of it in France. In 1917 shrapnel wounded Major Bader badly in the head. They could not get all the shrapnel out, but he recovered without home leave and went back into the fighting.

Douglas followed 'Derick to Temple Grove and fairly soon scored his first knock-out. A bigger boy twisted his arm and Douglas clouted him across the face with his free hand. Honour demanded a proper fight, in which the bigger boy rushed at him. Douglas stood his ground, ducked his head, thrust both fists out together, and the boy rammed his chin against them and went down, out cold for several seconds. Thinking he had killed him, Douglas knelt contritely by the body and was most relieved to see the eyelids flicker and open.

Temple Grove was a pleasant old school with plenty of playing fields. The regime quickly drew the new boy into organised games and overnight he seemed to flare up like a Roman candle with eagerness. It was the perfect outlet for his mercurial nature and he literally threw himself into rugger, a gritty and indestructible small boy bouncing up as fast as he was knocked down, which was often. Fast on his feet and fast-thinking, he shone as fly-half, and after the first few games was promoted to more senior teams, finding himself now, as in all his fights, matched against bigger boys. It only made him more determined to hold his own.

In the gym he limbered up on the parallel bars or the horizontal bar, the vaulting horse or in the boxing ring; he would try anything, not just once but till he had mastered it, hating to let anything beat him. Or anyone. People lost count of the times he fell off the parallel bars, but he learned to fall without hurting himself; in fact he lost all fear of falling, and that, as he later discovered, was one of the most important things that ever happened to him.

At home in the holidays without the outlet of sport, the favoured 'Derick talked his mother into buying them bows and arrows. They started shooting at each other first, and then as they became too accurate for comfort took to ambushing passers-by. A hedge ran along one side of the house just high enough for hats to bob invitingly over the top as men passed, and irate men with arrow-dented bowlers kept banging on the door-knocker.

Now the war was over but still they rarely saw their father, who was still in the Army, still on the Continent and busy helping repair war damage. Even after that he was retained in France on the War Graves Commission.

Meantime Hazel had married an R.A.F. flight lieutenant, Cyril Burge, who had flown most of the war in the Royal Flying Corps. He fascinated Douglas by the wings and ribbons on his tunic and his stories of the war. Burge was likewise attracted by the boy who seemed at times so vital as to be " almost on fire," a good-looking youngster with large clear blue eyes and frank gaze, a mouth that grinned easily, crisp curly hair and a square jaw, an oddly commanding face for a small boy. 'Derick looked very like him, but without quite the same intensity in the face.

Back at school, Douglas shone at cricket too, being a reasonable bowler, miraculously quick as a fieldsman and a batsman who believed that the ball was there to be hit, not blocked.

By tradition at Temple Grove all boys carved their names on desks. Douglas tried but made a botch of it, and 'Derick was a shade scornful. They were walking near the garden where the headmaster grew huge vegetable marrows. " I bet I could do a corker carving on that," Douglas said, not very seriously, eyeing the largest marrow.

" Bet you're not game," said 'Derick provocatively. " I dare you." Douglas carved " D. Bader " in large and immature print on the headmaster's prize marrow. He deserved no sympathy. Nor did he get any.

Though he always tried to the limit at games he never tried hard in the classroom. He did not really have to because his mind was quick and receptive; he picked up Latin and Greek with ease and was often top of his form, but never worked harder than just enough. Academically, he was lazy because he was not interested. Maths and other modern subjects he detested and did the barest minimum of work on them so that his reports usually said, " Very good, but could do better if he tried." He was turning out to be impregnably obstinate about things he did not want to do, having, like his mother, a will of his own.

The P.T. instructor, Crease, a retired chief petty officer with a beard, who looked like the man on a Player's cigarette packet, taught him to shoot. Crease drilled it into him to get his bead and shoot quickly before the sight became blurred with concentration, and he became accurate and fast in shooting (which years later cost men their lives).

Once they put him in a hockey team against some girls from a neighbouring school, and he played robustly, scorning chivalry. One of his shots missed either the goal or girl at which it was aimed and bounced off a slow-moving master's skull with a satisfying thud which brought Bader Minor some hero-worship. He was barred from playing against girls any more and that delighted him.

In 1922 a War Office telegram came to the house in Kew regretting that Major Bader had died of his wounds in St. Omer—the shrapnel which had wounded him in the head in 1917. Though the boys had seen little of their father, it did not make Douglas feel any more secure. Later, a more practical effect had to be faced. 'Derick had already gone on to King's School at Canterbury. Now there was doubt whether funds were enough to send Douglas to public school too. The one solution was a scholarship, and a very loath boy began studying, in the galling position of having to prove his reports: " could do better if he tried."

Not for a moment did he slacken his sporting activity. Not Bader Minor. In that last year he was captain of cricket, captain of rugger, captain of soccer, and in the school sports in the final term won every senior race he could enter for, the 100 yards, 220, quarter mile, half mile and hurdles, then set a new school record for throwing the cricket ball. At term's end the headmaster, with real pleasure, told him he had also won a scholarship to St. Edward's School, Oxford.

About this time Jessie Bader, dark and vividly good-looking at thirty-two, remarried. The boys' step-father was the vicar of Sprotborough (Yorkshire), the Reverend Ernest William Hobbs, who had been a gentle bachelor of thirty-seven before his life was so radically stirred up. Jessie was devoted to him but still had her outspoken wilfulness, while the two boys resented going up to Yorkshire to live in the rambling rectory with its eight bedrooms, two kitchens, servants' quarters (mostly empty), pump (no running water), lamps (no electricity) and all-pervading cold in winter. Acres of garden and elm-studded grass spread between the house and the handsome church that dated back to the eleventh century and, like the rectory, was too big for the small village of scattered cottages near Doncaster.

The vicar was too mild for his intransigent new family. He suggested that 'Derick and Douglas might like to mow some of the grass but they flatly refused, and that was that. Jessie was firmer, insisting that the two boys take it in turns to pump the water in the kitchen, and they did so. The vicar tried to institute family prayers after breakfast, but Douglas and 'Derick scuffled and fidgeted and giggled so much that he gave it up. Jessie was inclined to blame Douglas, and he began to feel more at home out of doors.

That summer he was packed off for a week with Cyril and Hazel Burge at Cranwell, where Cyril was adjutant of the Royal Air Force College (in fact, he was Cranwell's first adjutant, having helped open the R.A.F.'s equivalent of Sandhurst in 1919). It was not then the grand place it is now: no fine white façades planted four-square in tailored acres but a few weedy buildings and barrack huts straggling along the side of a large field which was the aerodrome.

From Hazel and Cyril the welcome was warm. Only just thirteen, Douglas had never been near aeroplanes before, and when the quiet, good-humoured Cyril sat him in the cockpit of an Avro 504 trainer the thick hair almost vanished as the boy bent over the controls and dials like a terrier. Later he stood for hours in Cyril's garden watching the bellowing Avros taking off over his head as the cadets practised " circuits and bumps." Every morning at 6.30 he joined the cadets in training runs, doggedly trying to keep up. He admired them enormously; they seemed so fit, and after a couple of days, he spent less time watching the flying and more time with the cadets at cricket and athletics.

When Hazel and Cyril were putting him in the train for Sprotborough he said with what sounded like a catch in his voice (though it was probably only the voice breaking), " Crumbs, I want to come back to Cranwell as a cadet." Cyril thought he had a convert then but he was a little premature. The flying bug was not in Douglas as yet. Interest —yes, as a boy likes dogs and catapults: but it was the games that drew him. Soon he forgot even that because he went to St. Edward's, and there was all the sport he wanted.

2

A MILE OR TWO along the Woodstock Road outside Oxford, St. Edward's School lay behind a high stone wall, a little world of its own. The boys seldom saw much of Oxford. If they went outside the gates in the stone wall it was usually to cross the road to the playing fields, acres and acres of rugger fields and cricket pitches, fives courts and a swimming pool. Behind the wall the school buildings stood around the quad with its clipped lawns and gravel paths, the Warden's house, School House, Big Hall, Big School, and the other houses. And a little apart, away from the road, Cowell's House, into which the new boy, Bader, in new blue suit and new bowler hat, walked on a late summer morning in 1923. The new boys always arrived a day before the school re-assembled. A dozen or so were allotted to Cowell's and for a while they and Douglas stood meekly in the lower hall, lonely and strange, waiting for their next directions. Upstairs, the housemaster had some guests for sherry before lunch. The matron was bustling around, too busy to be motherly. Douglas dropped his new bowler hat, which was part of the school uniform. He did not like it very much. He gave it a kick to express what he felt. Very satisfying. He kicked it again. And again. That was better. He kicked it round the hall, his shoes scraping and clumping on the stone.

A voice above said crisply: " Boy! "

He looked up. A lean face peered over the landing balustrade, cold eyes behind spectacles.

" Stop kicking your hat about. Pick it up and be quiet."

" Yes, sir," said the boy, abashed.

The face vanished. For seconds the hall was quiet. Then Douglas dropped his hat and kicked it once more to establish independent self-respect.

Above, the voice rasped louder: " Boy! "

In the hall the new boys froze. The face of the house-master, wise in the ways of boys, peered again over the balustrade where he had lingered a few seconds with unerring suspicion. " Come here, boy! " he said.

The sherry guests were impressed to see the housemaster return, excuse himself briefly, draw a cane from behind the grandfather clock and make his resolute exit. They did not witness the six strokes on the tightened trousers seat. Nor for that matter did they hear anything. Douglas never yelped. It was not in his character, though his first day at public school certainly was.

He lost any shyness at school within a couple of days. People liked his zest and transparent honesty, and he, feeling he was liked, responded warmly as always. With a willingness that might have surprised his mother he submitted to the rules, even to that mark of inferior status inflicted on all new boys of always having the three jacket buttons done up for the first term.

Games instantly claimed his interest and absorbed excess energy. He played house cricket down on the canal fields, clouted a punching ball in the gym and swam in the pool, screened by shrubs and hedges, where everyone splashed about naked. School became his real life, not only the playing fields but the little things in the background—the red blankets on the iron beds in the dormitories, the overgrown patch in the middle of the quad known as " The Jungle," the " San," the " Crystal Palace " (main lavatories), " Hell " (the mysterious basement room where the text-books were stored), and Hall, where they clattered in to the long refectory tables and ate and chattered like sparrows till the gavel rapped on the wooden block, and everyone stood while the Warden intoned a Latin prayer.

He had to " fag " for a prefect, which was a bore, but there was not much more to it than running messages or polishing a pair of shoes occasionally, and that left plenty of times for games. Or even for study? As winner of a scholarship he was expected to shine in the classroom but, as at Temple Grove, he did no more work than the minimum required to avoid trouble. His darting mind picked up lessons easily, and at prep., half-hidden from prefectorial eyes in the battered

" horse-boxes " of the day-room, his mind wandered to more sporting matters.

In his second term things were better in two ways—he could leave one button of his jacket undone and the rugger season was in. As fly-half in the House second team, he showed such dash that they promoted him to the House first team, though it meant playing against boys much bigger and older.

Back home for the holidays, 'Derick and Douglas bought air-guns, and a reign of terror began in Sprotborough until the day Douglas saw through a bathroom window the pale form of a noted local lady about to step into the bath. Someone dared him, and a moment later the pellet smashed through the splintering glass, followed by a squeal. The sharpshooter vanished and later had a heated argument with 'Derick about the suffering inflicted by an air-gun pellet. 'Derick demonstrated by shooting Douglas in the shoulder at point-blank range, and that started a scuffle which ended with Jessie confiscating the guns.

Douglas simply could not resist a challenge, even daring himself to do anything that seemed to daunt him. With the air-guns locked away, poaching attracted him, but night in the woods was alarming for a small boy, so he dared himself to enter them at night and forced himself to walk slowly through without turning or jumping at noises or shadows.

The year 1924 was trouble-free at St. Edward's because he was busy on the playing fields. At Christmas time the boys put on a Shakespearian play in Big School and a youngster called Laurence Olivier outshone the others so much that he came in for a little deprecating comment for ostentatious acting.

In 1925 Douglas was more games-mad than ever, and, as a corollary, more fidgety in class. It was not easy to pin charges on him because with no effort he still shone at Latin and Greek, showed interest in history and absorbed pages of poetry with obvious pleasure. (Shakespeare, however, he was inclined to resist because he felt it was forced down his throat; he preferred the astringent Swinburne.) Maths was his weakness; he still hated them and refused to bother, so that several times he was " carpeted " by his new housemaster, A. F. Yorke.

" Bader, you aren't doing any work in class."

" I'm awfully sorry, sir. I'll try and do better next week."

" That's exactly what you told me last week."

The boy used to become disarming then, confessing his sins with engaging simplicity and suggesting that Mr. Yorke cane him to teach him a lesson. Yorke could rarely beat him after that. (" I hardly ever caned him. It wouldn't have had any effect if I had. He had a *very* thick hide.") Yorke finally accepted that Bader had an incisive and sensitive brain and would never bother to exercise it hard academically.

Simple misdemeanours such as indoor rugger and debagging, combining with his academic reluctance, brought him occasionally to the attention of the Warden (headmaster), the Rev. H. E. Kendall, a ruddy-faced, brisk and cheerful cleric who tolerantly believed that boys have a right to be reasonably naughty. Punishments were minor matters of a hundred lines here and there because Kendall considered that Douglas, whatever his peccadilloes, was generally " on the side of the angels," an increasingly strong-willed boy who could only be reasoned into the mould, never pressed into it.

In the summer holidays 'Derick persuaded Jessie to let them have the air-guns again, and the boys used them for poaching, keeping a sharp eye open for Scott, the gamekeeper. An accurate snapshooter, Douglas once got a partridge on the wing, a rare feat with an air-gun. They were never actually caught red-handed, though Franklin, the village constable, and Scott were often on the rectory doorstep with suspicion. Jessie confiscated the guns again and scolded bitterly that their behaviour was undermining her authority as vicar's wife. That amused Douglas, which infuriated his mother all the more. The two boys were good friends now, making common cause against authority, though they were beginning to have affection for " Bill " Hobbs, the gentle vicar, who tolerated their peccadilloes with resignation and was not above taking off his clerical collar and going off to the races for the day.

Back at school, Douglas was " capped " for cricket, aged only fifteen and the youngest boy in the team. He finished the season top of both batting and bowling averages for the First Eleven (batting 34, bowling 41 wickets for 8.63 runs)

and set up a new school record for throwing the cricket ball.
For the first time he really had status in the hierarchy of his
world behind the stone wall on the Woodstock Road.

But it was winter he was waiting for. He liked the
aggressive rough and tumble of rugger above everything. On
the Thursday before the first game the captain pinned the
names of the First Fifteen on the board under the cloisters of
Big School, and Douglas, looking over the heads of the huddle
round it, saw his own name scrawled there as fly-half. He
did not shout or make any outward show, but a glow flushed
right through him and he walked away soaked with quiet,
fulfilled happiness. It was the warmest moment of life. Now
there was no mad hurry for the game. The list was up and
he was on it. Barring some appalling accident he was going
to play on Saturday, and for the next couple of days he kept
passing by the board, taking a little peek at his name. On
the Saturday he played, almost broke his nose in a tackle,
had blood drawn from a gashed lip, scored a try and thoroughly
distinguished himself by his fiery vigour. He was still only
fifteen, again the youngest in the school team, and thereafter
was never dropped except through illness.

A report in the *School Chronicle* of a match not long after
said, " Bader did as he chose and scored seven tries." (No
question now of him being second to 'Derick, or second to
anyone else.) The Warden clearly remembers his jaunty
figure striding around the quad, hands in pockets, " absolutely
full of beans."

Pride cometh before a fall. In the charabanc returning
from an away match he fell and hit his head on the edge of
a seat. It was rumoured he gave cheek to an older boy, who
then pushed him, but Bader insisted that it was his own fault;
that he had merely tripped. He was six weeks in the San
recovering from concussion before he took the field again.
The boys he played against, the seniors of other schools, were
older and invariably bigger so that he took more hard bumps,
but that only seemed to increase his ardour.

At Easter his mother told him she did not think they would
be able to keep him on at St. Edward's after the next term.
On a parson's stipend they could not afford the fees. 'Derick
was leaving King's School and though Douglas's scholarship

had helped so much, it still cost an extra £100 a year to keep him at St. Edward's. Though school was the only thing he cared about, Bader was not greatly upset. He was showing a peculiar capacity for shutting his mind to disagreeable things until he had to face them (maths was another example). He was clearly too fond of enjoying the present and ignoring the future.

Half-way through the next term, Walter Dingwall, a reserved young history master who also acted as bursar for the school, sent for him and said, " I'm very sorry, Bader, but we've just had a letter from your mother to say that she does not think you will be able to return here next term."

For a few minutes the words brought the reality unpleasantly close.

" Don't worry," Dingwall said. " I feel it would be a pity if you had to leave. We'll see what we can do about it."

A week later Bader had put it right out of his mind. He was playing for the First Eleven again, boxing and running for his House, and Yorke had just made him a House prefect. At the end of term he went home for the holidays, but no one said anything about leaving school and after the holidays he went back to St. Edward's again. By this time he had filled out and was giving as many bumps at rugger as he received.

The Warden made him a school prefect with the privilege of wielding a cane and of possessing a study in the " Beehive," a quaint little octagonal building where the rooms were tiny triangles just big enough for a boy, a desk and chair and a trunk covered with cushions. One or two thought Bader was getting bumptious, but the Warden felt it was mostly that he was too full of vitality to sit in the background. Underneath, Kendall detected a sense of responsibility that should be fostered. Other boys all respected him greatly, an acid test, and Kendall liked his spontaneous friendliness and the way he could talk to a master without being " on guard."

The authority in Bader's character developed fast. He seldom had to use his cane as a prefect; his mere presence in a day-room doorway compelled instant quiet in a scuffling crowd of boys. Sometimes his eagerness at rugger led him into individualism that amounted to selfishness: he would try to run through the whole of the opposition. Arthur Tilley, the sportsmaster, partly cured him of that by saying tartly, "You might get through five people, Bader, but the sixth will usually get you if you don't pass the ball out." Now he was also playing fives for the school. Without a glove, of course. That would not have been in character.

Early in summer he went to the San one day and said he thought he was getting 'flu. They found he had a temperature and put him to bed, and as he lay there he began to feel light-headed and then his heart began to pound. It got worse, every beat seemed to hammer through him, the blows coming faster and faster, vibrating in his ears till his body seemed to be thumping like a compression engine. He was drifting away from the room and reality, withdrawing into himself; vague illusions chased nightmarishly through his mind. The nurse found him delirious with rheumatic fever.

For several days he wandered in delirium, close to death. They sent for his mother and she came down from Sprotborough and stayed nearby. In the chapel the whole school prayed for him. Then the fever broke one night and the crisis passed. His memory of new consciousness starts when the Warden stood by his bed and told him that the school had prayed for him. A glow spread through him; there was something deeply warming in knowing that so many people had cared enough about him to do that. He had never had that before, unless one counted the occasional resented voice asking (as though it were hopeless) that God forgive him for his many sins.

The doctor told him as gently as he could that rheumatic fever affected the heart and that he must lie quietly for a long time and try to repair some of the damage, but the boy declined to accept that, insisting that he was perfectly well already and was going to play rugger in the coming season. It was a trying time in the San; Bader, feeling fit and confined to bed, was not tractable. The crisis came one hot night when the nurse found his bed empty. People rushed everywhere looking for him and finally saw him sleeping peacefully on the lawn, where he had dragged his mattress. It was cooler there, he said.

Out of the San he quietly began training again, swimming at first, then gym and running. Soon after the rugger season started the doctor examined him and, a little surprised, found he was fit enough to play. So fit, as it happened, that Arthur Tilley made him captain of the First Fifteen.

This was Bader's first real taste of leadership, and he seemed to blossom instantly. He lived for the team, full of a breezy, non-stop enthusiasm both on the field and off that infected everyone else. Some captains had been known to hold themselves a little aloof, especially from the lesser members of the team. Not Bader. Every player was a brother (slightly junior) to be exhorted and coached and fired with enthusiasm from dawn till lights out. Douglas lived for them—with one proviso: they must also live for the team, dedicated, tireless and fearless. If a boy did not, he was no longer on the team. It was as simple as that. Tilley noticed that Bader's paternal concern for his team was overshadowing his own ego; he was not so selfish with the ball now—only rarely when his exuberance carried him away. Being captain obviously nourished his sense of responsibility.

He sat near the Warden at lunch in Hall, and Kendall watched with interest how his will and generosity combined with his vigour to make a commanding personality. Here was no doubting Hamlet, but a young chieftain who evoked co-operation as well as obedience. At lunch one day the Warden asked him what he was going to do when he left school, and Bader said simply that he did not know. Lately he had begun asking himself the same question. Go on to Oxford? He could probably win a scholarship, but that would mean hard study, which was repulsive. Besides, what would he read at Oxford? Classics? History? Neither appealed. Certainly not maths. Anyway, too many undergraduates had long hair. 'Derick was talking of going out to South Africa in engineering but that did not appeal either. As he did so often with tedious things like text-books, he put the problem out of his mind and lived on in the agreeable present.

Shortly before Christmas an old boy, Roy Bartlett, now at Cranwell, visited the school, and Bader remembered his own visit there five years earlier, especially the games. Flying might be fun. That night he wrote to Uncle Cyril asking what his chances were of getting into Cranwell as a cadet.

Cyril Burge had left Cranwell and was now personal assistant to Air Chief Marshal Sir Hugh Trenchard, Chief of the Air Staff. With the satisfaction of a match-maker, Cyril wrote back saying that Douglas was just the type they wanted and he would do everything he could to help (which, from the p.a. to the C.A.S., sounded considerable). There was one catch—Cyril pointed out that it would cost Jessie and the vicar about £150 a year [1] to send him to Cranwell, and the course lasted two years. Could they afford it?

Douglas took the question home and Jessie quickly settled it. (a) She did not like flying, (b) she did not think Douglas should go into the Air Force, and (c) they could not possibly afford £150 a year.

She added, " You wouldn't even be at St. Edward's now but for the kindness of Mr. Dingwall."

" What d'you mean? " He was puzzled.

" I didn't want you to know yet," his mother said, " but Mr. Dingwall has been paying the rest of your fees since 1926."

The news staggered him, more so as he knew his mother had never met Dingwall, who was such a reserved person that he himself hardly knew Dingwall. He had never been in one of Dingwall's classes and had seldom encountered him.

Back at school he went to thank Dingwall, and the master, looking very embarrassed, shrugged it off with a deprecating laugh and got off the subject by asking him what he was going to do when he left. Embarrassed himself, Bader mentioned that he had hoped to get into the R.A.F.

" Something might be arranged," Dingwall said thoughtfully.

Shortly another letter came from Burge saying that six prize cadetships were given every year to Cranwell, which meant virtual free entry. Several hundred boys fancied them, there was a stiff eliminating examination and the academic standard was high. Did Douglas really think it worth trying? (It was tantamount to a dare—as Burge knew.)

Bader tapped on the housemaster's door. Did Mr. Yorke think he was good enough to win a prize cadetship?

" I think you *could* get one, Bader," Yorke said, a little meaningly.

" But I'm no good at maths, sir."

[1] In those days Cranwell was like a public school in that it charged fees. Now the system is different and no fees are charged; in fact, modern cadets are even paid properly.

" You're darned lazy at maths, I know that."

" If I worked hard, sir, and you coached, d'you think I could catch up? "

" If you worked hard," said Yorke, " I *know* you could do it. But I'm not going to waste time coaching you unless you *will* work. Are you prepared to? "

Bader took a breath and said, " Yes, sir, I'll have a shot."

He joined the small circle of boys, sometimes known as " the Army Sixth," whom Yorke coached in maths. They were all trying for the Services. After his day's work, duties and games, Bader spent a couple of hours every night " cramming " maths, hating it but sticking to it. By day he still exhorted and captained the rugger team, dispensed prefectorial justice, boxed, exercised as an under-officer with the O.T.C., shot with the school rifle team, played fives and even found time to be a leading member of the school debating society. He did not regard debating as a mental fag; it stimulated him because the element of contest was in it. In debate his mind had a habit of cutting through irrelevancies to the heart of the matter, sometimes imperiously, sometimes with a sudden charm that glowed out of him with compelling vitality, and always plausibly. In his face one could see signs of evolving character, a hint of pleased yet defiant pride, and in the bearing an amiable swagger. If beneath there was insecurity, it was well hidden, or well compensated; only if he were challenged did it flash out and make him combative. Whether, after schooldays, the mould would sufficiently curb the sparkling nature no one knew, though it was felt that the mould would have to stretch a little now and then.

That spring (1928) he became captain of cricket, then early in June a letter called him to London for R.A.F. examination, interview and medical. Another letter came from Cyril telling him what sort of answers the selection board usually liked to hear.

He sat for the exam in a comfortless room in Burlington Place, glad to find the papers were not difficult but knowing that scores of other boys were likewise rejoicing. The maths paper, happily, was almost a replica of those that Mr. Yorke had been setting for him, and he finished on time, reasonably content. After lunch he stood to attention in front of a long table while five elderly men in civilian clothes gazed steadily at him. Some of the questions seemed foolishly irrelevant: " How often do you brush your teeth? "—" What is the capital of Sweden? "—but all the time the eyes were on him. Some questions he was ready for (thanks to Cyril):

" Why do you want to join the Air Force? "

" I think it would suit my temperament, sir . . . and so does my housemaster."

(Satisfied nods.)

" What do you do in your holidays? "

" Oh, games, sir. *Team* games usually. Cricket or rugger. I like rugger best."

(True up to a point, but he had a sudden quaking fear that they might have inquired about him at Sprotborough and heard lurid tales about the poaching and the air-guns. Apparently they hadn't. They beamed.)

He came out knowing he had done well. (Out of a maximum of 250 points for the interview he had, in fact, scored 235, a figure which is seldom approached.)

Then to the doctors. They looked down his throat, into his eyes and ears, tapped his knees for reflexes, tapped him all over, made him blow a column of mercury up a fuse and hold it, holding his breath, listened to his heart and took his blood pressure. When it was over, the man in the white coat looked thoughtfully at the papers on his desk. " I see you've had rheumatic fever," he said. " I'm afraid it's left your blood pressure a little high."

Bader asked in dismay, " Does that mean I'm turned down? "

The doctor said, " Not necessarily, but high blood pressure is not very good for high flying. Come back in a few weeks and we'll see how it is then. I suggest you keep fairly quiet in the meantime."

He went back to school and for a while was almost sedate. Then back to London, where the doctor wrapped the cloth round his arm and pumped it up three times. He felt his heart beating with anxiety. The doctor scratched his chin. The seconds dragged. " I'm a bit keyed up," Bader said. " That might have affected it."

" Yes." The doctor closed the lid of his blood pressure

gadget with a detached professional air. "It's still up a bit, you know, but we'll pass you."

It was a good moment, till he remembered he still had to win selection.

About a week later another letter came from Air Ministry and he made himself open it slowly. The unemotional, numbered paragraphs told him he had come fifth in the examinations, had won a prize cadetship and would be required to present himself at Cranwell in September with a change of underclothes, bowler hat and toilet articles. Stilted prose has seldom had such an electrifying effect. Mr. Yorke, very pleased, said:

"I'm delighted for you, Bader, but remember you have another two years of academic work to do now."

He was proud when he told Dingwall.

"From what I know of Cranwell, all the chaps there have motor-bikes," Dingwall observed. "I think you'd better have one, too, as a reward for your work."

He pressed the point over the boy's reluctance with discreet insistence, and soon Bader had a second-hand, flat-twin Douglas motor-cycle for which Dingwall had paid £30 and fended off any thanks with his usual deprecating laugh.

A day or two later the school broke up for the summer holidays and Bader said good-bye to St. Edward's. The Warden had him to tea before he left and observed: "Don't become over-confident. Keep a hold on those high spirits of yours."

At Sprotborough his mother, though proud of him, was still dubious about the Air Force as a career. As 'Derick had gone off to South Africa, Douglas got more attention than usual and responded warmly to it.

In the second week in September, Douglas, boisterously cheerful, strapped two small suitcases to the pillion of the motor-cycle, rammed a new bowler hat rakishly over the headlight, kissed his mother, shook the vicar's hand, and pelted with exhaust blaring down the highway towards Cranwell. Two hours later, roaring down the Ancaster straight four miles from Cranwell, he saw a cow wander across the road ahead and swerved; his front wheel hit the grass verge and the motor-cycle kicked over the steep bank and cartwheeled on the other side. Thrown clear on the grass, he got groggily to his feet, shaken and bruised but otherwise, surprisingly, unhurt. Watched vacantly by the idiot cow, he hauled the motor-cycle upright, wheeled it back to the road and kicked the self-starter. The engine blurted healthily and everything seemed all right till he noticed the headlamp sticking through the top of the bowler hat where the crown had burst and a flap at the top gaped open like a tin lid. Instead of dismay he felt a wicked satis-faction, flung a leg over the saddle and roared off again. Eight minutes later he rode through the gates of Cranwell and into the Royal Air Force.

A confused couple of hours then, waiting, coming to attention and saying " Sir," filling in forms, saying a few brief and guarded words to other new boys, trying to size them up, and then a corporal led four of them like sheep to a hut, into an end room where four iron cots covered with khaki blankets stood thin-legged against the wooden wall. Rough bedside tables, four lockers—an impression of bareness.

" Like school, isn't it," said one.

They talked till well after Lights Out, and in the morning went on parade for the first time. Wearing bowler hats. Bader was not so happy about his hat now. He tried to tuck the loose flap inside the crown, but when they were snapped to attention on the gravelled square he had a feeling (later confirmed) that the torn flap was sticking up like a lid again. A warrant officer with a red and bony face walked down the line, inspecting each face. In front of Douglas he stopped and stared and the arid voice said, " And what is *your* name, sir? "

" Bader, sir."

The voice crunched again, " And what do you think you are, Mr. Bader? . . . A comedian? "

" I had an accident on the way yesterday," he started. . . . After five seconds or so the warrant officer cut him short. " I don't think I wish to hear any more." He gazed once more at the hat, once more into the young man's eyes, turned and walked frigidly down the ranks.

Bader stayed rigid and poker-faced, remembering his other bowler hat on his first day at St. Edward's and the six weals that it produced. But now they were not boys. They were

gentlemen on probation spending hours every day on parade
having discipline drilled into them by straight-backed N.C.O.s
who called them "Sir" and "Gentlemen" and blistered
their ears with invective. Cranwell had grown a little but
still looked much as he remembered it; still with the cavernous
hangars squatting beside the two landing grounds that straddled
the camp of long wooden huts.

On parade the N.C.O.s took it in turn to comment
raucously on Bader's bowler hat. He considered gumming
the lid down with sticky paper and then stubbornly decided
to leave it as it was, until, after a week when the joke had
worn thin, they got their uniforms, rough serge tunics (as still
worn), breeches worn with puttees and a cap with shiny
peak and the white cadet band round it. They paraded
again to draw flying kit and a new excitement stirred as he
stood in the Q.M. store and a sergeant slapped a Sidcot
flying suit on the counter in front of him, stood a pair of
flying boots beside them, added a scarf and gauntlets, slapped
a pair of goggles on the pile and handed over a helmet to try
on. It fitted snugly and suddenly he wanted urgently to try
this flying which was to be his career. He had never been in
the air yet.

A couple of days later—a sunny afternoon late in September
with the trees still in summer leaf—he reported to the flight
hangar with flying kit. A chunky little man came into the
cadet pilots' room and introduced himself in a quiet voice as
Flying Officer Pearson. Bader was to be his pupil. They
went out on the tarmac and Pearson led him, self-conscious in
his new flying kit, to a flimsy-looking biplane, fabric-covered
wings harnessed together with struts and wires. It was an
Avro 504, the same type he had sat in at Cranwell five years
earlier.

"We're going up for half an hour," Pearson said. "You
won't touch the controls this time. It's just to get you used
to the idea of flying." He explained briefly why and how
the machine flew, pointed out the controls, strapped him in
the rear cockpit (all open in those days) and slipped into the
front cockpit himself. The propeller spun into noisy life, and
in a little while they were bouncing across the field. Gently
the grass sank below, wing-tips tilted, and Douglas, leaning

over the leather-padded rim of the cockpit, wind whipping at his face, looked down on green country, exhilaration bubbling in him. Soon they dipped towards the landing ground, and the Avro, swaying a little in the afternoon thermals, slid down the glide-slope to check, check, touch the grass and rumble.

" How did you like it? " Pearson asked, and found his answer in gleaming eyes.

Next afternoon Flight Cadet D. R. S. Bader took the control column in the air for the first time, gingerly at first, then too tightly, till Pearson's voice nudged at him to relax. Stick gently forward and the nose dipped; gently back and it rose; stick to each side and it tilted. Then feet on the rudder bar and the first co-ordinated turns. Taut concentration for a few minutes: it was strange; one had to think before one could tentatively act. Then the athlete's eye, mind and muscle began to combine in harmony and he had the feel of it. Pearson himself was a classically smooth pilot who never showed off to his pupil like some other instructors. He kept quietly drilling into Bader: " Never be brutal with your aeroplane. Guide it. Don't shove it." And another time: " I never want to hear you call it a plane or a kite. The word is aeroplane or aircraft." (Never since that day has it ever been anything else from Bader's lips. Pearson taught him to look on an aeroplane as a man might regard his favourite horse.)

After a landing in October, when the pupil had had only six and a half hours' dual instruction, Pearson got out and said: " D'you think you could take it around on your own? " Douglas grinned and nodded, and Pearson casually waved him off, saying: " All right. Don't bend it." It is always done like that, before a pupil has time to start worrying. Bader did not worry; he opened the throttle and eased the Avro into the air, revelling to be up alone and guiding the vibrating thing round the perimeter. Gently he turned upwind, slanted her down towards the field and now memory and tension faded from the rapt and lonely moments as he jockeyed her down, flattening, holding off, off, as the tail sank until the little aeroplane settled in a velvety and somewhat flukey three-pointer, giving him the same stab of joy a man has at the click of his first perfectly hit golf ball.

" Pretty smooth," said Pearson tolerantly when he had taxied in. " I bet you don't do another one as good for a couple of months."

Pearson nearly took his words back because his pupil was consistently smooth in his flying, landings as well, and the instructor fairly soon realised that he had the eye and timing of a natural pilot. Perhaps too much exuberance? But under that lay a disciplined zeal to shine at the things that stirred him—in this case to fly with delicate accuracy. Some day rashness might for a few moments overrule the discipline. It happens among pilots trained for war who are not recruited for their caution; usually it happens only once to each—he lives and learns or, if they can reassemble enough of him, is buried.

Now he had gone solo, Flight Cadet Bader wanted to be a fighter pilot, and flying vied with rugger for his devotion. He liked Cranwell exceedingly. It was like school but even better because, in spite of the discipline, they were treated more as adults and did not have to behave responsibly like prefects. Sometimes they could stay out until midnight, they could ride motor-bikes (though cars were strongly forbidden), smoke and be men of the world. After a couple of puffs at a cigarette he had tossed it away with distaste. Besides, it was not good for one's fitness. He tried a pipe, liked it, decided it would not clog his lungs if he did not inhale, and soon was an addict, seldom seen (at permissible times) without a stub pipe between his teeth.

The only catch was the schoolroom part. Theory of flight, engines, signals, armaments and such things were reasonably interesting, but the maths! He ignored them. Besides, the rugger season had arrived. He was picked for the First Fifteen, and for the first time Cranwell beat both Sandhurst and the Woolwich Military Academy.

The flight cadets were paid £4 a month pocket money, but every twelve weeks the post brought Bader cheques for a further £12 from Walter Dingwall, with a brief note when the first cheque arrived saying that there was no reason why Bader should have less than the others. He wrote several letters of thanks, deeply touched and amazed at Dingwall's

B

generosity, and got pleasant little notes back, but Dingwall always stayed remotely in the background. One never seemed to know what he was thinking, but he seemed to find pleasure in quiet altruism. Bader never saw him after leaving St. Edward's, but he did discover that Dingwall had intended to pay his fees at Cranwell had he failed to win his prize cadetship.

He found a new pleasure in the schoolroom side of the course—reading the stories of the Great War "aces"— McCudden, Bishop, Ball and others. Their accounts of air fighting fired him more than ever with the ambition to be a fighter pilot, and his spirit thoroughly approved of their tenets—get up close as you can and let him have the lot.

In the air Pearson was initiating him into aerobatics, teaching him not to throw the Avro about but to coax her immaculately through every antic in the book. As well as the thrill, Bader began to find the joy of an artist, in a slow roll, for instance, of revolving her evenly about her axis without losing height. Yet not all his flying was copybook. An enterprising fellow-cadet named Hank More (who later won a D.F.C. and was killed in the Far East) evolved a hair-raising trick of climbing out of his rear cockpit in mid-air and crawling forward to tie a handkerchief about the joystick in the empty front cockpit, then getting back into the rear cockpit. One had to take one's parachute off to do it. A crony of Bader's, an old Etonian called John Chance, did it then. On his next solo flight, of course, Cadet Bader did it too, finding it diverting to be straddled across the fuselage like a bare-back rider, holding on with the heels while the hands were busy tying the handkerchief. Naturally then nearly every other cadet did it. One could not do it while an instructor was in the front cockpit because the instructor would (*a*) get in the way, and (*b*) have the cadet thrown out of the college. The riskiest part was considered to lie in the chances of being found out.

As well as flying and rugger, he was playing hockey now and also boxing. His first fight he won by a knock-out in the first round. A sergeant instructor had told him that if you hit a man on the chin very hard at the beginning of a fight, when he is cold, he would go "out" far more easily than later when he had warmed up and was sweating, when his body could absorb a punch better. Next fight Bader lunged out of his corner at the gong, bashed through the other man's guard with a storm of punches and knocked him out within a minute. His fights were on the same pattern after that, and word of his toughness spread. He had just the body and temperament for a middleweight fighter. By his twentieth birthday he had filled out to a muscular 5 feet 10 inches, with strong-fingered, square hands, ruggedly handsome with an arresting vitality in the eyes that seemed to glow vividly blue in large clear whites under the dark brow. Some of the other cadets were beginning to look upon him as a super-youth and some of the Cranwell staff as an *enfant terrible*.

The fact is that discipline alone was never enough to curb him. He needed responsibility or some positive purpose to harness him, but he lacked both and enjoyed the sport of flouting minor regulations. They " gated " him for roaring round the district at high speed on his motor-bike, and when he was freed from barracks he did it again, more culpably, by having John Chance or his particular friend, the dark, slight Geoffrey Stephenson, on the pillion (pillion riding was strictly forbidden). Chance bought an old Morris car for £50, and the three of them kept this banned luxury hidden in an old barn about a mile from the camp. Often they got back from Grantham after their midnight passes had expired, and climbed back to bed over the seven-foot spiked fence. More than once they were caught, but that only made the sport more attractive. It was all a game.

After a year they sat for exams. He struggled with his maths, hoped for the best, and afterwards, with Chance, Stephenson and Denys Field,[1] rattled off to a dance at Grantham in the old Morris. They arrived back at the barn with three minutes to sign in at the guardroom a mile away. Bader alone had his motor-cycle there, but that was a detail; all four festooned themselves on it, and two minutes later, after a crazy ride, he was pulling up a hundred yards from the guardhouse to let the others off to walk the rest when suddenly a torch shone on them, held by an advancing policeman. It was a fair cop. Service police came down from

[1] A big, excitable young man who could break evens for the 100 yards and became a scratch golfer before being killed over Hamburg in 1941.

the guardhouse and there was a solemn period of name and note-taking.

In the morning the four of them had a menacing interview with the squadron commander. In the afternoon Bader was fined £2 for being in improper control of his motor-cycle, and next morning the four of them went out in the car again. As they returned to the barn a hawk-eyed instructor coming in to land just overhead, spotted them. At this trying moment the results of the exams came out and Cadet Bader, scholarship winner, was nineteenth out of twenty-one.

This time he stood alone on the carpet in front of the desk, and after a crisp homily the squadron commander concluded by saying: " I'm fed up with you. If you don't change considerably I shall take steps to have you and your friends removed from the college."

There was no doubt he meant it. Bader emerged a disturbed young man and received a message to report to the commandant immediately. Unhappily he went.

Air Vice Marshal Halahan was a square-faced, grey-haired former heavyweight boxing champion who spoke in a quiet voice. Bader, rigidly at attention, listened to a dispassionate review of his misdemeanours and winced at the end when Halahan said, almost laconically: " You're young. I can understand your trouble, but the Air Force won't go on understanding. They don't want schoolboys here. They want men."

He almost crept out, feeling he had shrunk to about half size. To have his manhood challenged! And even worse, to know that Halahan was right! He was honest enough to face that. After a couple of days' heavy thinking Flight Cadet Bader was a different young man, with radically changed views of Cranwell and a potent desire to justify his place there. He even began studying maths.

Some of the staff regarded the transformation suspiciously at first, but eventually even they recognised that a permanent change had occurred. Like any convert, he steered a rigidly straight path, his maths kept improving and his flying, as always, was deft and accurate.

Now the course was flying single-seater Siskins, biplane fighters odd to modern eyes, but they made Bader keener than ever to be a fighter pilot. (Not much doubt that he would be. Fighter pilots are picked from individualists, and Cranwell knew an individualist when they saw one.)

He stuck to his studies, but without missing a moment from games, and in both his years at Cranwell got his " blues " for cricket, rugger, hockey and boxing. (Rupert Leigh, a cadet on the junior course, gave this appraisal of him: " To us he was a sort of god who played every conceivable game and was the best player on every team.")

Young tyros in the R.A.F. have not always been noted for temperance, but Bader was. Once he tried beer, and once each sherry and whisky, but never finished any of them. He did not like them; therefore he ignored them. In any case, at a party he had his own spirits to exhilarate him, and any temptations liquor might have held were easily repelled by the thought that abstinence would keep him fitter.

Everyone knew how fit he was. When the Sandhurst boxing team came to joust with them again the visiting middleweight climbed into the ring looking pale and ill-at-ease. Bader ducked through the ropes a few seconds later looking sure of himself and obviously relishing the coming fight. The gong sounded and in seven seconds the Sandhurst man was unconscious on the canvas. He spent the next two weeks in hospital with concussion. Rupert Leigh remembers Bader having about twenty fights at Cranwell, of which he won all on knock-outs but the last one. This last bout was against a man called Jock McLean, Inter-Services light-heavyweight champion and somewhat heavier than Bader. At the gong Bader rushed out in his usual way and within a minute McLean was down. But not out. He got up again and a fierce mutual slogging went on. At the gong for round two Bader tore out again, ran smack into a rigid fist on the chin and went down, out cold. When he came to he wanted to fight McLean again but it was too late. Playing rugger a few days later he tore a cartilage in his knee and that put a stop to more boxing. He has mourned ever since that he did not have a second try against the only man who ever beat him.

The damaged cartilage was a curb that helped him focus on less robust affairs, even maths, and early in 1930 his persistent new virtue was rewarded when he and another out-

standing cadet, Paddy Coote, were appointed under-officers of
" A " and " B " Training Squadrons. Once again he was a
leader with responsibilities and once again he rose to it,
tending his cadets with a firm and friendly hand and setting
an example even in studies.

In June they sat for their final exams and this time he had
no qualms about his work. A couple of days later, while
waiting for the results, he led " A " Squadron in the last
cricket match against " B " Squadron (whose team had nine
of the Cranwell First Eleven). " B " Squadron scored 238.
Bader took five of their wickets and opened the batting for
his own team. On a sodden pitch, wickets fell fast: soon
4 for 23. Bader began lambasting the bowling and in less
than an hour it was six for 126—Bader's share being 97 not
out. Three " ducks " followed, and the last man, Reed, came
in with the score at 135. The first ball shaved Reed's off-
stump. The next shaved his leg-stump. He never received
another ball. Bader kept jumping down the pitch slamming
at everything, hitting fours and sixes during the overs, and
singles or threes off the last balls. The 200 came up with
Reed not out, o, and Bader not out, 171. Excitement was
mounting continuously. Soon Bader clouted a ball to the
square leg boundary, bringing the total to 227. Two more
sixes would do it. Next ball, he jumped out of his crease and
drove it like a bullet knee-high to short mid-off, where Paddy
Coote held a brilliant catch.

The score-sheet read:

Emson	..	..	8
Morrison	..	..	5
Cleland	..	..	o
Bader ..	..	..	194
Doran	..	..	o
Moore	..	..	8
More ..	..	..	8
Andrews	..	..	o
Widdows	..	..	o
Edwards	..	..	o
Reed ..	..	..	o
Extras	..	..	4

Next day the exam results came out, and Paddy Coote just beat him for the Sword of Honour. No one could mind being second to a man like Coote.

In reticent official terms the report on Bader summed him up neatly: " Plucky, capable, headstrong." His flying rating was " above average," which is R.A.F. understatement for a natural pilot (the only higher rating is " exceptional," which is such a rarity as to be almost a myth.) Then the postings:

" P/O Bader, D. R. S., to 23 Squadron, Kenley."

He rode his motor-cycle to London and traded it in for his first car, a second-hand Austin Seven that looked like a lacquered biscuit box on pram wheels. In this, on an August morning in 1930, he drove to Kenley, brimming with content. No. 23 Squadron flew Gloster Gamecock fighters.

3

BEFORE THE age of runways Kenley was a large, grass field and behind the hangars on the rim lay the graces of a station built in peace for an Air Force that was small and select, like a club whose members in the red-brick officers' messes scattered across the land (and outposts) more often than not knew one another. Less encrusted by years than the Navy or Army, the R.A.F. accent was on youth: even the core, the 1914-18 veterans who had made its first traditions, were still young enough to play rugger. A mess waiter, with the deference reserved for qualified officers, showed Bader to his own room, an austere enough affair with an iron bed, leather chair and simple furniture which he viewed with pleasure. It was home: the life he wanted lay before him and down the corridor lived his friend Geoffrey Stephenson, posted to the same squadron.

In the morning B Flight commander sat him in a Game-cock and showed him "the taps"; not much to show, no brakes, no retractable undercart lever, no flaps, no variable pitch propeller, no gyro instruments, no trimming tabs. She was a tubby little thing and from the cockpit he felt he could almost touch the tips of the two braced and strutted wings. Top speed was 156 m.p.h., but the stumpy fuselage made her the most agile little aeroplane in the R.A.F. He took her up that morning, rolled and tumbled her about the sky for half an hour and joyfully agreed with that. For the past two years two of 23 Squadron's Gamecocks had been picked to do the combined aerobatics at Hendon pageant. Bader decided he wanted to be one of those two pilots next time.

He slid effortlessly into squadron life, perhaps a shade too confident for a new boy, but too friendly and vital to irk anyone. On "dining-in" nights when, immaculate in mess kit, they passed the port decanter, Douglas, strictly sober, joined as wildly and hilariously as anyone in the subsequent games of rugger in the ante-room with a waste-paper basket for a ball; or highcockalorum; or " desert warfare," when they grabbed assegais off the wall and stalked their fellow-men through oases of aspidistras on the floor while others beat tom-tom rhythms on the table-top. Life was idyllic, with flying, games and fellowship, buttressed by the tangible prestige and comfort of a permanent commission from Cranwell. Most of all he liked aerobatics in the Gamecock. That same August he arrived at Kenley he was picked for the R.A.F. cricket team.

A month later, when cricket was finished, the Harlequins, famous amateur rugger club, asked him to play in a trial game. The knee cartilage stood up to it well, and so the Harlequins acquired a new centre-threequarter. Thereafter in *The Times* one not infrequently read little headlines such as " Bader Brilliant," " Bader Excels," often with the remark that he was the best player on the field. A few weeks later he was picked for the R.A.F. Fifteen, and again as fly-half he was in both senses head and shoulders above the ruck. By his twenty-first birthday in February, 1931, his name was becoming widely identified with a sinewy, beautifully-tuned human machine that weighed eleven stone six pounds stripped, and had the temperament of a dynamo. His present to himself was to trade in his little Austin biscuit-box for an M.G. sports car, which he cherished.

All other fighter squadrons now had the Bristol Bulldog or the Siskin; only 23 Squadron was left with Gamecocks, and that was partly why they were chosen again to do the combined aerobatics at Hendon that year. Woollett picked C Flight Commander, Harry Day, to lead the team, and all the other pilots started training hard for selection. One man killed himself flying upside down, and slowly the selection narrowed. In April Woollett told Douglas that he was to be second man in the team, with the inseparable Geoffrey Stephenson as number three, in reserve. Harry Day was a lean, glint-eyed man who had fought as a youngster in the Great War, and now, a hawk-faced thirty, commanded instant obedience. Prone to occasional turbulence, he thought it was time to change Hendon's traditional aerobatics, so he invented five new routines of " synchronised aerobatics." The first was typical of the other four—two aircraft would dive together, then pull out in two consecutive loops, wing-tip to wing-tip (three feet between, Day said), then up again, stall-turn away on each side into a vertical dive, aileron turn inwards so that they faced and crossed each other, wing-tip to wing-tip again, then up, up and roll off the top of a loop together (going different ways) to dive to each side of the airfield, turn back and race at each other head-on to start a new routine which included some upside down formation. It was safe enough provided no one made a mistake and provided the wind stayed kind. Day would not have .tried it with pilots less cool and accurate than Bader and Stephenson.

Strict orders said they were not to go below 500 feet, though Bader made a nuisance of himself wanting to go lower. Typically, one of his favoured occupations was to do slow rolls " on the deck " at about fifty feet. One tends to lose height in a slow roll and the engine tended to cut upside down. The trick was not to fly into the ground, and part of the charm was that to try this trick was a court-martial offence.

During practice one day Stephenson fell out of a slow roll but luckily was just beyond the end of the Kenley escarpment and had enough space to recover. Another day his engine failed and he made a neat forced landing in the grounds of a large country house. Bader drove over to pick him up and met there the daughter of the house, a dark and vividly pretty girl whom we shall call Patricia. The attraction was prompt and mutual and they began to meet after that.

Day tolerated Bader's " press-on " spirit good humouredly. Other pilots might do bone-headed things on the spur of the moment, but he felt that Bader, even in his wilder moments, was always practical, would always know in advance exactly what he was going to do and would then do it with judgment.

There were still other activities—cricket, for instance. Early in June, Bader was picked to play for the Air Force again and soon there was a picture of him in the paper hitting a six almost out of the ground at the Oval. In that innings he hit 65 in thirty minutes—a six, a five and twelve fours made up 59 of that. Later that month Day confirmed that he was to be his number two at Hendon.

The Times said that 175,000 were inside Hendon Aerodrome
on the day of the display and that " hundreds of thousands
of others crowded hillsides and fields outside." In bright
sunshine they saw what *The Times* also declared was " the
event of the day " as Day and Bader in the Gamecocks " provided the most thrilling spectacle ever seen in exhibition
flying . . . ten minutes full of the cleanest trick flying, synchronised to a fraction of a second . . . the most successful of
the Hendon displays yet held."

Pilot Officer Bader was an object for youthful hero-worship
—dashing airman, brilliant rugger player and cricketer, and
vitally handsome, especially at a Service dance in the tight
blue trousers and the short mess jacket with blue silk lapels
and gilt buttons. Many young women sighed over him and
made what decorous advances convention allowed. From
time to time he played escort to several: Patricia, of course,
and there was a quiet, blue-eyed girl with classic features
called Hilda, a pert little blonde called June and a giggly
blonde as well. His main interests were still flying and games,
but he *did* enjoy the adulation and the Press notices—all very
stimulating to the self-confidence of a young man who was
once the somewhat rejected Bader Minor.

The aerobatics team flew north to Cramlington for a display, and on the way back, strictly against orders, Bader
dropped out of the formation to spend an hour skimming
over the hedges and along the floors of the valleys. When
they landed, Day read him an angry lecture on flying discipline,
though Bader turned on his usual disarming charm and
averted the worst of the wrath.

A couple of weeks later he heard through the orderly
room that he was on the " A List," a roster of young officers
due for posting overseas. That had nothing to do with the
low flying; it was routine that after a year on a squadron a
young permanent officer would go overseas. He seemed
slated for Iraq in the autumn, and late in summer, sitting in
the pavilion at Aldershot with the pads on waiting to bat, he
mentioned a little sadly to Squadron Leader Brian Baker,[1] of
32 Squadron, that it would probably be his last game in England
for a long time. Baker commented: " I don't think so. You

[1] Now Air Chief Marshal Sir Brian Baker.

probably won't be going till next year." Bader wanted to know why and Baker said he fancied they were going to keep him at Kenley all winter to give him a chance to get his " cap " for England at rugger.

Bader felt the electric thrill a man would get on drawing a horse in the Irish Sweep. Rugger for England was the summit of ambition, something breathtaking in the " too good to be true " class. Some overseas postings came out but he was not on them.

At last 23 Squadron was getting Bristol Bulldog fighters to replace Gamecocks. The Bulldog was the last word in fighters. She could do 176 m.p.h. There were minor drawbacks; she was not as manœuvreable as a Gamecock, for instance, being heavier, which gave her a tendency to sink faster on her back in the middle of a slow roll. Low aerobatics were strictly banned, though some people good-humouredly ignored that. Then one of the pilots spun into the ground and killed himself.

Squadron Leader Woollet left the squadron and Harry Day took over command for the time. Another pilot crashed and killed himself. Day called all the others together and read them a lecture on low aerobatics in the Bulldog. " Fighting Area Regulations say that you must not aerobat below 2,000 feet," he said. " Well, you know my views about some regulations—they're written for the obedience of fools and the guidance of wise men. Now if you're going to aerobat under 2,000 feet, first of all—don't. If you decide to ignore that advice, don't do it where any senior officers can see you. And remember these three things: first of all, make up your mind exactly what you're going to do, then get properly settled down, and *then get your speed right* so you don't spin off or lose height. The only thing you have to worry about then is if your engine stops. If it stops—you're dead, but if you're going to start worrying about that stop flying anyway."

It was sound advice, if a little ambiguous, but Day was not out to make decorous airmen; he wanted to turn out pilots with the " guts " and judgment for war. Otherwise the R.A.F. was meaningless. Besides, people were not in the habit of ignoring a warning from Harry Day.

Pilot Officer Bader did. In November a flight commander spotted him doing low aerobatics and " beating up " the airfield. Day had him on the mat and told him crisply and at length to watch his step and not to show off. After a chastened Douglas went out Day wondered whether perhaps he should not have slapped him down harder. Bader was getting into the dangerous phase of over-confidence which comes to many pilots after a year or two. What with his Hendon success and other things on top of the volatile nature he was too outspoken. One or two resented the " white-haired Cranwell boy " and thought he was conceited. Day recognised it more as a coltish, super-vitality and also recognised what others did not always see, that under the buoyant front lay sensitivity. Perhaps he could be slapped down too much? You could not force him —he would only become stubborn. Very likely, with a little firmness, he would correct things himself. But the red light was there. It was a problem. Day was still thinking about it (and other squadron problems) when he went on leave.

As it happened, Day's remark about " showing off " had given Bader the sort of jolt he had had from Halahan at Cranwell; he began to watch what he was saying and shy away from ostentatious aerobatics. Also the Springboks had arrived from South Africa for a series of rugger tests against England, and with that goal in front of him he was training harder than ever before. He wanted his " cap " so much he wouldn't even admit he had a chance for it.

On Saturdays he played for the Harlequins, knowing that the international selectors were watching, and was dismayed to feel that he was over-trained and not playing well. The other pilots kept reassuring him, telling him he would be out of his misery as soon as the selectors named the Combined Services team to play the early match against the Springboks. Last season's England fly-half was also fly-half for the Navy. If they chose Bader instead of him for the Combined Services—he was probably in for England.

At the end of November the Combined Services team was named and there it was—"Fly-half: D. R. S. Bader." It was like the moment he had seen his name on the board for the First Fifteen at school; the same kind of brimming joy, but even deeper. For days he savoured the prospect, and on the Saturday played with a dashing, high-geared vigour. Just after half-time he flung himself at a huge Springbok who was trampling for the line, brought him down, but broke his own nose at the same time. They'd be picking the England team in about three weeks. Too much at stake to worry about a broken nose: he played on.

The following Saturday he played again for the Harlequins, not even bothering to plaster his nose first, and though he tried his hardest, kept fumbling passes and spent the rest of the week-end worrying about his uneven form.

The Monday morning, 14th December, 1931, was bright and clear with a nip in the air and a little scattered cumulus about 4,000 feet. About ten o'clock Bader was curing his gloom with some aerobatics not far from the airfield when he saw two Bulldogs taking off and remembered that two of the pilots, Phillips and Richardson, were flying over to Woodley Aerodrome near Reading to see Phillips' brother, who helped to run the aero club there. Bader tacked on to make a threesome, and half an hour later they settled on the grass in a neat vic at Woodley. In the clubhouse some young pilots, drinking coffee and talking shop as usual, asked Douglas, the Hendon star, questions about aerobatics, and then someone suggested he give a demonstration beat-up of the airfield. Bader said, no, he didn't want to. The Hendon show had been in a Gamecock and the Bulldog was not quite the same (and uncomfortably he remembered Harry Day's " show-off " remark). The matter was dropped until they were leaving, and a young man suggested it again. Bader again said no, and someone grinned and made some barbed joke about being " windy." He made it sound like a dare.

Richardson took off first, and then a tight-lipped, angry Bader. As Phillips left the ground Bader was banking steeply, turning back, and slanting down for a low run across the field. A knot of young men watched from the clubhouse. Just above the grass, rocking a little in the thermals, the Bulldog, engine bellowing, swept across the boundary fence, rushing at a spot beside the clubhouse. The nose lifted a fraction and she began rolling to the right.

He had the stick well over . . . a little top rudder to hold the nose up . . . stick forward to keep it up and as she rolled upside down throttle back to keep the engine alive. He felt her starting to drop.

Stick *hard* over now; the wings were vertical, glinting in the sun, and she was dropping fast. Grimly he was reefing her round and she was rolling out of it fast when the left wing-tip hit the grass and jerked the nose down. As propeller and cowling exploded into the ground the engine tore out, bouncing in a cloud of flying dirt, and the Bulldog seemed to crumple and cartwheel into a tangle very fast. Pinned by his straps, Bader did not feel anything but heard only a terrible noise.

All the airfield was suddenly still, except for the fierce boil of dust round the awkward heap in the middle that looked like crushed brown paper. As the dust began to drift the men by the clubhouse were running.

4

AFTER THE noise everything was suddenly quiet and still. The cockpit was tilted. That was odd: it leaned him sideways. He must have crashed; but it was only a hazy idea and not very interesting because pain was stabbing his back. Slowly it ebbed, leaving a passive torpor, and sitting in the straps, hands in his lap, he was placidly aware of the cockpit: beyond that, nothing.

Gently as the mind came into focus he was aware that his knees were buzzing as though he had hit his funnybone. The eyes wandered down and absorbed with curiosity that his legs were in peculiar positions. At least his right leg was. He could not see the left leg and forgot about it. (It had buckled under the collapsed seat so that he was sitting on it.) His right foot was tucked over in the far, right-hand corner and the clean white overalls were torn at the knee and staining in blood that was pumping in slow little squirts and spreading in filmy waves. There was his knee through the blood, and something sticking through it. Looked a bit like the rudder bar. Very odd. He regarded it in an abstracted way, and for a while it made no impact until an ugly thought crystallised: "Damn! I won't be able to play rugger on Saturday."

After a while that did not seem to matter so much and he was content again.

For the first time he became aware of things beyond the cockpit: voices, and people moving, but they seemed shadowy and remote.

A man in a white coat was standing beside the cockpit. Right at his elbow. There was a face and a white coat and a hand holding out a glass. A voice said: "Here you are, sir. Have a bit of this brandy." (It was a steward from the club-house.)

Automatically, with no effort, he answered casually: " No, thanks very much. I don't drink."

The man leaned over to urge him and saw the blood spurting in the cockpit. He turned very pale and then he stood back and drank the brandy himself.

A big ruddy-faced young man stood there instead of the man in the white coat, and leaned in and started undoing his harness, saying things in a gentle voice. He let him go ahead, and then became unconscious for a while.

Jack Cruttenden, the big man, an Australian student pilot at the club, found he could not lift Bader out of the crushed cockpit. He started tearing at bits of the wreckage and other men did the same. Someone brought a hacksaw and cut away a twisted centre-section strut. Bader partly came to and sensed more than knew that Cruttenden was gently lifting him out.

Consciousness was lapping and receding in waves. He was lying on the grass. Someone was taking his shoes off. Cruttenden's hands were doing something to his right knee: they felt very strong and were covered in blood. He felt no pain. A little to one side two white doors with red crosses opened and the crosses went out of sight. He supposed it was an ambulance.

Then he was lying in it on a stretcher and men were bent over his legs. He tried to sit up but could not get very far and watched the men with detached interest. The legs of his overalls and trousers had gone somewhere, and Cruttenden's fingers seemed to be in his right knee (holding the femoral artery). After a few moments he got bored with watching. He could feel the ambulance was moving and wanted to see what was happening outside. He said to Cruttenden: " Look, I think I'll get up now. I want to get out of here."

He started struggling up on his elbows and Cruttenden said: " Take it easy. Won't be long now."

Bader said petulantly: " Oh, to hell with this. I want to get out now. This is damn' silly."

He tried to struggle up again, and Cruttenden took one hand from the knee and pressed it gently against his chest to hold him down.

Being held down by a stranger was irritating. He twisted

a shoulder off the stretcher, hooked his right fist up and hit Cruttenden on the chin. He felt he could not hit very hard lying down.

Cruttenden, looking at him with a pacifying grin, said: " Ease it up, mate."

Having hit him, Bader felt suddenly feeble and foolish. But honour was satisfied—he'd made the gesture—and anyway he'd completely lost interest in getting up now. He lay back and did not remember any more.

The ambulance weaved swiftly through the Reading traffic, swung into Redlands Road and stopped in front of the Casualty door of the Royal Berkshire Hospital. Within a minute he was on a table with the duty doctor tying the artery and swabbing the pulpy mess in both legs where the bones had torn through. The right leg looked nearly off at the knee and the left shin was broken and badly splintered, the torn flesh full of oil and dirt. The patient's pulse was getting weaker, very thready, so that the doctor could hardly feel it and broke off to give a heart stimulant. He straightened both legs and put them in box splints, then got Sister Thornhill in Benyon Ward on the house phone.

" There's a young man coming up with multiple injuries, shock and loss of blood from an aeroplane crash. Get him warm in bed to ease the shock. I don't think there's much we can do." (Sister Thornhill recognised the tone. After messages like that the patient was sometimes dead by the time he arrived.) Soon they wheeled Douglas in, now deeply unconscious, and she packed hot-water bottles and blankets round the body, which was very cold.

The resident surgical officer examined him briefly. No chance of operating yet, he said when he straightened up. Perhaps later, if he lasted, but there was no real hope.

Thornhill remembered that Leonard Joyce, who was probably the best surgeon in England, was operating at the hospital that day and rang the theatre, but they said he had just left. Hurrying as fast as she dared, she found him in the entrance hall putting on his coat to go. She said: " Excuse me, Mr. Joyce, but we've just admitted a young Air Force officer after a bad crash. Could you have a look at him? "

The rest was understood: she had assisted Joyce at many

operations and he was a man of few words. He took his coat off and followed her back to the ward, and shortly was saying that he would wait and see if the patient came out of shock enough to try and operate. He was young and strong. They must at least try.

When Harry Day rang the hospital from Kenley they were very guarded and he understood perfectly clearly that Bader was dying. He sent a telegram to Jessie, at Sprotborough, and, on the hospital's advice, to Cyril Burge, who was at Aldershot and could reach the hospital in an hour.

About two o'clock Sister Thornhill noticed that the patient was breathing more noticeably and his pulse was also stronger. Gradually his condition kept improving, and Joyce, surprised, put it down to his physical fitness. At 3.30 he decided to try and operate, and on the way to the theatre they first wheeled the patient into the X-ray room.

On the operating table Bader came to and lay looking up at a large light and a white ceiling, not knowing where he was or caring, becoming aware of a hospital smell and a man in a long white surgeon's coat and cap standing by his head who looked scholarly and said in a quiet voice: " Hallo, old chap. I see you've had a bit of an accident. Don't worry. Just lie back and we'll soon have you fixed up."

Bader looked at him vaguely, and as this sank in he said: " Don't give me an anæsthetic, will you. I can't stand the stuff."

" Don't worry," the man said, " we'll see things are all right." He seemed to exude warmth and compassion.

Afterwards Bader could not remember getting the anæsthetic. As he was going " under," the plates came in from the X-ray room and Joyce held them up, still wet, to the light. First the right leg. He passed it almost instantly to the nurse, saying briefly: " That must come off." He hesitated over the left leg and finally passed it across without comment. The plates of the abdomen and head showed only two ribs broken, though the face was gashed and a tooth had come through the upper lip.

Joyce worked fast. The patient was too shaky for thorough surgery; there was time only to try and patch things temporarily in a race with the imminence of more shock and fatal collapse. He severed the right leg above the smashed knee, but that did not take long because it was almost off already. When he turned to the left leg the patient was sinking and there was just time to clean the torn mess and seal it, hoping no infection would set in, and inject a saline solution. Bader was close to death when they got him to a private room and started working on him for post-operative shock.

Cyril Burge reached the hospital and waited. By nine o'clock Bader was still alive, but shock was draining him of the last resistance and he was nearly pulseless, cold to the touch and still deeply unconscious. Joyce told Burge he was not expected to live till the morning and a matron gave Burge a room to sleep in, promising to call him when the time came. He lay on the bed in his clothes to wait.

A nurse woke him out of a doze about 2 a.m. and said softly: " Will you please come down now." He got up and followed her without a word. Outside the patient's door two girls stood, both crying. One was Patricia and the other Hilda, though in the emotion of the moment there were no introductions. He put his head in the door and saw two doctors in white coats and two nurses bending over a bed doing something to the shape in it. One of the doctors saw him and came over and murmured: " Would you wait outside, please? He seems to be holding on."

Half an hour later the doctor came out again and said they might as well go and rest for a while. He would call them if anything happened. The girls went away. Burge went back to his room and was called again an hour later, but when he got there the doctor said the patient had suddenly rallied again, and after a while Burge once more went back to bed.

In the morning Bader was still alive but it seemed only a matter of time. His mother, Mrs. Hobbs, arrived but was so overwrought that the matron gave her a room and a sedative. At nightfall Bader was still holding on, but at midnight they called Burge again, then sent him back to rest. By morning the patient still lingered with a finger-tip hold on life. He had not recovered consciousness since the operation. Joyce told Burge that if he lasted another day he might have a chance, provided the left leg did not become septic.

There might even be a chance of saving the remaining leg.

Twenty-four hours later Bader's eyes quietly opened and gave him an extraordinary experience that started with knowing again and seeing things for the first time like a puppy at the moment its birth blindness lifted. It was like being born again, being alive without knowing what alive meant, unaware of the world or even his name. Sunshine flooded the room. He was conscious of objects that meant nothing for a while but then slowly focused into meaning: a cream ceiling, white sheets and then a tall girl in white with a red cape standing by a window with her back to him. It was like a fade-in of a film scene that suddenly stops and is frozen. Imperceptibly comprehension came without any effort, and the film came to life and meaning, but with no pain and no concern, no backward memory to give depth or disquiet. After a while he murmured: " What the hell am I doing here? "

Sister Thornhill turned and came over smiling. She had been given Bader as a " special " and had been with him nearly all the time. He saw she was about twenty-five, nicely rounded with a strong, capable face, healthily attractive.

" Oh, you're awake, are you? " Her voice was pleasant and steady. He looked up at her impassively.

" You've had an accident," she said.

" An accident? "

" Yes. You crashed in an aeroplane."

" Oh, did I? " He pondered vacantly. " What a bloody silly thing to do."

She laughed and said she must go because Mr. Joyce wanted to see him as soon as he was awake.

He did not know who Mr. Joyce was nor care if he came. Nothing seemed to matter. He became aware that there was an enormous mound in the bed-clothes, and remembered a similar mound when 'Derick had broken his leg at prep. school and they had put a cradle over it.

" Must have broken my leg," he thought. But he was not really interested.

The door opened and Joyce came in, but he did not recognise the pointed, sensitive face.

" Hallo," Joyce said. " Glad to see you're awake."

Bader looked at him composedly but did not speak. Joyce

made a few more cheerful sounds and then said: " I'm very sorry, old chap, but I'm afraid we've had to take off your right leg."

Bader gazed placidly at him. He had heard and understood the words but not the meaning. Politely he said: " That's all right. I hope I haven't been a nuisance."

Thornhill leaned over his body to block his view while Joyce lifted the bed-clothes and started unwrapping the dressings. It gave Bader his first reaction: an urgent curiosity to see this most interesting sight of a severed leg. But he did not want to look while the others were in the room: for some crafty quirk he wanted them outside so he could lift the bed-clothes in privacy.

Joyce looked at the right stump first. It seemed all right. He unwrapped the dressing on the left leg and saw the red puffiness of incipient septicæmia and the dead, grey signs of gangrene. After a while he wrapped it up again, smiled at Bader: " I'll see you again soon," and went out to find Mrs. Hobbs and Cyril Burge.

As soon as the door had closed, Bader lifted the blankets and looked. Yes, there it was. A short stump of thigh with a rather bloody bandage round it. He thought it would look like that. They hadn't given him any pyjama pants.[1] Oh, well . . . he put the blankets down, not even noticing the left leg.

Mrs. Hobbs collapsed into a chair when Joyce told her the second leg had to come off. In near hysteria, she wanted everyone to go away and leave Douglas alone so she could look after him herself.

Joyce found Cyril Burge and told him the situation plainly and lucidly. The boy would certainly die if the left leg stayed. He would probably die from operative shock if they tried to take it off, but it was the only chance. It would have to be done immediately. Burge nodded.

The door opened and Joyce walked into the sick-room again and said: " We've got to re-set your left leg, old chap. I'm awfully sorry about that. It might hurt a bit, so we'll put you to sleep for a while." He looked like a sympathetic housemaster.

---

[1] He never wore pyjama pants again because trouser legs get tangled round a short stump.

"That's all right, Doc," Bader murmured obligingly, supremely placid. It did not seem to be particularly his business. Other people had charge and he was drifting with the stream.

A burly man in a violent check suit and yellow pullover came in. He had a big nose, a cheery face and a tremendously breezy and matey manner that made Bader feel like getting up to shake hands. Commander Parry Price, R.N.R. (Ret'd.), the anæsthetist, said: "By Jove, old boy, you look fine. Now let's see, what do you weigh?"

"I used to box at eleven stone six."

"That's fine. Just about what I thought you were."

Price went out, and soon Thornhill came in with a phial of pink liquid that she injected into him. Soon he felt consciousness withdrawing to a little speck in the back of his mind, and then he was asleep.

In the operating theatre Joyce worked fast again, taking the left leg off about six inches below the knee. As he lifted it away a young nurse started crying, and then as Joyce was sewing the flap of skin over the bone, Parry Price, who had been watching like a hawk, said quietly: "The heart's stopped."

Joyce looked up, motionless. The room was suddenly still. In a dead silence Price jabbed with a needle and took the wrist. The silence lingered on, and then Price felt the little thready flutter start again.

Joyce finished quickly and they wheeled him back to the room. Every ten minutes they kept taking his pulse and it kept palpitating with thin, fast persistence.

Some time in the night, about eighteen hours later, Bader's eyes opened. Vaguely on the rim of a dim circle of light that played round him a nurse was sitting. It was soothing to feel that he was not alone, and the eyes closed and he sank into oblivion again.

Six hours later he came to again, conscious only of pain. His left leg was hurting with a bitter, steady ache that sharpened the torpid mind and began to distress him. After a while Sister Thornhill came in and said: "Oh, you're awake."

"My left leg's hurting," he complained, and she said soothingly that it would probably ease after a while. The leg kept on hurting keenly and remorselessly. Thornhill gave him a little morphia to ease it, but it seemed to make no difference: the terrible hurting went on, stabbing stronger and stronger till it was shredding his nerves all over and beginning to obsess him with agony to the point of feeling he could stand no more. But he had to stand it because it went on and on, and there were no defences and no relief. The mind was sharper now, but still not caring about the loss of the right leg, only about the cruel pain in the left. Sweat began to glisten on his face, and then he was sweating all over and groaning now and then. Thornhill gave him more morphia and the pain went relentlessly on.

By nightfall his eyes were sunken and restless in dark hollows, and the face was grey and waxy, glistening with a film of sweat. For a while he slept under more morphia, but soon awoke to more pain. The following morning he drifted into unconsciousness but now and then revived for brief spells, when his eyes rolled with the constant ache and his mind wandered in a vague half-world. Once he was briefly aware of his mother sitting by the bed, and then she had changed into Cyril Burge. Joyce looked in and told Burge that they were giving all the morphia they dared and doing all they could, but he did not sound hopeful. It would depend on the patient's youth and constitution; in short, his lasting power and resilience.

That night they sent for Burge again at the hotel where he was now staying, but Bader did not die and towards dawn Burge was able to go back to his own room.

Later the young man woke and the pain had gone. He could not feel his body at all, but for some reason his mind was perfectly clear. He lay still, eyes open and head raised on a pillow, looking straight out through the top of a window at a patch of clear blue sky, and into his mind crept a peaceful thought: " This is pleasant. I've only got to shut my eyes now and lean back and everything's all right." Warm peace was stealing over him, his eyes closing and his head seeming to sink into the pillow. It did not occur to him that he was dying; only that he was letting go, drifting down and wanting to. In a dreamy haze the mind was shrinking into a soft, deep pinpoint.

Through the slightly open door of the room a woman's

disembodied voice slid into the receding clarity: " Sssh! Don't make so much noise. There's a boy dying in there."

The words quivered in him like a little electric shock that froze the drifting dream and sparked a sharp thought: " So that's it. Hell, am I! " Feeling began flickering out through his body like ripples from a pebble tossed in a pool. He stopped letting go and the mind was clearing; the body did not move but the brain began gripping thought and reality. It was the challenge that stirred him. His eyes opened and, instead of looking unseeing through the window, began moving, taking note of things in the room. Sister Thornhill came in. He noted her stiff white cap and dress under the red cape. She stood by the bed looking down at him and then smiled and moved away.

As he lay thinking, quite clear-headed, the pain came back to his leg. Somehow he did not mind this time; it was almost satisfying because he felt he was normal again and had slipped away from the ethereal spirit that had been floating him to Limbo. Another thought came: " I mustn't let that happen again. Apparently it wasn't as good as it felt."

Some instinct told him that he had been dying in that moment. (Ever since then he has been convinced of it, and from that moment has never been frightened of dying. Later this was to have a vital effect on his life.)

The pain began to increase agonisingly again till it gripped him so that he wanted to die because it was unbearable, but now he could not die because the tortured mind could not sink back in peace. Thornhill gave him more morphia.

That night delayed shock took effect and he sank into unconsciousness that lasted two days. His mother and Cyril Burge were asked to keep in close touch with the hospital. Joyce was non-committal about the prospects. Thornhill kept rolling him over in bed from time to time to avoid lung congestion that would lead to pneumonia. It had become a personal fight with her and other nurses to save the young man's life. Usually they were impartial and impersonal about patients, but this one somehow was different. He seemed too young and handsome to die, and everyone kept asking about him. On the second morning she was turning the limp body with the help of another nurse when he suddenly sat up and kissed her, then sank back into unconsciousness again. She was petrified with amazement. "Not so unconscious after all," observed the other nurse slyly. Thornhill lifted his eyelid back with a gentle thumb but he *was* unconscious.

Later, Joyce (who had heard from the other nurse about the incident) came round on his inspection and asked whether the patient had shown any signs of reviving. Thornhill, still a little confused, said no, there hadn't been, and Joyce looked at her and said dryly to no one in particular: " Sister isn't giving much away this morning, is she? "

Bader came to that afternoon and they kept injecting so much morphia into him that he lay in a drugged stupor for two more days. Several times in the nights he had moments of near clarity, aware of a pretty young probationer giving him a drink out of something with a spout that she held in his lips. Every time he opened his eyes she seemed to be leaning over him and he thought she was wonderful.

Slowly the shock subsided and he came out of the coma. Morphia helped deaden the pain of the leg and the face lost some of its greyness, though it was still waxy, with eyes sunk in dark sockets and a dark stubble of beard. Thornhill changed the dressings that day, and he rose up with a sharp and quivering groan of agony as she whipped away the last lint that stuck bloodily to the raw wound. She leaned her body carefully over so that he could not see that he had lost both legs. The whole hospital seemed to be aware with a sort of fascinated dread that he would have to find out soon. Thornhill was frightened that he would find out accidentally himself and be thrown back into danger by the shock.

The next day he winced as usual when she was changing the dressings and asked: " How are they? "

Now! she thought. Do it casually.

In an off-hand way she said: " Well, they took one off the same day and the other one came off below the knee a couple of days later when septicæmia set in. Don't worry about it. A man with your guts can overcome that. They've got pretty good artificial legs nowadays."

She waited nervously for the answer and was amazed when he said quite casually:

" I suppose so." He was quite calm about it, and after

the moment of relief and anti-climax she wondered how he had known.

In fact, Bader had not known, and still did not know. He had heard her words and answered automatically, but they had not registered a meaning in his drugged mind because he could still feel his toes and did not know anything about the phantom sensations that lead a man to feel his foot so realistically after losing his leg that he can waggle his toes in his mind. With the phantom feeling he was in a never-never land of unreality, as in a dream when anything can happen, when a man can lose both legs and still walk on them.

Later that day when Cyril Burge sat with him and the left leg was hurting again, he said despairingly: " Why does it hurt so much? Why don't they cut it off like the other leg? " Burge, a little sick at heart, did not try to tell him.

It was the following day that the boy found out, and he only discovered it then because in spite of the morphia he was in torment that sharpened the brain into a little clarity. Squadron Leader Woollett had come in to ask how he was, and Bader said: " All right, sir, but my left leg's hurting like hell."

" I expect it's bound to hurt for a bit," Woollett said sympathetically.

" Well, I wish to God they'd cut it off like the right leg," he groaned, " that doesn't hurt at all. I'm sick to death of this left one."

" Would you really like them to cut it off? " Woollett asked.

" I don't give a damn what they do as long as they stop it hurting."

" You mightn't want it off if it didn't hurt."

" I don't know what I'd want if it didn't hurt. All I know is that I'm sick of the damn' thing now and I wish to God it were off."

Sitting on the chair by the bed, Woollett leaned forward, elbows on his knees, and he said quietly, nervously aware of the drama: " As a matter of fact, Douglas, they *have* cut it off."

5

THAT TIME it sank into his brain, but distorted with the morphia and the pain, it made no impact. Only the pain mattered: nothing else. He only said petulantly: " Well, why does the damn' thing hurt so much? "

It shook Woollett and he switched to the safety of squadron gossip, though he did not mention that most of them felt it would have been better for Bader to have been killed outright.

The impact of losing his legs never hit Bader in one moment, or even in a day or a week. The realisation formed slowly in a doped mind, which was merciful. Against the agonising urgency of the pain it was only a detail, and when the pain ebbed and allowed other things to matter his feelings were cushioned by dope that left him floating easily and somewhat detached in a tranquil unreal present, unmindful of any future. Joyce came in later that day and said: " Sorry, old man, but I had to take the other leg off below the knee. I couldn't save it. You're really lucky to be in the world still."

" That's all right, sir," Bader said. " I'll get some longer legs. I always wanted to be taller."

Next day, Christmas Eve, as the patient seemed disinclined to die yet, Joyce had him moved a hundred yards across a courtyard from the main hospital to Greenlands, the private nursing home in the hospital grounds. They put him in a friendly little room on the ground floor looking out on the lawns and a green deodar tree. There were gay curtains, deep chairs and a bookcase to give it warmth of atmosphere. Nurses kept injecting dope to quell the outraged nerves in the left leg, and Christmas Day was a blank to him. So were the next two days. Joyce was still afraid he would die from either thrombosis or sepsis.

On the fourth morning he was conscious of a new nurse

by his bed saying that she would have to change his dressings, and he started sweating again, remembering the last times, but she brought hot water and spent twenty minutes soaking them off so that he did not feel a thing. It endeared him to the new girl from that moment. Dorothy Brace was petite, with a friendly laugh and used her hands tenderly.

The pain was under control now, and about this time he remembered talking to his mother for the first time, though she had been sitting by the bed for days dabbing sweat off the grey face. They never mentioned the legs and most of the talk was a stilted fumbling for safe subjects. Patricia and Hilda came to see him too, both overflowing with a girl's warmth and sympathy for a wounded warrior, though Patricia, the more attractive of the two, was normally a rather brittle type. The more sensible Hilda said: " Look, Douglas, don't worry about losing your legs. If you'll take me as a typical young woman, the fact that you've lost your legs doesn't make any difference at all. You're still my favourite boy."

" I don't give a damn about losing my legs," he said amiably. " Honestly, it doesn't worry me a bit." In his drugged state he obviously meant it. Another time he said to Hazel Burge: " I can't always believe I've lost them, you know. I can still feel my toes."

Just before New Year Joyce took the stitches out. Bader braced himself for it, but there were only a couple of snipping sounds and a faint but painless sensation when the threads were pulled out. Suddenly and quite rapidly he began to get better. The face filled out and got some colour, and the dark rings went from round the eyes. So did the pain in the left leg and they tapered off the morphia. He felt well and alert, yet still unconcerned about the loss of his legs.

There were several reasons for this. Over the days through the soothing morphia and the monopolising pain the loss had slowly infiltrated his mind so that he had digested it gradually, absorbing it into his mentality through a cushioned pressure that did not jar. By the time it had clarified into reality he was already temporarily adjusted to it.

Another reason was that he did not—yet—miss his legs. He was comfortably in bed where legs were only remote extensions, and surrounded by attractive girls who brought him anything he wanted like devoted and adoring angels. There was no need to move a finger; he had chicken and egg-flips, fruit and cream, books, friends paying court, and a gramophone which gave him bliss by grinding out " Trees " or " Abdul the Bul-Bul Emir," nearly all day. Old friends from the squadron popped now and then through the window, assuring him by their presence that he still belonged and making jokes about his beard, which, as no one had shaved him yet, was beginning to look impressive rather than scruffy. Harry Day said: " You look like one of the apostles," which shocked Bader's firmly religious mother. Hilda stroked his brow. Dorothy Brace was a cheerful and gentle lieutenant who gurgled at his jokes and was deliciously horrified at bolder things he frequently said. He lived most agreeably in the present.

The past was past, the present was good and the future had not yet intruded. Let it wait. His nature, nearly always so practical, still had the capacity for dealing with first things first and shutting out others. The first thing was to get well again and that he was obviously achieving.

Possibly the most powerful reason lay in the kindness that enveloped him (largely due to Sister Penley-Cooper, who ran Greenlands, hand-picked his nurses and relaxed hospital rules for his benefit). The warm and reassuring affection on all sides satisfied a deep need that he was not consciously aware of. To all the nurses, as well as to Hilda and Patricia, he was inevitably attractive, not only because he was young, virile and handsome, but because he was a heroic figure cheerfully enduring tragedy with a courage that stirred deep feminine feelings in their normally impersonal and professional bosoms.

With the two girls (plus occasional others) and his mother always popping in there was seldom a dull moment. Mrs. Hobbs did not wholeheartedly approve of the girls, nor they of each other. As none would submit to the indignity of calling by roster it fell to Dorothy Brace to juggle the callers in the interests of peace, so that when one was in session with the patient she kept guard and diverted any others of the female sex. There was one hectic day when the two girls arrived within a minute of each other while Mrs. Hobbs was with her son. The nurse had no sooner steered Hilda into a waiting-room than Patricia arrived, and she bundled Patricia quickly into a refrigerator room, thinking: " That'll cool her off."

Dorothy Brace much preferred Hilda, who was devoted and completely unselfish, though Douglas, as a young man will, was becoming a little smitten by the more glittering, if less enduring, Patricia.

On 15th January he got up for the first time—a month and a day after the crash. He put on a dressing-gown in bed, Dorothy Brace pushed a wheel-chair to the bed and he heaved himself into it with his hands and sat there beaming with satisfaction. He wheeled himself to the window and sat looking out, but found he quickly became tired and was put back to bed in a couple of hours. Yet within a week he had the bandages off his stumps and was able to wheel himself down the ramps into the garden and spin around talking cheerfully to the gardeners.

At the end of January, Joyce said he could have a peg-leg on the left stump and try getting about with crutches. Bader wanted to start off with a " real " artificial leg, but Joyce said that would be a waste because the stump would probably shrink later. The real reason was that he had to operate on the stump again to cut more bone away, but he did not mention that.

A thin-faced little man in a white coat came into the room next day to take a plaster cast of the stump for the socket into which it would fit on the peg-leg (he called it a " pylon "— that was the trade name). Bader bared his stump and the man slapped the plaster on. In five minutes it had set, and as the man pulled it off all the hairs of the stump were dragged out by the roots with it, in a thousand little pinpricks of torture. Taken by surprise, Bader's shocked bellows of agony reached to the farthest cranny of the hospital and the language made people blanch. The little man apologised, nearly in tears; he had forgotten, he confessed, to put a thin sock over the stump first.

The little man was back in a couple of days with the " pylon," a short smoothly turned piece of wood, painted black, and with a rubber pad on the bottom. At the top was a leather socket made from the plaster cast and above this two metal arms stuck up on each side, hinged where the knee went and ending in a leather corset to be laced round the thigh. Bader strapped it on, with the little man explaining that the weight was taken on the sides of the leather socket, not on the bottom of the stump.

It felt very odd when he put it on. The stump fitted neatly into the moulded leather, but it felt strange to the unaccustomed skin, and the thigh corset gripped firmly. Sitting on the edge of the bed with the little man, Dorothy Brace and a big Irish nurse watching, he bent his knee to waggle the pylon and get a little used to it. Brace passed him a pair of crutches and said:

"Now don't forget, you won't have any strength in that leg at all for a while."

One on each side, they helped him up from the bed to ease his weight on the crutches. Tentatively he let his weight sink on to the pylon and the knee buckled like a piece of paper. It had no strength at all. They held him up while he shuffled each crutch forward in turn, and like that they lurched all over the room, giggling. It seemed a great joke. After half an hour he was tired out. Later he tried again and again, but it was three days before he was able to hobble a couple of steps without help, with the left knee feeling it would collapse at any moment. Apart from that the strangeness was going and it did not seem very difficult. He took to new crutches with rings round the elbows instead of pads under the armpits and they were more manageable.

A day or two later came a milestone in his career when he was able to stump down the corridor and take a bath—the first since his accident. He had worked out in advance how he would get into it—sit on the edge, unlace the pylon and then lower himself into it with hands on each side. Sinking into the hot water was ecstasy and he lay there a long time and got Brace to scrub his back. Getting out was not very difficult either. When he heaved himself up with a hand on each side, he was surprised to find how easy it was and remembered that Joyce had told him he would be about thirty pounds lighter without his legs.

Soon he was independent of outside help and spent hours stumping about the garden. It felt really good to be moving

round again, and in the limited world of the garden the loss of
his legs still did not seem at all serious, though the skin over
each stump was contracting and stretching tightly over the
bone-ends that he could clearly feel protruding. Joyce said
one day: " We'll have to trim these off a bit soon, you know.
Otherwise they might split the skin. We didn't have time to
do them properly before and you can't get your proper legs
until the stumps are all right."

" Another operation? " Bader asked.

" Yes. But it'll be all right this time. You're as strong as
a young bull." Joyce's manner seemed to be trying to soothe
him, but it was unnecessary, partly because Bader had complete faith in him and partly because his mind was still comfortable and secure from the weeks of protective kindness.

He said flippantly: " That's all right, Doc. I'm all for
you having your fun."

Joyce, professional dignity ruffled, remarked a little
severely: " It isn't exactly fun, old chap."

" Well, I don't mind, Doc. You can cut my head off if
you like."

" Would the day after to-morrow suit you? " Unused to
this attitude, the surgeon was a little formal.

" Fine. Any time you like." He genuinely felt no ner-
vousness at all.

On the chosen morning Parry Price breezed in again in
the same check suit. " You look disgustingly fit," he boomed.
" What d'you weigh now? "

" Ten stone two."

" Getting disgustingly fat," boomed Price and breezed
out again.

Brace came in with the pink liquid and injected it. Bader
said: " That sugar water won't send me to sleep."

" Won't it," she said. " You wait and see," but there
was no answer from the sleeping patient.

Joyce sawed about two inches off the bone of the right
stump, pulled the muscles down over the bevelled edges to
make a pad at the base and sewed them underneath. On the
left leg he took about an inch off the fibula, the little bone
behind the shin. There was no hurry this time; the patient
stood it easily.

Bader woke drowsily back in his bed, noted that the blankets were humped with the cradle again, and drifted off to sleep again. Hours later, nagging pain brought him more sharply awake; this time it was the right stump. The pain grew till it was like sharp teeth gnawing and tearing ceaselessly at the raw nerves and he was rolling his head from side to side in instinctive and futile struggles to get away from it. Dorothy Brace gave him morphia, but soon the pain cut through the drug and he began to sweat and make little involuntary sounds.

At intervals that he longed for, the morphia gave brief relief and then the attack started again, focused round the blunt end of the stump, where some major nerve seemed to be stretched on a rack. His mother and other visitors came, but, obsessed with the pain, he could not talk properly to them and did not want to be bothered. Even the top of the thigh seemed to have a sore patch, though they discovered the reason for that the first time Dorothy Brace changed his dressings; he flinched when she pulled out the top safety pin and she saw that the bandage had been pinned accidentally through his flesh.

The pain kept on and after a day or two visitors were discouraged. The patient was going downhill again, losing weight rapidly, the face growing grey and waxy under the sweat and the eyes sinking into the dark sockets. After a while his mind wandered into delirium and they began to get worried and increased the morphia to a maximum until he was unconscious for long stretches until resurgent pain or nightmares brought him out of it.

Night and day had no meaning and the nightmares came even in the stupor. Brace always knew when one was starting because he began twitching, then he would start waving his arms in front of his face as though he were trying to ward off something and call out: " Get me out of here! I can't get out! I can't get out! " It was nearly always the same, but there was no escape from the pain. Joyce guessed that internal sutures must be pressing on the sciatic nerve, and it was a question of time until the sutures absorbed and relieved the pressure.

It was nearly a week before the pain began to ease, and

then one day when Joyce looked at the stump he said: " You've got a bit of hæmatoma here, old chap."

Bader was too weak and exhausted to bother about what a hæmatoma was.

" Hang on to something," Joyce went on. " This might hurt a bit." Almost before Bader was aware of it, he was sliding something sharp into the wound, and in the shock punch of agony, Bader grabbed the back of the bed in such a frenzied spasm that he bent the iron frame. The pool of blood that had been trapped tightly inside began seeping out, easing further pressure, and from that moment the last of the pain began to ebb. The fluid seeped for ten days, gradually turning almost white before it stopped. By that time the stitches were out and the physical battle was over. Then the mental battle started.

Perhaps it would not have been so bad if everyone had not tried so hard to reassure him. He himself had accepted that he was legless and in some ways the future was a challenge that was almost exciting. That perennially stimulating aspect made him eager to be out of bed and into the world to get at it; also a lot of encouraging pamphlets had arrived in the post from artificial limb-makers and they had braced him. Perhaps, through a little wishful thinking, he had read into them a little more than the authors intended or perhaps they were too rosy anyway. At any rate he had the feeling that when he got his new legs he would be able to carry on a reasonably normal life, not, perhaps, playing rugger, but playing cricket (with a chap to run when he was batting), maybe some squash, certainly walking and dancing (with a bit of a limp perhaps), driving a car, of course, and flying too. No reason why not. Flying was mostly eyes and hands and co-ordination, not feet. He'd be able to stay in the Air Force. After all, he knew of a Service pilot who had lost a leg in the war and still flew. Thornhill used to come over and tell him about a friend of hers who had lost a leg and still played tennis. One leg. Two legs. No legs! What the hell! He had strength and balance and with the latest tin legs he would be quite mobile.

Lying in bed he had begun working out a way to drive his car again. The short right stump would probably not be sensitive or quick enough to guide a leg working both accelerator and brake. But his left leg would. All right—he'd have the outside pedals transposed; work the clutch on the right with his right leg and use the left for both foot-brake and accelerator. The seat would slide back on runners so that he could climb in easily and then lock it in the driving position.

But gradually the drip-drip of grave but well-meant encouragement began to have a sinister effect.

" Of *course* you'll be all right," they said. " Of *course* . . ." trying just too hard to be convincing. . . " Of *course* they'll let you stay in the Air Force . . ." (They'll *let* me stay . . . Charity!) " Even if you can't fly, they'll let you do a ground job."

" For God's sake they *can't* throw me out of the R.A.F.," he used to say. " I *know* I'll be able to fly still."

" Of course you will," they said soothingly.

The thought of a ground job while his comrades flew revolted him. They kept telling him about one-legged people who had made successes but he began to notice that no one seemed to know of anyone who had lost *both* legs and made a go of it. His mother said he was not to worry because she had signed a paper to look after him for the rest of his life, and his insides seemed to twist at the thought of always being dependent on her. He began having dreams, and always in them he had his own legs, dancing or flying, playing rugger or running around doing all sorts of carefree things as he used to. It was such a cruel shock when he woke and remembered where he was. That kept happening night after night because his subconscious knew nothing about life without legs and so it ignored the loss.

Dorothy Brace noticed he was getting less open and cheerful, and sometimes for hours would lie back with his eyes open, silent and moody. It worried her because she guessed what was happening. The first spoken sign came on a day when he heard that Johnson, a friend on the squadron, had crashed and was killed.

She said to Douglas: " You're darned lucky you didn't do that," and he turned his head and said bitterly:

" *He's* the lucky one. He's dead. I'd rather be killed outright than left like this."

Sometimes he was his cheerful self and at others, when he thought too much, the moodiness and silence would settle. He swung like an uncertain pendulum between the two. Out of the blue he said to Brace one day:

" They won't have me back in the Air Force, you know. And they won't give me a pension because they'll say it was my own fault."

" You don't *know* anything of the sort," she answered with practical sense. " Anyway, you could still make yourself a new career in an office."

" An office," he said scornfully. " Shut up in an office all day, tied to a desk and getting constipated on a stool! There'll be no life for me if I have to leave the Air Force."

In one way separation from the Air Force would hurt him more than separation from his legs. The Air Force became a kind of symbol: return would mean that he was a normal man: rejection would mean that he was a helpless cripple.

Yet Brace was the only one who ever saw his depression and bitterness, and with unflagging warmth and an instinctive sympathy that never hurt she unobtrusively soothed, cheered and encouraged him in the way that is a woman's special gift. The two were so closely identified that they were virtually fighting the battle together (to such an extent that Bader ever since has claimed that Dorothy Brace saved his life). To others, the other nurses, his mother, Hilda, Patricia, Cyril Burge or his squadron friends he always cracked hardy, putting on a brash front, saying that he would rather lose both legs than one hand, that he was not disfigured, not helpless, and that he had seen chaps with one leg gone who were worse than he would be. There was never any self-pity and he never looked back thinking, If only I hadn't done it. He *had* done it, and knew it, and it could not be undone. It was that attitude which made his future possible.

Only once he said wryly to Dorothy Brace: " Never do anything in a temper."

He took to reading his old favourite, Swinburne, who appealed to some secret and cynical streak bred of juvenile hurt.

" Listen to this," he said once and read to her:

> *"Thou hast conquered, O pale Galilean; the world has*
> *grown grey from thy breath;*
> *We have drunken of things Lethean, and fed on the*
> *fullness of death.*
> *Laurel is green for a season, and love is sweet for*
> *a day;*
> *But love grows bitter with treason, and laurel out-*
> *lives not May . . .*
> *For the glass of the years is brittle wherein we gaze*
> *for a span;*
> *A little soul for a little bears up this corpse which*
> *is man."*

" He doesn't know love," Brace said, giving the woman's viewpoint. " I don't know whether you know it, but Hilda has been in love with you for a long time. The legs might worry you but they'll never worry her. She's ready to marry you, you know. You've only got to ask her."

" Yes," Bader said, " I know. She's so utterly decent and kind. If I asked her to marry me she would . . . out of pity. They're all stirred by pity and hers would last, but I couldn't face it. If I ever marry it's got to be someone I meet for the first time just as I am now. Or no one." Then he covered up with a brazen laugh: " And if no one'll have me—hell, I'll marry *you*," which reduced her to demonstrative indignation.

Yet he was increasingly attracted to Patricia and she, in her own impulsive way, to him. About this time her mother took her away to South America for three months. Neither she nor Douglas had any illusions about the reason for the trip. Her mother liked Douglas in an abstract way but did not approve of her growing feeling for a legless man; a trip away might be the best solution. It was a practical thing for a mother to do but it hurt Bader for a while, increasing his moodiness.

Slowly he began to emerge from his brooding. A stream of affectionate letters from the ship helped and so did the prospect of artificial limbs, but the greatest and most constant factor in his endurance and resilience all through the months since December lay in his eternal and aggressive response to any challenge, the quality in him that is least elegantly and most effectively expressed as guts.

Senior Air Force officers visited him at the hospital to hold a court of enquiry into the accident. It did not promise to be a cheerful affair and, impressed by the braid and alarmed for her patient, Brace whispered to him: " If you're getting in an awkward spot ring the bell and I'll come in and say you're not well and they must go."

The door closed on the court and she spent a troubled hour until the bell suddenly rang and she hurried grimly in to protect him. The officers were sitting round the bed, everyone laughing and joking in great humour. Bader called: " Ah, tea for four, please, Nurse," and, fear somersaulting into feminine umbrage, she said severely: " What d'you think this is—a Lyon's café " and swept primly out.

The Court of Enquiry's finding slid adroitly round the question of blame, considering that whatever had happened, Bader had suffered more than enough.

Soon he was up in the wheel-chair again, and a week after that was stumping about the hospital garden on the pylon (luckily the left stump still fitted into the leather socket). Now it was late March and stimulated by the sunshine, the early spring air and the first green buds, he was feeling eager to face the world again. One day he went outside the main gate into Redlands Road, into the world again for the first time, and as he stood on the pavement a peculiar sensation of naked insecurity suddenly welled up as though a strong light were beating on him. He made himself stump a hundred yards down to the other gate and thankfully went inside again to the safe, home pasture. Trying it again that afternoon, he got the same feeling of exposed vulnerability as soon as he got outside the gate, and this time it was a shade worse because two people passed him, staring at the peg-leg and the right trouser leg pinned high above the knee. But after doing the same thing for three days the unpleasant feeling eased a little.

The day came when he had to cross the road to meet Hilda, and as he stood on the kerb a car whizzed past and a wave of dread chilled his insides. It felt like stepping help-lessly into a snakepit, but he made himself do it, waiting till no cars were in sight and then hobbling across as fast as he could, dimly realising that there would be a lot of strange and terrifying plunges to take from now on and that, for a while at least, there would be as many mental barriers to overcome as physical ones.

One important day Dorothy Brace and another nurse called a taxi and took him to a cinema in Reading, and he was like a small child bubbling with glee until the taxi pulled up outside the cinema. As he struggled out in a tangle of peg-leg, crutches and helping nurses, people stopped and stared: he did not see them until he straightened up, and then the cod-like eyes seemed to hit him. Clustered faces of pity and vacuous curiosity gave him the feeling of nakedness again, and he hobbled into the foyer shrinking from it. Inside the darkened auditorium he sank into a seat and felt all right again, normal and belonging with all the others, but later, as he ran the gauntlet across the pavement to a waiting taxi, he heard a woman say: " Oh, look, Jean, he's lost both of them."

Dorothy Brace squeezed his hand in the taxi and said: " Don't worry. You'll get used to it."

After a few more days swinging along Redlands Road he found that he did, at least to some extent, being able to shut his mind to the curious stares almost completely.

About this time Audrey and Adrian Stoop several times drove him for tea to their home at Hartley Wintney about sixteen miles from Reading, and these sallies into the world were noteworthy for their pleasantness. Adrian Stoop, secretary of the Harlequins, was one of the best fly-halves ever to play for England, and his home was a lovely rambling red mansion set in acres of lawns and parkland where Bader was surrounded by friendliness with no prying eyes to stare.

In the middle of April came the time to leave Greenlands for good. He was still the Air Force's responsibility and they sent a car to take him to their hospital at Uxbridge. The nurses seemed more affected than the patient; most of them gathered on the steps, some in sentimental tears, and he kissed them all with his cheerful enthusiasm and was driven off to face whatever the future held.

6

UXBRIDGE WAS pleasant enough, but different. They were mostly male nurses, enlisted men, respectful but remote. In the ward, however, he was among old chums again; Flying Officer Victor Streatfeild with his arm in a cradle, Odbert, who had played rugger with him and was in with a slipped cartilage, and others of his own ilk, all barely mobile " crocks " in some way so that he felt naturally at home among them. In fact, the R.A.F. *was* his home; no other place gave him the same feeling and it linked him again with the past to which once more he belonged.

For a few days the usual Service restrictions irked a little, especially the hot day he stumped three-quarters of a mile to the Group Captain's house for " elevenses " and struggled sweatily all the way back to arrive five minutes late for lunch. At the door a senior doctor, a wing commander, greeted him testily, " Oh, Bader, I do wish you'd try and be on time for meals. It's an awful nuisance for the staff when you people come in late."

He said, " Yes, sir," thought, " You ——! " and stumped into lunch fuming. It would never have happened at Greenlands; but then again, he thought philosophically, he would not have had quite the same companionship there. In any case, if he wanted to be a normal chap again he should expect that sort of thing.

His mother drove down from Yorkshire in the family car for a fortnight and took him for a drive most afternoons. The first time they went out she was driving along a quiet stretch of road in Great Windsor Park when he said: " Stop a minute, Mother, will you? "

She stopped, and he said: " Now let's change places. I'd like to have a crack at driving."

She looked at him in horror but he bullied her until before

she quite knew what was happening he was in the driver's seat
and she was sitting in the passenger's, saying: " But you can't.
And what will happen if the police catch you? "

" We'll have a damn' good argument," he said. " Now,
just put your foot on the clutch, will you? "

After more vain protests she did so. He selected the gear
(the car had a pre-selector gear on the steering wheel) and
said: " Right. Now let it up." She lifted her foot slowly, he
pressed his peg-leg on the accelerator and off they went. It
worked like a charm and as they went along he worked out a
drill for changing gear. He'd say, " Mother! " Her foot would
go on the clutch, he would select the new gear, say " Right,"
her foot would come up and that was all there was to it, apart
from practice, concentration and co-ordination. After a couple
of hours the team-work was quite good and his mother became
enthusiastic. " What a pity you can only drive with a partner
beside you," she said.

Pondering this limiting factor he thought out loud: " If
only I had something to prod the clutch with."

" Well, dear, would my umbrella do? "

" Yes! That's a wonderful idea."

She passed across her short, black umbrella, a very practical
implement. He took it in his left hand, selected the next gear,
held the wheel with the right while he felt for the clutch with
the ferrule, pressed it down, let it up again and the car had
changed gear smoothly. For several days he drove his mother
like that and it seemed to open new windows in his limited
world. This was being normal!

But there was still a catch. He could only use the umbrella
on a car with a pre-selector gear. There was no way on a
normal car of working both umbrella and gear lever with his
left hand at the same time.

Patients at Uxbridge were not supposed to have cars but
Peel, a young flying officer with a broken left leg in plaster,
had an old Humber parked in a garage a few hundred yards
away and he suggested to Bader and Streatfeild that they
should go for a surreptitious spin. In the safe period after lunch
when the doctors had vanished for coffee the three cripples
clumped down the road to the car. Peel's claim that he could
still use his plastered leg on the clutch pedal turned out to be

correct and cheerfully they cruised about the district. As the car had a normal gear lever Bader had no ambitions about driving it until going through Windsor Great Park again he noticed that it had a hand throttle on the steering wheel. It occurred to him that a hand throttle would spare the peg-leg to work the clutch.

" I could drive this car," he said. " Pull up and let's have a go."

Peel very agreeably did so and left the engine running while Douglas slid behind the wheel. Streatfeild in the back started muttering: " God, if I'm going to have my arm broken again I'd rather have a surgeon do it." Bader pressed the clutch down with his peg, put the gear lever into first, and let the clutch up again, working the hand throttle, and they moved off smoothly. After a while he found that changing gear with two movements of the clutch called for tricky co-ordination but with occasional crashes from the gear box, winces from Peel, and insults from Streatfeild, he managed reasonably well, though in due course they ran into Slough where the traffic was heavy and he began sweating with the concentration of slowing, stopping, restarting and slowing as they moved jerkily and noisily in the stream. It was easier to try and keep the car moving at all costs, even if only slowly in first gear, so he ploughed remorselessly on, butting, weaving and honking, carving a kind of bow-wave of squealing brakes on other cars and pedestrians jumping like startled springboks out of the way. Shouts of abuse rose in their trail but they blundered on with Streatfeild leaning out the back yelling: " So are you! So are you! So are you! "

In due course, in great good humour, Streatfeild said: " It's four o'clock. How about stopping somewhere for a cuppa? "

" Good idea," Peel said. " Stop at the next place Douglas." Bader promised to do so if he could.

As they came over a little bridge on the outskirts of Bagshot, Streatfeild said: " There's the Cricketers pub. Let's stop there."

But the pub was on the other side of the road and just as they neared it a stream of cars came the other way making it too awkward for the unpractised driver to ease up and swing behind them, so he took the easy way and said: " Oh, hell. Let's go on a bit. Bound to be another place soon."

Chance hangs on such slender threads. It was purely fortuitous that the other cars should be passing at that moment to force him on, but it was the luckiest thing that ever happened to him. A hundred yards on he saw a sign hanging out on the same side as the car: " The Pantiles." " Morning coffee. Lunches. Cream Teas." He eased the car and swung off the road on to the gravelled apron in front of an attractive converted barn with leaded windows, surrounded by garden, shrubs and ornamental trees. Outside, people, mostly elderly women, were sitting sedately at little tables in the sun sipping their cups and delicately pronging bits of cake into their mouths. Streatfeild got out of the back with his arm in a cradle and they all looked up at him with mild curiosity. Peel stiffly clambered out of the front passenger's seat with his conspicuously plastered leg, hobbling with a pair of sticks, and the converging eyes softened in sympathy. Streatfeild leaned in, took the crutches out of the back and handed them to Bader as he got out, and when the women saw the third cripple emerge from the driver's seat and prop himself up on the crutches and a single peg-leg, the eyes stuck out like organ stops and an awed silence seemed to echo round the place.

No one said a word while the three hobbled to a table as though everything were quite normal, sat down and distributed sticks and crutches around them. They looked up as a waitress arrived at the table and the interest of all three quickened. She was a slim girl with a delicately modelled face and a sensitive, expressive mouth—very good looking. Bader was first off the mark, flashing his glowing smile and saying: " Can we have three teas, please? "

" Cream or plain? " asked the girl.

The three men giggled faintly. " Cream," Bader said. (He never forgot the first words that he and the girl spoke to each other. It always seemed such a ludicrously banal start.)

As the girl went away Bader said to the others: " And very nice too! "

" Wonder if there are any more like her," Streatfeild said, looking round, but deciding soon that there were not.

The girl came back with the tea and laid it out in a faintly strained silence, conscious of being watched. Later when she came back with the bill Bader made a couple of facetious comments and once, briefly, she permitted herself a faint and dignified smile.

As the strange procession stumped back to the car everyone gaped again, especially when the one with the peg-leg got back into the driver's seat. With a grinding of gears the car jerked into motion and vanished into the traffic. The girl watched it go from the serving-hatch, feeling that the bold-eyed one with the peg-leg had an arresting personality.

On the way back to Uxbridge Bader was both concentrating on driving and thinking about the girl.

Next day when his mother took him out he artfully contrived that they should arrive at the Pantiles for tea and sit at the same table. The girl came over looking more attractive than ever and after some cogitation and discussion Mrs. Hobbs decided on cream tea. As the girl went away Douglas said as casually as he could: " That looks a jolly nice girl," but his mother only said absently: " Yes, dear. Rather a sulky mouth, though." He concluded that she had not really noticed the girl at all.

A day or two later came the moment he had been waiting for. One of the Uxbridge doctors said: " It's about time you got your new legs, Bader. Your stumps should be all right by this so we're sending you over to Roehampton for measuring."

Roehampton was a hospital in London where the Ministry of Pensions carried out its obligations. In the grounds were several wooden huts occupied by artificial limb makers, some specialising in legs and some in arms. The R.A.F. car took Bader to the hut of the Dessoutter Brothers who used to make aeroplanes until Marcel Dessoutter lost his leg in an early crash and became interested in artificial limbs. Bader was introduced to the other brother, Robert, a short, thickset, vivacious man with a big face and a shock of dark, grey-streaked hair.

" You *are* an ass getting both of 'em messed up," Dessoutter said. " Let's have a look."

Bader took his trousers down and showed the stumps. Dessoutter inspected them professionally and said: " By jove, those are good. Who did them for you? "

Bader told him about Leonard Joyce and added: ". . . so

now if you can trot me out a pair of your pins I'll bung 'em on and get cracking."

" Ha, we don't take 'em off the peg," Dessoutter said. " We tailor 'em to the stumps pretty carefully. It'll take a couple of weeks. How tall used you to be? "

" Five feet ten and a half in socks."

" I see." Dessoutter did some measuring and then slid thin socks over each stump and slapped plaster over them. Ten minutes later when he slid the casts and socks easily off, not a single hair came away. Bader watched the procedure with interest, beginning to be fascinated by the business.

" Right," said Dessoutter when he had finished, " I'll let you know in a couple of weeks when we're ready for a fitting. Send me an old pair of your shoes so I can give you the right-sized feet."

" Get 'em fixed as soon as you can, would you? " Bader asked. " There's rather a nice girl I want to take dancing."

" We'll do the best we can for you," Dessoutter said, thinking, incorrectly, that he was joking.

During those next two weeks Bader, unlicensed and un-insured, drove the Humber a lot in defiance of Air Force and Civil regulations, becoming quite competent and usually steering it to the Pantiles for tea till it became a kind of ritual which Peel and Streatfeild bore tolerantly. The girl always served him and every day the little chit-chat between them increased, though legs were never mentioned.

She was becoming rather important to him and he was beginning to realise that the situation was raising a new mental hurdle. Driving a car with companions in the normal world had lifted him out of the bitter moods of Greenlands but a girl, in the serious sense, was a different thing altogether. Though not depressed he was well aware that his future relationship with life was uncertain and somehow he did not feel justified yet in making any sort of advances. With confidence and bravura he could pat any other girl's bottom and kiss her till she giggled and said: " Stop," unconvincingly, but this girl was different and disturbing. He wanted to make advances and yet shrank from it, feeling that first he must sort things out, and also not wanting to spoil things by an ill-timed approach. All very complicating. Besides, there were Hilda and other girls, and affectionate letters coming from Patricia in South America. Outwardly as brash as ever, he was confused inside.

Some of the other girls took him driving and usually he steered them blandly to the Pantiles where the slim waitress, already very conscious of him, brought tea and went away thinking dubiously he was somewhat of a Casanova, legs or no legs.

The new legs might be his solution—when he got them! He yearned for the day they would be ready and he could put them on and walk out of Dessoutter's hut, free and exultantly independent again, almost like he used to be, except, he supposed, for a bit of a limp. He could stand with other people, with equality and with the blessing that they did not have of appreciating what it meant to be like them, however ordinary. He would drive his own M.G. straight to the Pantiles, walk in with full-length trousers and no crutches and sit at the old table. Then it would be different. He wrote to the garage at Kenley where the little M.G. was stored and told them to change the brake and clutch pedals and have it ready.

Dessoutter rang one day. He was ready for a fitting.

The first thing Bader saw when he stumped into the hut on the pylon were the new metal legs standing up incongruously without a body by the wall. Unpainted, they looked shiny and new and covered in little rivets, nuts and screws, and he was amused to see that they wore socks and his own shoes.

"Ah," said Dessoutter; "handsome, aren't they? Look at those muscular calves."

Bader grinned.

"You'll be about an inch shorter than you used to be," Dessoutter went on.

The grin faded. "Why?" Bader demanded indignantly.

"Gives you better balance. We always do that. If you want them longer we can always lengthen them."

"As long as I can be as tall as any girl-friend."

"You can marry an Amazon if you like," Dessoutter said. "We can make you seven feet tall."

They went into the fitting-room, a long rectangular place with large mirrors at the end and what looked like parallel bars, but so low that a man could walk between them, holding on to the bars for balance. A middle-aged very fat man was standing there in shirt tails with a strap over one shoulder and a belt round his bulging abdomen to which a tin leg hung by straps. He looked so odd that Bader said with youthful and tactless impudence: " I must say you look damn' funny."

Justifiably annoyed, the fat man said: " You won't think it so damn' funny when you try these things." He stumped clumsily along to the far end and began pulling on his trousers.

"Sit down here." Dessoutter indicated a stool and Bader, with a hand grabbing a crutch and another on the stool, eased his rump on to it and began the aggravating task of wriggling his trousers down over the buttocks he was sitting on. Dessoutter introduced two of his white-coated assistants, a jovial little man called Charlie Walker, and Tulitt, a big man with glasses. They made him strip to vest and underpants and then Walker, the " below-the-knee " specialist, pulled a short woolly " sock " over the left stump and slid it into a leather socket sunk in the calf of his new left leg. Above the calf, metal bars came up on each side like the ones on the peg-leg, hinged at the knee and ending in a lace-up leather corset. Walker laced the corset round the thigh.

" You'll find it a bit different to the pylon," Dessoutter said. " You've got ten inches of fairly rigid foot sticking out at the bottom and you'll have to lift your leg a bit higher to get the toe clear."

" All right," Walker said. " Hups-a-daisy." He put the crutches under Bader's armpits and he and Tulitt helped him up. Bader stood firmly on the leg and it felt fine. Just fine. Much more solid, somehow, than the pylon. Leaning experimentally on it he felt a slight " give " in the foot and Dessoutter explained that it was hinged at the instep with little rubber pads inset to allow a faint, resilient movement. The toe was jointed with a rubber pad too. Confidently Bader took a pace forward on the crutches and the wooden left toe caught on the mat and he nearly tripped.

" See what I mean about the stiffish foot," Dessoutter said.

He tried again, lifting his leg like a high-stepping horse, and walked up and down the room like a one-legged man with crutches. " Right," he said with satisfaction. " Let's have a go at the right leg."

Tulitt brought it over. The thigh was a shaped metal cylinder that came right up to the groin and strung to it were straps leading up to a thick belt, with more straps looped on the top like a double military Sam Browne. Tulitt pulled a " sock " on the right stump, eased the stump into the deep socket of the thigh and then buckled the belt to which it was attached round Bader's lower abdomen over his underpants. Over each shoulder he buckled the leather braces and then strapped the thigh corset of the left leg to the body-belt.

Bader sat in growing dismay, feeling he was being trussed into a strait-jacket. There seemed to be strap after strap and he felt irksomely constricted and uncomfortable.

" I'm afraid you'll have to have all this harness," Dessoutter said; " but you'll get used to it. Everybody does."

Tulitt stepped back. " All right," he said. " You'll do. No, never mind the crutches. Hups-a-daisy."

This was the moment!

Walker and Tulitt took each arm round their shoulders and hauled him to his feet for the first time. As his weight came on both, especially the right stump, it was the worst shock he ever had. He felt absolutely hellish, wildly unbalanced and strange. His right stump was utterly helpless and uncomfortable to the point of hurting and the harness itself seemed to cripple him.

In stung despair he burst out: " Good lord, this is absolutely impossible."

" That's what they all say the first time," Dessoutter said. " You get used to it. Don't forget your right stump has done no work for nearly six months."

Bader said grimly: " I thought I'd be able to walk out of here and start playing games and things."

" Look," Dessoutter said gently. " I think you ought to face it that you'll never walk again without a stick."

Bader looked at him with tense dismay, and then as the challenge stirred him he said pugnaciously: " Damn that! I'll never, *never* walk *with* a stick! "

In his stubborn anger he meant it.

" Try a step or two," Dessoutter suggested.

Feeling he would be more secure staying on the left leg he tried to swing his right leg forward, but it did not move.

"How the hell do I get it to move?" he demanded.

"Try kicking the stump forward," Dessoutter said. "The right knee will bend automatically. Then when it's forward, kick the stump downwards and it'll straighten out on the heel. It's like cracking a whip."

He kicked the stump forward and the metal knee bent as the leg went forward. He jerked the stump down and the knee straightened as the heel hit the mat.

"That's better," Dessoutter said. "Now come forward."

Bader suddenly felt paralysed, unable to move. It was like having a chair back stuck under a door handle.

"How the devil *do* I?" he asked irritably. "I *can't* move."

"That's the big lesson you've just learned," Dessoutter said. "You haven't got any toe or ankle muscles now to spring you forward as you used to. That's the secret of it. Or the catch. That right leg is a firm barrier that you have to push yourself over, on top of, by leaning forward and by your momentum when you're moving."

Bader said to Tulitt and Walker: "Pull me forward over this damn' leg."

They heaved him forward till he was precariously balanced on the weak right stump. Having his own knee, he was able quite easily to swing the left leg forward and then he stuck again, unable to push forward with toe and ankle.

"Pull me, for God's sake," he said.

They pulled and he flicked his right stump forward again, and they pulled him on to it and he got his left leg forward once more; so it went on in clumsy, stiff, jerky movements as they pulled him the length of the room. There was no natural automatic movement at all; he had to think each step out in advance and then signal his mind to make the move. Whenever they eased the forward tug he felt that the stiff leg out in front would push him over backwards. At the end he lowered himself on to another stool and uttered with grim feeling: "This is—awful."

"It always is the first time," Dessoutter said. "Don't be too depressed. The first steps always feel like that. It's learning to walk all over again with an entirely new system and you can only learn it by practice, like playing the piano. Don't worry. You'll do it, but it might take you six months."

Bader looked at him with a humourless grin. " Don't be silly. There's a girl I want to see in a couple of days and I want to be walking on these things then."

Dessoutter broke a slightly appalled silence: " You'll find a stick useful in pushing yourself over the leg in front."

Bader stuck his jaw out aggressively. " Not me! Come on, you two. Let's have another go."

They hauled him to his feet again and this time they took his elbows instead of having his arms round their shoulders. " Try taking very short steps,"[1] Walker said. " It'll be easier to lean forward over a short step."

He tried that and the improvement was immediate. They still had to pull him forward, but he did not get quite the feeling of coming to a dead stop whenever he put a leg forward, especially the right leg. They went up and down the room several more times and slowly, subconsciously, he began to get the hang of it, leaning the top of his body well forward so that his unbalanced weight tended to carry him on to the leg placed just in front.

Dessoutter said after a while, " Let's try taking half an inch off that right leg. Might make it a bit easier."

Bader sat down and unstrapped it. Walker and Tulitt took it away for half an hour and lowered the thigh about half an inch into the knee socket. Bader put it on again and without so much height to overcome found that he could transfer his weight with a little less trouble. It was not so much that it was easier but just a little less impossible, still wildly clumsy and un-nerving. They helped him up and down the room several more times and then he said: " All right, now let me go." They were too cautious to do so, so he shrugged his elbows to push them away and took his first steps alone, three or four jerky stumbles that ended with him just grabbing the parallel bars before he fell over. He hung on to them, grinning all over his face where the sweat was shining again. Turning to Dessoutter, he said: " There you are. You can keep your damn' sticks now."

Dessoutter was laughing in genuine delight " I've never even seen a chap with *one* leg do that before first time," he said.

---

[1] This is one of the real secrets at the beginning.

Walker and Tulitt were openly surprised, obviously not pretending.

" I think you've done enough for to-day," Dessoutter said; " you must be feeling pretty tired."

That was true enough. He was hot, and sweaty, beginning to feel exhausted, and the right stump was stiff and sore. As he strapped on the peg-leg again Dessoutter suggested he come back for more practice in a couple of days; meanwhile he would " pretty up " the legs with paint and other finishing touches. Bader got up with his crutches to leave and this time the peg-leg felt strange in an unpleasant way, unsteady and uncomfortable. Back at Uxbridge when he hobbled in Streatfeild bellowed: " Hallo, here's Long John Silver again. I thought you were coming back on your own two pins this time? "

" I was going to," Bader said; " but I forgot to take a clean pair of socks."

Thinking in bed that night, he did not feel so flippant. It was not like he thought it was going to be at all. Little needles of doubt were pricking him. He supposed, a little doubtfully, that it would be all right with practice.

Back at Roehampton in a few days he found the legs painted a smart yellow. " Looks more natural than any other colour through a thick sock," Dessoutter explained. " Don't ask me why."

Walker and Tulitt walked him up and down the room again and it was still hellish, but not quite as bad as the first time he had tried. After a while he made them loosen their grip and with their hands hovering by his elbows he was able to walk the length of the room. Standing facing the wall he found a new problem—he could not turn. In exasperation, hands steadying him against the boards, he said to the wall, " What the hell does a man do now? " The others turned him round and back at the parallel bars the same thing happened. It seemed impossible to turn his feet round. He lurched back to the other wall and this time as he neared it he teetered round in a tight semi-circle, fending himself off against the wall. For two hours he practised that morning until he was almost too tired to stand.

" I honestly think you're incredible," Dessoutter said as he unstrapped the legs. " None of us has ever seen anyone like you before."

Walker and Tulitt inspected the stumps for raw patches or chafing, but they seemed all right. Bader wanted to take his legs away there and then, but Dessoutter said there were still a couple of adjustments he wanted to make.

It was a glorious spring morning when Bader drove back to Roehampton to take delivery and his spirits were soaring at the prospect. He thought it must be the way a woman felt on her way to pick up a new fur coat. Dessoutter had a set of three shallow wooden steps with banisters in a corner of the room and when he had put the legs on and tried a couple of circuits round the room, he made his first attempt at the steps. With the banister to support him, it turned out to be relatively simple—hand on the rail to steady him, left foot on the first step, bring up the right foot to the same step, and then lift the left foot again. Thank God he still had one knee left to raise himself with or it would have been impossible. Coming down was the same thing. He called it the " dot-and-carry " system and has never used any other for stairs. That morning he learned how to get up out of a chair without help too—lean forward, a good shove on the seat of the chair with both hands and the left knee took the strain and lifted him.

" Well, there you are," Dessoutter said. " They're all yours. It's a bit soon to let you have them really, but I suppose you'll only start complaining if you don't take them." He grinned. " Shall I wrap them for you? "

" Not on your life," Bader grinned back. " I'm walking out on 'em. Here, catch this. . . ." He threw him the peg-leg and nearly fell over in the process. " You can do what you like with that."

" Now what about a stick," Dessoutter suggested persuasively.

" Never! " he answered crisply. " I'm going to start the way I mean to go on."

For the first time he began putting the rest of his clothes on over the legs and harness, the shirt over the belt and shoulder straps, the trousers over the legs. Ah, here was another catch! He had to lift the right leg with a hand round the thigh to do it, and then found that with the foot sticking rigidly out he could not point his toes to slide into the trouser leg. The heel and toe caught and he had to ease the foot through the cloth by tugging on each crease alternately.

" Oh, another point," Dessoutter said. " Never try and walk barefoot. It's difficult and you'll probably fall flat on your back. You'll notice that the feet slope down at a slight angle. That's because shoes have thick heels and you'll always need a heel underneath to put you on an even keel."

He put on his tie and jacket, stood up and teetering round, looked at himself in the mirror. He looked *quite* normal. It was a terrific moment. Heart-swelling! He was *standing up*—dressed like an ordinary chap—looking like one. And, after seven months, suddenly feeling like one again. Perhaps he looked a bit shorter than before, about five feet nine and a half now so that the trousers crinkled slightly at the ankles. A detail. With great satisfaction he said: " It looks damn' good to be standing up like this again."

As Walker and Tulitt helped him totter out to the waiting car he became irksomely conscious of the harness. Under his clothes it seemed worse than before, cripplingly uncomfortable, as bad as walking with a stone in one's shoe . . . in the circumstances a ridiculous comparison, he thought wryly. But he'd have to wear it for the rest of his life! A grim thought. Maybe he'd get used to it. . . .

As they handled him into the car Dessoutter said: " Don't worry if you have a bad time for a while. You've done amazingly well so far, but don't expect it to go on as fast as that. Everyone feels desperate for a while." They shouted " Good luck! " through the glass and the car moved off. He relaxed, satisfied, on the soft seat and discovered a new catch. He could not cross his legs.

7

WHEN THE car pulled up just before lunch in front of the Uxbridge hospital doors an orderly helped him out and the wing commander who had once ticked him off for being late for lunch was standing by the door talking to another doctor. Bader pushed away the orderly who was fussing at his elbow and lurched with tense concentration about six paces to the door feeling smugly proud like a girl in a new party dress which is bound to be noticed.

The wing commander briefly turned his head, said curtly: "You ought to have a stick, Bader," and turned back to the other doctor. Bader tottered angrily through the door, praying that he would not fall.

In the dining-room the greeting was hearteningly different. There were roars of welcome and ribald remarks. Streatfeild bawled: "Long John's got his ruddy undercarriage back." He walked across to them, concentrating too much to make any answer and feeling that he was going to spoil his entrance at any moment by making a three-point landing and denting his tail-skid. One of them pulled out a chair and he just made it. Lunch was eaten in great jollity.

"No doubt any moment now you'll be wanting to dash off to the Pantiles," Streatfeild suggested banteringly.

"Not on your life," he said. "I'm going to learn to walk on these pins first and the next time I go there I'll be driving my own car."

His ward was on the first floor and after lunch he tottered out to the stairs. They looked appallingly high and steep, but he dragged himself up and was sweating at the top. In the ward he tried to give a demonstration of walking, lurching a precarious way from bed to bed, grabbing each bed-rail as he reached it, and encouraged by cheerful barracking from patients in the beds. But after a few minutes he was so tired he could hardly stand and the right stump was trembling and aching with weakness. He tried again an hour later but after one circuit sweat was soaking him all over and the right stump was threatening to collapse under him, the muscles shrunken, weak and flabby after so long without use. He was beginning to realise that it was not going to be so easy and for the rest of the day he relaxed to give the stumps a chance to recover.

At dinner-time he was able to struggle downstairs, but when he went to climb back he just could not do it; the strength was drained out of him and he was aching all over. A burly orderly carried him up with Bader's arms round his neck, body dangling over his back, and lowered him on to his bed. Lying there, Douglas undressed and with enormous relief unstrapped his harness and carefully leaned the legs against the wall where they would be nicely within reach. He thought it was smart of him to remember that, but the thought was interrupted by a minor clatter as the legs fell over on to the floor, looking obscene and disembodied with shoes and socks on. Too tired to pick them up, he swore and crawled between the sheets.

Shortly another thought stirred. Damn! He hadn't cleaned his teeth. Oh, let it go till morning for once. A little later he came out of a doze wanting to go to the toilet. Damn! He'd forgotten that too. Well, it would *have* to wait till morning. Sinking down again he wanted to blow his nose and found he did not have a handkerchief. That was the last straw and he started muttering unprintably. In that mood there was not going to be any sleep and at last he testily reached out for his legs but could not reach them on the floor. He rang for an orderly who picked them up and offered to carry him, but no —he laboriously strapped on all the harness, got a handkerchief, tottered into the bathroom and did all he wanted to, then tottered back to bed, making sure this time that the legs stood up within reach. Very tired he was drifting off to sleep when he began to feel thirsty. Firmly he put it out of his mind and rolled over, but the desire for a drink of water crept insidiously back and the more he tried to forget it the more he wanted a drink and the angrier he became. Damn and blast! No drink —no sleep, that was obvious. But he was damned if he was going to strap that flickering harness on again. Tossing the blankets back, he lowered his rump on to the floor by taking his weight with hands on the bed and the bedside table, then swinging himself along on his hands and bottom he got to the bathroom.

Then he couldn't reach the tap.

Muttering, he pulled a stool across, hoisted his rump on to it with a hand on the edge of the bath, took a drink from a tooth-glass and "walked" on hands and rump back to his bed where with a last strenuous effort, hands on bedside table and bed, he hoisted himself back on to the sheet. Temper cooling off as he drifted tiredly into sleep he realised that going to bed would have to be an organised ritual before removing the legs.

In the morning as he woke he remembered with satisfaction that he was mobile and, after the previous night's lesson, lay a while planning procedure. Was it worth putting on his legs to walk to the bath, taking them off and putting them on again afterwards? No. He went to the bathroom on his rump and put his legs on afterwards. Clutching the banister rail he dot-and-carried alone down the stairs to breakfast and after that teetered out into the garden, where he got another shock as he stepped on to a patch of grass and instantly felt as dismayingly insecure as the first time he had stood on the legs. It was fairly level grass, but it was no firm level floor and he felt that he would topple if he moved. He took a step, the right toe immediately hit a clump of grass and he pitched forward—his first fall. He took the shock on his hands. That part was all right, but now he had to get up again. He lay for a while thinking about it. A man came running up and said sympathetically: "Hang on to me, old boy. Soon have you up."

"Go away," he snapped. "I'll do this."

He took his weight on his hands and lowered the rear weight on to his left knee, then pushed hard. In a moment he had fallen back on his hands again. He tried again, pushing up on the left toe, straightening his left knee, and pushing his hands back towards the toe, and came uneasily but without too much difficulty to his feet again. Then he took another step and fell again.

That morning he fell at least twenty times but managed to stumble up and down the grass again and again, arms flailing to keep his balance like a novice on ice skates, but

persisting until his legs were aching and trembling with
exhaustion again. Worse, the right stump was sore in spots—
obviously chafing. The difficulty of walking on anything but
the smoothest floor was worrying him. That was the worst
part of all. There would be more rough paths than smooth
paths in life, and the airy confidence he had had was rattled.

After lunch he got the orderly to carry him upstairs to the
ward where he practised from bed-rail to bed-rail again. Soon
he was in agony from the chafed right stump and had to
struggle to his bed. Unstrapping all the harness and taking off
the stump sock he found that the skin round the groin was
rubbed raw in a couple of places. If the future was going to be
like that . . .

With a sudden idea he called an orderly to bring him some
sticking plaster and taped it over the raw parts, put his legs on
and tried again. It was a little better, but then the whole
stump was so stiff and sore that it was hard to tell which part
hurt most. That evening a nurse put some of her cold cream
on the raw patches and it was very soothing.

In the morning a car drove him back to Roehampton.

"I thought you'd be back about this time," Dessoutter
said. "Let's have a look at those stumps." He, Tulitt and
Walker spent about two hours adjusting the sockets of the
legs.

"Remember it's darned hard for you to tell yet whether
there's anything wrong with the fit," Dessoutter observed.
"They'll feel awful for a while anyway, like false teeth when
you first put them in. Later, you'll know anything not fitting
in a moment."

Bader went back to Uxbridge to try again, but they seemed
no better. For two days he stumbled about, continually falling,
curtly refusing any help and getting up unaided to lurch and
fall again. Mostly he fell forward, sometimes backwards, two
or three times sideways, sometimes on hard floors, often on the
grass. As he did not fall on the stairs where he had a banister
to cling to the others kept suggesting he use a stick but he
refused tersely. From the parallel bars at prep. school and the
years of rugger he had no fear of falling and that was the big
thing that helped. If he had worried about falling he would
probably have been beaten.

Hour after hour he doggedly kept at it when other men would have given up to rest or despair. Moving the stiff, chafing and aching stumps was continual torment but he made himself keep on doing so, his face running with sweat that poured off all over him, soaking his underclothes and, unfortunately, the stump socks too, so that they lost their woolly softness and began chafing again, rubbing the skin off in new spots. The good-humoured barracking that had greeted his first efforts died away as people became aware that they were watching a man battling to do something that had never been done successfully before, with only his guts to help him and a crippled life ahead if he failed. It was something that could not be laughed off.

Refusing to accept that it was impossible kept him going. He insisted that he *knew* he could learn to manage the legs with practice. In a way he was like a man trying to run before he could walk because he would *not* stop trying and the right stump was not strong enough to take the punishment. The more he forced himself to walk the more it hurt, tending to become a vicious circle and making it even more difficult. Now and then he *had* to rest a little because the stump would not hold him, and then he tried again.

Soon, stumps plastered like a quilt, the car took him to Roehampton again where Dessoutter found that the right thigh seemed to have shrunk. In due course, he said, they would rivet the metal a little tighter, and meanwhile he slipped a second stump sock over it. That felt better, and then Dessoutter found a hard muscle developing at the back of the thigh and with a little hammer Tulitt tapped out an almost imperceptible indentation in the metal to accommodate it. To reduce sweat and chafing Dessoutter suggested keeping both stumps well powdered. Then Walker lacquered the leather socket of the left leg so that the sides would not hold perspiration. Bader found it fascinating to watch their ingenious approach to each new problem.

But the main problem, the sheer clumsiness, they could not help. Dessoutter, who had noticed the new grimness in Douglas, said: " Look, in this business I've seen that only people who've actually lost a leg can know the shock of awkwardness when they first try an artificial one; it's just a thing they have to work on till they develop a new skill. Most of them take months to learn. Some never do. In a way it's like a chap starting to play tennis from scratch and having to work up to Wimbledon standard. Chaps who lose one leg have still got a good one to rest and hop on and an ankle and toe to give them spring when they're walking. You haven't, so you've just got more to learn. And it's still harder for you because there's no one with no legs to teach you. There aren't any text books either."

Back at Uxbridge he kept trying but it seemed impossible to acquire balance and natural movement, and still he kept falling. Gradually he found the right stump did not ache so much, as the flabby muscles hardened with use and the chafing came under control, but that eased only the pain; the legs were as unwieldly as ever, yielding no fraction to practice and bringing growing disillusionment and anguish as he woke from the dreaming expectations of normality and cricket. Mentally, it was the worst time since the accident. His nature, in any case, rejected defeat and now the menacing implications produced obsession to master the legs. The others learned not to try and help him up or steady him as he lurched, realising it was a battle that he himself had to fight. Besides, trying to help only produced rebuffs. He wanted passionately to be independent as much as he wanted to be mobile. It goaded him to think of having to ask help in the simple, physical things of life and he shrank from the idea that people in due course would politely prefer to avoid him as being a nuisance.

He began dreaming about his legs again, not as at Greenlands, about having his real ones back, but something more wickedly subtle. In these new dreams he had his artificial legs —he could see them and they had the nerveless artificial feel— but he was using them easily like his real ones, running around exuberantly, leaping up and down stairs and even, on one bitter-sweet occasion, kicking a football. Waking up was not pleasant.

And then, about ten days after he got his legs, he detected the first hint of automatic control. It was a little like a man learning a strange language that sounds like gibberish until one day he catches a phrase and understands it. As though some barrier had been removed, he began walking a little more easily and after that the improvement was rapid. In five days he was lurching about without having to concentrate so hard either on movement or balance; some automatic instinct seemed to have taken over part of the work. It was not easy, far from it; it was still hard work, but not intolerably hard. He still fell, but not so often. The stumps still chafed, but not badly, and they did not ache or twinge any more. The legs still felt uncomfortable when he strapped them on but after a few minutes he became a little more used to them, though the harness remained just plain, bloody uncomfortable. Best of all was the change in the mental climate as hope, a little qualified, came back. It was strengthened when he went all through one day without falling and also learned to turn by spinning on his right heel.

He telephoned the garage at Kenley and asked them to drive his car over (the doctors gave him permission to have it —good occupational therapy, they said).

" Off to the Pantiles? " Streatfeild asked, and he nodded.

" Ah, well, jolly good luck to you. I kept telling you you'd be all right but all you did was be ruddy rude. There's only one thing you've got to learn now and that's to change your socks now and then. It's getting a bit noticeable already."

" Why should I," Bader grinned. " I haven't even taken my shoes off for two weeks."[1]

" Please yourself," said Streatfeild; " but I can just imagine people some day muttering to each other, ' Don't go too near Bader, he's still wearing those same purple socks he had on at Uxbridge twenty years ago '."

Changing into his best clothes that morning while waiting for the car, Bader did take his shoes off and was amazed to see that his socks had practically no feet on them. Not only the heels and toes were worn away but almost the whole of each foot as well. He realised that it must be because there was friction now on each side of the sock where before there had been soft, yielding skin on one side. Changing his socks, he hobbled out and got a thrill as he saw the familiar old M.G. with the red wings swing through the gate.

" Cor, I 'ad a time driving it over," the mechanic said.

[1] As another man pulls on his shoes and laces them up, Bader pulls on his legs and buckles and laces them up.

" Kept putting my foot on the brake to change gear and then treading on the clutch to stop. Be careful with it, sir."

" You seem to have made it all right."

" Yes, sir," the mechanic said. " In the end I crossed me legs and drove that way."

Bader heaved himself into the seat behind the wheel. His feet seemed to fit easily enough over the pedals. He pressed the clutch down with the right leg—it was purely a thigh movement with no feeling in the leg or foot at all but he *could* feel the pressure of the clutch against his thigh with enough sensitivity to control it and let it up slowly. He tried the left foot on brake and accelerator and found there was enough feeling in the shin to switch the foot from one to the other. That was strictly a knee movement, but the whole thing seemed to be easier than he had expected. He felt no tendency to use the accelerator with the right leg because it felt obviously too remote, in the way that a man who had lost his right arm would not try to steer with the missing arm. He started up and drove slowly round the asphalt parade ground: no trouble in keeping an even pressure on the accelerator and no tendency to do the wrong thing. For a quarter of an hour he drove in figure eights, stopping, starting and reversing, and was highly gratified. It was almost literally driving a car by the seat of his pants and rather a good augury for the time he started flying again. Doubts were vanishing fast. Now he knew he could go anywhere he liked at any time and was even more mobile than people who had only their legs and no car. Altogether a most prepossessing day. With his old confidence he said to Streatfeild: " Like falling off a log. Now we're off."

" God be with you," Streatfeild said. " I suppose they'll bring you back without a head this time."

He steered out of the gates and drove in a sunny mood and at a cautious speed to Kingston Police Station where he lurched with care up to a uniformed man behind a desk and said: " I'd like to take a disabled driver's test, please."

" Certainly, sir," said the constable.

" It's just that I've got no legs, but I can handle the car perfectly well."

He might have been remarking that it was a nice day for all the reaction he got; one would have thought that legless men popped in for driving tests every day. Soon a man in civilian clothes came out and got into the car with him. Bader drove away from the kerb explaining the transposed pedals, but the man did not seem interested. After a couple of hundred yards he said: " Stop and reverse across the road, will you, please? "

Bader stopped, looked behind to see if everything was clear and reversed as directed.

" Glad to see you look behind first," the man said. " Last chap didn't do that. If you'd like to drive me back to the station you can fill out the form and we'll give you your ticket."

It was as easy as that.

Blithely he set off for the Pantiles and pulled into the gravelled apron about quarter to four. This time as he got out and lurched to the usual table hardly anyone looked except the girl. Out of the corner of one eye he saw her over by the serving hatch, staring, but he kept looking straight ahead concentrating on appearing casual about his metamorphosis. She came across to the table looking very bright and he switched on the glowing grin. With a little less reserve than usual she remarked that he had not been there for some time and he was delighted that she was too discreet to mention the legs, though he had been quite sure that she wouldn't. But it made everything so natural, as though there were nothing at all remarkable about his walking. He chatted before he ordered and chatted again when she brought the tea, and again when she brought his bill. He paid her, got up, stumped over to the car, praying that he would not fall, turned round—she was still watching— and gave her an enormous wink. As he drove away he wondered what her name was.

Now with the car and able to walk, even if still precariously, life took on a new savour and he drove out every day to sample it. Most days he arrived at the Pantiles for tea and the friendship with the girl progressed quietly and decorously with no particular move on either side. He still had to find out where he stood in regard to life.

Patricia wrote from the ship in Madeira, just a brief note to say that she was due back in a fortnight and hoping he was getting along well. That was something more to sort out.

Kendall, the Warden of St. Edward's School, had been

writing to him constantly and encouragingly ever since the
accident and Bader wrote to let him know how successful the
new legs were. Back came a suggestion from the Warden:
Why not play in the Old Boys' cricket match in a few weeks?

Just that little touch gave Bader a thrill and he wrote back
a joyful acceptance.

Several times in this period he went to the Stoops at Hartley
Wintney and once stayed the night, scaring the life out of a
maid in the morning by bouncing down the stairs on his rump
and hands because for some small unremembered errand he
could not be bothered to put his legs on. They were still uncomfortable, especially the wretched shoulder straps that seemed
to tie him up so that he felt hobbled. Now and then the stumps
still chafed or hurt in other ways, but he was able to control
those things with powder and sticking plaster. Yet, all the time
he was becoming more sure of them, though he still fell from
time to time. Audrey Stoop said one day, " Honestly, Douglas,
no one would know that you haven't got your own legs."

" Oh, don't be silly," he said. " Anyone would know."
But, absurdly pleased, he got down on his knees and turned a
somersault on the lawn. " I've been dying to do that," he
beamed.

From time to time the Stoops introduced him to other
visitors who were never told, at least till later, that he had no
legs, and they were therefore quite natural with him, regarding
him only as a young man with a bad limp. Natural reactions
like that were good for him; he was already aware of a subtle,
constrained atmosphere with some strangers who already knew.
They took him one night to a nearby party where someone
started playing a gramophone and couples began dancing.
Bader, aflame with a new challenge, had to try. He asked a
girl to dance; she smiled and got up, and as they started he
caught his toe and fell, luckily not dragging her down with
him, but as he got clumsily to his feet she said tartly: " You're
drunk," and left him. Later she was horrified when she found
out, but she need not have worried because the incident did
not trouble Bader, who was too practical to have any pity for
himself.

At Hartley Wintney he met a young flying officer who had
had an accident which left him with a stiff knee so that he

could not fly any more. Bader picked up his own right leg and waggled the knee. " There you are," he said. " Have it off, old boy. Have it off." It became his standard joke to anyone with a sore leg.

The Stoops had a testy old wire-haired fox-terrier called Worry who was half-deaf and jealous of his little privileges such as lying in the same spot every night under the dinner-table. Bader was dining with them one night when he moved his legs under the table too near Worry and jerked them away again as a menacing growl came up. Then he remembered and put them back in the objected place. The dog growled again and suddenly snapped at his ankle, bit on the metal and recoiled from under the tablecloth with the hair along his back bristling with shock.

About the middle of June he suggested some sick-leave, and O'Connell, the young doctor who was looking after him, said it was a good idea. He'd better take a couple of months and get really used to life outside again. Rather than go all the way home to Yorkshire straight away Bader said he would go to Kenley for a couple of weeks so that if anything more went wrong with the legs he would be within easy reach of Roehampton.

With nostalgic eagerness for the familiar faces and atmosphere he drove himself to Kenley and walked into a deserted mess, full only of empty memory. A waiter he did not recognise said that most of the pilots were away on an air-firing course at Sutton Bridge. Then Harry Day, who was waiting for a posting overseas, walked in and saved the moment. " Hey, hey," Day said cheerfully. " What've we got here. Good lord, you look like a drunken sailor." Then the mess sergeant came along beaming with pleasure and said he could have his old room back.

He felt a queer moment of pleasure when he looked again at the spartan bed, the lino, rug, chair and the bookshelves. It was even his old batman who answered the bell, and said warmly: " Why, Mr. Bader, sir, it's good to see you back."

Bader shook his hand. " It's good to *be* back," he said. " I'm staying for a while. Have you still got my kit here? "

" Yes, sir," said the batman. " All safely in store. I'll go and bring it straight up."

Soon he was back with the trunks and Bader rested in the chair while the batman began hanging up the clothes and stowing shirts and things in drawers. There was an awkward moment when, delving into a trunk, he pulled out a pair of rugger boots; their eyes met for a moment and the batman put the boots back in the trunk. A little later Bader said: " Bring up my cricket-bag, will you? "

Next afternoon was very hot and Day suggested he join his family for a swim—Day had a lovely home with a handsome, blue-tiled swimming-pool on a Surrey hill near Kenley. That raised a new problem. He also had three children.

Bader asked awkwardly: " Will the youngsters mind if they—er—see me? "

" Good lord, no," Day said. " They'll probably be fascinated."

While the others changed in the house Bader walked the hundred yards across the lawns to the pool, took his legs off and changed under a tree, then rump-walked to the edge of the pool and lay on the grass waiting. When the children came down—girls of eight and three and a boy of six—he was feeling uncomfortably self-conscious but the youngsters, apparently well briefed, did not seem to notice anything unusual.

" Slip in over the side," Day said, " and I'll stand by in case you're top-heavy and turn upside down."

" Hell, no," he said. " I'm going in off the springboard."

At the deep end the springboard jutted over the water from a platform on stilts about eight feet high. He rump-walked to it and hauled himself up the short ladder with his hands (his arms were getting very strong now) holding his weight between hauls with the right stump on the rungs. Then he swung to the end of the springboard, stood on his hands and dived in. Spouting water and grinning, he surfaced (right way up), finding himself more buoyant in the water without his legs, though swimming seemed more tiring because he could not kick to help himself along and, instead of being top-heavy, his rump tended to sag in the water instead of trailing in the normal flat position. But they were details; just being in the water felt glorious.

Having tea on the grass afterwards the children's curiosity overcame their briefing and they stared frankly and with great interest at the stumps, but so innocently and naturally that he was not in the least embarrassed. All afternoon they alternately swam and lay in the hot sun which was good to feel on his bare and pallid skin after the months indoors.

Round about seven the family went back to change and Douglas dressed on the lawn. As soon as he started walking back to the house he felt the shoulder straps chafing his shoulders and realised with annoyance that he was sunburned. By the time he reached the house they were beginning to hurt. He was up against a new problem. Even sitting down at dinner the straps chafed and irritated, and by the time he got back to his room in the mess he was glad indeed to take them off.

In the morning when he got up the shoulders were red and very tender. He strapped the legs on but as soon as he stood up the straps bit into his shoulders like hot bread-knives scraping on the nerves and he sat down hurriedly, wincing, and slipped them off with relief, swearing with frustration. From a little thing like that he was helpless again, unable even to get to the dining-room for breakfast unless he submitted to the unthinkable indignity of the rump-walk in public. More than ever he loathed the shoulder straps.

In desperation he unbuckled them from the belly-belt hoping he might be able to struggle out cautiously without them. After pulling the belt fairly tight, he eased himself up from the bed and gingerly took a few steps; to his amazement and delight the legs felt better than ever before and just as secure. For several minutes he stumped about the room, an odd sight in creaking legs, vest and underpants, and everything he did felt better. After that he tossed the shoulder straps into a corner, dressed and stumped out to breakfast. (He never wore the shoulder straps again.)

Patricia was due back and he rang her home. The butler said yes, she had returned and went to find her, but came back soon to say she was not in. " Ask her to ring me, would you? " Bader said.

No call came in the next three days, but on the fourth morning a letter arrived from her. It was only about four lines and the line that mattered was, " I don't think it's any good us going on any longer . . ." It was the first time that he felt he did not belong, was not exactly a wallflower, or a leper, but a man apart. Years later he told me it bounced off his back. It didn't. In an unguarded moment it brought him facing a stark and ugly possibility that he had refused to admit into his controlled thoughts, though it had always haunted the background. The girl herself did not mean a great deal to him but bitterly he felt that she might at least have made some other excuse than hinting so baldly that the trouble was that he had lost his legs. That letter rubbing it in loosened some of the roots of his robust but none-too-firmly planted confidence. Outwardly he was as breezy as ever when the pilots came back from air firing but in private he had hours of encroaching doubt which, in the end, only made him more stubbornly set on making no major concessions to life and requiring the same important things as anyone else. Several times he went to the Pantiles and the fact that the girl was so clearly glad to see him, accepting him as he was, strengthened his morale.

A pleasant note came to him from the Under Secretary of State for Air, Sir Philip Sassoon, inviting him for a week-end at his house near Lympne. Clearly it would be not only a pleasant week-end but a chance to find out where he stood for his future in the Air Force: once at Cranwell he had briefly met Sassoon and everyone in the R.A.F. seemed to like and admire him for his hard-working helpfulness. Sassoon even suggested that he bring a young man from the squadron with him as companion so he drove down in the M.G. with Peter Ross, a thickset, lively young pilot officer with whom he had become friendly.

Sassoon was a millionaire and his house was a mellow old mansion set among cypress trees on a slope beside Lympne Aerodrome where 601 Auxiliary Squadron was busy flying Hawker Demon two-seater fighters on its annual summer camp.

The Saturday afternoon they spent lying beside the swimming pool with the Demons taking off and noisily climbing just over the pool and the tree-tops. As one of them roared over Bader said wistfully: " By gosh, I wish I were up there again." He turned to his host and added: " You know, sir, I'm quite sure I could fly perfectly well now. It'd be easier than driving a car—not so much footwork."

"Well, they've got an Avro 504 on the aerodrome," Sassoon said. "Would you like to have a shot at it?"

"I'd *love* to," Bader said, exhilarated and hardly believing, and Sassoon promised to arrange it. Bader spent the rest of the afternoon in nervous hopes that Sassoon would not forget, but at dinner that night Sassoon said: "I've had a word with the C.O. of 601. The Avro will be ready for you in the morning, and Ross can go with you in the other cockpit." They were the most melodious and exciting words he had ever heard.

8

I N THE morning it felt wonderful just to be putting on overalls, helmet and goggles again and to be walking up to a well-remembered Avro.

"Take it as long as you like," Norman, the C.O. of 601 said. "All I ask is bring it back in one piece."

Getting into the cockpit was not the trouble he thought it might be. He put his foot into the slot at the side of the rear cockpit and Ross gave him a heave up. Then, clutching the leather-padded rim of the cockpit with his left hand it was simple to grab his right calf and swing it over into the seat. He eased himself down, delighting instantly in the old, familiar smell of an Avro cockpit, the blend of castor oil, dope, leather and metal that rolled the months back more subtly and potently than any other sense. Sitting in the familiar seat, eyeing instruments and crash-pad and taking the stick in his hand, sent a flush of enchantment through him. He set each foot on the rudder-bar and pushed each end in turn—it was easy; nerveless in the foot but sensitive in the shin and right thigh. He'd literally be flying by the seat of his pants.

Ross climbed into the front and shortly his voice came through the earphones: "Shall I start her up from here, Douglas?"

"No," he said; "just turn on your switches and take your hands off. Leave everything alone. I'll do it."

The Huck starter backed up and turned the propeller; the warmed-up engine caught smoothly and throatily and the aeroplane was quivering with life. He ran up to test magnetos, set the cheese-cutter trim in neutral, waved the chocks away and taxied carefully downwind, jabbing the rudder and finding it easy to steer. Turning at the hedge he saw the grass stretching down to Romney Marsh, pushed the throttle forward and the engine let out a deep, hearty bellow. She started rolling, and as the tail came up and she yawed with the torque he prodded automatically at the rudder and she straightened, gathering speed. Pure joy flooded him at that moment; he knew already he was completely at home. At about 55 m.p.h. he let her come gently off the grass, climbed a little, turned and circled the aerodrome and then steered for Kenley. The old touch was back and as she cruised over the familiar fields he was sublimely happy. A circuit over Kenley and then he was slanting in to land. This was the acid test.

She swayed and dipped docilely as he nursed her with delicate and quick little movements of stick and rudder so easily that he did not notice how simple and automatic it was to hold her straight. Quite unconscious of the legs he flattened, held back, back, back, and then she touched gently on three points. On the landing run he was conscious of his legs again but held her straight with ease and turned and taxied to the tarmac apron in front of the squadron's hangar, full of satisfaction. Ross turned his head back from the front cockpit. " Not bad," he grinned. " Not bad at all. I couldn't do much better myself."

He helped Douglas out, guiding his left foot into the slot because the wooden foot could not feel it. A lanky figure sauntered across the tarmac to them. " Hey, hey," said Harry Day. " Peter been giving you a taste of the air again? "

" No, he hasn't," Bader grinned. " I was just giving him a lesson."

" *You* were," Day said. " Well, I might have known it was you from that ruddy awful landing."

After an extremely cheery lunch in the mess Bader flew Ross in the Avro back to Lympne and made another neat landing. That afternoon he was happier than he could remember. At the house Sassoon asked how he had got on, and he said: " Absolutely fine, sir. Honestly, no different at all to flying with my old legs." Later he added carefully: " I've got to have a medical board, sir, to see if I can fly again. I was rather hoping you might let them know in advance that I actually have flown again and that it's perfectly simple with these legs."

Sassoon said: " You let me know before you go for your board and I'll see to it."

That was all he needed. The clincher! All worries fell away in that moment. He'd be back on the squadron flying again as though nothing had happened with the full life he wanted so badly stretching out in front of him. In that faith a glow suffused every part of him.

After that wonderful week-end he drove to St. Edward's with his cricket-bag for the Old Boys' match. The Warden and the masters were amazed to see how mobile he was and, changing into flannels, he felt on top of the world. The Old Boys batted first and Bader went in third wicket down with a man by the square leg umpire to run for him. As soon as he had the bat in his hand taking block at the crease he felt natural, but when the first ball came down, pitched a shade too full on the off, and he tried lunging out to drive it he suddenly felt hobbled and helpless, and the ball flashed by the wicket-keeper. The same thing happened next ball; it was as bad as having the ankles tied together. He knew then that his old habit of jumping down the pitch was finished : he would have to wait for the ball and swing cautiously from the shoulders, and even then it had to be a limited swing or he would over-balance. He could block them all right, but that was only negative. Still, the eye was as keen as ever and shortly he broke his duck by glancing one to leg. It was easier to pull balls than stroke them out to the off. He got another single, then a two, and cheering broke out round the ground as he pulled a fast one to the leg boundary. Shortly he did the same again and had scored 18 before he flicked one on the off into the wicket-keeper's gloves. Walking back, he was cheered to the pavilion.

So far, highly gratifying, but when he went to field in slips he was useless unless a ball came high into his hands; he just could not get down to stop a grounded ball in time and if he tried too hard he only fell over. In the outfield it would be worse because he could not throw without falling over. Then his stumps began aching from the constant standing in one spot. He refused to give up but by the time the side came off the field he was exhausted and felt unhappily that he could only be a passenger in any side. It was not a defeat for the legs that day, but neither was it a victory; it left him with a mildly depressed feeling that he would rather not play seriously again, partly because the contrast with the old days would be hurtful and partly because he felt he could not pull his weight on any team.

Later that week he drove home to Sprotborough and relaxed for several weeks in peace, irked only towards the end of the period by an itch to be active again and doing something about the future. His mother asked him one day what his plans were, and he answered: " I'm going to stay on in the Air Force, Mother. I'll be flying again and everything will be fine."

" I thought you might have had enough of flying now."

" Good gosh, no," he said. " I've had my crash now. I won't have any more." In fact, at that time he did have an illogical faith (later destroyed) that he had had his issue of crashes: a little like an artilleryman's theory that a shell never lands in the same place as another. Besides, he pointed out tactlessly, if he crashed again like the last time it would not matter because he had no more legs to lose.

Back at Kenley a telegram arrived telling him to report for his medical board and he drove down to the Central Medical Establishment in Kingsway, filled with confidence and delighted that things were getting under way again. He went the rounds of the doctors who examined his eyes, whispered at the other side of the room to test his ears, looked up his nose and down his throat, listened to his heart and chest and tapped him here and there. One of them absentmindedly took up a ruler to tap his knees for reflexes and then dropped it with a foolish laugh. " Sorry, old boy, I forgot. We'll take your reflexes as read." The doctor who took his blood pressure looked up and mused, " That's interesting. Your blood pressure's down; quite normal now." He decided it must be because the lack of legs reduced the distance that the blood had to be pumped and added: " You'll probably be less inclined to black out in steep turns and dives too, because you've got less extremities for the blood to sink into." Then, with a grin: " Something to be said for losing your legs after all."

The senior doctor, a wing commander, glanced over the findings, and said: " Well, you seem to be in pretty good shape so we're passing you out as A2H, which means restricted flying at home. I'm afraid you won't be able to go solo with

that, but we'll recommend you for a posting to the Central
Flying School at Wittering and see what the flying boys think
of you."

Bader accepted the finding equably. He knew he would
have no trouble with the flying boys, and while waiting for a
posting went back to Uxbridge (the depot, not the hospital, this
time) and did normal duties, taking parades, acting as orderly
officer and so on. It made staying on in the Air Force seem so
natural. Several times he went to Roehampton for more
adjustments to the legs and also kept driving over to the
Pantiles for tea as often as he could, though he still did not
know the girl's name and, affected by dormant self-doubt,
hesitated to make any overt move. Yet he felt the friendship
was ripening very agreeably so that it came as a shock one day
when she mentioned that she was leaving the Pantiles soon and
going back to live with her parents in London.

It disturbed him more than he thought it would. Time he
did something about it. Also it irritated him because with any
other girl, waitress or lady, he could have turned on the bold
banter at the drop of a hat and had her giggling and liking it
in no time. Yet he did not think of her as a waitress (though it
was normal for regular officers in England of the 1930's to
consider such questions seriously).

Then the posting arrived, ordering him to the glowing new
horizon at the Central Flying School, but his pleasure was
tempered by the knowledge that Wittering was far away. One
last time he drove to the Pantiles resolved to do something
about it and said to the girl when she arrived:

" I'm going away too."

" Oh," she said, sounding politely interested but not
ostensibly crushed.

" Going up north to Wittering to start flying again." He
tried to be offhand about it, but she clearly guessed its importance because she smiled with pleasure and said: " Oh,
you'll like that, won't you? I *am* glad."

This was the moment. He said, trying to sound casual
again:

" I was wondering if you'd care to come out with me one
night in London if I can get down."

" That would be nice. I'd love to," she said, sounding

neither too eager nor too cool, but observing the rules for young women impeccably.

(What the devil was her name?)

He said blandly: " Would you give me your address and telephone number in London? "

The girl knowing quite clearly what he was thinking, printed on the back of a tea ticket:

> Thelma Edwards,
> 12, Avonmore Mansions,
> Kensington, W.14.

" Oh, thanks awfully," he said, relieved. " My name's Douglas Bader."

(She had known that for weeks. Three of her cousins[1] were Air Force officers and she had asked them a lot of questions about the interesting young man who had lost his legs. Bader did not discover that till later, when he also found that her father had been a wing commander, that her step-father was a colonel and that the girl had been a young woman of leisure until her beloved pet dog had died and she had gone to stay with a grandmother at Windlesham and taken the Pantiles job to get her mind off her grief about the dog.)

For a while he was too joyfully occupied at Wittering to get up to London. His very arrival there on a flying course filled him with thrilling content. First they gave him dual in an Avro 504 and he was so obviously competent that on the third morning his instructor took him up in a two-seater Bulldog. When they landed the instructor said, apparently in ignorance of the doctor's ruling, " Nothing at all wrong with you, old boy. You might as well take her up by yourself after lunch."

After four years in the Service Bader did not volunteer the information that he was not allowed to go solo, but went smugly into lunch where, by the sheerest chance, the station doctor observed with appalling clarity in the hearing of the instructor: " I hear you're doing frightfully well, old boy. You must be *very* fed up at the doctors not allowing you to go solo."

What made him more furious than ever was that Freddie West, who had lost a leg above the knee winning a V.C. in

[1] The Donaldson brothers, who all rose to senior rank and won eight decorations between them (each won a D.S.O.). Teddy Donaldson also broke the world speed record after the war in a Meteor.

the war, was at Wittering doing a refresher course and flying solo every day. And what was more—he walked with a stick.

As consolation the instructor promised him a week-end's leave and he wrote to Thelma saying that he would be in London on duty during the week-end. Would she care to go out with him to the Café de Paris on Saturday night? A decorous note came back accepting and asking if he would care to call for tea beforehand. The flat, she pointed out, was under the name of Addison, her step-father's name.

On the Saturday morning he set out early in the M.G. with boiled shirt and his tails in a little case. Avonmore Mansions, he found, was six storeys high and the name Addison was under the heading: " 6th Floor." There was no lift. Carrying his case, he dot-and-carried up the stairs, twelve flights, ninety-six steps. He counted them and arrived at the top breathless and heart pumping. As he rang the bell he wondered what it was going to be like. He didn't give a damn if she *was* a waitress, but he was annoyed at being breathless. Might make him seem nervous. He wasn't nervous. Hell, no. Ridiculous thought.

The door opened and a uniformed maid showed him into a pleasantly furnished sitting-room where the girl, looking very fetching in a green dress, rose from the sofa. He'd never seen her without the waitress overall on before. She introduced him to her mother who looked young and agreeable and a tall, lean man, her step-father, Lieutenant-Colonel Addison. The girl leaned over the tea things and asked, with a tiny smile: " Cream or plain? " and after that he felt very much at home.

Later, feeling debonair in tails for the first time since the crash, he took her to the Café de Paris in a taxi. The dinner was good, the girl was utterly charming, and sitting at the little table for two with his legs tucked safely away beneath, the music lilting away in a straight, pre-war rhythm, stimulated a mood of glowing zest. On the spur of the moment he leaned over, and said: " Would you like to dance? "

Just for a moment she looked uncertain and then she smiled and nodded.

He got up and lurched round to help her up. He hadn't meant to dance at all: the idea had just slipped out but there was no drawing back and suddenly reckless he thought: " Dammit, if I can walk all right, I can certainly walk clutching a girl."

" I didn't know you danced too," she said appreciatively as they reached the floor.

" Oh, it's quite easy," he said airily. " If I trip I hang on to the girl."

He took her in his arms, waited a moment for the beat of the music and then hopefully lurched off.

It *was* quite easy—if not especially graceful. He held her a little away to give him space for kicking the right leg forward and for a while he was really only walking in approximate time to the music, steering round the bends still in a walk, but it was so uncomplicated that it was almost an anti-climax. Emboldened he tried a mildly fancy turn and it came off. He tried another one and stumbled but instantly she was unobtrusively steadying him and they danced on. " You seem very good at supporting men," he grinned.

Now and then his right knee tapped her left knee cap as he jerked the leg forward, but she soon learned to move her own leg a little more smartly than usual After a couple of numbers they were moving round the floor quite impressively until suddenly he collided with her and she came to a dead stop, her face tight with pain.

" What's the matter? " he asked anxiously. " Are you all right? "

" Yes," she said torn by apology; " but you're standing on my left foot."

He jumped off in horror, torn by apology himself, and they danced on. Soon the music changed to a waltz. He had a stab at it but very nearly tripped, taking her with him, on the first half-step. " Sorry," he said. " Afraid I can't cope with this one. Let's go and sit down."

They went off the floor arm-in-arm and as he dot-and-carried up the two shallow steps to their table his other hand missed the banister and he overbalanced backwards, landing heavily on the floor and nearly bringing her down with him. People turned round and stared down their noses as if he were drunk.

She helped him up and they got to the table where he

grinned to cover up his inward mortification—he had never fallen in front of her before. She leaned across and put her hand on his arm. " You know, I think you're really amazing," she said. It was the first time she had ever even obliquely referred to the loss of his legs and she did it so warmly and naturally that it really endeared her to him.

They danced several more times after that and he blissfully ignored the fact that his legs were aching and that patches on the stumps were rubbing raw. About 2 a.m. he took her home, bade her a decorous good-night and drove off very pleased with himself in the M.G. to the R.A.F. Club where he had to tape the chafed patches on his stumps before he went to bed. On the Sunday he took her for a drive in the M.G. and un- obtrusively she managed to convey to him that she genuinely admired the way he drove and got around on his legs. Driving back to Wittering that night he was sure he had found the girl he wanted.

Next week-end he drove to London again and took her to the Ace of Spades roadhouse near the Kingston By-pass. They danced again and on the way back he stopped the car and kissed her. (She had been wondering when he was going to do that.) To his delight, after an appropriate time, she kissed him back.

On the Sunday he drove her to the Stoops' and Audrey Stoop, who approved very much, invited both of them down for the following week-end.

That week at Wittering he was doing aerobatics again in a Bulldog as well as ever he had, though still irked by the com- pulsory presence of the instructor in the back cockpit. Once or twice he assuaged this affront to his dignity by brashly criticising the instructor's own aerobatics and giving him a few tips, though the instructor got his own back a day or so later when a gust caught the aircraft in a cross-wind precautionary landing and the Bulldog swung in an incipient ground-loop till the instructor quickly corrected with his own foot on the rudder bar. He made a few ribald comments, but Bader's flying was so invariably immaculate that resumption of full flying duties seemed " in the bag." On the strength of that he traded in his M.G. for a later model that week, though it took the last penny out of his bank account.

On the Saturday he drove Thelma down to the Stoops' and, when he kissed her good-night at Avonmore Mansions on the Sunday evening, he knew he was in love with her and that she was at least extremely fond of him. He floated back towards Wittering in the usual bliss of a smitten young man, unconscious of a scene that concerned him deeply in the Addisons' flat.

Thelma's mother said guardedly to her: "You and Douglas are becoming quite a twosome. Is it serious?"

"Yes, it is rather," Thelma said. "You like him, don't you?"

"Yes, I do," her mother said. "He's charming. But how could you marry a man with no legs? Have you thought of that? You must be very sure."

"I'm already sure. Without his legs I still like him much more than anyone else."

"You might have to be a sort of nurse to him," Mrs. Addison warned.

"Not," said Thelma confidently, "with Douglas."

She had no qualms at all about a future with him and though, as an unusually attractive girl, there were also in the offing a naval officer, an army officer and a young stockbroker, they seemed stodgy and even pompous compared to the zest and sparkle of the legless one.

The Chief Flying Instructor sent for Bader and said: "Look, you're wasting your time up here. There's nothing more we can teach you about flying and there's no point in your mucking about not able to go solo."

"That's what I was sent here to find out, sir," Bader said. "Once I'm passed by you the medical board can decide on my flying category."

"All right," said the C.F.I. "I'll write and tell 'em."

The answer came back surprisingly quickly—a call for Bader to appear for another medical. He drove to London savouring the moment that evening when he would see Thelma and tell her he was going back to a squadron. In the Kingsway building the rotund warrant officer receptionist who had seen so many accident cases come up for medical check, welcomed him. "Hallo, sir. Back again. Just a moment, sir, and I'll get your file."

He was back with it shortly, saying: "You don't have to see the doctor after all, sir. Only the wing commander."

Good, Bader thought. Only a formality. He went into the wing commander's office and the man with the detached professional air behind the desk said: "Ah, Bader, nice to see you again. Sit down, will you?"

He sat, waiting equably for the good news. The wing commander cleared his throat and glanced at some papers on his desk. Clearing his throat again he said: "I've just been reading what the Central Flying School says about you. They say you can fly pretty well."

Bader waited politely.

"Unfortunately," the wing commander went on, "we can't pass you fit for flying because there's nothing in King's Regulations which covers your case."

9

OR A moment it didn't sink in, and then a cold feeling slowly spread through him. He sat in stunned silence for a few more moments and then found his voice: "But of course there's nothing in King's Regulations, sir. That's why I was sent to C.F.S. To see if I *could* fly. They were the only ones who could give a ruling. I mean . . . doesn't that fit the case?"

The wing commander cleared his throat again. "I'm sorry. I'm very sorry indeed, but I'm afraid not. We've thought about it a lot and I'm afraid there's nothing we can do about it."

Forgetting discipline, Bader flared angrily: "Well, why the hell did you send me there to be tested?"

Embarrassed, the wing commander said apologetically: "Well, you were very keen to have a shot and I'm just terribly sorry it turned out like this."

It was then it occurred to Bader that the whole question had probably been decided before he went to Wittering. They had expected him to fail at the flying test—let him see he can't fly and then he won't mind. Now they were embarrassed by it. A little longer he argued the point, but it was obvious that the decision was official, probably made at high level, and he had been in the R.A.F. long enough to know that trying to reverse official decisions was like kicking at a wall of blubber. One could never even track down their source.[1]

Too sick with disappointment and anger to argue any longer, he pushed himself to his feet, said stiffly, "Thank you

[1] Some time later he discovered that while he was at Wittering an article had appeared in a Sunday paper asking rather querulously about the waste of taxpayers' money in giving a flying course to a man without legs. It also pointed out how unfair it was to mothers whose sons might have to fly with this man. Presumably people who saw it were too tactful to show it to him at the time. Whether it had any bearing on the R.A.F.'s decision he never discovered.

very much, sir," and stumped out. Dimly he realised that it was probably not the doctor's fault and they had probably meant well in sending him to Wittering. But that did not help. As he passed the warrant officer he said, " The bastards have failed me," and walked out.

Tight-lipped he drove to Avonmore Mansions, walked up the ninety-six steps again and found Thelma sewing in the sitting-room. Surprised and pleased, she asked what had brought him from Wittering, and he told her, barely controlling his anger. She listened quietly and asked: " What's the situation now? "

" I haven't the slightest idea," he said moodily. " I suppose they'll offer me a ground job."

" Well, you'll still have a career in the R.A.F.," she said consolingly and he burst out violently:

" I'm damned if I'd take the job. I'd rather leave."

She talked to him for a couple of hours before he promised to wait a while and see what happened. A week later—it was November now—he was posted to Duxford, a fighter station some forty miles north of London in Cambridgeshire, where he found 19 Squadron flying Bulldogs, some instructors training the Cambridge University Air Squadron, and a precise, immaculate wing commander in charge of the station, who said: " Glad to have you here, Bader. You're taking over the motor transport section."

The job was simple enough: not much more than sitting in a little office all day drinking tea, signing chits and giving orders about lorries. He knew several of the squadron pilots and he thought it would not be difficult to talk them into giving him some flying. Officially he was still classed as " General Duties," the flying branch, and stubbornly he felt there might still be a chance of getting an airborne job—how, he didn't know. They asked if he would like to be reclassified " Administrative " or " Equipment," and he said no. Vaguely unhappy, he soon knew that he could never stay in the R.A.F. doing a ground job because his unhappiness came from watching others flying.

He became friendly with Joe Cox, one of the instructors training the Cambridge undergraduates, and one December day when the wing commander was away Cox took him up in an Armstrong Whitworth Atlas, an Army co-operation biplane. Cox let his passenger do most of the flying and was impressed. Several times after that when the coast was clear they went up together, and after Cox's reports the other pilots were indignant that bureaucracy limited Bader to flying on the sly.

They were discussing it in the mess one night when Cox said: "Look, come out and watch Douglas do a tarmac landing to-morrow." (Tarmac landings consisted of coming in so slowly and with such fine judgment that the aircraft touched down on the short tarmac apron and stopped before running on to the grass. They were not officially approved of and therefore popular.)

Next morning at eleven o'clock the pilots watching by the hangar saw the Atlas waffle down with Cox's arms ostentatiously held high out of the back cockpit to demonstrate that Bader was doing the flying. At the critical moment as the Atlas touched neatly on the tarmac the wing commander walked round the side of the hangar, saw the performance and guessed grimly from the instructor's upheld arms that he was allowing a pupil to do a tarmac landing. As Cox climbed down his grin faded to see the wing commander standing next to him like an outraged schoolmaster. The wing commander opened his mouth to speak, and then Bader pushed up his goggles in the front cockpit and was recognised. The senior man said coldly:

"Was that you flying this aircraft, Bader?"

"Yes, sir."

"But you're not allowed to fly!"

"No, sir."

The wing commander turned to Cox. "Don't you know Bader isn't allowed to fly, Cox?"

Bader cut in. "No, sir," he lied. "Flying Officer Cox had no idea. I should have told him, I know."

The wing commander said grimly: "Well, Cox, if you didn't know before, you know now. Bader is not to fly again." He turned to Bader. "I shall decide later what action to take about you."

Apparently he was sporting enough to forget it because Bader heard no more and the weeks passed tediously. Cox suggested they might fly again but Bader vetoed the idea for Cox's sake. The only diverting incident was the time four of his lorries in convoy collided nose to tail on a wet road when the front one had to brake sharply. Bader's report exonerated the drivers and blamed the R.A.F. for fitting all the lorrries with solid rubber tyres that skidded easily. The wing commander told him tersely that it was not his job to tell the Air Force what they should do with their lorries, and he saluted and withdrew, thinking there was one further recommendation he would like to make about the lorries to his seniors.

One week-end on leave Adrian Stoop took him and Thelma to see the Harlequins play Richmond at Twickenham. Bader was very excited until the match started, and then in the first couple of minutes as a scrum triggered off a Harlequin wing movement that ended in a try, he suddenly became quiet and did not open his mouth for the rest of the match. Stoop knew that he had made a mistake and that it would be an even worse mistake to suggest that they leave. In that hour Bader felt more bitterly than ever before the loss of his legs. All his old friends were playing and it really hurt. Driving back to the house they talked of other things, and later that evening he told Thelma that he would never go and see another rugger match. (Nor did he.)

Towards the end of April he was sent for by Squadron Leader Sanderson, C.O. of 19 Squadron and acting station commander in the senior man's absence. Sanderson had been adjutant at Kenley before Bader lost his legs, and when the young man walked into his office and saluted, the good-natured Sanderson said: "Douglas, this is the worst thing I've ever had to do in the Air Force. I've just received a letter from Air Ministry . . . here, you'd better read it yourself." He passed the letter across. Bader took it and read:

Subject: Flying Officer D. R. S. Bader.

(1) *The Air Council regrets that in consequence of the results of this officer's final medical board he can no longer be employed in the General Duties Branch of the Royal Air Force.*

(2) *It is suggested therefore that this officer revert to the retired list on the grounds of ill health.*

(3) *A further communication will be sent in respect of the date*

of his retirement and details concerning his retired pay and disability pension.

Sanderson said: " I'm terribly sorry, Douglas."

" That's all right, sir," he said, and after a while he saluted and stumped out. There did not seem anything else to say. In a way he had been expecting it but it was still a shock and left him with an odd numbed feeling. Shortly it began to seep through that he would soon be unemployed, possessing no skill that he could profitably use and mobile only so long as he could afford to buy petrol for the M.G. Yet they were giving him a pension—that was quite decent of them—though he knew it would not be much, especially for a man used to pleasant things.

He drove down to see Thelma and told her.

" But you could still stay in on the ground, couldn't you? " she asked.

He said bluntly: " I suppose I could, but I won't. It's no good being in the Air Force unless you're of it, and as far as I'm concerned you're not of it unless you're flying."

" Do you have any idea as to what you'd like to do? "

" Frankly," he said, " no."

He took her out to dinner at the Indian Restaurant in Swallow Street, just off Piccadilly, and they sat close together over curry. After a silence he said obliquely: " I'm not much of a proposition for anyone, you know. No legs. No job. No money."

" Don't worry," she said. " We'll make out. I could always make a few pennies at the Pantiles."

There was not much more said than that. No blunt question. No blunt answer. Just a delicate understanding that sent him back to Duxford quietly happy, knowing he was not alone.

Shortly another letter came from Air Ministry, impersonal but not unkind, granting him £100 a year total disability pension and £99 10s. a year retired pay. That was not too bad in those days—at least for someone content to exist quietly. Bader wasn't.

For a fortnight he was clearing up the ends of his Air Force life, handing over his job to another officer and packing his civilian clothes: the latter part was easy—he had only one blue suit, a sports jacket and some grey flannels. His uniforms and cricketing kit he gave to Joe Cox. One day he visited the Officers' Employment Bureau at Air Ministry. The Bureau's task was to find jobs for Short Service Officers when they had finished their five years' commission. A brisk, cheerful man asked him what he would like to do and he answered: " I really have no idea."

" Would you like to go abroad? "

" Not very much. I wouldn't be any good in the tropics with these legs anyway. It's no good when they start to sweat."

The man said at last: " Well, leave it to me and I'll have a look round and let you know if anything turns up."

Getting his clearances brought one last-minute hitch: six lorries were missing and the transport sergeant who knew all details was away on leave.

" I can't sign your clearance," said a worried adjutant. " These lorries are worth £6,000 and if they aren't found you'll have to pay a proportion, you know."

" It'll be a damn' small proportion and you'll have to take it out of my end of the month pay," Bader said, not caring greatly. " I've only got forty-five bob at the moment."

Then the sergeant came back and they traced the lorries to a repair depot.

The last few days were trying. Suddenly tired of the whole business, he wanted only to get the final agony over and be away to face what he had to face. Then there was only one more signature to get; and that night he took his last uniform off for the last time and handed it to Joe Cox with no visible sign of emotion. In the morning he dressed in his sports coat and flannels, looked over the Rooms to Let column in the *Daily Telegraph* and marked a few likely ones with a pencil, then dumped his two suitcases in the M.G. and about ten o'clock drove to station headquarters for the final moment of separation. It was quite undramatic. He said to the adjutant: " Here are my clearances, sir. Would you put your mark at the bottom, please? "

The adjutant signed and said: " Well, there you are, old boy. All clear."

In that moment he had left the Air Force. His mind deliberately dulled, cushioned by expectation, he said: "Thank you very much, sir," and walked out.

He drove straight past the guard-room out of the gates and turned left on the road to London; even in that moment feeling no pang, only a numbness. It was some minutes before he began to think again, and it occurred to him first that now he had no home. In the Air Force he could have gone to any officers' mess in the country and been welcomed and given a room. Now they were all closed to him, and all he had was a copy of the *Telegraph* with some pencil marks. He began to realise what a warm shelter the Air Force had been, and drove thinking: "I can't go back there. I can't go back there." Shortly he tried to make himself accept that there was nothing behind him that would ever come back, but his mind kept reminding him that neither was there anything in front.

One of the places ticked in the *Telegraph* was 86 Boundary Road, St. John's Wood, roughly on the way to Avonmore Mansions. Turning into Boundary Road, he liked its plane trees in fresh spring leaf, pulled up outside a house, a typical, three-storeyed solid affair, and rang the bell. An attractive blonde woman opened the door. Yes, Miss Markham said, she had a room for a guinea a week with breakfast, and he followed her up the stairs. She saw his dot-and-carry movement: "Oh, you've hurt your leg?"

"Well, no," he said. "I haven't got any legs actually."

After an embarrassed pause she said: "Oh, I'm so sorry."

"That's all right. I don't mind a bit."

She said she was sorry the room was two floors up and he said he didn't mind that a bit either.

He liked the look of the room immediately; it was nicely kept and furnished, with a divan bed and good wash-basin, and the window looked out over the plane trees: rather pleasanter than the usual officer's room on a station.

She said apologetically: "I'm afraid it's a little small."

"I like them small," he said. "I can reach everything more easily."

He took it on the spot and brought his two suitcases up: their contents, the month's pay in his pocket and the car outside were all he had in the world. After paying Miss Markham for a week in advance he drove off to see Thelma and took her out to the Ace of Spades.

" Well," she said, over inexpensive bacon and eggs, " how do you feel about things now? "

" Not too bad," he said. " I'll find my feet."

The following week brought him for the first time in his life a proper taste, a real mouthful, of the unsheltered world where there were few rules and fewer privileges and you scrambled with all the others for your share. It was a cold awakening, facing a future which was the equivalent of facing nothing. This was the neo-post-depression period when the jobs-required columns were full of appeals for permission to sell vacuum cleaners and he was too fresh with past dignity to be bothered with that sort of thing. And yet, for the likes of him, there was no opening in the miniscule jobs-vacant column.

On the Monday at the Officers' Employment Bureau the cheerful man said: " Got a few feelers out, old boy, but nothing in sight yet. I'll let you know if I hear anything."

On the Tuesday he drove all over London, but not looking for a job; just driving. On the Wednesday he did the same, not accepting yet the drop in status and the need to scramble. Mixed with this was an attitude, inchoate but stubborn, that he was not going to drop his standards. As at school he had disliked maths and declined to do them until forced to, so now he disliked looking for a job and declined to exert himself in the search until circumstances pressed. It was essentially an English attitude, somewhat head-in-the-sand, slightly snob, and rather deceptive. So far the challenge had not yet stirred. On the Thursday he drove Thelma down to the Pantiles for cream tea. The place had charm for them both. On the Friday he called for her again and she brought out a Thermos of tea and a packet of sandwiches. " We might as well get used to things," she said. " If you won't watch the pennies, I will."

On the Saturday he began to feel he was in a puzzling vacuum. He wanted to do something but there was nothing to do, nothing to catch hold of, and it began to disturb him.

He went back on the Monday to the Officers' Employment

Bureau, where the man was still cheerful but devoid of prospects.

After that a man in the R.A.F. Club suggested he might try journalism and gave him a note of introduction to the assistant editor of a London morning paper. Bader took it along to the paper and found the assistant editor was a slightly overdressed man with sharp features and a brisk manner. Without excessive enthusiasm the man asked: " What made you think you'd like to work on newspapers? "

" I really haven't the faintest idea," he answered, " but I've got to get a job and as I know sport pretty well I thought I might be able to do something along those lines."

The editor explained that they already had special sporting correspondents and most of them were international names. He thought for a while: " What about special contacts? D'you know a lot of society people who could give you gossip stuff? "

" Hell, no," Bader said fastidiously, and lost interest in newspapers. Going out, he thought with satisfaction that at least the man had no idea he had no legs.

In the mornings now, without especially admitting it to himself, he took to looking at the jobs-vacant column in the *Telegraph* but nothing attracted him there. Then a letter came from the Officers' Employment Bureau suggesting he go along to see the staff managers of Unilevers and the Asiatic Petroleum Co. He went to Unilevers first and they told him about soap and its by-products, and offered him a job starting at £200 a year in London before going out to West Africa. He explained that his legs would bar him from the tropics. They said that might not matter, though it might limit his career with them.

Then the petroleum company, where a scholarly, elderly man like a university don also suggested a job that would mean going to the tropics for promotion. Depressed, he explained about his legs. The scholarly man thought for a while. " We've got a little aviation section growing up here," he said. " They might have a vacancy. Would that interest you? "

At the word " aviation " Bader was extremely interested. The man took him along to the office of the aviation department, where the manager said magically, yes, he could do with a smart young man. It would be a job in the office helping sell aviation spirit to airlines and governments. Bader began almost literally praying they would take him on. He really wanted the job. Then they took him to the home staff manager, who sized him up in a chat for a while and then said abruptly: " Well, we'll pay you £200 a year and start on Monday. How's that? "

Bader said cagily: " I'd like to think about it, sir."

All the way down the corridor the aviation manager kept saying: " Of course you'd be foolish, you know, Bader, if you don't take the job. It's a wonderful chance."

Though he was jumping with delight inside, Bader would say neither yes nor no. He was damned if he was going to look like making a dirty dive for a job in commerce.

He drove immediately to tell Thelma he was now employed, and they went on to the Ace of Spades, where, over a more expensive curry, he said with unromantic and irritating masculine directness: " I suppose we can start thinking about getting married now."

She looked at him in the odd, half-smiling tolerant way that was coming naturally to her. " How much do you think we'll need? " she asked.

" Oh, I don't know," he said. " I suppose at least £500 a year."

That seemed reasonable enough. They were only twenty-three, and with his job and pension he now had £399 10s. a year. " I'll make damn' sure the pay from the job goes up smartly," he said, rather cockily, and they settled down to an engrossing discussion about cost of flats and food and engagement rings. Thelma suggested with exquisite tact that he should forget about an engagement ring for a while and have a secret engagement to preserve domestic content at her home. Bader knew that though her parents liked him they would justifiably worry about the idea of her marrying him. Thelma knew Douglas didn't have a bean to buy an engagement ring with.

In the morning he rang the aviation manager and said he would report for work on Monday. He was very happy that morning: being engaged to Thelma and having a job had lifted him suddenly out of the vacuum, and already he was feeling eager for Monday.

When the day came he put on his blue suit and drove hatless to his new office just off Bishopsgate in the City of London. (He had thought about buying a bowler hat but the symbolism revolted him.) The manager showed him to a desk with a green top and swivel chair backed against another desk. All told there were eight desks and eight pink and shaven young men. One showed him on a map where all the petroleum installations were, and he listened politely and largely uncomprehendingly while others explained what the organisation did. Then they gave him a mass of documents to read about aviation spirit, prices, marketing and so on, and at the end he was little wiser. " Take it quietly," the manager said. " You'll pick it up in due course." He lunched in the staff canteen, drank tea at four o'clock and drove to see Thelma at 5.30.

" Well, darling," she asked, " how was it? Tell me all about it."

" Actually," he said, " I don't rightly know, but they seem a good bunch of chaps."

After a couple of weeks he gradually got the hang of things, and was concerned mainly with prices and delivery of aviation spirit and oils to Australia. It was remote and dull, a tenuous, vicarious and somewhat hollow association with flying.

In the third week a senior young man gave him his first specific job to do, handing him a letter from a branch in Australia and saying: " Look, old boy, write them back and say so and so and thus and thus." For the first time Bader pressed the buzzer on his desk and a girl came in from the typists' pool, sat by his desk with her notebook and pencil poised and waited. And waited. And waited.

For the first time Bader was completely tongue-tied with a girl. After a considerable silence he said: " Ah . . . Dear Sir."

" To whom shall I address this? " asked the girl.

" Oh . . . ah . . ." He looked at the address on the letter and gave it confidently to her. Another long silence. At last he said: " Ah . . . Dear Sir." The girl waited, pencil still poised, and slowly, word by agonised word, the letter took shape, a whole paragraph long.

Later the girl came back with the typed letter and he took it from her with what he hoped was convincing composure. As he read it he could not quite remember what he had said but thought a little smugly that it was rather clearly put, and sent it to the senior man for signing.

Soon the man came over with the letter. "Look," he said, "this is a bit abrupt, you know."

Bader turned on the luminous smile. "I'm so sorry. What have I done wrong?"

"Well, it's a bit like a telegram," the man said. "You want to wrap it up a bit to the chaps out there, you know: make it a bit longer and use expressions like 'We would suggest' and 'Perhaps you have already considered.'"

Bader said: "I'm awfully sorry, but I've been used to writing letters in the Air Force so chaps would understand what you were saying."

Distinctly ruffled, the man said: "Well, you'll have to get used to different ways here. You'd better do it again."

Bader pressed the buzzer again, and when the girl came in they struggled together over it for half an hour. The finished article was a full page long and reading it over he thought he had buried the meaning rather well.

"That's the stuff," said the senior man. "Just the sort of thing we want."

As the months rolled slowly by he sank gently into the rut of the job. For a while it was painless enough and he thought he had found the secret of it—never commit yourself; never be forced into a position where you have to make a clear decision; always leave yourself with a let-out. It began to irk him.

One September week-end he drove Thelma up to Sprotborough and was delighted that his mother liked her from the start. So did Bill Hobbs, the vicar, and later that week the young man and the girl began thinking about getting married in a few months if he got his Christmas rise in pay. They could just marry on his present income of a little over

£7 10s. a week, but there were two barriers. First, he had
to run a car and use it extensively, which was expensive.
Standing in tube trains crowded at peak hours was not recommended for a legless man who stubbornly refused to use a
stick and just as stubbornly insisted on giving up his seat to
any woman, young or old. In that latter habit lay the clue
to the second barrier. He lived determined to make no concessions to the loss of his legs but to carry on with touchy
pride on the same basis as anyone else. No one must help
him because he declined to admit even to himself that he ever
needed help. It was the hard way and the only way not just
to overcome the handicap but to rub it off the slate. Associated
with this principle was a resolve, growing into an obsession,
that he would not drop his standards. He was a Cranwell
man, still an officer on the retired list; so by God he'd live
as an officer like all the others who had been his friends and
equals. Ostensibly he might be apart from them but
spiritually he was still with them and of them. That was not
so much snobbishness as a rigid, foolhardy and admirable
refusal to accept any fraction of defeat. On his present
income he felt he could not support Thelma in marriage as
he should. Therefore, he would wait till he could. She suggested gently that she should go out and work, even at the
Pantiles, but that he firmly vetoed and she did not press the
point, sensing that for him a wife who worked carried the
bitter seeds of partial defeat.

There were other practical considerations. He had, for
instance, just £2 in the bank. And what, for example, would
happen if the car were damaged? It was only insured " third
party " because the companies seemed to look dourly on Air
Force officers with fast sports cars, especially when they had
no legs. However warily they viewed the car, Bader cherished
it not only for its usefulness but for its symbolism as fitting for
a vital young man who loved flying. On the Saturday morning
when he hosed and washed it carefully to take Thelma to the
Stoops he was wondering if they dared marry if the rise did
not come through.

Soon he forgot that in the joy of driving along the Great
West Road at his usual 70 m.p.h., Thelma as usual enduring
the speed tolerantly because she trusted his driving. Passing

the spot where London Airport is now, a large Humber
pulled out ahead on the other side to pass a lorry, and Douglas
eased his foot on to the brake to give it time to swing in again.
The brakes had not the slightest effect (brake-drums full of
water from the hose washing). Suddenly alert to danger, he
tried to swing in, but another lorry was parked ahead on the
left and the little M.G. darted at uncontrollable speed for
the narrow gap left between the lorry and Humber on one
side and the lorry on the other, all unfortunately abreast at
the same moment. The gap was not wide enough.

10

EVEN AS fright alarmed the mind the M.G.'s offside front wheel sliced along the Humber's running-board as they came together at about 100 m.p.h. In a screeching flash the front wheel had gone, the door by Bader's elbow vanished, the rear wheel tore off and the M.G. lurched crazily on to its brake drums and screeched along the bitumen. By some luck it ran straight, slowing up on the drums, and then it was motionless and the noise had gone. Thelma relaxed her grip on the seat as Douglas said "I'm sorry, darling," and she had enough wisdom and calm left not to rebuke him at the moment. He got out, surprised to see that his door and two wheels were gone, and realised that he was extremely lucky.

The Humber had pulled in to the other side of the road, apparently all right, about 200 yards away, and in it an admiral's wife was shaken with shock but otherwise unhurt. Two daughters comforted her, and the third daughter, a forthright young woman who had been driving, got out and began striding towards the M.G. Oddly enough she was an acquaintance of Thelma's, being a neighbour of her grandmother at Windlesham. She arrived and said stormily to Bader: "Were you the lunatic driving this car?"

"Yes," he said, "but I should prefer you not to be rude because I shall only be rude back."

The two bristled at each other and then the daughter recognised Thelma sitting on the bank of the road. "Hallo, Thelma," she said, "were you in this?"

"Hallo, Maisie," Thelma said. "Yes, I was." She thought it not exactly the moment to introduce Douglas as her fiancé. The moment was odd and confused. A big chauffeur-driven car pulled up and a large businessman got out and entered the conversation with a statement that the young man had driven past him a couple of miles back going like a maniac.

He growled angrily: "It's not safe for a man's wife and children to be on the roads these days."

"Well, they shouldn't be on the roads," Bader said truculently. "They ought to be on the blasted pavement."

The businessman made it clear that he would be delighted to give evidence for the admiral's daughter. Everyone exchanged names and addresses. The businessman drove off and the daughter went back to the Humber, which was crumpled along one side but still able to drive away. A man brought along one of the M.G. wheels he had found in a field a hundred yards away. They could not find the other wheel (it took a garage man two hours the following day to do that). An agreeable young man gave them a lift back to London, and on the way Bader rang a friend who had a garage and asked him to collect the M.G. The affair was going to be expensive and he thought wryly that he didn't have a leg to stand on. Well, one thing: it gave him the answer to the marriage question. No!

For the next three weeks he travelled to work by tube or by bus, standing, which was misery and brought it forcibly home to show how much he depended on the car. It was even awkward going to see Thelma, and by the time he reached Avonmore Mansions the ninety-six stairs seemed higher than before and endless. It was a new reminder of what it meant to lose one's legs.

The bill for the Humber came in—£10 (an insurance company paid the rest). Then the M.G. was ready and he went to collect it. They gave him the bill at the same time—£68. The friend said sympathetically that it was as low as he could make, but he could pay it off at £1 a week or what he could manage. He drove it to Avonmore Mansions and took Thelma to the Ace of Spades for dinner (this time back to scrambled eggs and bacon.) He began to feel a little better there at their usual table in the olde worlde barn atmosphere with a tinkling piano, tiny dance floor, and coloured lights round a swimming pool through the window. They danced, and as they came off the floor the piano struck into " Stormy Weather."

"Very apt," Thelma said dryly. "How long do you think it will take to pay it all off?"

He said that if he got his rise he might be in the clear by next June.

Thelma said comfortingly: " Never mind, darling. It'll give us good practice for saving for a wedding."

He thought gloomily in silence for a while and then burst out impulsively: " Look, why don't we get married anyway now? "

" What would we live on? " asked the practical Thelma.

" We won't starve," he said eagerly. " Look, we aren't going to change towards each other, so we might as well be married as not."

Thelma suggested that there might be a little reluctance from her parents.

" Why tell them? " Douglas asked. " Why tell anyone? "

" Well, darling, even in this day and age you can't live together and just not tell people you're married."

" We can't afford to live together," he said, " so no one'll have to know. If we get married at least we'll have some object in life."

They discussed it, oblivious to the piano, and Thelma began to like the idea. After a while she said: " All right, darling. Let's do it. When? "

" Next Saturday," he said. " Sooner the better. I'll hop in and get a licence."

At Hampstead Registry Office he said to the clerk without preamble: " I want to get married next Saturday."

The clerk said yes, that would be all right. He could do it with a special licence for twenty-five guineas.

" Good grief," Bader said. " I haven't got twenty-five shillings."

The clerk said that then he would have to wait three weeks and it would cost only thirty shillings. Bader found he actually had just over £2 and settled for that. With a new idea he went back to the office, and with hardly any wheedling and without telling them he was getting married, got a fortnight's holiday to start in three weeks. Back at Avonmore Mansions that evening, when the others were out of the room he whispered to Thelma: " Zero hour October 5th."

" Oh lord," Thelma said, after a pause, " I haven't got any clothes."

He told her about the honeymoon.

" Oh, my gosh," she said, " what am I going to tell the parents, going away with you? "

That was another problem. The solution was quite fortuitious. They happened to meet Thelma's uncle just back from a holiday at Porthleven in Cornwall, where he had stayed at a most respectable guest-house.

" I've got some leave coming up," Bader said artlessly. " D'you think I'd like it there? "

" You'd love it," Uncle said. " So would Thelma. Why don't you both go down for a while? "

With that recommendation it was easy.

In the next two weeks Thelma spent her Pantiles savings on some new clothes.

On Wednesday, 4th October, Douglas got the next day off from the office for " urgent private business."

At 10.30 on the Thursday morning Mrs. Addison went out shopping, and Thelma rang Douglas and got into her new dress. By eleven Douglas had arrived and they were off to Hampstead.

In a drab, lino-floored office a strange man muttered from a book and at last looked up and said in almost the same monotone: " Well, congratulations, Mr. and Mrs. Bader." Something obviously had to be done about the witness, who was a bored-looking clerk dragged in for the occasion from a next-door office. It was almost the last straw for Douglas, who had had to calculate his honeymoon budget to the last penny.

Driving off in the M.G., both were shaken by the unemotional nature of the ceremony and neither felt really married, though neither said so. Douglas merely observed after a quiet spell:

" We'll have that done again in a church next time," and Thelma agreed feelingly.

They lunched at a hotel on the Eastbourne Road and Douglas ordered a bottle of champagne. It was the first time he had really had a drink in his life, and as the glow spread through each they began at last to feel happily married. He drove her back to London, dropped her at Avonmore Mansions, and she took the wedding ring off and put it in her purse before she went home. A few hours later he called at the flat for dinner as though he had just come from the office.

That night they announced their engagement to the family, promising, slightly tongue in cheek and with bare technical truth, that they would not be arranging a wedding for some time until he could support her comfortably. Everyone seemed quite happy about that; in fact, Mrs. Addison no longer noticed that he had no legs. After he had gone to Boundary Road that night she brought out an old diamond ring and gave it to Thelma, saying: " Look, darling, I don't suppose Douglas has many pennies to buy a ring, but this old one of Granny's has some nice diamonds and he could probably get them re-set."

On the Saturday morning *The Times* announced the engagement and the happy couple drove off towards Porth-leven for their honeymoon.

It rained all the way down and nearly all the fortnight they spent in the grey, Cornish stone house where the upright and unsuspecting landlord woke each in their separate rooms at eight o'clock every morning with a cup of tea. With each other and a sense of humour they enjoyed it, driving off with a picnic lunch every day round the sodden countryside, and it was even vastly funny when the seagulls choked on pieces of the landlady's adamantine rock cakes and bashed the pieces with their beaks against even harder rocks to break them up into swallowable size.

On the last Sunday they drove back to London to start married life. He left her at Avonmore Mansions and went back to Boundary Road. Thereafter he saw her nearly every evening, either having dinner at Avonmore Mansions or taking her out for scrambled eggs to the Ace of Spades. On Christmas Eve the manager said to Douglas: " We're very satisfied with your work, Bader, and I'm happy to tell you that we are raising your salary by £50 a year."

It helped in paying the car bills, but as winter dragged on he began to feel bogged down in a morass, increasingly frustrated by the dull and undemanding job and the virtual and indefinite separation from Thelma. The job offered no challenge and as he was barred from going overseas offered few prospects either except interminable, safe dreariness,

bound to debt and a desk as one of the eight pink and shaven
" bog rats," as they called themselves. There was not even a
game he could turn to for relief. His legs still troubled him:
he could never walk far without weariness and chafing, and
sometimes he had to go back to Roehampton for adjustments.
Always he was conscious of the legs, their discomfort and
limitations and the pain they often caused, though he never
complained about them, even when he fell, which was not
often now.

Thelma was the one bright spot. She was soothing and
undemanding, knowing instinctively how to cope with his
moods which were a form of rebellion against circumstances.
Often the moods led him into extravagance to relieve the
drabness and also to maintain the standards he was bent
upon. Maintaining those was like hanging on to a lifebelt in
the morass. It was hard to save. Sometimes he spent as
much as £4 in a week-end, yet any resistance at those times
would have driven him to further excesses. She never nagged
him but always waited quietly till his own conscience stirred
and then unobtrusively steered him in the right direction and
encouraged him to relax and carry on. He could hardly have
married a more suitable girl. She was utterly unselfish.

One day she lured him into going to a fortune-teller,
getting him, after his first grumbles, to treat it as a joke. He
went into a dark and dingy room and shortly a wrinkled old
woman shuffled in, took his palm and surprised him by saying
that he was destined to have trouble with his feet and legs.
She added: " There is a period of difficulty in front of you,
but you will be a great deal happier in due course. You will
become famous and be decorated by your King." Then she
made him sign her book which she kept for people who were
going to be famous. In it she showed him the name of David
Beatty, who had signed as a sub-lieutenant in 1904 and
laughed when she told him he was going to be a famous
admiral. Despite himself, Bader was a little intrigued because
he knew she had not seen him limp in. Then he forgot all
about it.

About that time 'Derick was killed in an accident in
South Africa. The Bader family seemed to be out of luck.

On a spring Saturday at Hartley Wintney, Adrian Stoop

and Tinny Dean, a Harlequins and England scrum-half, were
going to play golf at a local nine-hole course and suggested
that Douglas and Thelma go and see them hit off. Perhaps
Douglas could walk a couple of holes with them. After they
drove off Douglas said he would potter about the fairway
until they returned, so Stoop handed him a seven iron and a
ball and suggested he potter about with them. When Stoop
and Dean had gone on he dropped the ball on the grass and
took a swing at it, but the club missed the ball by inches and
he overbalanced and fell flat on his back. He got up and tried
again and the same thing happened. The same thing happened
the third time and the fourth time. He tried changing his
stance and his swing, and the same thing happened. Luckily
the turf was soft and painless. He got a stubborn feeling
that he *must* hit the ball and keep his balance before he gave
it up.

Again and again he fell until about the twelfth attempt
the club hit the ball with a sweet click and, lying on his back
a moment later, he could still see it in parabolic flight. Something about that click was very satisfying. He tried again,
missed and fell over. He kept falling over and missing every
time until, on about the twenty-fifth shot, he hit it for the
second time (or rather, topped it) and fell over again. In
the thirties he hit it twice more, one of them another exciting
click, but still fell as before. After he had fallen about forty
times Thelma said persuasively: " Now come on, I think
you've had enough."

Next day he tried the seven iron again on the Stoops'
lawn, this time with Stoop coaching. Several times he hit
the ball but still he kept falling over. It was remarkable how
precarious the balance was as soon as the swing of shoulders
and arms took his weight a fraction over the straddle of his
feet. There was no instinct or agility to correct. He had fallen
about twenty times again when he tried a shorter and slower
swing, hit the ball and just kept his balance. As he looked
up with a triumphant grin Thelma said: " Good, now you'll
be satisfied."

" Not on your life," he said, got the ball back and kept
on trying. Shortly he hit it without falling again, and did it
several times more after that.

The following week-end he tried again at the Stoops, until nine times out of ten he was hitting the ball and not falling. It had started off as a determination to do it once and now it was something more, part obsession to be able to do it every time and part pleasure from the feel and the sound of the click when he hit it cleanly and saw it arc away. Stoop said: " You're getting the bug, Douglas. Be careful, there's no cure for it."

Next week-end he improved still more, his brain absorbing the instinctive reflexes needed to keep his balance and thus freeing him to concentrate on hitting the ball. A couple of week-ends later Tinny Dean took him over to the golf course and handed him a three-wood on the first tee. Acutely aware of the concentrated eyes of the usual first-tee onlookers, he desperately wanted to hit the ball, stay on his feet and not let them know he had no legs. " Don't worry," Dean assured him. " Everyone misses on the first tee."

With taut concentration he braced his feet wide apart, took a slow swing and connected. Stumbling, he still kept his feet and saw the ball flight about a hundred yards, fading with a little slice.

" That was a hell of a good shot," said Dean.

" It was a hell of a fluke," muttered Bader, vastly satisfied.

He walked down the fairway with Dean, borrowed a couple of clubs and more or less hacked his way to the green, though he did not finish the hole. He hit off the next tee without any strange prying eyes, and then Dean went ahead to do his round, leaving him a couple of clubs to practise with up and down the fairway. Later he returned to the clubhouse, stumps chafed and aching and glowing with satisfaction and perspiration.

All that week Bader found he was looking forward with longing to the week-end's golf practice. Dean took him to the North Hants course at Fleet and he struggled round the first two holes, falling over only once, then staying to practise on the third fairway. Already the muscles of the stumps were developing and he learned the trick of smearing zinc ointment on spots that were likely to chafe, then powdering and taping them. He was hitting drives consistently over a hundred yards, sending them farther and farther as he developed more instinctive balance and could put more effort into the swing.

The odd thing was that though he sometimes mis-hit, his good shots sailed dead straight, probably for the simple reason that where normal men tried to " press " with wild and sloppy swings, Bader *had* to keep perfect balance and control—or fall over. Where other men overbalancing could grab at the ground with toes, or steady themselves with ankle muscles or two knees, Bader had to keep his head still and down, without excessive body sway. It made his strokes look a little stiff, but they were clean-cut and even and had behind them the strength of shoulders, arms and wrists that had been strong before and had developed more since he had lost his legs. Then again, he had the born athlete's co-ordination of eye, mind and muscle and fanatical tenacity. He had always shone at games and it was an irritant to his ego to feel like a novice, even compared to plump lady battlers of the " Good shot, Gladys," school.

He and Thelma went two or three more times to North Hants and it was like a window opening on a new world. They met a lot of people there, and now, as well as the joy of hitting a ball, there was the pleasure of a new social life with fellow addicts. After a month he got to the stage of doing three or four holes every Saturday and Sunday, feeling stronger and hitting the ball longer each new week-end. On anything except very even ground he still had to worry about keeping his balance and therefore often mis-hit, but now and then he did a hole in four or five, and one day coming off the course with Thelma after practice he said: " You know, this could be a game I might play on level terms with anyone."

The club secretary suggested he might become a member for a year at nominal rates to see how he got on, and he joined with delight. Then he started wondering how he could afford to buy clubs.

" My dear chap," Dean said, " spring along to the Railway Lost Property Office. You can pick 'em up there for a song."

He did so and bought six good steel-shafted clubs for 7s. 6d. each and a light bag. Thelma became an enthusiastic caddy and never stopped encouraging him. Already she could see he had a new and absorbing interest in life.

Towards the end of August he was playing six holes at a

time. In early September he played nine holes for the first time, though towards the end as he got tired and erratic he gave up counting. The following week he did twelve holes. The legs did not ache or chafe so much now and he found himself less and less tired. His drives now were reaching out nearly 200 yards (though not always in the right direction), and he got some satisfaction from the astonishment and admiration of the first-tee spectators.

It was at the beginning of October—nearly the first wedding anniversary—that he played his first straight eighteen holes. Back at the clubhouse, delighted, he said: " You know I feel so fresh I could do another nine."

" No, you don't," Thelma said. " You come and have some tea."

He resolved after that to play eighteen holes every time, and at the end of November he broke 100 for the first time. One would have thought he had won the Irish Sweep. Next week-end he played twenty-seven holes in one day, and then in December he played eighteen holes one morning and eighteen in the afternoon, returning to the clubhouse utterly exhausted, with the chafed stumps hurting him, sweat pouring off, but grinning all over his face. Even on cold days the sweat ran off him, evidence of the tremendous effort that he had to exert in getting round. That was the only outward sign that told people how hard he had to work at the normally simple process of walking. He felt now that he was a golf slave for life and that delighted Thelma, who was no golf widow but carried his clubs for him on every round.

There was one further complication about playing golf with artificial legs: the feet had a little fore and aft movement but no lateral " give " at all, so that when he straddled his legs to play a shot the ankles were quite stiff and he stood uncomfortably on the inside of each sole. He lamented of this defect at Roehampton, and the ingenious craftsmen there designed and fitted a kind of universal joint in the ankles, allowing lateral " give " against rubber pads, so that he could stand with legs apart and feet flat on the ground. It felt instantly better the first time he tried it, until at the fourteenth hole his right foot fell off. Luckily he had thought of that possibility and brought a spare pair of legs in the car, so he had only to lie beside the green until Thelma came back with another leg. At Roehampton they redesigned the joint and the new model gave no trouble thereafter.

That Christmas he got a rise of £25 a year. He was out of debt now and it brought his total income to £475 a year, so that they could really start saving for a second wedding. Yet by this time the passionless decorum of the office was reducing him to restive desperation and he began talking fretfully about throwing it up and trying to get something less stultifying. Leaving the job would certainly mean postponing the church marriage again, but Thelma was patient and unselfish about that. Her attitude was that if he were not happy and they married " officially " he would have no chance then of leaving the company and would be unhappier than ever. Still, the only other jobs that seemed available were the revolting hawking of vacuum cleaners which would be defeat.

Several times he spoke to friends who might know of other jobs, but they all advised him depressingly to stay with the company where the future was safe, if unspectacular. If he had had his own legs still he would probably have resigned, married Thelma again publicly and battled for a new career, but psychologically the loss of legs forced him into unnatural caution because no lowering of present standards could be tolerated. He heard there was a vacancy in the company for aviation manager in Cairo. The lucky man would have a little aeroplane to fly around in and he fairly raced in to ask about it. " My dear chap," said a London executive, " they'll never let you fly. Your future is in the London office." ·

One morning (this was 1935) he opened the *Telegraph* and saw a headline: " Royal Air Force To Be Expanded." Under it was a speech by Mr. Baldwin announcing that Britain's frontier was on the Rhine and that Britain must re-arm to keep pace with Germany.

A bigger Air Force meant they would need more pilots!

All morning he thought about it, and after lunch he dropped his work and wrote to Air Marshal Sir Frederick Bowhill, now Air Member for Personnel, who had been his A.O.C. when he crashed.

An answer came back in a few days, sympathetic and understanding. Sir Frederick said that if it were left to him he would have Bader back in the Service, but there was no chance of persuading others to agree.

Golf was the opiate that made life bearable after that. By late summer he was good enough to start playing competition, his scores ranging between 90 and 110, with a handicap of 18. A few weeks later he won a silver jam spoon in a bogey competition and they dropped his handicap to 16. Now he could hit drives consistently 200 yards, often down the middle, and was sometimes getting into the high eighties.

By some miracle they had still been able to keep the secret of their marriage. Living apart was a thing one got used to—after all, husbands and wives in the Services were often separated for years. Usually they managed to be together the whole of each week-end, either staying at some pub not far from Fleet (which was the usual reason for his week-end extravagance) or staying with Thelma's grandmother at Windlesham. They preferred a pub when they could afford it because at Windlesham they had to keep pretending they were only engaged.

As well as golf, North Hants had several tennis courts near the clubhouse, and one day in summer Tinny Dean suggested: "Come and have a shot, Douglas." Bader did not need much persuading, though he had to play in heavy crêpe-soled golf shoes because his artificial feet needed a thick heel under them (tennis shoes would have toppled him backwards).

He partnered Dean in doubles and found it surprisingly and refreshingly easy after the tremendous labour learning to play golf. He was limited in his movements, of course, and out of practice as he had not held a racket for years, but the balance he had learned in swinging a golf club also worked at tennis. Once or twice he tripped and fell through trying to move faster than his lurching walk allowed, but as usual, falling was only a detail. When a ball came within reach he was very accurate, with a smashing forehand drive, yet, as with cricket, he felt he could not pull his weight properly. In doubles he could only get to a ball that came reasonably within reach and his partner had to do a tremendous amount of running. He tried singles but that was unsatisfying because his opponent always had to hit the ball back at him and he hated the idea of people playing down to him.

Still, it was another successful activity and he played often until he was able to enter for tournaments. One day at Fleet he played seventy-two games on end in a tournament, partnered by a Cambridge golf blue, Horton Row, who ran himself almost down to his knees going for the one's just outside Douglas's reach, spurred on by the breezy whiplash of the Bader tongue in full cry.

The main reason he liked tennis was that he could play with Thelma, though golf remained the first love. His fame reached the ears of the urbane and witty Henry Longhurst, author, golfing journalist and addict, who came down to Fleet to play with him. A former captain of Cambridge, Longhurst, who had been rubbing shoulders with the world's greatest golfers for some time and seen just about everything possible to see in golf, was astounded at the first tee when Bader hit a screaming drive. No mean performer himself, being a scratch man, Longhurst was most impressed that day as Bader finished with a card of 81. They played often after that and Longhurst soon learned that Bader did not like being helped up when he fell, though he was prepared to accept a tug up a hill or a shoulder coming down. Usually they played thirty-six holes a day, and even if his legs were raw after the first eighteen, Bader would never call off the second round unless his partner made the first suggestion. On the coldest winter days, with icy winds blowing, Longhurst, rugged up in sweaters and blowing on his hands, used to marvel at him playing in a thin, short-sleeved shirt, still sweating freely, impervious to the cold.

Longhurst began to notice that Bader always hit good second shots on the fifth hole, where the fairway sloped gently up to the green. He mentioned this and Bader said he had noticed the same thing and thought it was because the uphill stance gave better resistance to his left side against the impact of the club-head hitting the ball and following through. Longhurst thought it was the fact that the uphill lie made it easier to get squarely behind the ball, but they both agreed that it would be a terribly clever thing to do to take half an inch off one leg so that he could get the same effect even on level ground. " Wish I could do the same," Longhurst said.

At Roehampton when Bader went along to get the leg

shortened, Dessoutter looked dubious and said that one short leg might lead to curvature of the spine, but Bader said golf was much more important than that and so the deed was done on the set of legs he used for golf. Next week-end he felt the benefit immediately, being able to punch the ball farther and more consistently on level ground than before. He told Longhurst that it worked, and Longhurst wrote a marvelling article in London's *Evening Standard* about the man who had taken half an inch off his left leg to play golf with a permanent uphill lie.

Bader saw it and rang Longhurst in great dudgeon. " You goat," he said, " I had it taken off the right leg, not the left one."

" Good god," said Longhurst, " you've taken it off the wrong leg."

They started arguing about it and have been arguing ever since, though the reason has long since vanished, because Bader had the leg restored a year or two later when his golf had improved permanently.

At Christmas he got a rise of £30 a year, bringing total income to £505, the mark he had been aiming at, and they began saving more conscientiously, planning to be married again as soon as they had £100. By May they were nearly half-way there, when driving back from Hartley Wintney one Sunday he noticed a knock in the engine. It got progressively worse and soon he had to pull into a garage, where a mechanic diagnosed a broken crankshaft.

For a week Bader travelled by bus and tube again. Then the repaired car was ready. He collected the bill at the same time—£30. When he drove away a loud and unpleasant grating came from the back. Smashed crown wheel and bevel! That brought another bill.

Eventually, driving it back to London with Thelma, they came to an accident at the top of the hill by Virginia Water, where two cars had collided and he stopped to see if he could help. Before he could get out a motor-cycle combination pelted over the top of the hill, swerved to avoid the damaged cars, and the sidecar rammed the M.G. head on. In the jolt Thelma's face jerked against the ignition key, cutting her nose badly, and the front of the car was stove in, but neither

Douglas nor the motor-cyclist was hurt and there was no one in the sidecar. Ambulance men bandaged Thelma's face, which was streaming blood, and he took her back to London in a taxi. She was more or less all right in a day or two, apart from a black eye, but Bader was without the car for nearly a month. Luckily the motor-cyclist's insurance covered most of the damage, but it still left Douglas with some £15 to pay taxis, doctors and incidentals. The savings were wiped out and so were any chances of setting up home together for another six months.

Then in August (with another friend in the car this time) he was approaching a rise near Rugby at about 70 p.m.h. when the driver of a large Rolls Royce in front waved him on. As he pulled out to pass, a car came over the rise. He braked and pulled in sharply behind the Rolls, but the Rolls was braking, too, and the M.G. rammed its rump very hard. Geoffrey Darlington, the passenger, copied Thelma, cutting his face on the ignition key and getting a cut nose and brow and a black eye. Everyone got out of the cars and all were remarkably polite about the affair, but that did not help a great deal towards paying the bill of £30 for the M.G. Thelma was haunted for weeks by the guilty note in her fiancé's voice when he rang up and confessed: " Darling, I've busted the car again."

At Christmas he got a rise of £35 and said: " Come hell or high water we're going to get officially married this year."

11

BY MARCH he was out of debt again and the money began
to mount in the bank. Prodded by Thelma's common
sense he was beginning to realise that however much he
hated his job it was not so much the job's fault as his own anti-
pathy to that sort of life. The petroleum company was the
great Shell organisation and it was Thelma who pointed out
to him that if he did get another job it would be the same sort
of life as in the Shell Company and probably not as good a
job. He faced it, reluctantly but with resignation.

It was Thelma's idea, too, that they should get married
again on 5th October, fourth anniversary of the uninspiring
Hampstead ceremony. She found a flat in a new block going
up in West Kensington and at the end of September the
fluctuating bank account was drained again, this time to pay
for the furniture.

Only one mild hitch happened at the last moment: at a
wedding rehearsal at Avonmore Mansions on the evening of
4th October he bent to kneel in the prescribed way and tipped
flat on his face. Everyone laughed amiably: he tried again
and tipped forward once more, realising then for the first time
since he had lost his legs that he could no longer kneel on both
knees because the wooden feet would not bend and enable him
to sit on his heels. It was a great joke until he said: " What
the hell do I do to-morrow? " Geoffrey Darlington, who was
to be best man, said he would buttonhole the vicar beforehand
and get permission to stand.

Next morning they were re-married, standing, in St. Mary
Abbott's Church, Kensington, Douglas looking very dapper in
cutaway coat and sponge-bag trousers, and Thelma weakening
at the last moment and uttering the word " obey " which she
had vowed she would not do. All the relatives and friends
were so warmly happy to see the couple at last married after

so many difficulties. Neither "bride" nor "groom" disturbed their sentimental illusions (which have endured to the present day).

Afterwards at Avonmore Mansions the champagne flowed freely and for the first time in his life Douglas joined the others at the trough. As was his nature, he tackled it with rather more zeal than other men, and after seeing him sink the second tumbler, Mrs. Addison said: "Douglas, that *is* intoxicating you know."

Beaming, his eyes more electrically alive than ever, he boomed: "Yes, isn't it wonderful," adjusted a woman guest's hat over her startled eyes and grasped another tumblerful. Colonel Addison counted five tumblers all told, and was amazed that a man could absorb so much and still stay on his feet, especially artificial ones. Later, Douglas lurched unassisted to the car with Thelma and drove off for a second honeymoon in Cornwall.

At Farnborough they stopped to break the news of the wedding to friends in the Royal Tank Corps mess, where they were refuelled with champagne and sped on their journey. He cannot remember seeing another car on the road till they reached their hotel at the Lizard (neither wished to sample again the Porthleven rock cakes.)

He woke in the morning issuing low moans, with the leaden pulsing head of the first and last hangover of his life, and for two days he was unusually tractable. Four years earlier no one had guessed they were on a honeymoon, but this time everyone knew because there had been a photograph in the *Daily Mirror* of them walking out of the church at the wedding with the caption "This Man Has Courage," and a local shop had hung it up in the window. It was exasperating to sense that everyone was smirking tenderly at them as honeymooners when they were really a veteran married couple. Back in London after a fortnight it was glorious to be able to walk into their own flat and shut the door on the world.

Settled in their own home, Thelma soon noticed that his depressed moods which had sometimes gone on for days were becoming rare and brief. Besides, his golf handicap was down to nine and he had started playing squash at the Lensbury Club, a pleasant recreation spot for Shell Company staff near

Teddington. She was a little worried about his playing squash; he put so much energy into it that sometimes he came back with eyes sunk in dark sockets from sheer fatigue. His partners had a gentleman's agreement to try and return the ball just out of reach and Bader lunged furiously about the court, taking some terrible tumbles and with legs thumping and creaking on the protesting floor. Rivets often popped out of the legs under this treatment, and one day the knee bolt of the right leg snapped and, as he fell, the right shin and foot, complete with sock and shoe, shot across the court.

Hitler had never meant much to him until Munich; it was then he realised there was going to be a war and that war was his chance. He wrote to Air Ministry asking for a refresher flying course so that he could be ready when war came, and a polite note came back saying that the doctors still thought that the legs made him a permanent accident risk. Would he consider an administrative job? He wrote back: No.

About April, 1939, when Hitler was marching into the rest of Czechoslovakia, Geoffrey Stephenson was posted to Air Ministry. Stephenson was friendly with the personal staff officer to the new Air Member for Personnel, Air Marshal Sir Charles Portal, and soon, by arrangement under the " Old Chums Act," Bader wrote to Portal asking the same old question. He got what looked at first like the same old answer: " I am afraid that during peace time it is not possible for me to permit you to enter a flying class of the reserve." And then he came to the last exciting sentence: " But you can rest assured that if war came we would almost certainly be only too glad of your services in a flying capacity after a short time if the doctors agreed."

It was not perhaps the accepted thing to do, but part of him began almost praying for war. Thelma, full of dread both at the idea of war and of Douglas trying to fly in it without legs, tried miserably to get him to give up the dream, but he would not listen. She tried to calm herself by thinking that they would never take him. Colonel Addison suggested that he would never get past the people in Whitehall and Douglas answered fiercely: " Well, by God, I'll sit on their doorsteps till I do get in."

The day after Hitler marched into Poland he sent Thelma

away to join her parents in the country for a few days in case masses of bombers came over when the whistle went. (The family had recently taken over half a bungalow attached to the Pantiles.) He had to force her to go because she had a feeling of impending doom which was not soothed by his eager satisfaction at the turn of events. Next morning, washing up his breakfast things, he heard Chamberlain's tragic voice announcing war. He left the washing up, sat down and wrote to Portal's secretary again.

On the Monday the Shell Company began evacuating some offices to the Lensbury Club, and Bader's boss told him that he would be based there on the list of indispensable workers debarred from call-up.

Bader immediately said: " Would you mind taking my name off that list, sir. I'm not really indispensable and I'm trying to get back into the R.A.F. I don't want to risk my pitch being queered."

" They'll never let you fly," the executive said.

" I'm still going to try, so please whip my name off the list."

" My dear chap, you don't have to do that. No one's going to give *you* a white feather."

Angry at that, Bader pressed the point and shortly his name was removed from the list.

Down at the Lensbury Club he began telephoning and writing peremptory notes to Stephenson and another friend at Air Ministry, Hutchinson, to get things moving for him, but weeks passed and he got restless and even more tersely demanding. Then, early in October, a telegram arrived: " Please attend Air Ministry Adastral House Kingsway for selection board Thursday 10.30. Bring this telegram with you."

Eagerly on the Thursday he found the right room. A dozen other men were waiting and he thought they all looked rather old for flying. A corporal called his name and he followed into an inner office where, to his surprise, he came face to face with Air Vice Marshal Halahan, his old commandant at Cranwell. Halahan got up from his desk and shook hands. " Good to see you, Douglas. What sort of job would you like? "

It almost took his breath away.

" General Duties,[1] of course, sir."

Halahan said: " Oh! " and looked dubious. " I'm very sorry but I'm only dealing with ground jobs here."

His stomach sagged a little. " It's only a flying job I want, sir. I'm not interested in anything on the ground."

Halahan looked at him steadily and silently for some five seconds and then, apparently making up his mind, stretched out, took a piece of paper and began writing on it. No words were said. He finished, blotted it, sealed it in an envelope and handed it across.

" Take that across to the medical people," he said, " and good luck."

They shook hands again and Bader stumped out. Dying to know what was in the letter he felt strung up with fearful hope. The feeling mounted as he crossed Kingsway and went up in the lift to the bitterly remembered medical unit. Guarding the sanctum was the same stout and kindly Cerberus who had seen so many men broken from crashes come in and try to talk their way back to A.1.B.—full flying category. The warrant officer recognised him:

" 'Ullo, sir. I thought you'd be along. What's it this time? "

" Same again," Bader said. " I think they might pass me this time."

" Not A.1.B., sir. Never."

" We'll see. Would you please give this to the wing commander." He handed over the letter from Halahan.

After a while the warrant officer came back and got out a new file for him. " Come along, sir," he said. " We'll get you done as quickly as possible."

Bader always remembered the sequence of events after that. He wrote them down:

> " *I didn't know any of the doctors this time, but everything went perfectly except for the chap with the rubber hammer who tests your reflexes by knocking you on the knee and seeing how quickly your foot and shin jerk. I'd been stripped except for my trousers, and he said: ' Just pull your trouser leg up and cross your knees.' I said ' I can't and it's no good.' I explained the position and we both*

[1] Flying.

had a good laugh. He had a look at them while I walked and professionally was very interested. He tested my reflexes by hammering the inside of my elbows instead. Seemed much the same.

"*I visited the various rooms in turn; eyes, ears, nose and throat; blood pressure, heart and lungs—never a shadow of doubt. I asked the last doctor, ' Am I all right for flying?' and he gave a short laugh as though I had been joking. Finally, my file was complete and the wing commander sent for me. He also was a different chap, slightly bald but with quite a pleasant face. I sat down. I could see he was looking at my file as though he were thinking, not reading. Then he looked up and said: ' Apart from your legs you're a hundred per cent.' He pushed a bit of paper across to me, and said: ' Have you seen this?' It was Halahan's note. I said: ' No, sir.' I looked at it and as far as I remember it read:*

"' *I have known this officer since he was a cadet at Cranwell under my command. He's the type we want. If he is fit, apart from his legs, I suggest you give him A.1.B. category and leave it to the Central Flying School to assess his flying capabilities.'*

"*I handed the note back without a word. I looked at him. I had the feeling of being tremendously alert at a terribly important cross-road. I think I stopped breathing. I remembered 1932—the same scene, different circumstances, different man behind the desk saying there was nothing in King's Regulations to let me through. The silence seemed to go on. I don't know whether it was a second or ten seconds. I had the feeling the doctor wanted to look away, but I was not going to let him. I was looking directly at him, willing him to think my way. He said, ' I agree with Air Vice Marshal Halahan. We're giving you A.1.B. and it's up to the flying chaps. I'll recommend they give you a test at C.F.S.' "*

It was too big to show emotion. He felt a serenity pervading him, turning into a glow like a man who feels his fourth whisky flooding him with soft fire. His face hardly changed, except that he took a deep breath, said correctly: " Thank you very much, sir," and walked out, feeling that the wasted years were cancelled and he was picking up life again from the moment he had crashed, back on a par with the chosen few.

In that mood he drove to the Pantiles. The fact that a war had opened the gate never crossed his mind; personal content was too deep to bother about externals that could not be changed. As he walked in the doorway the family was listening to a gramophone, the tea things still on the table. Thelma switched off the music and said: " Hallo, what are you doing here? Lost your job? "

" No," he said. " I'm getting my old one back."

It was her turn to feel that the moment was too big to show emotion, though, as a matter of fact, ever since he had known her she had always retired into a studied restraint in moments of crisis. The deeper the feeling the less she allowed it to show and the most she said this time was, miserably: " I suppose you'll be very happy now."

Back at the Lensbury Club a few days passed with no more word from the R.A.F. and he became intolerably impatient. It was not that he wanted to burst straight into action because there was no fighting except far off in Poland. He just wanted to get back into the R.A.F., into an aeroplane and get the feel of the life back again, especially now that there was a purpose in it. He took to ringing Stephenson and Hutchinson in the old peremptory way, bullying them to make someone do something immediately. All the latent vigour banked up for years was bursting out. On 14th October a telegram came from the Central Flying School at Upavon, " Suggest report for test 18th October." He drove down next morning.

It was over seven years since he had flown—he was bound to be rusty—but only on the way down did the insidious, disturbing thought cross his mind that he might fail the test. He tried to put the thought out of his mind but it would not go.

It was odd at first walking into the grey stone mess in flannels and sports coat while everyone else walked about confidently in uniform. He felt awkward and out of place until he came across Joe Cox there, and also the thickset, amusing Rupert Leigh whom he had last known as a junior cadet at Cranwell.

" You're my meat," Leigh said menacingly. " I am the maestro of the refresher flight and I give you your test. I know you will behave courteously towards me."

That demolished the insidious fear. Under " The Old Chums Act " it was in the bag unless he made some unthinkable blunder.

After lunch Leigh took him out to a Harvard advanced

trainer on the undulating grass field. This was going to be different from the old Bulldog: the Harvard was a sturdy monoplane, its cockpit crammed with a hundred instruments and knobs compared to the twenty odd in the Bulldog. It had all the modern things he had never encountered before, flaps, constant speed propeller, retractable undercarriage and brakes. Brakes! To his horror, when he got into the cockpit he saw that the Harvard had foot-brakes and they were a physical impossibility for him to manipulate sensitively as well as the rudder pedals. Leigh soothed his truculent lament:

" Forget about the brakes. I'll work them. You won't have to worry about them after to-day because the Harvard's the only aircraft in the Service that hasn't got a hand-brake on the stick."

Leigh explained the cockpit, climbed into the back seat and started up. " I'll do a circuit first," he said, " and then you have a stab."

He took the Harvard off with a surging, satisfying bellow and explained what he was doing all the way round. After landing he taxied back to the downwind perimeter and said: " Right. She's yours."

Bader was too busy to feel that This Was The Moment. He went through the cockpit drill, turned into wind and opened the throttle, and as she went away with a roar and picked up her tail there was no swing. Soon she lifted, docile in his hands, and he remembered to change pitch as she climbed. Just for a minute or two it felt a little strange, but as he flew round for a quarter of an hour the " feel " came back, dispersing the last wisp of unease and filling him with joy. With Leigh's voice jogging his mind about pitch, undercarriage and flaps he turned in to land. She was heavier than he realised and he undershot but tickled her over the fence with a bit of engine and flattened, easing back and back till he cut the throttle, held her off and then cut her tail down as she settled. She touched smoothly and ran without swinging. Surprised that she was so easy to fly, he took her off again and spent an hour doing two more landings and then climbing for a roll and a loop before landing again, exultant.

When they taxied in and got out Leigh's first words were, " Well, it's damn' silly asking me if you can fly. However, I'll humour them and write recommending that you be re-admitted to the fold and posted here for a full refresher course."

He went back to the Lensbury with warm content that changed to growing impatience, and as the days and then the weeks passed without word he started pestering Stephenson and Hutchinson again.

The news came, and saddened him, that Harry Day, his old flight commander, was missing from a semi-suicidal daylight reconnaissance over Germany.[1]

Towards the end of November an Air Ministry envelope arrived. He ripped it open and there it was in detached official language: they would take him back, not on the Volunteer Reserve but as a regular officer re-employed in his former rank and seniority (which meant higher pay). His retired pay would cease but his hundred per cent disability pension would continue. (That was a droll touch—hundred per cent fit and hundred per cent disabled.) If the terms were acceptable would he kindly state when he was prepared to report to C.F.S. for duty. That day was a Friday. He wrote back, naming Sunday, rang his tailor to demand a new uniform within a week, and left his desk for the last time.

That gave him a final day with Thelma at the Pantiles and he could not disguise his glee until, on the Sunday when he had put his bag in the M.G. and was ready to go, Thelma, for the first time since he had known her, gave way, and the tears began trickling down her face as she stood by the car. Then she turned and ran into the house. He drove away greatly sobered, and the mood stayed until he turned in past the guardroom at Upavon: at that moment he felt back in the Air Force again.

In the morning he drew flying kit, which was deeply satisfying. Along with the new log-book, helmet, goggles, Sidcot flying-suit, and other things, the quarter-master corporal pushed a pair of handsome black flying-boots across the counter and Bader pushed them back, saying: " No, thanks, Corporal. You can keep these. I don't get cold feet."

" But you've *got* to have them, sir," said the corporal, puzzled, so he took them to give to Thelma.

---

[1] Day was later reported a prisoner-of-war.

At the refresher flight he reported to Leigh with a smart " Good morning, sir," and they both started laughing because Leigh, who had been his junior, was now a squadron leader and Bader was still only a flying officer, one of the most senior flying officers in the R.A.F. After lunch another old friend, Christopher Clarkson, took him up in an Avro Tutor for his first flight as an active officer since the crash. Clarkson handled her for the first " circuit and bump " and then let Bader have the controls. The Tutor was an aeroplane he knew—a biplane: none of this variable pitch propeller nonsense or flaps or retractable undercarriage. A sensible aeroplane! His first landing was workmanlike and his second a neat three-pointer. As he turned downwind again Clarkson hauled himself out of the cockpit and said: " She's all yours, chum."

" *This, then, was the moment. At last I was alone with an aeroplane. 27th November, 1939—almost exactly eight years after my crash.*

" *I turned Tutor K3242 into wind and took off. I remember the afternoon as clearly as to-day. It was 3.30, a grey sky with clouds at 1,500 feet and a south-west wind. A number of aeroplanes were flying around. I went a little way from the crowd . . ."*

Shortly the telephone rang in Rupert Leigh's office and Leigh picked it up and heard the cold voice of Wing Commander Pringle, the chief flying instructor: " Leigh! I have just landed. On my way down I passed a Tutor upside down in the circuit area at 600 feet."

Leigh froze with foreboding.

The frigid voice continued: " I *know* who it was. Be good enough to ask him not to break *all* the flying regulations straight away."

When Bader landed and taxied in he found Leigh beside him, saying: " Don't do it. Please don't do it."

" Do what? "

Leigh told him what had happened but Bader could not very well explain to him that on his first solo flight he *had* to turn the aeroplane upside down at forbidden height. At the time he did not know himself that it had any connection with his last flight in the Bulldog.

" I had a new flying log-book then. I look at it to-day and read:
1939. *November 27th*
Tutor K3242.   Self   F/Lt. Clarkson.   25 minutes
Tutor K3242.   Self   ———   25 minutes
*These are the two entries and I recall exactly the feeling of the
schoolboy looking at the notice-board and seeing his name in the
team for Saturday."*

After that flight and after meeting some of the others in
the mess he did not feel so strange even in his civilian clothes.
Many of them were former Short Service officers of about his
own age, recalled to do refresher courses like himself, or an
instructor's course. Just for a day or so he felt like an old boy
back at school as a pupil with his former class-mates as masters
and then, just in the way he had got the feeling of flying, so
he slipped easily into the old atmosphere again. The last touch
was when his uniform arrived and then he was really back at
home, belonging as much as anyone else, more deeply content
than he could remember.

He flew the Tutor several times more, sometimes under the
hood[1] learning to use the new-fangled blind-flying gyro instruments. Then he took her up at night which had a tonic
effect on him, making him feel completely alone, master of it
all with the blacked-out land quiescent below, lit palely by
moonlight. The only awkward thing that remained now was
the possibility of being forced, some time, to bale out. Landing
by parachute is the equivalent of jumping off a 12-ft. wall,
and coming down on the right leg would probably be like
landing on a rigid steel post that would split his pelvis horribly.
He decided to worry about that if and when the moment came.

On 4th December for the first time he flew a modern,
operational aircraft, the Fairey " Battle," a single-engined,
two-seater day bomber. She was heavy to handle, approaching
obsolescence and not approved for pupil aerobatics (though
after a couple of days he was quietly looping and rolling her
away from the aerodrome and prying eyes at 7,000 ft.). He
preferred a lighter aircraft, but being put on to the Battle did
not bother him; he knew he was going on to fighters. No one

[1] A canvas hood which was pulled over the pupil's head so he could not see
outside the cockpit but had to fly on instruments. The instructor was always in
the other cockpit at these times to take over in case of trouble.

had said so, but it was obvious—with his legs it would have to be a single-engined aircraft carrying only a pilot.

On the Battle he quickly mastered the modern gadgets and never looked like committing the classic boobs of landing with undercarriage up or trying to take off with propeller in coarse pitch.[1] Upavon boasted a single Hurricane and a single Spitfire: he was burning to fly them, but so were thirty others, and he had to practise on other types first.

Like most of the others, he did not think a great deal about the war. There was not much, in fact, to think about in that respect: in Poland the fighting had ended in tragedy and the enemy seemed locked behind the Maginot Line as approaching winter called its own temporary truce.

A letter reached him from Air Ministry dated 8th December, and with a great red stamp " SECRET " on it. " Sir," it said, " I am commanded to inform you that a state of great emergency has arisen . . ." It went on to inform him that he was posted to Upavon some weeks previously and enclosed a rail warrant. It was another endearing little touch that the Air Force had not changed.

Time continued to slide by with flying every day and comradeship in the mess at night, often developing into exuberant impromptu parties which revived the old spirit he had missed so much, though still he never took anything stronger than orange squash. Not in the least did he mind others drinking, but for himself, his attitude was, " If I can't be cheerful without a drink I'm not much good." In fact, he was tremendously cheerful, in his element day and night. Thelma came down to stay with Joe Cox and his wife for a week and found Douglas happier than she had ever seen him. After that she did not mind him being back in the Air Force so much, though the thought of the future still terrified her.

One night at a mess party an army officer guest from a nearby unit buttonholed him, and said: " Hallo, chum, didn't you used to grind my face in the mud at inter-school rugger? "

" You look familiar," Bader said, and then recognised David Niven, the actor.

Winter froze hard that year. He got out of the M.G. at the

[1] Almost guaranteed to cause an accident. The aeroplane runs fast but not quite fast enough to lift off the ground.

mess steps one night and instantly slipped and fell on the icy ground. He got up and slipped over again, soon finding it impossible to keep his balance on the slippery ground. At last there was no help for it: he was forced to crawl his way to the steps on hands and knees and then crawl up them, unfortunately just as two brother officers came out and said: " Good grief, look at Bader! Bottled as a coot." Everyone pulled his leg about being a secret drinker and his grinning amusement changed to annoyance in the morning when he found the ice still on the ground so that he was marooned in the mess unable to walk about outside like the others. Joe Cox got a brain-wave and suggested he put his socks *over* his shoes instead of inside them: he tried it and found he could walk on ice quite easily.

Early in the new year he began flying the Miles Master, the recognised last step before going on to Spitfires and Hurricanes. Then, a couple of weeks later, he got his chance at the Hurricane. Just getting into the solitary cockpit roused his blood. Another old Cranwell friend, " Connie " Constantine, pointed out the " taps." It was common in those days to feel a little qualm before one's first flight in a Hurricane or Spitfire as there could be no trial " circuit and bump " with an instructor. Bader felt only deep peace as he taxied out alone. It was such a satisfying aircraft for an individualist. He opened the throttle slowly, corrected a slight drift to port as the tail came up and then he was in the air. From the start he felt a part of the Hurricane: she was the most responsive aircraft he had yet flown and after twenty minutes feeling her out he made a smooth landing. On his next flight in her he tried aerobatics; she felt better than ever and he began to fall in love with the aeroplane. Several times more he flew her but never got a chance at Upavon to fly the lone Spitfire because George Stainforth, a former Schneider Trophy pilot and speed record holder, passed out in it through oxygen shortage at about 23,000 feet. Not far from the ground he came to, pointing straight down at 500 m.p.h. and reefing her out, just in time, strained the wings.

At the end of January Joe Cox said to him: " Well, *we're* happy about your flying if you are. You might as well crack off to a squadron."

Bader immediately rang Geoffrey Stephenson, who had

deftly eased himself out of Air Ministry and was now commanding 19 Squadron at, of all places, Duxford, where Bader thought he had said good-bye to the Air Force for ever. The squadron had Spitfires and Stephenson set about getting him an immediate posting to it. It did not matter that he had not flown Spitfires: the main thing was to get to a squadron, particularly one whose commander would not be dismayed at having a pilot with no legs.

Before he went on end-of-course leave he saw the reports on his flying. Rupert Leigh wrote:

" This officer is an exceptionally good pilot . . . he is very keen and should be ideally suited . . . to single-seater fighters."

Cox's report said: " I entirely agree with the above remarks. When flying with this officer it is quite impossible to even imagine that he has two artificial legs. He is full of confidence and possesses excellent judgment and air sense. His general flying (including aerobatics) is very smooth and accurate. I have never met a more enthusiastic pilot. He lives for flying."

As O.C. Refresher Squadron, Stainforth noted: " I am in full agreement with this report," and then in Bader's log-book under the heading " Ability as a pilot," he wrote: " Exceptional."

On 3rd February Bader drove to the Pantiles for his leave and the next four days were not cheerful. Thelma, unable to mask her feelings as well as usual, was worrying about him, and he was restless day and night wanting to get on with it because he'd feel *really* back in the Air Force again when he got to a squadron. A telegram ended the waiting: " Posted 19 Squadron, Duxford, w.e.f. February 7." The date was already 7th February. Thelma, the stoic again, packed his kit and within two hours he was on his way in the M.G., feeling happier than he could remember.

12

DUXFORD WAS different. About teatime he drove in past the guardroom which he had so poignantly left behind in 1933, but now it was a different guardroom, new and bigger. The mess, too, was new and bigger—not so intimate—but the main change lay in the faces there; they all looked about twenty-one. Yet so they had been in 1933 too; Bader, sitting alone in the ante-room, became sharply aware that he would be thirty in exactly a fortnight and that it was he who had changed most. Geoffrey Stephenson was away for a couple of days and he felt out of it all, unable to retrieve the spirit of the dream.

His only cheerful moment in the mess that evening was meeting again Tubby Mermagen. Years ago he had known Mermagen as a pilot officer, but Mermagen now commanded the other squadron at Duxford, No. 222, which flew Blenheims. It was fun to talk over old times, but when he took off his legs to go to bed he felt again a comparatively elderly flying officer.

It would be all right as soon as he got into a Spitfire; but in the morning the pilots flew off to do convoy patrols from an advanced base and no serviceable Spitfire was left. He flew a Magister instead. The same thing happened next day. Then Stephenson came back and Bader greeted him with a glad cry. Next morning he climbed into a Spitfire and a boy of twenty showed him the cockpit. Above the throttle quadrant were the switches of a T.R.2 radio set. Bader had not used radio in the air yet. The boy prattled on about R/T procedure, making it sound so complicated that Bader impatiently cut him short and said he'd do without it this trip—just concentrate on the flying. She started easily and he took off without any nerves, feeling instantly that she was extremely sensitive fore and aft. The long, mullet-head cowling that housed the Merlin engine made for restricted vision, but he rapidly got the feel of her and liked the way she handled like a highly-strung thorough-bred. On the downwind leg he started his drill for landing and found he could not move the undercart selector lever into the " down " position. No tugs, pushes or fiddlings would budge it.[1] Disconcerting! Only one thing to do—" ring up " and get advice. He switched on the radio and like many of the ill-tuned early models it crackled and popped and buzzed, so that he could not hear a word from the control tower. That was more disconcerting! He tried with the undercart selector lever again and after some time fiddling with this and the pump handle finally got things working and the two green lights winked reassuringly as the wheels locked down. After that the landing was an anti-climax, but neat.

Old emotions were stirring. In this élite of beardless youth he had more seniority than anyone, twice as many flying hours as most and was years older. Long ago he had been the golden boy of such a squadron and now he was the new boy—the " sprog." Like a tide in him rose the need to prove himself equal to the young pilots who could play rugger and wore their uniforms with such blithe assurance. Not for a moment did he admit there was anything he could not do as well as they (apart from rugger, which he accepted), but there are other impulses in the mind than those of the conscious.

The old challenge. A new struggle.

That was part of it. There was also an old-fashioned zeal to get his teeth into the enemy, though there seemed few prospects of fighting in sight. Duxford was on the southern frontier of 12 Group which was charged with the air defence of England's vital industrial Midland from a line just north of London. Even the boys in 11 Group guarding London and the Channel were bored.

On 13th February his flight commander, an unblooded veteran of twenty-five, led him aloft for his first formation flying in a Spitfire, and Bader, by god, was going to show him —and anyone else who cared to see. Like the old days in

[1] The young lad of twenty had omitted to tell him that the undercarriage always hung on the withdrawal pins and a couple of pumps removed the weight of the wheels and allowed the selector freedom to travel into the " down " position.

Gamecocks, he tucked his wing in about three feet behind his leader's and stuck there, rocklike, through the whole flight. It takes quick hands and rapt concentration to do that; you watch your leader, not where you're going. Coming in to land the flight commander dipped low beside a wooden hut. Some instinct made Bader look ahead for a second and at the last moment under the Spitfire's long nose he saw the hut and that he could not miss it. Shoving on throttle he yanked back on the stick and the fighter reared up, squashing, engine blaring, and the tail smashed into the inverted—V wooden roof, and ploughed through, losing the tail wheel. The rocking fighter was still flying and he steadied her, brought her round again and landed her on the naked rump of the tail, inevitably tearing the metal some more.

The flight commander came across laughing, and said: " I'm awfully sorry, ol' boy. Most extraordinary thing—d'you know not long ago I landed a chap in a tree just the same way."

He never forgot the blunt details which Bader told him about his character in the next few minutes.

At dawn a few days later the new pilot made his first operational flight—a convoy patrol. After take-off, according to the drill, he turned the ring of his gun button from " safe " to " fire " and that was a good moment, the first time he had ever done it on business. It was exciting to feel there were eight loaded machine-guns in the wings, cocked to obey a thumb on the button. This was war and he had come a long way for it, his life usefully dedicated in a cause for which an Englishman may feel deep and private emotion. In that cause he flew among the vanguard, armed, strong and as fleet as any.

For an hour and a half they flew over a dozen tiny ships crawling over the grey water of the East Coast and saw nothing else in the sky at all. Before landing the gun button went back to " safe," and that was that.

Most days they spent practising the three officially approved methods of attacking bombers, known as " Fighter Command Attack No. 1, No. 2, and No. 3." In " Attack No. 1," for instance, the fighters swung into line astern behind the leader and followed him in an orderly line up to the bomber, took a quick shot when their turn came in the queue and swung gracefully away after the leader again, presenting their bellies predictably to the enemy gunner. Long ago the theoreticians at Fighter Command had decided that modern aircraft, especially fighters, were too fast for the dog-fight tactics of World War I. Bader, his head full of McCudden, Bishop and Ball, thought that was all nonsense and that the three official attacks were likewise absurd.

"There's only one damn' way to do it," he growled to Stephenson, ". . . that's for everyone to pile in together from each side as close to the Hun as they can and let him have the lot. Why use only eight guns at a time when you can use sixteen or twenty-four from different angles."

Stephenson and the others argued: "But you don't *know*, do you? *No* one knows."

"The boys in the last war knew," he said, "and the basic idea is the same now." Anyhow, he added, they'd damn' well soon find out if they tried the Fighter Command attacks, but they probably wouldn't get back to report it. When he got an idea into his head he wouldn't budge.

"No Hun bomber's going to stooge along in a straight line and let a line of chaps queue up behind and squirt at him one after the other," he said. "He'd jink all over the place. In any case, it won't be one; it'll be a lot of bombers sticking together in tight formation to concentrate the fire of their back guns. Why the devil d'you think our bombers have got power-operated turrets?"

Probably after the first pass or two the bomber pack could be split up, he considered. There'd be single bombers around then, but the fighters would be split up too and there'd be dog-fights all over the sky, every man for himself.

"The chap who'll control the battle will still be the chap who's got the height and sun, same as the last war," he said. "That old slogan of Ball, Bishop and McCudden, 'Beware of the Hun in the sun,' wasn't just a funny rhyme. Those boys learned from experience. We haven't got the experience yet, so I'll back their ideas till I find out."

Some of the other pilots ragged him about being pre-war vintage and old fashioned (especially on his thirtieth birthday), and Stephenson soothed him, saying in reasonable tones: "You might be right, Douglas, but we've got to keep on doing what we're told until we find out for ourselves."

So Flying Officer Bader kept dourly and sometimes profanely following his leader in dummy attacks on Wellington bombers which stooged obligingly in a straight line and never fired back. In those circumstances it was easy enough, until one day, diving in line astern on a hedge-hopping Wellington, one eye on his leader and the other eye on the Wellington, Douglas ploughed into a tree-top at about 250 m.p.h. and the Spitfire shot out the other side in a shower of broken branches with one aileron torn and bent. She was controllable, but veering to the right with one wing low and he had a busy and awkward ten minutes nursing her down to firm ground again without further damage.

Stormily he said to Stephenson: " That silly clot led me into a tree."

" Well," said Stephenson affably, "*you're* the silly clot. It's up to you to see where you're going. He can't fly the aeroplane for you."

With Churchillian grunts, Bader lurched off, convinced for all time of the superior virtues of individual attacks and dogfights, as against unwieldy processions. At the very least, he thought, if they had to line up in these damn-fool processions they ought to have good leaders. After that he began to watch carefully where he was led and a few days later, returning late from a convoy patrol in bad weather, noted with disgust that the leader had lost his way. It was dusk, with low cloud—a bad time to fly aimlessly. Bader, who had been map reading and knew exactly where they were, pulled across in front waggling his wings, turned the formation on to course and led them back to Duxford. That evening, in the privacy of his quarters with Stephenson, he said: " Look, I don't feel happy flying behind some of these young chaps. I'm more experienced and older, although I've not so many hours on Spitfires. Don't forget what we were taught in the old days in 23 Squadron that bad leading always causes trouble. I've had it twice now in a short time and I'm sick of it. I prefer to be killed in action, not on active service. Isn't it about time . . ."

The name of F/O Bader went up on the squadron readiness board next day as leader of a section of three.

He handled his section with confident pride on convoy and lightship patrols, practice battle climbs and even, conscientiously, in the official Fighter Command follow-my-leader attacks (though on the ground later he still scathingly condemned them).

It was the " phoney war " period, and Thelma, still at the Pantiles, was soothed by it, getting used to the idea of Douglas flying on a squadron—he had not told her about hitting the hut roof and the tree. To him none of this time was dull; he was flying and leading—that was enough for the time being. The fighting was bound to come in the end and as long as he was sure of that he did not mind, even though they did not yet have either armour plate behind the cockpits or self-sealing petrol tanks.

He flew over Cranwell one day and a wave of sentimental affection flooded his mind as he looked down. As he circled it the place seemed to take on a personality and he genuinely felt it was looking up at him, and saying: " I trained you for this and I trained you well. Don't forget what I taught you."

Tubby Mermagen's 222 Squadron at Duxford was changing its Blenheims for Spitfires and some of the crews were being posted away. In the mess one night Mermagen buttonholed Bader and casually said: " I want a new flight commander. I don't want to do the dirty on Geoffrey, but if he's agreeable, would you come? "

Beaming, Bader remarked with vigour that he would be delighted.

" Good show," said Mermagen. " I'll talk to Geoffrey and then fix it with the A.O.C."[1]

Convoy patrol next day had a new savour. Barring accidents Air Vice Marshal Leigh-Mallory was almost sure to approve. In the morning Bader led his section over to the advanced base at Horsham to await convoy patrol orders, and they had been on the ground only about five minutes, sipping at cups of tea, when the operations phone rang and the orderly who answered it shouted an urgent order to " scramble " (take off immediately) to cover a convoy. An unidentified aircraft had been plotted near it. Bader put his tea down and lurched as fast as he could after the other running pilots to his Spitfire. Unidentified aircraft! Perhaps at last!

[1] Air Officer Commanding.

Quickly he clipped his straps and pressed the starter button; the still-hot engine fired instantly and he was still winding his trimming-wheel as the plane went booming across the grass. The other two Spitfires were shooting past him, pulling away, and he sensed vaguely at first, then with sudden certainty, that his aircraft was lagging. A quick glance at the boost gauge; the needle was quivering on 6½ lb.—maximum power. She must be all right; but she was still bumping over the grass, curiously sluggish, running at a low stone wall on the far side of the field. The fence was rushing nearer, but still she stuck to the ground. He hauled desperately on the stick and the nose pulled up as she lurched off at an unnatural angle, not climbing. His right hand snapped down to the undercart lever but almost in the same moment the wheels hit the stone wall and ripped away. At nearly 80 m.p.h. the little fighter slewed and dipped a wing-tip into a ploughed field beyond; the nose smacked down, the tail kicked—she nearly cartwheeled—the tail slapped down again and she slithered and bumped on her belly with a rending noise across the soft earth.

As years ago in the Bulldog memory fled from the jolted mind. She jerked to a stop in a cloud of flying dirt and the perspex hood of the cockpit snapped forward and hit him on the back of the head, maddening him, though other emotions were momentarily frozen. The brain started working again and began wondering what had happened as he sat there with everything so suddenly quiet he could hear the silence and the hot metal of the engine tinking as it cooled. Automatically his hand went out and cut the switches and then he was motionless again apart from the eyes wandering round the cockpit looking for the answer. It stared back at him—the black knob of the propeller lever on the throttle quadrant poking accusingly at him, still in the coarse pitch position.

His stomach turned. Oh, hell, not that classic boob! He couldn't have!

But he had. Angrily he banged the knob in.

Apart from the aggravating crack on the head he himself seemed to be undamaged and he hauled himself out of the cockpit, noticing sardonically how much easier it was to get out of a Spitfire when it was on its belly. Stepping over the hole in the wall which he had knocked down he started walking back across the aerodrome just as the ambulance and fire-truck appeared. Men jumped out and ran up and when they asked whether he was all right and what had happened, he only grunted surlily: " Coarse pitch." They drove him back to the operations hut with his helmet and parachute; another Spitfire was parked there and he stumped over to it, climbed in, started up, waspishly pushed the propeller into fine pitch and took off to join the other two aircraft.

Over the convoy he found them sedately orbiting and circled with them for an hour and a half without seeing any sign of the unidentified plane. By the time he landed at Duxford he had a splitting headache. Geoffrey Stephenson said wonderingly: " Why the hell did you go and do a silly thing like that, taking off in coarse pitch? "

" Because I forgot to put it into fine, you stupid clot," Bader snarled, and stumped off towards his room. He must have hurt himself somewhere—he could hardly walk. In his room he undressed to lie down and when he took his trousers off realised why he had been walking so shakily: the shins of both artificial legs were smashed in—deep dents that made both legs bend forward like bows. They must have been jammed under the rudder pedals in the crash. He hadn't felt a thing. Sitting on the edge of the bed gazing at them, it occurred to him what would have happened if he had not lost his real legs. Not hard to imagine: both broken and probably the bones splintered. He'd probably have been on the operating table now with a doctor shaking his head over them. Perhaps reaching for the knife and the saw to take them off.

He unstrapped them and took them off himself, feeling more amused. Strapping on his spare pair he went to the door and bellowed for his batman, and when the man came running, handed him the damaged legs.

" Here," he said, " pack these up in a box. They'll have to go back to the makers."

Satisfied at the look on the batman's face, he went back and lay on the bed to soothe his aches and pains. A minute later something else occurred to him and he uttered an extremely strong word.

Neither Leigh-Mallory nor any other A.O.C. was likely to make a flight commander of any prune stupid enough to take off in coarse pitch. He uttered several more uncouth words.

Days passed and no word came from Leigh-Mallory. Then the A.O.C. visited Duxford on a routine inspection and sent for him. Bader walked in, saluted and stood to attention. The thickset square-faced man behind the desk regarded him sombrely.

" Bader," he said. " Squadron Leader Mermagen wants you as a flight commander."

Bader's face stayed expressionless, but inside he was suddenly alert, like the time he had waited for the doctor to speak at the medical board months ago. Leigh-Mallory seemed to be thinking and the silence dragged. Bader had a wild frail hope that he had not heard of the Spitfire.

" I see you took off in coarse pitch the other day and broke a Spitfire," Leigh-Mallory said.

(Hell!)

" Yes, sir."

" That was very silly, wasn't it? "

Another silence, very sheepish. Leigh-Mallory was looking at a piece of paper which Bader recognised as his accident report.

" I'm glad to see you've made no attempt to excuse yourself," Leigh-Mallory remarked in quite a reasonable voice.

" There wasn't any excuse, sir."

" No, there's no excuse for that sort of thing," said the A.O.C. A pause. " Anyway, you're going to 222 Squadron as a flight commander."

There were prompt results of Bader's promotion to flight lieutenant.

He brought Thelma from the Pantiles to stay at a pub just outside Duxford.

He lost the awkward feeling of being an Old Boy returned to school to pass his exams again.

He told the pilots in his flight that the Fighter Command attacks were no damn' good except as training for flying discipline.

Thelma's landlady at the Duxford pub was a formidable

woman known locally as "The Sea Lion" because of a tendency to a straggling black moustache. She dominated everyone and Thelma was getting a little restive until Douglas gave The Sea Lion the benefit of his overwhelming personality, fixing her with his glittering eyes and speaking a few forceful words. The Sea Lion and he became great friends after that and Thelma was happy.

Even in the shadowed times Bader's presence had tended to command a room and now, once more with responsibility and leadership, he spoke with unmistakable authority; not the bombast of a weaker man trying to assert himself but a compelling aura of will-power and confidence. Like the time he became captain of rugger at school he ran his flight with an enveloping gusto. For some days he led his pilots into the air to do the official Fighter Command attacks. In turn he sent each pilot up as a target aircraft, telling him to turn round in the cockpit and watch each fighter in the approved procession pop up one by one and break away in the same direction, presenting his belly for a sitting shot.

When they came down he said: "Now, you can see what's liable to happen to you." Then he took them up for his own style of fighting, leading two or three at a time, darting down out of the sun on each side of a target plane and breaking sharply away forwards and underneath. After that came hours of dog-fight practice interspersed with routine operations like convoy patrols, which were always dull. He led his men also in a lot of formation aerobatics as the best way to teach them complete control of their aircraft. On his own he tested his nerve and skill with illegal low aerobatics, though the Duxford wing commander at one stage said ineffectively: "I *wish* you wouldn't do that. You had such a *terrible* accident last time."

Some of the pilots were getting restive. The war had been going for eight months and none of them had even seen a German aircraft. It was a little better on the several days they flew up to Sutton Bridge for air firing, the first time Bader had fired his guns since he had shot part of his propeller away in the Gamecock. They no longer dived at white targets on the water but at a drogue towed by another aeroplane and that was much more thrilling. Eight guns, and no interrupter gear to go wrong!

A firm prod with the thumb on the button and the Spitfire quivered as the guns roared out in a tearing rattle.

Early in May a new squadron arrived at Duxford, No. 66. Its commanding officer, pint of beer in hand, cheerfully hailed Bader in the mess.

" Ha," he said; " fiddled my way out of Training Command."

It was Rupert Leigh. Odd how the old Cranwell chums were getting together—Stephenson, Leigh and Bader.

After a week even Leigh was bored with training and convoy patrols.

On 10th May he drove over to pick Thelma up at the pub and drive her back for lunch at the mess with Douglas (who was on readiness).[1] Climbing into the car, Thelma commented: " You look very gay this morning, Rupert."

Leigh said excitedly: " Haven't you heard. The war's started."

" What war? Another one? "

Gleefully Leigh said: " No. The balloon's gone up. Jerries are on the move."

He started telling her about Hitler's attack on France and the Low Countries, and she listened and said quietly: " I suppose you'll all be very happy now."

In the mess Douglas waved to her from a crowd of jubilant pilots, stumped over, put his arm round her and hugged. " Good show, darling, isn't it? " he exulted. " Good show. Now we can get at them." He was nearly on fire with joy.

She said unenthusiastically: " I suppose it had to start some time."

They all thought it would soon be over.

Yet nothing seemed to happen at Duxford except the same old stuff, practice flying and convoy patrols. The only diverting incident was when Bader was booked for speeding in the M.G. through Stevenage. Most of the pilots began complaining that the war would be over before they got their chance. They really thought that. The papers and the radio were full of the confused battle in France, but with the blindness of a small,

[1] On duty by his aircraft to take off at a moment's notice.

select and dedicated circle the pilots almost ignored the ground fighting and enviously read about the Hurricanes tangling with the Luftwaffe in France. Like hunting dogs they strained at the leash, too excited to worry that the quarry might have sharp teeth. The war was an heroic sport spiced with danger and they were still on the sidelines. Some of them began talking about transferring to Hurricanes . . . and then as the days passed the news changed and they were quieter, beginning to understand.

May 22 ended the hiatus but not agreeably. A staff car careered up to dispersals, pulled up with a jerk and Mermagen jumped out yelling: " Squadron's posted to Kirton-in-Lindsay. Everyone ready to leave by 1500 hours."

After a few stunned moments people started to move.

" Where's Kirton-in-Lindsay? " a young P/O asked Douglas as they scrambled into the flight truck.

" Up north, near Grimsby," Douglas said.

" Oh, gawd! " said the P/O. The battle lay the other way.

By three-thirty, after busy hours, the eighteen Spitfires were taking off for Kirton while the ground crews were still packing the lorries to go by road. No one seemed to know what the move was all about, and it was next morning before they found out.

Convoy patrols.

Day after day it was the same, lolling in the sunshine at dispersals while the battle raged across the Channel, waiting for a call that would send them stooging aimlessly in an empty sky over a few small ships. They did not feel heroic. In France the armies were being thrust back into unprepared positions.

On the afternoon of the 27th a lorry pulled up at A Flight dispersal and a flight sergeant jumped down and said to Bader: " We've got some armour plate for your aircraft, sir."

Everyone clustered round curiously. Men manhandled the plates of flat steel over to the planes and the pilots helped screw them firmly behind the bucket seats. They had never seen armour plate before and were highly pleased—not so much because of the protection (which seemed so academic), but because it made them feel in a way that they too, were almost " operational." Bader went early as usual to bed.

In darkness he came up out of sleep. A hand was shaking his shoulder and a voice saying: " Wake up, sir. Wake up! " The light clicked on and he blinked and scowled at the batman who stood there.

" Squadron's got to take off for Martlesham at 4 a.m., sir," said the batman. " It's three o'clock now."

" What the hell for? "

" Dunno, sir, but they said it was very urgent."

Still half-asleep and irritable he reached out and strapped on his legs, then thumped the other pilots awake. Mermagen arrived, and said: " I don't know what it's about but we're heading south and not taking any kit. Must be a flap about something."

13

DAWN GLOWED in the east as the squadron shook themselves into formation in the still air, and half an hour later they were landing in sections through feathers of waist-high mist on Martlesham Aerodrome, near Felixstowe, on the East Coast. Another squadron of Spitfires had already arrived, their pilots sipping mugs of tea in a group nearby. Bader strolled over and asked " the form " from a slim, handsome flight lieutenant, elegant in white overalls and with a silver name-bracelet round his wrist.

"Haven't got a clue," said the debonair young man, who had aquiline features like a matador, a thin black moustache and a long, exciting scar down the side of his face, the type of young blade, Bader thought, who would make a young girl think of darkened corridors and turning door handles. His name was Bob Tuck.[1]

Mermagen bustled over and said almost casually: " Patrol Dunkirk, chaps, 12,000 feet. Take-off as soon as we're refuelled."

"What the hell! " Bader said. " What's happening over there ? "

Mermagen shrugged. " Haven't the slightest idea. Something about evacuating, I think."

One of the pilots said in an injured voice: " I must say it's damned early to go junketing over there. I haven't even seen a paper yet."

It seems odd now that the word Dunkirk did not mean a thing then. The Army had laid a screen of secrecy over the plans for the evacuation and people did not realise that the beaches were filling with exhausted men, least of all the fighter

[1] A few months later Tuck was famous as a wing commander with a D.S.O., three D.F.C.s and thirty German planes to his credit.

pilots from the north who had not seen the war yet. At least they were going across the water to the edge of France—that was something—but the transition from peace to war is often cushioned and unreal. They did not quite grasp the idea that they might run into German planes over Dunkirk: and, in fact, that day they didn't.

Mermagen led them off in four neat vics of three; they climbed steadily and about 9,000 feet vanished into a layer of fluffy white cloud that stretched beyond the horizon. At 10,000 feet they popped like porpoises out of the cloud and levelled off at 12,000, still in tidy formation . . . unblooded. A Messerschmitt coming up behind could have shot the whole lot down. Far ahead Bader saw a strange black plume floating hugely through the limitless froth they were riding over. Mermagen's voice crackled over the radio: "That looks like it. That smoke. Must be burning oil tanks." For a long time they circled the smoke and ranged over the cloud. Mermagen wanted to dive below the cloud but the controller had said 12,000 feet and such orders (in their inexperience) were orders. They saw nothing else in the sky, and after an hour and a half Mermagen led them away. Under the cloud blood was staining the sand as the Stukas dive-bombed and the Messerschmitt 109's and 110's strafed.

On the way back 222 Squadron was told by radio to land at Manston, and after that were told to fly to Duxford, and at Duxford were ordered off again for Hornchurch, a fighter base just north of the Thames and a dozen miles east of London. "Typical shambles," they grumbled, blasé about the war. At Hornchurch they gazed, startled, and then with mild derision at pilots of other squadrons walking around with pistols tucked in their flying boots and as often as not with beard stubble. The others had been flying over France for several days and were quiet and preoccupied. Still the impact did not strike the 222 pilots, who considered the pistols and heard stubble as "line-shooting."

At 3.30 a.m. Bader was shaken awake again.

"Take-off at 4.30, sir," said the batman.

It was getting beyond a joke.

Unbroken cloud lay over the land at about 4,000 feet, but this day they flew at 3,000. Skirting the North Foreland to pass Dover on the right, he looked down on the grey sea with amazement. Out from the Thames estuary, from Dover and the bays little boats were swarming, slowly converging, heading south-east till they stretched across the sea in a straggling line, trailing feathers of foam, yachts and tugs, launches, ferries, coasters, lifeboats, paddle steamers, here and there a destroyer or a cruiser. It was unbelievable. " God," he thought, " it's like the Great West Road on a Bank Holiday." Far ahead the black smoke rolled thickly up from the edge of Dunkirk, where the oil tanks lay, and all the way in between the swarm of little boats streamed white tails across the water. Hundreds of them.

Mermagen led them across the dirty sand by Gravelines and swung along the beaches towards Dunkirk. At first the men in the distance looked like a wide stain of ants teeming over a flat nest and then, as the planes swept nearer, like flies, thousands and thousands stuck together, packing the sand. No holiday beach was ever like that, but this was no holiday and Bader began to understand that this was war. In the green shallows crawled the vanguard of the little boats, and black lines that were the heads of men threaded the water towards them.

A voice on the R/T said: " Aircraft ahead." Bader saw them in the same moment, about twelve of them, about three miles ahead and a little to the right. He wondered who they were . . . not Spitfires or Hurricanes, and a surprised voice said in his earphones: " Christ, they're 110's! "

A shock sparkled through him. They were coming head-on and in seconds he could see the twin-engines and twin fins. The Messerschmitts veered sharply left, climbing for the cloud . . . must be carrying bombs, avoiding a fight. Mermagen in front pulled up his nose and cartridge cases streamed out of his wings as he fired. But he was a long way out of normal range.

One of the 110's suddenly streamed black smoke, dipped out of the formation and went straight down, flaming. She hit and blew up behind Dunkirk. The other Germans had vanished into the cloud and the sky was clear again. It stayed clear for the rest of the patrol, and when they landed back at Hornchurch everyone clustered round Mermagen excitedly.

" Well I must say," Mermagen said, " I was *most* surprised when that thing fell down."

" I must say," said Bader, " so were the rest of us."

But it had been the real thing—if only a taste.

Next morning out of bed at 3.30 again for Dunkirk, and this time not a sign of enemy aircraft, only the ants on the beach and the little boats nosing bravely into the shore. So it was the next day, except that the town was burning and guns flashing round the perimeter. Dunkirk was beginning to mean something. Other squadrons excitedly reported running into packs of Messerschmitts and Stukas, and the bloody fights they had with them. Bader listened intently and with impatience.

Again in the morning up at 3.15, and from the cockpit at 3,000 feet he could no longer see the canals that threaded through the flaming town—smoke brooded heavily and drifted across the stone breakwaters of the harbour. But no German planes. They came and bombed and killed just after the squadron had turned for home. The afternoon was even more frustrating. He led his flight once more over Dunkirk, and after half an hour the engine started misfiring, shaking the plane horribly. For the first time on a battle flight he had to turn back early, and landed in a temper about the war that was raging and always eluded him. A letter awaited, bidding him to answer the charge of speeding at Stevenage. He wrote and asked if they would defer the case for a few days.

In the morning he felt dog-tired when the batman woke him at the same time. Same routine. An odd haze stretched like a ribbon towards London from Dunkirk, and even in the cockpit at 3,000 feet he smelt burning oil and knew what the haze was. Down below the same brave little boats streamed over the water. Dunkirk ahead . . . and over Dunkirk, about three miles away, a gaggle of swift-growing dots. He knew what they were instantly. The 110's wheeled inland without dropping their bombs, but the sky was empty of cloud and the Spitfires leapt after them, blaring on full throttle. No time for thinking, but as he turned his reflector sight on and the gun button to " fire," he knew he was going to shoot.

A glance back through the perspex; the straining Spitfires were stringing out in a ragged line and up to the left four grey shapes were diving at them—Messerschmitt 109's, the first he had seen. From the beam they flicked across in front like darting sharks, winking orange flashes in the noses as they fired.

He rammed stick and rudder over and the Spitfire wheeled after them. A 109 shot up in front; his thumb jabbed the firing button and the guns in the wings squirted with a shocking noise. The 109 seemed to be filling his windscreen. A puff of white spurted just behind its cockpit as though someone had used a giant flit-gun. The puff was chopped off . . . for a moment nothing . . . then a spurt of orange flame mushroomed round the cockpit and flared back like a blow-torch. The 109 rolled drunkenly, showing her belly, and in the same moment he saw the black cross on its side. It was true. They did have black crosses. Suddenly it was real and the 109 was falling away and behind, flaming.

Exultation welled sharply up, a fiery thrill running through him as he swung back towards the squadron—but the squadron had gone: not a plane in sight except the plunging torch on the end of the ribbon of black smoke running down the sky behind.

Turning back towards Dunkirk, he did see a plane. From nowhere it seemed a 110 was tumbling down half a mile in front. Incongruously the twin tail was snapped off but still hung to the plane by the control cables, spinning madly like a chimney cowl. Wide-eyed he watched the broken plane erupt into the ground below.

The heady joy of the kill flooded back as he slid out over the water towards England. A glow of fulfilment. Blood runs hotly at the kill when a pilot wins back his life in primitive combat. He had fought a plane and shot at it, impersonally, not seeing the man, and longed to get back and tell everyone, but when he taxied in the joy died. Two of the others were missing.

That afternoon, thirsting for more, he flew back to Dunkirk with the squadron, and on the fringe of the little boats off the breakwater saw a shadow diving on a destroyer. Another shock—black crosses on the wings as a Heinkel 111 swept over the funnels. A white core of water erupted just behind the destroyer and her stern kicked up, the screws foaming out of the water. He was peeling off after the Heinkel, which was swinging back to the coast. Little flashes came from the bomber's glasshouse, and Bader pressed his own gun button and the flashes stopped. Good! Killed the gunner! The Heinkel steep-turned sharply inside him. As he pulled up to swing in again two more Spitfires were closing on the bomber, already a mile away. Amazing how fast everything went. No chance of catching them in time. He looked for the rest of the squadron, but they, too, had vanished.

There was the destroyer though, and he banked over to see if they were all right. They seemed to be; they were flashing at him, and then he saw tiny black spots darting past and knew where the flashes came from. A multiple pom-pom. The Navy took no chances in those days. Bader shot away in the other direction. It was, he thought, rather rude of the Navy.

The squadron stayed at Hornchurch. Morning after morning up at 3.15 for the dawn patrol, and other patrols, but always it was the other squadrons that found the enemy, which was infuriating. All Bader saw were the rearguards on the beaches, embattled and dwindling, and it was not pleasant. When not flying the squadron sat all day by their planes, till nearly 11 p.m. when the last light went. Geoffrey Stephenson was missing. They said he had tried a copybook Fighter Command attack No. 2 on a Stuka and the single rear gun had stopped his engine, forcing him down, streaming glycol, in enemy territory.

On 4th June the Prime Minister ordered a last patrol and Bader flew on it. The beach by Dunkirk was empty and the crumbling town lay inert under the smoke. Out of the harbour tacked a single yacht with a little white sail; it must have been the last boat out of Dunkirk and they circled it protectively till low petrol forced them home.[1]

Dunkirk was over and Bader, suddenly exhausted, slept nearly twenty-four hours, waking to find a grim new mood lying over England. You could see what the pilots were thinking by their faces—if it was fighting they wanted they

[1] He always wondered what happened to that little boat.

were going to get it. Sobering, but not too daunting. Unreasonably, the country refused to see that it was beaten. Bader went a stage further, refusing to believe that he would, therefore, probably be killed. The possibility, or rather the theory, lay in his mind but he ignored it and like a dried pea it never took root. Having tasted blood, he thought only of flying, fighting and tactics, things he had wanted so long that nothing else mattered, and the thought never obtruded consciously that no one now could think of him with pity or as second to a man who could run. He lived for the coming fight, Britain's, as well as his own.

A letter came from the court in Stevenage saying " Guilty " and fining him £2 10s. Furious, he sent a cheque and a stiff note regretting his inability to attend as he had had to go to Dunkirk.

On a week-end pass he drove down to Thelma, who had gone back to the Pantiles. He had to tell her Geoffrey Stephenson was missing, and after that they did not talk about the war.

The fight seemed a long time coming and the days were unexciting with training—formation, dummy attacks, night flying. The squadron moved north again to Kirton-in-Lindsay and Thelma stayed at the Pantiles. At least for the time being, she thought, nothing was likely to happen to Douglas.

Towards midnight on 13th June Bader was 12,000 feet over the Humber looking for an unidentified aircraft that had been tracked in from Germany. Peering out of the little cockpit he could see nothing but a few pale stars and knew there was little chance of seeing anything else. The Spitfire, with its tiny perspex hood and long nose, was not good for night flying, and seeking a raider in the dark was like being blindfolded and chasing a rabbit in the woods. But then there were no other defences.

" Red One, Red One," the controller's voice said, " weather closing in. Return to base immediately."

He swung steeply down towards the blacked-out land, but the rain cloud moved in faster. On a homing course he was only a few hundred feet up, and right over the airfield before, dimly, he picked up the flarepath suffused through a veil of rain, and swung tightly round it to keep it in sight through the rain-filmed perspex. He floated past the first flare . . . too high. The second flashed behind . . . and then the third before he touched on the downhill runway. The tail was not down and he knew he had misjudged. Stick hard back in his stomach but still the tail stayed up and the flares flashed by. In the same moment he knew he was going to overshoot and that it was too late to open up and take off again; then the tail was down and the brakes were on as hard as he dared.

In front there were no more flares . . . only blackness. An agony of waiting, and then a tearing crash as the plane jolted, slid her belly over the low wall of an aircraft pen, sheering the undercart off, and jarred to a stop. Bricks were suddenly raining down on the metal, and the mind for a moment was a blank. No fear, no shock. He just sat there as he had twice before.

Then he said one short, unprintable word.

A car screeched along the perimeter grass. He took off his helmet and heard the rain pattering on the wings. Tubby Mermagen loomed out of the darkness.

" Douglas," he called anxiously, " are you all right? "

" No," Bader growled. " I'm bloody furious."

" Serves you right," Mermagen said, relieved. " That was a ruddy awful approach."

In the morning Mermagen greeted him with a sly grin and a significant remark: " Well, Douglas, we're losing you."

Bader stared, remembering last night's accident, and thought with a chill of being grounded.

" Where? " he demanded. " I don't want to leave."

" It's all right," Mermagen said soothingly. " You're getting a squadron."

Bader stared again.

" It's not a joke," Mermagen grinned. " Or perhaps it is. Anyway, L.M. wants to see you."

The surge of incredulous joy was cut off a moment later when it occurred to Bader that Leigh-Mallory could not possibly have heard of the latest accident.

He drove to 12 Group Headquarters at Hucknall and stood once more before the A.O.C. Without preamble Leigh-

Mallory said: " I've been hearing of your work as a flight commander. I'm giving you a squadron, No. 242."

(Better get it over!)

Bader said: " Yes, sir. . . . Sir, there's one thing I should tell you. . . . I broke a Spitfire last night. Overshot landing."

Leigh-Mallory said mildly: " Well, that happens sometimes, you know."

Wearing his hair shirt to the last, Bader went on : " Sir, the point is that last time you promoted me to flight commander, I'd also just broken one."

Leigh-Mallory looked grave, then grinned. " Don't worry," he said. " Your new squadron has Hurricanes."

Brisk again, the A.O.C. went on: " 242 are a Canadian squadron, the only one in the R.A.F. Nearly all the pilots are Canadians and they're a tough bunch, They're just back from France, where they got pretty badly mauled and lost quite a few aircraft. They were messed around quite a bit; it wasn't their fault and now they're fed up. Frankly morale is low. They need a bit of decent organisation and some firm handling; someone who can talk tough and I think you're the chap to do it. We may need every fighter squadron we've got on the top line soon. The Luftwaffe seems to be gathering across the Channel."

The squadron was at Coltishall, near Norwich, Leigh-Mallory said, and Squadron Leader Bader was to take over as from that moment. He stood up, shook Bader's hand, and said: " Good luck in your first command."

Squadron Leader Bader! Or at least Acting Squadron Leader! How unemotional the interview had been and how deep the content it stirred. Eight weeks ago he had been a flying officer! It hardly even occurred to him that he had caught up with his contemporaries; he was longing to flex his muscles in his first command.

By evening he had driven a hundred miles back to Kirton, packed his kit, telephoned Thelma and was steering the M.G. towards Coltishall. Low cloud hung over the sky and he felt his way in darkness. About 11 p.m. a policeman outside Norwich told him how to get to the aerodrome. Five minutes later he was lost. He saw a man on the road and asked the way but the man did not know. Then he saw a woman and she, fearful of his intentions, fled when he spoke. Not a sign-post anywhere (all taken down in case of invasion). He found another man who said suspiciously: " How do I know who you are? You might be a spy. I dunno where the aerodrome is." An hour later, content dissipated, he came to a barbed wire barrier across the road and behind it, in the light of a red lamp, stood an R.A.F. sentry. At last! Pleasantly conscious of dignity he said: " I am the new commanding officer of 242 Squadron," and waited for the barrier to rise.

The sentry did not move. Stolidly he said: " Can I have the password, sir? "

" How the hell do I know the password," exploded the new commanding officer. " I've never been here before."

" Sorry, sir, but I can't let you through without the password."

The new squadron commander simmered by the barrier for another twenty minutes until the guardroom phone located the duty officer, who ruled that he was admissable.

Almost the first man he saw at breakfast in the morning was Rupert Leigh. 66 Squadron, apparently, was now also stationed at Coltishall. Shaking his hand on hearing of the promotion, Leigh said: " Now you won't have to call me ' sir ' any more. Not that you ever *did*, but it'll be a comfort for you to go on being rude with a clear conscience."

After breakfast the " station master " at Coltishall, the pipe-smoking, phlegmatic Wing Commander Beisiegel,[1] told Bader about his new squadron, and was not comforting. The ground crews were about half English, three or four of the pilots were English and the rest were Canadians. Wild Canadians, the least tractable young officers he had ever seen, and most allergic to commanding officers! God knows what they would think when they heard that the new C.O. had no legs. Already unrest had affected the whole squadron. They needed someone pretty strong and active to discipline them.

It occurred to Bader that he was still wearing only the two rings of the flight lieutenant round his sleeve; he had not yet had time to get the third, thin ring sewn in between, and that would make him look very much a new boy.

[1] Known far and wide, naturally, as "Bike."

" If you don't mind, sir," he said, " I'll drive into Norwich and get the extra braid sewn on before I make my entrance."

He went off in the M.G. and while he was away the news of his arrival reached the squadron. One of the pilots encountered Bernard West, the squadron " plumber " (engineer officer) and said: " Have you see the new C.O.? "

" No, I haven't." West was greatly interested and a little wary. " What's this one like? "

" Bit unusual," the pilot said cryptically. " I don't suppose we'll be seeing much of him. He's got no legs."

West, a warrant officer of twenty years' service who had seen most things in the Air Force, gaped and groaned.

14

WHEN BADER got back the pilots were all down at the dispersals, on readiness. He had a long talk about them with his new adjutant, Flight Lieutenant Peter Macdonald, an industrious, imperturbable man who had been an M.P. for fourteen years and still managed to sandwich his parliamentary duties in between trying to pull the squadron together. At last Bader said: " Well, let's go down and meet these chaps."

" A Flight " dispersal was a wooden hut on the edge of the airfield, and he pushed the door open and stumped in unheralded, followed by Macdonald. From his lurching walk they knew who he was. A dozen pairs of eyes surveyed him coolly from chairs and the iron beds where pilots slept at night for dawn readiness. He had had a vague idea that they would all stand up respectfully; that was the usual thing. But no one got up; no one even seemed to move except that a couple rolled over on the cots to see him more clearly. Even the hands stayed in the pockets and the room was silent. Watchful. The duel seemed to last a long time.

At last he said, not aggressively but firmly: " Who is in charge here? "

No one answered.

" Well, who's the senior? "

Again no one answered, though the eyes turned and looked at each other inquiringly.

" Isn't anyone in charge? "

A large dark young man said: " I guess not."

Bader eyed them a little longer, anger flaring under his collar. But it was not the moment to get tough. He turned abruptly and went out.

In " B Flight " dispersal the unresponsive eyes again stared silently.

" Who is in charge here? " he asked.

After a while a thick-set young man with wiry hair and a face that looked as though it had been roughly chipped out of granite rose slowly out of a chair and said in a strong Canadian accent: " I guess I am."

He wore only the single ring of flying officer braid round his sleeve.

" Isn't there a flight commander? "

" There's one somewhere but he isn't here," said the young man.

" What's your name? "

" Turner." And then, after a distinct pause, " Sir."

Bader surveyed again the watchful eyes and again turned and walked out. A dozen yards from the door a Hurricane crouched with the hump-backed, bow-legged look of all Hurricanes. He headed for it and pulled himself up on the wing. A parachute, helmet and goggles already lay in the cockpit and he lifted his leg over the side, hauled himself in and pulled on the helmet. If they thought the new C.O. was a cripple there was one damn' good way to make them think again. He started up, pointed the Hurricane's snout across the field and opened up.

Right over the airfield for half an hour non-stop he tumbled the Hurricane round the sky, doing the old fluent routines of Hendon, one aerobatic merging into another, without pauses to gain height again, two or three loops in a row, rolls off the top, rolls, stall turns, finishing up with a Gamecock speciality in which he pulled up in a loop, flick-rolled into a spin at the top, pulled out of the spin and completed the loop. When he dropped her on to the grass and taxied in all the pilots were standing outside the hut watching, but he climbed out unaided, did not even look at them, got into his car, drove off to his office in a hangar and sent for Bernard West.

He liked the solid, north-country look of West as soon as the veteran warrant officer walked in and saluted.

" What's our equipment state? " he asked.

" Eighteen Hurricanes, sir," West said. " They're all new."

" Good. I want good serviceability on them."

" I'll keep them flying as long as I can, sir," West said,

" but that won't be for long. We have no spares and no tools. I'm scrounging what I can, but if you do any operations they'll all be grounded in no time."

" What d'you mean, no spares or tools? " Bader demanded.

West explained that they had all been lost in France. Only one of the fitters had brought his own personal tools back in his kitbag. The rest seemed to have brought back only cigarettes. He sounded angry.

Bader, looking grim, asked: " Have you requisitioned for a new issue? "

West said yes, he had. The indent forms and vouchers and all the duplicates made a pile six inches high, but the station stores officer said they had to go through the normal channels in their turn. West considered that the channels were well clogged.

" Well," said the new commanding officer grimly, " we'll ruddy well unclog them."

In the morning he called all the pilots to his office and they stood there bunched and shuffling in front of his desk while he, this time, eyed them coolly and silently, noting the rumpled uniforms, the preference for roll-neck sweaters instead of shirts and ties, the long hair and general untidy air. At last he spoke:

" Look here . . . it is *not* smart to walk about looking like mechanics who haven't washed the grease off their hands. I want this to be a good squadron and you're a scruffy-looking lot. A good squadron *looks* smart. Just for a start I don't want to see any more flying boots or roll-neck sweaters in the mess. You will wear shoes, and shirts and ties. Is that perfectly clear? "

It was a mistake.

Turner said unemotionally in a deep, slow Canadian voice:

" Most of us don't have any shoes or shirts or ties except what we're wearing."

" What d'you mean? "—aggressively.

" We lost everything we had in France." Evenly, with just a trace of cynicism, Turner went on to explain the chaos of the running fight, how they had apparently been deserted by authority, separated from their ground staff, shunted from one place to another, welcome nowhere, till it had been every man for himself, each pilot servicing his own aircraft, scrounging his own food, and sleeping under his own wing; then searching for enough petrol to take off and fight as they were forced back from one landing ground to another. Seven had been killed, two wounded and one had had a nervous breakdown—nearly fifty per cent pilot casualties. The commanding officer had been missing most of the time, but had managed to get his Hurricane back to the South of England. When the end had come the rest had flown themselves back across the Channel and been sent to Coltishall. Since then things had not greatly improved and they were drifting, without steerage way. It was not a heartening story but there was no self-pity, only a kind of restrained anger.

When he had finished Bader said: " I'm sorry. I apologise for my remarks." A brief silence. " Have you claimed an allowance for loss of kit? "

Apparently they had, and it was assumed, with another tinge of cynicism, that the claim was drifting quietly along one of the proper channels.

" Right," Douglas said. " To-morrow the whole lot of you go into Norwich, to the tailors. Order what you want. I'll guarantee that it's paid. O.K.? "

A shuffle of assent.

" Meantime, for to-night, beg or borrow shoes and shirts from someone. I've got some shirts and you can borrow all I've got. O.K.? "

" That's fine, sir," said Turner, who seemed to be spokesman by common consent.

" Right! Now . . ." (briskly) " Relax and take it easy. What fighting have you had and how did you get on? "

The next half-hour was a lively discussion on various aspects of the trade, and afterwards Bader interviewed each pilot in turn, finding, with one or two exceptions, that he liked them very much. Suddenly, they were keen and co-operative, though one pilot, an Englishman, seemed unhappy and thought he would be more suited to Training Command. After talking to him for a while Bader burst out angrily: " The trouble about you is you don't want to fight. I'll have you posted off this squadron in twenty-four hours." The remaining flight commander he also summed up swiftly as unsuitable, and as soon as he was alone telephoned Group and asked them to send him the best two flight commanders they could find. For one of them, he suggested Eric Ball, of 19 Squadron. Group said that would be fine, and for the second chap they recommended a young man called Powell-Sheddon.

" What's he like? " asked Bader.

" Stutters a bit," said Group, " but he's very good type."

" Stutters! Stutters! " the phone vibrated in Group's ear. " That's no damn' good to me. What's going to happen over the radio in a fight? "

" I should have thought he'd be just the chap for you." Group sounded slightly injured. " It's not a bad stutter and he's good leader material . . . ex-Cranwell."

" Cranwell," boomed Bader. " Just the chap. Send him along."

When he put the phone down he sent for West again, and West marched in to find the new C.O., pipe clenched in his teeth like Pop-Eye, leaning thoughtfully back in his chair with his right leg stuck up on his desk. Bader grabbed the trouser leg and dropped the leg with a thud on the floor, leaned forward on his elbows, fixed West with a flinty eye and said: " Mr. West, I want you to tell me what's been going on in this squadron."

Just for a moment West hesitated before he said: " D'you want the truth, sir? "

" That's *just* what I want."

" Well, sir . . ." and West explained, confirming all that Turner had said and adding some extra facets. He added that he himself had been going to ask for a transfer before the new commanding officer arrived. Already between the two men was the indefinable bond that comes from mutual respect and long service in the same cause. Otherwise West would never have added:

" If I may say so, sir, I think the first thing you need are two new flight commanders."

" Already got 'em," Bader said. " They're on the way. Now, any more word about your spares and tools? "

West said no, there wasn't.

Three minutes later the stores officer, working serenely on vouchers in his kingdom of shelves, saw two square hands descend palm down on his desk. He looked up into a pair of glowing eyes. Politely enough, Acting Squadron Leader Bader asked about the tools for his squadron, and the stores officer, shrugging at the masses of paper work, explained that he was nearly snowed under. Coltishall was a new station and there were masses of things to be acquired for the stores . . . blankets, soap, boots . . . The depots only supplied them in their own good time and only if they got all the copies and the correct forms.

" I literally haven't got enough staff to type out the forms," he said frankly.

" To hell with your forms and your blankets and your blasted toilet paper," Bader said wrathfully, " I want my spares and tools and I want 'em damn' soon."

The discussion raged for some time and was not agreeable to either party. Bader went to Wing Commander Beisiegel and explained that until he got tools and spares and the pilots trained under new flight commanders there was no point in regarding the squadron as operational. This was not happily received.

After lunch he began leading the pilots up in twos for formation, and was pleased to see that they knew how to handle their Hurricanes, though their formation (by his standards) was rather ragged. Though they had done more fighting than he had, he had already decided to train them for future fighting according to his own ideas. That night in the mess all of them were reasonably neat in shoes and shirts and ties, and he turned his sparkling charm on them. Soon the ice was broken and his pilots clustered round, laughing and talking, taking swigs at their beer and getting to know him while he, orange squash in hand, was further summing them up. His breeziness was like a shot in the arm to them, and towards the end of the evening one of the pilots put down his empty pint-pot and said: " Hell, sir, we were really scared you were going to be a passenger or another goddam figurehead." The evening progressed with great hilarity.

By the second morning there was already a feeling of direction about the squadron. People were neater and earlier and everyone seemed to be busy. For the first hour or two the new C.O. was appearing everywhere, at dispersals, in the maintenance hangar, the radio hut, instrument section, armoury. By ten o'clock he was leading sections of Hurricanes into the air again, and this time his voice came snapping crisply over the R/T when any aircraft lagged or waffled a few feet out of position. Later in the dispersals hut he parked his rump on the end of a bed, lit his pipe and called them around.

"That formation was better," he said. "Next time I want it better still. It's the best training for co-ordinated flying and air discipline." Then he gave them his first talk on the ideas of fighter tactics which he had been expounding at 19 and 222 Squadrons. "I haven't been able to test them properly yet," he said, "and you chaps have seen more fighting than I have, but I'm certain Bishop and McCudden and the others were right." He emphasised other refinements of battle too: never follow an enemy down, never straggle, aim steadily with plenty of deflection, and a host of others, finding an intent and intelligent audience.

In the afternoon Eric Ball and George Powell-Sheddon arrived. Both were English. Ball was lean and firm-jawed with a little moustache above good, smiling teeth. Already he had something to remember the war by—a scar furrowed through the fair curly hair where a 109 bullet had " creased " him at Dunkirk. Powell-Sheddon was shorter and was solidly built. Almost thirty, he was going slightly bald and was a steadfast type with thoughtful eyes. Both, Bader felt, had the " good school " background which he valued and would lead with authority. Not that he thought for a moment any the less of the Canadians. Englishmen do not require a " colonial " to have been to a " good " school, but respect him for other virtues (and because a " colonial " does not give a damn whether he has been to the right school or not). He would have been happy to promote a Canadian as flight commander, but none yet had enough leadership experience and he had old-fashioned ideas about that, though they became flexible ideas, not confined to Cranwell or the old school tie.

Ball took over A Flight and Powell-Sheddon B Flight, and that afternoon both were leading their pilots in formation.

Within a couple of days there was a perceptible impression of the whole squadron clicking into position as a team.

Bader kept trying to get the tools and spares, bickering daily with the stores officer. Many words were spoken but no equipment materialised. About the seventh day he sent for West and asked if there was any more word about the tools and spares.

" No, sir," West said. " The stores chaps started quoting A.P. 830,[1] volume 1, paragraph something or other; some regulation that says you have to wait three months before you can start the procedure for hastening new tools."

" They say *that* now, do they? " grated the C.O. Shortly after he stamped across to the station commander and said: " Look, sir, the boys are fit for anything now, but we still haven't got our tools and spares. As the equipment chaps don't seem inclined to do anything about it I've sent this signal to Group." He handed across a slip of paper and Beisiegiel read the curt message with mounting distress:

" 242 *Squadron now operational as regards pilots but non-operational repeat non-operational as regards equipment.*"

" Good god," the wing commander was appalled. " Why the devil didn't you show it to me first? "

After a heated scene there, Bader went back to his office and showed it to West, whose eyes widened as he read. He wondered discreetly whether the station commander would pass such a blunt signal. Bader said that the station commander *had* been a little perturbed, especially when he heard that the message had already gone.

With masterly understatement, West observed: " It's . . . a bit unusual, sir."

" I'll take the kicks," the C.O. said. " Is there anything you'd like to take back about our need for tools and spares? "

" No, sir."

" Good."

" There'll be an awful shindig at Group, sir," West suggested.

" There'll be an awful shindig from Fighter Command, too," said Bader. " I've sent a copy there as well."

---

[1] Equipment Regulations for the R.A.F.

West broke a few moments of pregnant silence:

" Well, sir, we'll either be getting our tools or a new C.O."

The upheaval was immediate. Bader was playing snooker in the mess with his pilots that night when an orderly announced he was wanted on the phone. He picked it up and the voice of a squadron leader (equipment) at Fighter Command Headquarters said coldly:

" Squadron Leader Bader, what is the meaning of this extraordinary signal you sent to-day? "

" It means exactly what it says," bluntly. " We haven't got any tools or spares and I'm going to keep this squadron non-operational till I get them."

" But you *must* have *some* tools there surely."

" About two spanners and a screwdriver."

The voice observed with severity that these were difficult times and tools and spares were short. He was having a gruelling time organising things, and surely a resourceful squadron commander could borrow things and make do till his requirements could be satisfied. Moreover, there was a proper procedure for obtaining new equipment and if everyone ignored such procedure and did what Squadron Leader Bader had done there would be frightful chaos.

" I've carried out the correct procedure and nothing has happened," Bader snapped.

" I'm quite sure you can operate with what you've got."

" Look, don't you tell *me* what I can do. I'll tell *you* what I want and until I get it this squadron stays non-operational."

" You don't seem to care what trouble you cause," snapped the equipment officer. " Well I can tell *you* that signal of yours is going to bring you trouble. The Commander-in-Chief is furious about it."

He nearly had the receiver slammed down his ear.

In the morning a little communications aeroplane landed on the airfield and Leigh-Mallory got out.

" I just dropped in to see how you were getting on," he said to Bader and did not mention the other matter till he had half finished his inspection of the squadron. They were leaving dispersals for the maintenance hangar when he said non-committally: "Your non-operational signal caused a mild sensation at Group. What's it all about?"

Bader told him of everything that had been done. Leigh-Mallory himself inspected the miserable little collection of tools they had been able to borrow and had a few words alone with Warrant Officer West. Afterwards he sent for Bader again and said:

"Well, you've stuck your neck out but I can see why. I'm afraid you're going to be sent for by the Commander-in-Chief about that signal and you can tell him what you've told me. Don't take it too much to heart—his bark is much worse than his bite."

The summons came a day later. Bader flew down to Hendon and drove from there to Bentley Priory, the fine old house at Stanmore that was Fighter Command Headquarters. Waiting to be ushered in to the C.-in-C., he did not regret what he had done but was acutely conscious that he was only an acting squadron leader. A corporal appeared and said: "He'll see you now, sir."

15

BEHIND A tidy desk sat the austere Air Chief Marshal Sir Hugh Dowding, eyes pale and cold under tufty eyebrows and lips pursed in the craggy face. Known as " Stuffy " because he could be very stuffy, he gazed unwinking and said baldly: " What's all this about equipment and that signal of yours, Bader? "

Bader explained that he had done everything he could to get tools and spares, and then decided he would have to do something extra because if the Germans attacked, his squadron would soon be unable to get off the ground. Without a word Dowding passed a typewritten report over and Bader saw it was from the equipment officer—an account of the phone conversation. He glanced over it and said:

" I did have an acrimonious conversation with an equipment officer, sir, but it was between two officers of equal rank. He tried to shake me by saying you were furious about my signal and that annoyed me."

" Oh, he said I was furious, did he? " Dowding pressed his buzzer.

In a minute the equipment squadron leader came in. His eyes flickered at Bader, whose eyes flickered back.

" Did you say I was furious about the signal from 242 Squadron? " Dowding asked.

" Yes, sir," said the squadron leader. " I knew you would be very angry about such a signal."

Dowding said coldly: " I will not have any officer taking my name in vain or predicting my emotions. Your job is—or was—to help the squadrons in the field. You will be off this headquarters in twenty-four hours."

After the equipment officer went out Dowding seemed to relax. He pressed another buzzer and shortly a grey-haired air vice marshal walked in—" Daddy " Nichol, who looked after all equipment for Fighter Command. He listened to Bader repeating his story and then took him by the arm, and said cheerfully: "All right. Now you come with me and we'll fix this up."

At Coltishall the following day Beisiegel held an inquiry into the affair of 242 Squadron's equipment, and next morning, even before the Coltishall stores officer, too, had finished clearing his desk for his successor, the lorries were rolling past the guardroom and up to the maintenance hangar where West, with brisk good humour, supervised his fitters unloading crates of spare wheels, spark plugs, oleo legs, spanners, files, piston rings and about 400 other assorted bits and pieces. By evening, after the last lorry had gone, West was surrounded by piles of boxes.

"Have you got enough, Mr. West?" Bader asked.

"Enough?" declaimed West. "I've got enough here for ten squadrons, sir. What I want now is somewhere to stow it."

"That's your problem," the C.O. said. "I'm leaving the aircraft side to you now while I get busy with the pilots. This is going to be the best squadron in the command if it kills me."

He drove to his office and sent a signal to Group, with a copy to Fighter Command:

"242 Squadron now fully operational."

As a matter of fact, the pilots already thought they were the best squadron in Fighter Command, a distinct change from their opinions of a few days before. Now the Hurricanes were hardly ever out of the air, ranging over Norfolk in formation and cloud flying, climbing on practice interceptions, diving on air firing and tangling in mock dog-fights. Even when they were on the ground there was always something to do, generally listening to the C.O. expounding with the fervour of an evangelist the finer points of air fighting. He was a dogmatist preaching dogma of a bygone day and because he believed so ardently, they believed too. He made every pilot lead a formation in dummy attacks and barked at him like an exuberant mastiff if the pilot did anything "clottish." It was learn by practice, by example, by seeing for yourself, and more practice. As long as one tried, his bark, one felt, was worse than his bite, and they all tried because one also felt that if he *did* bite the wound would be nigh on fatal.

Once he tried to loop the whole squadron in line astern, but only the first four got over the top and the rest stalled and spun off. The C.O. did not mind; they had tried. Even in the mess they tried, taking a perceptible interest in their appearance.

The first time he did dawn readiness with a section he slept as usual with the rostered pilots on the iron cots in the dispersals hut, taking his legs off and parking them beside the cot, complete with shoes, socks and trousers on them [1] It was the first time they had seen him with his legs off and surreptitiously they eyed them, fascinated, in a slight hush. No one, of course, made any remark but it was uncanny to see that the man who was so vital and energetic actually *did* have artificial legs. The legend was true.

A squadron in war is a sensitive body. The men who fly find glory and die young. The men on the ground live long with little acclaim but their work is endlessly exacting, and if they fumble once a pilot is likely to die. There must be mutual respect and trust, and it is the commander who must inspire this delicate balance. (I was once on a fighter squadron when a new, weak commander arrived, and in days the close-knit comradeship and teamwork frayed and split into aimless isolation and lack of confidence. It added up to low morale and happened fast.) Within a fortnight 242 Squadron was a cohesive unit, trusting in and loyal to the new C.O., and therefore loyal to their corporate selves. They knew just what they had to do, and why, and when, and it all made sense, and they knew the C.O. would be loyal to them.

Bader, in fact, looked on his squadron with a fierce possessiveness. (" I felt they were *mine*, all the pilots and troops. I used to get furious if anyone said anything about them or did anything to them, and I arranged with the Norwich police[2] that they never put my chaps on a charge in a civil court, but sent the charge to me to deal with. I was tough with them myself, but always closed the ranks if anyone else tried to interfere. I suppose I was unreasonable in my attitude about

[1] In this way Bader could dress ready for action before the others could put on their shoes and socks.
[2] With the urbane help of Peter Macdonald, M.P.

The Prefects with the Head Master, St. Edward's School,
Oxford, 1928.

The Gamecock, 23 Squadron, Kenley, 1930.

The aerobatics team for the Hendon Air Display, 1931. Bader,
Day, Stephenson (reserve). Ten years later they were to meet in prison
camp in Germany.

Douglas Bader with members of the Canadian Squadron. Left to right: Crowley-Milling, Tamblyn, Turner, Saville (sitting on the wing), Campbell, McKnight, Bader, Ball, Homer, Brown.

The Squadron Emblem. Left to right: Eric Ball, Douglas Bader and William McKnight. Ball had just received the D.F.C. Bader the D.S.O. and McKnight a bar to his D.F.C.

Bader is allowed to sit in the cockpit of an ME 109. Note the German officer holding a pistol.

Harold Russell (star of the film "The Best Years of Our Lives") pours out a cup of tea for Douglas Bader.
On the right
McGonigal.

Christie Street Hospital, Toronto.
Douglas Bader and a patient discuss their approach to a common problem.

Douglas Bader can go round a course with a score that would be envied by many a golfer not handicapped by artificial legs. His swing is a bit restricted, but he can make a drive of 200 yards.

Thelma, Douglas and Shaun.

the squadron, but it was an obsession with me and I would not brook interference.")

Often he worked the ground crews like beavers for long hours to keep the Hurricanes flying and in return defended them aggressively from the station commander, who was a stickler for rectitude according to the book. Bader and Rupert Leigh often marched together into the wing commander's office to assert their points of view. All three were Cranwell men and among them was a strictly unofficial tradition that if junior and senior officer took off their hats they could argue with more freedom than discipline normally allowed. Hatless they had some crisp debates, especially when some of the men were a little late back from leave or careless about the blackouts in the huts.

Now when the 242 pilots went out in the evenings to absorb beer it became a habit to go in a homogeneous group with the teetotal C.O., who did not mind how many pints they sank so long as they were fit in the morning. He brought Thelma up to a house in Coltishall and her presence helped ensure that the evenings were decorous enough, though not excessively so. A favourite game was "The Muffin Man," where a man has to balance a pint of beer on his head and turn around, singing and bobbing his knees, without spilling the beer. With his legs Bader could not play it but Smith, a young Canadian flying officer, taught him to sing "Little Angeline" and he became crazy about the song.

Command now had sublimated the last traces of the frustrated years. He lived for his squadron and expected all his men to do likewise. The somewhat swashbuckling figure with the lurching walk was liable to appear anywhere on the squadron at any time, a masterful and undisputed head of the family seeing that his house was in order. As Stan Turner, of the granite-chipped face said to West: "Legs or no legs, I've never seen such a goddam mobile fireball as that guy."

The muscular Turner himself was not a mild man, having a large capacity for beer and a penchant for firing off a large revolver in public. The wing commander had suggested to Douglas: "You ought to get rid of that chap Turner. He's too wild."

But Bader saw eye-to-eye with Turner, who was a first-class

pilot, and fearless and decisive. Turner stayed; in fact, Bader made him a section leader and found that responsibility curbed his wildness.

Leigh-Mallory had been shrewd when he sent Bader to command 242. The Canadians lived with an informal and sometimes noisy vigour, respecting a rule or custom only for its usefulness and never for its age or its index number in a book of regulations. They respected the same qualities in Bader and understood the contradictions in him when his own exuberance clashed with his sense of discipline. Bader's sense of discipline was deep-rooted when it was a matter of obeying an order from Bader, or from anyone whom he respected; it was less predictable in some other circumstances. Often he was bullying with his tongue but his victims had forgiven and forgotten in five minutes, knowing that he likewise would have forgotten.

Already he had his eye on several of the pilots as future section leaders, in particular Hugh Tamblyn, of the firm jaw, steady eye and dry good humour. The handsome Tamblyn had an air of utter reliability about him, and so did Noel Stansfeld, of the fair, curly hair and good looks, and Laurie Cryderman, who was tall and slight with crinkly hair and a cheerful charm. Two years before Cryderman had been leading a jazz band and was still only about twenty-four. Norrie Hart was a different type, shorter, firm-faced, quick of wit and speech delivered in a hard, dry accent. On the side of his Hurricane he had painted a chamber pot with swastikas falling into it. John Latta was again different, with a drawly voice, a dark, slight young man who occasionally showed the dourness of Scottish forebears. Ben Brown was very handsome, very brave and a very bad shot. Neil Campbell was even more handsome. Bob Grassick was compact and blithely imperturbable.

All the Canadians seemed fearless and none more so than Willie McKnight, a flinty-eyed little dead-shot of twenty from Calgary, who had already knocked down several German aircraft in the shambles over France. Under the tender lips he was a tough little man with a D.F.C. and a weakness for soft music; he had a large collection of Bing Crosby records and played them endlessly in the mess in the evenings, being greatly irritated when Cryderman sang over the top of the velvety Crosby.

Apart from Bader and the two flight commanders, the only other English pilot on the squadron was Denis Crowley-Milling, a sturdy blond pilot officer who looked about seventeen but was, in fact, twenty-one. Then there was also Roy Bush, a steady-eyed New Zealander, yet apart from accents no one noticed nationality any more; they were too busy training as a team, and life under the new C.O. was stimulating, though no fighting seemed in sight. One never saw a German aircraft. Once in a blue moon a lone raider might flirt round the coast in cloud and they said there were masses of them gathering in France, but unless Hitler tried an invasion it looked as though the war had bogged down. Pity, in a way.

But always in the background echoed Churchill's recent words:

" The battle of France is over. I expect that the battle of Britain is about to begin. Upon that battle depends the survival of Christian civilisation. Let us therefore brace ourselves to our duty and so bear ourselves that if the British Commonwealth and Empire last for a thousand years men will say—this was their finest hour."

On 11th July a sudden blanket of cloud sagged over Coltishall and streamed all morning, grounding the squadron. Bader was dozing in a chair in dispersals when the telephone rang and Operations said they had a plot of a suspicious aircraft flying down the coast from the north. Could they get a section off? Bader grabbed the phone, and said: " No, we can't get a section off. The cloud's right on the deck, and ·I won't send my pilots up in weather like this. It's impossible."

" Isn't there any chance? It's heading for Cromer and we're pretty sure it's enemy." Ops sounded anxious.

Oh, the temptation!

" All right, I'll have a go myself." He dropped the phone and sloshed out through the rain to his Hurricane.

It was almost an instrument take-off through rain that drifted in a veil across the field, and within seconds the cloud closed clammily round him. He called up Ops. for a course to intercept, but water had leaked into the radio and no sound came back. Climbing on instruments there was not much point in going on unless he broke soon into the clear. The

needle was pointing at just over 1000 feet when abruptly he
came out of the cloud like shooting into a new world, and down
below saw the coast. More cloud hung close overhead and
without word from Ops. there was little chance of seeing anything in the broken sky, but he swung north towards Cromer,
more to clear his conscience than anything else. Finding an
enemy over England was about as likely as finding a burglar
in one's room.

Far ahead a dot appeared in the sky and began to grow
larger, approaching very fast with the combined speeds, a little
higher, just under the cloud. It could not be an enemy, unless
a very rash one, or semi-blind, as it was flying straight on
towards him. With a queer and abrupt shock he saw the thin
body had twin fins. A Dornier!

Heart thudding he wheeled up towards it as the Dornier
slid by above a couple of hundred yards away and the Hurricane
was already standing on a wing-tip when the Dornier saw it
and lifted for the cloud. Pin-pricks of light flickered from the
rear gun and then Bader was lining up the luminous bead of
his reflector sight. He jabbed his thumb on the gun button in
a long burst, then fired again. The rear-gunner stopped and
then the Dornier fled into the cloud and the Hurricane lunged
after it, still firing. He saw nothing but milky mist and ranged
furiously about the cloud, but it was a limitless yielding ocean
and after a while he knew it was no good, dropped out below
and hedge-hopped back to base, muttering unprintable things.
At dispersals, in a temper, he rang Ops. and told them what had
happened, then flopped back in his chair in no mood for dozing.

Five minutes later the phone rang again.

" You know that Dornier," Ops. said, excited and triumphant. " Well, an Observer Corps chap saw it dive out of the
cloud and go straight into the sea. You got him! "

That night in the mess they had a party, but Bader still
stuck to orange squash. Any further stimulus he needed he
found in the fact that he had got the squadron's first enemy
bomber in weather which was too bad for him to let the other
pilots fly. Now, he thought, he really *had* proved himself to
the boys.

But then, he always thought he had to go on proving
himself. It was never conscious. The exterior was always.

masterful but underneath hid the little demon born in him, aggravated in his childhood and again when he lost his legs. He just had to be better than anyone to find the deepest and unconsidered assurance. Such demons never stay content for long, but must be pacified with more evidence. Great men have them, though the demon himself does not make the greatness; he is only the spur for the other qualities of the mind, the body and the spirit.

Outwardly he exuded so much confidence that it was catching. Even Thelma had caught it now; he looked so virile and competent in everything that it did not seem real that he could be killed. The pilots had certainly caught it. Such a leader is precious to a squadron because pilots are young and human and often frightened under the carefree surface. The shrinking mind keeps saying: " It can't happen to me," but logic also says it can and it is good to be buttressed by invincible example.

Now the squadron had eighteen Hurricanes and three more young men came to bring the pilots up to twenty-one. Oddly enough they were naval types lent by the Admiralty because the R.A.F., short of pilots, was manning the ramparts for the battle. One of them, Midshipman Patterson, was about nineteen, still with the fuzz of youth on his cheeks, and the others were a year or two older, Sub-Lieutenants Dickie Cork and Jimmie Gardner. Cork was a rugged, laughing six-footer and Bader often put him in his own section, the third man being the hawk-eyed little Willie McKnight.

On 8th August, off the Isle of Wight, sixty Stukas dived out of the sun on a convoy. Two hours later a hundred more attacked the same convoy. Fighters swarmed up from Tangmere and other fields and dived on the enemy. Aircraft spun smoking into the sea and two ships went down in flame and smoke. In the afternoon 130 German aircraft savagely bombed a convoy off Bournemouth. The storm had burst and in the great crook of hostile airfields off south and east England, Goering had 4000 aircraft. Fighter Command's squadrons in the front line had 500 pilots and aircraft and there were not many reserves.

The Stukas swept in again and bombs crashed down on

Portland and Weymouth and convoys off the Thames Estuary and Harwich. Goering was going for the vulnerable ships and testing the strength of the air opposition. Then eleven waves of two hundred bombers attacked Dover. Portsmouth was next, and then Portsmouth again, and now the enemy was sending over 400 aircraft in one day. The fighters of 11 Group around London and to the south tore into them and the Luftwaffe had lost over 200 planes. Across the Channel R.A.F. bombers were attacking the gathering invasion barges.

The defences were stronger than Goering had thought. He had to cripple the R.A.F. by mid-September—Hitler planned to launch twenty-five divisions to land between Folkestone and Worthing on 21st September. On 15th August the bombs came down on the fighter fields of south-east England—Dover, Deal, Hawkinge, Lympne, Middle Wallop, Kenley and Biggin Hill. Next day nearly six hundred bombers raided the fighter fields at Kenley, Croydon, Biggin Hill, Manston, West Malling, Northolt and Tangmere, and scores of aeroplanes, German and British, went down blazing.

Bader and 242 Squadron saw none of this, though every day they waited " at readiness " by the Hurricanes. It was 11 Group's battle and 12 Group was held back to cover England's industrial heart north of London. Burning for the fight, Bader rang Leigh-Mallory and pleaded to be embroiled but Leigh-Mallory told him: " We can't put all our eggs in one basket, Bader. You've got to hang on and wait. No doubt the enemy would be delighted to draw our fighter cover away from the Midlands. In any case, I can't send you in until 11 Group calls for you."

It was hard waiting.

There came another lull and England, shocked by the bombing, waited. Goering, shaken by his losses, was reconsidering. And then the weather closed in.

Bader was not in dispersals the day the controller scrambled a section to cover a convoy when thick and heavy rain cloud almost on the ground had stopped flying. Young Patterson was in that section and did not return. Someone on the convoy reported seeing a Hurricane dive out of control from the cloud into the sea and Bader, almost berserk, drove over to the controller and for ten minutes the bull-like voice flayed the man for sending out his pilots in impossible weather. One would have thought it was a father who had lost one of his sons.

Next day (it was 21st August) the weather was better and Bader, bringing a section back over the airfield from a practice flight, had just broken them away by R/T to land when he heard a voice saying: " Rusty Red Leader calling. Rusty Red section airborne."

And then the controller: " Hallo, Rusty Red Leader. Bandit angels seven over Yarmouth. Vector one-one-zero."[1]

Yarmouth lay fifteen miles to the south-east and Rusty was the call sign of Rupert Leigh's 66 Squadron. As soon as it had registered, Bader's throttle was wide open as he streaked for Yarmouth.

He came to the coast north of the town but saw nothing else in the air. Rusty section had not arrived yet. A layer of strato-cumulus cloud covered the sky at about 8000 feet. Might be something above that! He lifted his nose and bored into the cloud; twenty seconds later he lifted out of the grey foam into brilliant sunshine and there unbelievably in front of his eyes flew a Dornier 17 with a glistening pale-blue belly. She was about 700 feet above, going from left to right only a couple of hundred yards in front. As he wheeled up, the Dornier spotted him and dived for the cloud, but Bader was between the cloud and the enemy.

Closing fast, he fired, seeing the tracer flick out. The rear gunner was firing. He was nearly straight behind now and something came suddenly away from the Dornier like a little chain with weights on,[2] and then it had whipped past under him. He had his thumb on the button in a long burst when the Dornier slid into the cloud and he followed, still hosing bullets into the greyness.

Suddenly he shot into the clear beneath. No Dornier. He circled under the white ceiling, breathing hard, eyes above the oxygen mask darting everywhere, but still no Dornier. In a rage he turned back to base.

[1] Enemy aircraft 7,000 feet over Yarmouth. Steer 110 degrees magnetic to intercept.

[2] A new weapon which the Germans threw out of bombers. The " weights " were grenades, to explode on contact with a fighter. They were not effective.

The lull ended on 24th August. That evening 110 German fighters and bombers moved towards London, but were intercepted over Maidstone and fled. Next day they were bombing Portsmouth and Southampton, savagely attacked by defending fighters. Then it was Dover, Folkestone, the Thames Estuary and Kent. Time and again the great formations ploughed steadily across the Channel and clashed bloodily with the spearheads of 11 Group. But 11 Group's losses were heavy too; they fought in squadrons, twelve aircraft against fifty or a hundred or two hundred because there were not enough squadrons and some had to be held in reserve. Air Vice Marshal Park, the A.O.C., never knew where the next attack was coming from, or when. The plot of a hundred plus on the board now might be a feint, to draw all his fighters up so that when they had to land to refuel and re-arm the main attack could sweep in unopposed.

Day after day while the fights raged Bader alternately sulked and stormed in the dispersal hut at Coltishall, where he and the pilots sat restlessly at readiness like pining maidens waiting for the phone call that never came. Ops. ignored them and it was intolerable to Bader that others should be plunging into the fire of battle (not to mention honour) while he was held impotently on the ground. It hardly occurred to him that he might be killed up there, and he kept railing at the stupidity of keeping them on the ground while outnumbered squadrons had to engage a massed enemy. Blunt and dogmatic, he snapped at anyone who questioned him. Training had wrapped a cloak of correctness round the ebullient spirit, but now the spirit was bursting the seams again. So might a tribal warrior, sniffing the battle, shed the veneer of the mission school.

Some of the 242 Squadron " erks "[1] had been careless about the blackout in their huts again and the station commander, worried about the bombing of aerodromes, decided to make an example and ordered them to carry their bedding over to the hangar and sleep there. Bader was furious that anyone should punish his hard-working men without consulting him. He stumped into Beisiegel's room, saluted, took off his hat and sent it spinning across the room, sat on the edge of the wing commander's desk, tapped his pipe out noisily on his

[1] Aircraftmen.

metal knee, leaned across glaring, and said: " I think you're a ——! "

Beisiegel, slightly empurpled, recovered his phlegm, and said, half philosopher and half martyr:

" D'you know, I thought you'd come and say that."

On that basis the debate waxed vigorously until Bader exploded: " All right. If the erks have to go and sleep in the hangar, the officers will too—the whole damn lot of us."

The erks and the officers continued to sleep in their own quarters. Beisiegel, in fact, was beginning to admire the revitalised squadron.

The intelligence officer buttonholed Bader in the mess, and said: " You know that Dornier you pooped off at the other day? "

" That——! "

" I thought you might like to know," said the I.O. " They've fished a couple of bodies out of the sea off Yarmouth. Their log-books show they were in a Dornier on the day in question and their watches had stopped just after the time you said you shot. Obviously you got him. It all clicks."

It was pleasant to be credited with a kill that one had not even claimed.

Thelma, anxious about the renewed and savage air fighting, tried to curb his eagerness, suggesting that there would be plenty of battles to come and he was not immortal.

" Don't be damn silly, darling," said her husband. " I've got armour plate behind me, tin legs underneath and an engine in front. How the hell can they get me? "

It was hard to argue with him.

On the morning of 30th August the phone rang in dispersals and Ops. said: " 242 Squadron take off immediately for Duxford! "

Duxford lay south—not far from London—towards the battle.

Bader grabbed the phone and demanded: " What's happening? "

Ops. said they didn't know, but a bit of a battle was going on down south and 242 Squadron might have to do readiness near the scene, just in case. Whooping wildly, the pilots were running for the Hurricanes. Bader, ablaze, bellowing to rouse the ground crews, moved as fast as his legs would go to his Hurricane parked only five yards away from the door. He was the first man strapped in and within two minutes was leading them off in an impatient, thundering stream.

Half-way to Duxford the controller's voice came coolly over the R/T ordering them back to Coltishall immediately.

Irritated, they flew back to base and Bader harangued Ops. over the phone. An hour later Ops. ordered them off to Duxford again, and this time there was no recall. By 10 a.m. the Hurricanes stood scattered round a corner of the familiar Duxford field and Bader and his men waited in a restless knot nearby. And waited. From Ops. they heard that the Luftwaffe was storming over southern England in waves, but still 11 Group sent out no call. Lunch-time came—and went. They had sandwiches and coffee by the aircraft. Bader sat by the phone in the dispersal hut, cold pipe clenched between his teeth, seething. At a quarter to five the phone rang and he grabbed it.

Ops. said crisply: " 242 Squadron scramble! Angels fifteen. North Weald."

He slammed the phone down and was outside the door, yelling.

16

As the wheels, still spinning, folded into the wings and the rest of the pack thundered behind, he flicked the R/T switch. "Laycock Red Leader calling Steersman. Am airborne."

A cool and measured voice answered: "Hallo, Laycock Red Leader. Steersman answering. Vector one-nine-zero. Buster.[1] Seventy plus bandits approaching North Weald." He recognised the voice of Wing Commander Woodhall, Duxford Station Commander.

Behind him the squadron slid into battle station, four vics line astern, and climbed steeply south through haze. Holding a map on his thigh, he saw that 190 degrees led over North Weald fighter station. The sun hung in the orb of the sky over the starboard wing and he knew what he would do if he were the German leader: come in from the sun! From the south-west.

This was no damn' good. He wanted to be up-sun himself. Disregarding controller's words, he swung thirty degrees west. Might miss the enemy! One usually obeyed a controller.

Hell, he'd made up his mind the way he thought was right, and now the brain was cool and clear, and only the blood ran hot. Soon, please God, the guns too. At 9,000 feet he was boring steeply up over the haze in steady air, eyes probing to the left, seeing nothing.

"B-b-blue Leader calling Laycock Leader. Th-th-three aircraft three o'clock below." Powell-Sheddon's voice.

Over the rim of the cockpit he saw three dots well to the beam. They might be anything.

"Blue section investigate." He did not bother to identify himself. They knew his voice.

[1] Full throttle.

Powell-Sheddon peeled off to starboard, followed by his two satellites. Nine left, against seventy plus.

South-west of North Weald a glint, then another, and in seconds a mass of little dots grew there; too many to be British. The skin tingled all over as the blood pulsed and in the same moment he shoved his throttle forward and called tersely: " Enemy aircraft ten o'clock level." Young Crowley-Milling on his right noticed that his voice was harsh and vibrant. The Hurricanes were suddenly bellowing.

Now the dots looked like a swarm of bees droning steadily north-east for North Weald, stepped up from a vanguard at 12,000 feet. The bombers were in tidy lines of four and six abreast, and he was counting the lines: fourteen lines—and above and behind them about thirty more aeroplanes that looked like 110 fighters. Above them still more. Over a hundred. The Hurricanes were above the main swarm now, swinging down on them from the south-west out of the sun, a good spot to start a fight if the 110's had not been above. The main swarm were Dorniers. Must go for them. Too bad about the Messerschmitts above. Have to risk them. He called:

" Green section take on the top lot."

Christie led his vic of three up and away to the right.

Bader again: " Red and yellow sections, line astern, line astern." From a thousand feet above he dived on the swarm of seventy followed by the last five Hurricanes, and now among the Dorniers saw more 110 fighters. A gust of rage shook him. " The bastards—flying over here like that. It's *our* sky." On the spur of the moment a demonic compulsion took him to dive right into the middle of that smug formation and break it up. He aimed his nose into the middle.

Black crosses! Glinting perspex! Wings that spread and grew hugely, filling the windscreen. He was on them and suddenly the drilled lines burst in mad turns left and right out of the sights, out of the way. He swept under and up swinging right. A ripple was running through the great herd, and then it was splitting, scattering. Glimpse of Willie McKnight hunting left, Crowley-Milling lunging ahead, and three 110's wheeling in front. The last was too slow. Just behind, he thumbed the button and almost instantly, as the bullets squirted, pieces flew off the 110. Fire blossomed at the wing roots, spurting into long flames as it heeled over.

The blood was fired too, nerve and muscle taut and the roused brain racing like an engine in the capsule of the cockpit which bore him through the torrent. Above to the right another 110 was slowly curling out of a stall-turn and he reefed his nose up after it, closing fast. A hundred yards behind, he fired for three seconds; the 110 rocked fore and aft, and he fired again. Pieces flew off the wing near the starboard engine. Flames suddenly burst along the starboard wing and the 110 was going down blazing.

Full of the fire of the kill, he looked for others and exultation chilled; in the little mirror above his eyes a 110 poked its nose above the rudder, slanting in. He steep-turned hard and over his shoulder saw the 110 heeling after, white streaks of tracer flicking from its nose past his tail. The Hurricane turned faster and the 110 dived and vanished under his wing. Bader spiralled steeply after, saw the 110 well below, streaking east, and dived and chased it, but the 110 was going for home like a bat out of hell and it was hopeless. He was startled to see that he was down to 6,000 feet, sweating and dry-mouthed, breathing hard as though he had just run in a race. He pulled steeply up, back to the fight, but the fight was over. The sky that had been so full was empty and he wondered again—as all fighter pilots wondered—that a mass of raging aircraft could vanish in seconds. Plumes of smoke were rising from the distant fields. The pyres of victory. All German, he hoped, with joy, and with a sudden stab that some might be his own men. Climbing back to 12,000 feet, he called Duxford and was told "Pancake at base."

A lone Hurricane appeared on the left, and he ruddered towards it, formating alongside till he saw the big scythe, dripping blood, painted on its side. Willie McKnight! Grinning under his oxygen mask, he raised two fingers to indicate that he had got a couple. McKnight nodded vigorously and then three of his fingers were spread above the cockpit rim. Three! Round the field Hurricanes were coming in. Hard to see how many. He swept down to the grass and Woodhall, the station commander, was standing beside the Hurricane when he climbed out. "Did you get among 'em?"

The old exuberance bubbled up as he told the story. All the Hurricanes were back, the pilots coming in from dispersals hanging on the sides of the flight-trucks, cheering and yelling to each other. "Did you get one?" Drunk on high spirits they babbled out their versions and bit by bit the battle was pieced together: a Dornier had crashed into a greenhouse, another into a field full of derelict cars, a 110 had dived into a reservoir, another Dornier exploded into a ploughed field. Two to Bader, three to McKnight; Turner got one, Crowley-Milling had shot the belly out of a Heinkel, Ball had got one ... several others. They totted up the score—twelve confirmed and several more damaged. The rest had dived and fled home. Not a single bullet hole in any of the Hurricanes.

And not a bomb on North Weald.

Later Bader explained to Woodhall why he had disobeyed his R/T instructions. "From all the combat reports I've seen the Huns seem to be using the sun. After all, they always did. In the mornings they've usually come in from the south-east with the sun behind them, and in the afternoons they swing round to the west or south-west and come out of the sun again."

He expounded his views with the usual vigour.

"It's no good trying to protect North Weald or other targets over the top of them. In the morning they must be protected from way down south-east and in the afternoon from south-west. We've got to catch them before they get to their target, not when they've got there and are dropping their bombs. If the controller will tell us where they are in time—direction and height—we'll sort out the tactics in the air, get up-sun ourselves and beat hell out of them before they can bomb."

"I'm with you," Woodhall said. "I think you're dead right. It certainly worked to-day and from now on I'll be on the other end of the radio every time you're up, so don't worry. I'll tell you your patrol line and then keep telling you where the Jerries are so you can use your own judgment." He added grimly: "We may be sticking our necks out a bit."

"Someone's got to," Bader said. "No one knows much about this game yet and we've got to learn."

"Nelson put his telescope to his blind eye and got away

with it," Woodhall observed. "They'll like you if you get away with it too, but they won't if you don't."

"Trust the Jerries," Bader said grimly. "They'll use the same tricks every time."

From the start he had the comfort of feeling able to talk frankly to Woodhall. The two had plenty in common, though Woodhall was older, a World War I veteran, grey-haired and stocky with a lined and leathery face. A monocle gleamed in one eye but he was no stuffed shirt, being known as a " character " who could turn a glassy blind eye to the book of rules at the right time. That afternoon his voice had come over the R/T as clear as a bell, with unruffled poise.

Bader led the squadron back to Coltishall in tight formation at 200 feet, turning in his cockpit to make rude and hilarious two-finger gestures at everyone.

Leigh-Mallory flew over that evening full of congratulations and Bader took his chance to broach a new idea: " As a matter of fact, sir, if we'd had more aircraft we could have knocked down a lot more. Other squadrons in the group have been standing by like us. Would it be possible for us all to take off together? "

"How would you handle them in the air?" Leigh-Mallory sounded interested.

"It'd be easy to lead, say, three squadrons," Bader said. "I haven't worked it out, sir, but surely the whole object of flying in formation is to get a number of aeroplanes in the same place together. If I'd had three squadrons this afternoon it would have been just as easy to get them to the enemy, and we'd have been three times more powerful. That's all you want, sir. Get as many as possible into the fight together. Once it starts there's nothing more the leader can do.

" I think the thing is to dive into these bomber formations and break them up, and the quicker the better. Then it'll be a free-for-all, and the fighters will have the advantage of eight guns against an isolated gun or two."

"Sounds splendid," Leigh-Mallory said.

" I think it would save our casualties too," Bader went on. "One squadron against a formation of a hundred or more is pretty sticky. We were lucky to-day because we were above and up-sun."

Leigh-Mallory said he would think about it.

Next day 242 Squadron, flushed with success, were scrambled three times to patrol North London again, but each time was an anti-climax—no trace of the enemy. It seemed 242 were only sent up at lunch-time or tea-time to give 11 Group a spell when no German aircraft were about. It was frustrating but in the evening Bader felt better when Leigh-Mallory phoned and said:

" To-morrow I want you to try this large formation scheme of yours. We've got 19 and 310 Squadrons at Duxford. Take your chaps there and see how you get on leading the whole three squadrons."

With great warmth for Leigh-Mallory's decisive ways, Bader spent three days practising take-offs with the three squadrons and leading them in the air. 19 Squadron flew the faster Spitfires so he had them flying above and behind as top cover with the 310 Hurricanes staggered behind 242 on the same level. In those three days he also led 242 on several more patrols round North London, but again saw no trace of the enemy. Exasperating!

Once Powell-Sheddon thought he saw something. They heard his voice on the R/T—" Th-th-thousands on the left! "

A silence as the eyes darted across, and then a cold and scornful voice: " Barrage balloons, you clot! "

Farther south the Luftwaffe was still smashing at southern England and 11 Group seemed to be hogging the battle. Intolerable! Bader said so repeatedly.

On one abortive patrol a plot came on the board just as the wing had to turn back short of petrol. It was maddening. Far below he saw a lone squadron climbing hard to intercept the plot, and hoped very hard that they could get height in time and that there were not too many enemy.

At Group's request he wrote a report on how to break up an enemy formation. " They can be dispersed by shock tactics of the leading section fighters diving into their midst as close as possible . . . risk of collision is there, but the fact remains that the effect of a near collision makes German pilots take violent evasive action which, of course, immediately breaks up any tight formation. Apart from giving the fighters their chance, it also ruins the enemy's chance of accurate bombing."

He kept drumming that into the pilots of all three squadrons, and adding: " Another thing—keep one eye in your mirror the whole time the scrap's on and if you see a Hun in your mirror, break off fast! " By 5th September he had the " scramble " time down to a little over three minutes in getting his thirty-six fighters off the ground. In the air, skipping formality, it was, " Hallo, Woodie," and " Hallo, Douglas." Leigh-Mallory flew down to watch them practise, and said: " All right, Bader. Next time 11 Group calls on you, take your whole team."

Next day, Goering, for the first time, turned the Luftwaffe on London.

Since dawn waves of bombers had been battering through the defences to the city and Bader, on readiness with his squadrons, heard the reports coming through and was stamping with impatience. All day he railed at Group, at Ops. and the imperturbable Woodhall, demanding to be let off the leash, but it was not until a quarter to five that Ops. rang and electrified him by saying, " Scramble! "

In the air Woodhall's calm voice: " Hallo, Douglas. There's some trade heading in over the coast. Orbit North Weald. Angels ten. If they come your way you can go for them."

They climbed fast and hard, and Bader disobeyed instructions again, going on past 10,000 feet to 15,000 in his eagerness to be well on top of anything they sighted.

Nearing North Weald Woodhall again: " Hallo, Douglas. Seventy plus crossing the Thames east of London, heading north."

Far to the south-east a cluster of black dots stained the sky. Somehow they did not look like aircraft but he swung his squadrons towards them. Flak bursts! That meant only one thing. As he searched the sky, McKnight's voice, sharply: " Bandits, ten o'clock above."

He caught the glint and in seconds saw the dots. Damn! A good 5,000 feet above. Throttle hard on, he kept climbing and the Hurricane was vibrating and thundering, clawing for height on full power. Soon he saw there were about seventy Dorniers and 110's mixed up. And more glints above—Me 109's. Behind him the squadrons were trailing, unable to keep up; though the Spitfires were faster they did not climb so well. Only Dickie Cork was anywhere near. It was going to be sticky. Attacking in a straggle from below with the 109's on top. No chance to break them up. No time for tactics. He closed fast and the flanks of the Dorniers were darting by. A quick burst, but the Dornier had only flashed across his sights. Turning under the tails of the rear section, streams of tracer were streaking at him from the rear gunners. Cork was with him—then " Crow "—the others well back. He lifted his nose and a 110 floated in his sights. A quick squirt. He fired again and his eyes caught the yellow spinner of a 109 in his mirror. A second to spare for one more quick burst at the 110—triumph as smoke streamed from it, and then a horrible jarring shock as cannon shells slammed into the Hurricane and jolted it like a pneumatic drill. Instinctively he broke hard left as fear stabbed him, horrible paralysing fright like an ice-block in the chest. Crashes and chaos and the cockpit suddenly full of reeking smoke. For a moment he was frozen rigid, then thought and movement switched on—he was on fire and going down! His hands shot up, grabbed the twin handles of the cockpit hood and hauled it back. Must get out! Straps first! He yanked the pin of his straps and suddenly the cockpit was clear of smoke— sucked out by the noisy slip-stream. No fire. Must have been only cordite smoke. No panic now. He was all right, but furious at having been frightened he slammed the hood shut and looked back, hunted and sweating. No Messerschmitt behind.

The Hurricane was in a screaming diving turn and he eased her out. A 110 was sliding below and he peeled off in chase. It seemed to move towards him as he overhauled it and fired three sharp bursts. The 110 fell away on one wing, nosed straight down, and seconds later dived into a field by a railway line and exploded.

He became aware that his Hurricane was crabbing awkwardly, left wing dropping, and he had the stick hard starboard to keep her level. With a little shock he saw out on the wing that the left aileron was tattered and hanging almost off and there were holes on the right of the cockpit. His Sidcot flying-suit was gashed across the right hip, spilling chewing-gum out of the pocket. Near thing! For the first time in his life he had known the sickness of fear.

After nursing the aircraft back to Coltishall he taxied straight in to the maintenance hangar and climbed out, yelling brusquely: " West, I want this aircraft ready again in half an hour."

West had a quick look at it, and said: " Sorry, sir, but this job won't be flying again for a couple of days."

" That's no damn' good, I want it in half an hour."

West, who understood his C.O., said soothingly but doggedly: " More like a week, I'm afraid, sir. Apart from the aileron you've got four bullets that I can see through the petrol tank. You're lucky it's self-sealing, but it still stinks of petrol. Shells've also smashed your turn and bank, rev. counter and undercart quadrant. There are probably other things too. Sorry, sir, but I won't let it fly."

Bader's anger was cut short. Cork was taxi-ing in and got out painfully, eyes screwed up and face bleeding. Shreds were hanging all over his Hurricane and the cockpit was a mess where 109 shells had smashed it. Glass splinters from shattered instruments, reflector sight and windscreen had hit him in the face and eyes. He said he was fine but Bader sent him away in the ambulance. West marked another aircraft as unflyable. Three other damaged Hurricanes landed.

One by one the pilots reported. Turner had got another and had also seen Bader's first 110 burst into flames and crash. McKnight had also got two; Ball, one; Tamblyn, one—and others. Jubilantly they added the score. Eleven confirmed. But the other two squadrons had been so far behind that they had virtually missed the fight.

Young Crowley-Milling and Pilot Officer Benzie were not back. By dusk they were still missing.

Then a phone call from Crowley-Milling, who had been shot up and cut his face crash-landing in Essex. No word from Benzie. He was dead.

In the morning, a little grimmer, 242 flew again to Duxford, but no call came from 11 Group, though the bombers again were storming London. He could visualise those single 11 Group squadrons climbing up under the German packs, vulnerable to the hovering 109's while they tried to get at the bombers. Often they were picked off like pigeons, and for all the shiny stories of success there were also stories of squadrons which had been almost wiped out in a week. They used to post them north to reform then, and bring down a fresh squadron which might also have to be pulled back north for reforming a week later.

After lunch Leigh-Mallory flew in, and Bader said:

" It didn't come off yesterday, sir. We were too low. If we'd been higher we could really have got among them and the Spitfires could have covered us from the 109's." Angry that the squadrons were kept so long on the ground, he added: " R.D.F.[1] get these plots of bombers building up over France. If only we could get off earlier we could be on top and ready for them. Why can't we do that, sir? "

" The Germans might want us to," Leigh-Mallory suggested. " If they can decoy our fighters up they can hold back for an hour till the fighters have to go down to refuel again and then send the bombers in."

" It's worth taking that chance, sir."

" So it might be," said Leigh-Mallory; " but it's 11 Group's decision and they feel they should wait till the Germans start moving in. That doesn't give them much chance to scramble big formations then, but your score yesterday seems to justify the experiment, so carry on with the three squadrons. After all, it was only the first try. We'll try and get you off earlier in future so you can get your height. Let's see what happens then."

Next morning to readiness at Duxford again with three squadrons for another day of impatient waiting, and about five o'clock Sector Ops. reported that R.D.F. was showing a build-up of enemy aircraft over the Pas de Calais.

Bader rang Woodhall. " For Christ's sake let's get off in time and catch these —— on the way in."

" Keep your hair on, Douglas," Woodhall said. " I'm prodding them hard as I can."

Soon Woodhall rang back. "Bombers heading in. Scramble fast as you can! "

And then in the air: " Hallo, Douglas. Looks like they're

---

[1] Radio Direction Finding—soon to be developed into Radar.

heading for London. Will you patrol between North Weald and Hornchurch, angels twenty."

(" Will you patrol . . . ? " Woodhall left that part open.)

Bader looked at the afternoon sun and thought: I know damn' well they'll swing west and come out of the sun. He forgot North Weald-Hornchurch and climbed his three squadrons south-west over the fringe of London; ignored the " angels twenty " too, climbing till they were specks at 22,000 feet over the reservoirs at Staines, still climbing.

And then a few miles in front the sky glinted and around the spot like a film coming into focus the dots appeared; two great swarms of them cutting across fast in front, heading for London. About the same height. (Just as well he'd ignored " North Weald-Hornchurch " . . . and the " angels " too.) Looked like sixty odd in each bunch. He wheeled to cut them off, still climbing, swinging higher now and between the swarms with the sun behind him and calling 19 Squadron urgently to climb higher and cover their tails. Then to the rest: " Line astern, line astern. We're going through the middle."

In the corner of his eye a scatter of fighters darted out of the sun and he thought with a surge of joy that more friendly fighters had arrived: only a few pilots behind saw that they were 109's and wheeled back to fight them off. Diving now on the first swarm he saw they were mixed Dorniers and 110's. A Dornier was slightly in front leading, and he plunged for it, firing almost point-blank for two seconds, then diving past and under, pulled up again, but the leading Dornier was falling over on its back, smoke pouring from both engines. Other bombers above! He kept zooming up like a dolphin, squirting at them, seeing flashes as the armour-piercing incendiary bullets hit. The mind was racing again in the deadly confusion of high-speed battle.

To the side another Dornier was diving, trailing fire and smoke, and a voice shouted in his ears, " F-f-f-flamer! " Powell-Sheddon had scored. Black twisting bombs were suddenly falling on Bader as the bombers jettisoned over the fields and turned south-east to flee. He steep-turned out of the way of the bombs, seeing that only about twenty of the bombers still clustered in ragged formation, the rest straggling over the sky, hunted by darting fighters.

Half a mile ahead was a Dornier; he chased it and was soon pulling it back. Five hundred yards now. Two Hurricanes suddenly dived in from each side in front of him converging on the Dornier. Damn! Daylight robbery! Swiftly the two fighters swept together behind the bomber, and he suddenly screamed into his microphone: "Look out. You're going to collide." A moment later they did. The left wing of the Hurricane on the right folded and ripped away, and it spun instantly; the other Hurricane, crabbing crazily on, smashed into the Dornier's tail and the air was full of flying fragments. The two broken aircraft wrenched apart and spun, followed by torn pieces twisting and floating down. It was over in seconds.

A big Heinkel was fleeing about a mile away and well below, and he dived in chase. It seemed to be stupid or helpless, making no effort to dodge as he swept nearer—must have been shot up. It filled his windscreen—a beautiful target. As usual he held his fire until almost point-blank he jabbed the button and heard only the mocking hiss of compressed air through the breech-blocks. Out of ammunition! He flamed with outraged fury and swung across the Heinkel's nose, but it took no notice, lumbering wearily in. He slammed round behind it again raging with a crazy impulse to ram it—cut off its rudder with his propeller—and then sense returned and he turned away.

Back at Duxford two of the pilots, Brimble and Bush, said they saw Bader's first Dornier go down in flames and only one of the crew had baled out. Bush had also got one. McKnight had collected a couple more . . . and others too, Eric Ball, Powell-Sheddon, Turner, Tamblyn had scored . . . eleven confirmed to 242 Squadron.

But Sclanders and Lonsdale were missing.

The other two squadrons added a further nine enemy destroyed, but two of 310 Squadron had not returned.

Later Lonsdale phoned. He had been shot down, baled out and landed in a tree in the grounds of a girls' school, hurting his leg, and could not get down because of his leg. Uncomfortably, he had roosted in the branches for half an hour while the girls stood underneath giggling until the local constable came and brought him down a ladder.

Sclanders was dead.

Then Gordon Sinclair, of 310 Squadron, phoned from Caterham on the other side of London. He had been in one of the Hurricanes that collided and had managed to bale out. Bader grabbed the phone. " How are you, Gordon? "

" Utterly amazed, sir," Sinclair said. " D'you know, I lobbed slap in Caterham High Street and I was picking my parachute out of the gutter when a chap walked up, and said: ' Hallo, Gordon, old boy. What are you doing here? ' And I'm damned if it wasn't a chap I was at school with."

The pilot of the other Hurricane, a Czech, did not bale out.

But the mathematics were good—twenty enemy destroyed for the loss of four Hurricanes and two pilots. In September, 1940, only the mathematics mattered.

Still Bader was not satisfied. He flew to 12 Group H.Q., at Hucknall, and told Leigh-Mallory: " Sir, if we'd only had *more* fighters we could have hacked the Huns down in scores."

" I was going to talk to you about that," Leigh-Mallory said. " If I gave you two more squadrons, could you handle them? "

17

FIVE SQUADRONS. Sixty plus fighters! Even Bader was startled. He collected himself:

"Yes, sir. When a fight starts we'd break up anyway. I'd have the Spitfires on top to hold off any 109's, and a mass of Hurricanes below with nothing to worry about on their tails could crucify a pack of bombers."

"I thought of that too," said Leigh-Mallory.

He seemed to understand so well that Bader took the plunge and told him about disobeying controller's instructions, not to clear himself but with a proselytising zeal, expounding his ideas.

"The formation leaders might make a mistake and miss the enemy altogether," suggested Leigh-Mallory.

"The controllers are already doing that, sir. They can't help it. R.D.F. is inaccurate about height."

"You think the advantages outweigh the risks?"

"Yes, sir, I do." Bader was emphatic.

"So do I," Leigh-Mallory said. "I'll put this up to the right people and meantime you might as well carry on with your theory. It seems to work."

There was more to the conversation than those extracts, of course. It lasted over an hour, and Leigh-Mallory did not accept all that Bader said without reservations, but he recognised the square-jawed man with the glowing eyes and manner as an individualist with a direct approach that impatiently threw out minor details and concentrated on the elementals. With equal zeal he could be abysmally wrong or brilliantly right on any problem. In this battle, where the right answers had to be won by bitter experience, the A.O.C. thought Bader was right. He added that he was also spreading Bader's gospel of breaking up enemy formations by diving into their midst. Bader had done it the first time on the spur of a moment of anger—from that moment was born a new tactical method that was against all the teachings. Leigh-Mallory called 242 the "disintegration squadron."

Up before dawn next morning for Duxford. And the morning after. Several more patrols to relieve 11 Group but nothing seen. Everyone complained of boredom but that was only the fashionable, elaborately casual pose. In the past fortnight 231 pilots had been killed or badly wounded, and 495 Hurricanes and Spitfires destroyed or badly damaged (mostly 11 Group). The factories only turned out about a hundred new ones a week. Pilot replacements were also fewer than the losses and many of the new pilots too raw for battle.

Among the survivors fear and tension lay under the surface like taut sinews in a naked body, but always decently covered with understatement: protection against showing emotion, either fear or unseemly elation at being the only instrument between Hitler and the conquest of Britain. Life was a brutal contrast. Off duty they could joke in a pub and sleep between sheets, to wake in the morning to a new world of hunters and hunted, sitting in deck-chairs on the grass, waiting by the aeroplanes with needles in the stomach. Other men who knew they themselves would still be alive at night brought them sandwiches for lunch and coffee, but any moment the phone might go and they would have to drop the cup: half an hour later they might be trapped in a burning aeroplane crashing from 20,000 feet.

Only Bader had no pose. He swashbuckled around as though he were about to step into the ring and knock out Joe Louis with one punch and without even bothering to change. His exuberance, the way he utterly ignored the danger, was contagious and infected every other pilot. Morale was extraordinary. He loved the battle and talked and thought tactics, fascinated by them. Insensitive to fear, he never had what was known as "the twitch" like the others. For the Germans (hidden in their aeroplanes) he conceived an impersonal hate, but he passionately loathed "those aeroplanes with the black crosses and swastikas dropping their filthy bombs on *my* country. By the same token I felt a great love for every single English person I met on the ground."

About this time he designed the squadron emblem— a figure of Hitler being kicked in the breeches by a flying boot labelled 242. West cut a metal template of it and the ground crews painted it on the noses of all the Hurricanes. The ground crews were working devotedly day and night to keep the aircraft flying.

Off duty, Bader did not mind anyone letting off steam violently. Peter Macdonald helped by turning on a champagne party for the pilots one night. Leigh-Mallory came over and entered into the spirit of things by forsaking his dignity and doing a Highland Fling on a mess table. It all ended hilariously with a crowd of young men squirming on the floor in mock scuffle, punctuated by occasional sharp yelps when one of Bader's flailing tin legs hit someone in ribs or head. Leigh-Mallory seemed to be on duty all the time; he had a weakness for cold baths and midnight conferences and was often working till 3 a.m., usually rising again at 6.30. He had been known to spend twenty-seven hours in the operations room, and then go and talk to pilots on windy tarmacs when they came back from a flight. After that he would probably take them into the mess, stand drinks all round and listen to any complaints or suggestions.

Bader slept in the mess at Coltishall but used to go and see Thelma every evening to let her know he was all right. On 13th September he was having dinner with her at the house in Coltishall when the phone rang for him in the hall. Leigh-Mallory's voice greeted him courteously: " Oh, hallo, Bader. I wanted to be the first to congratulate you. You've just been awarded the D.S.O."

A great glow suffused him, and then in the emotion of the moment he could think of nothing to say until at last he managed an automatic " Thank you, sir."

" And another thing," Leigh-Mallory added a few moments later. The next morning 302 Squadron (Hurricanes) and 611 (Spitfires) would also be flying into Duxford. Would Bader be good enough to include them in his formation, which was now to be called the ' 12 Group Wing.'

Bader managed to convey that he would be delighted to.

It is good form to be offhand about decorations, but nothing can dim stirring inner pride. One always feels it and

no one more fiercely than Bader, who was living so wholly
for the fight. And for the consummation of himself. It was
too fierce a moment to be offhand about, or even to mention.
He sat holding it to himself for an hour before mentioning it
quietly to a flight lieutenant known as Poggi, who was also
in the house. Poggi went delightedly to Thelma and said:
" Isn't this wonderful about Douglas's D.S.O."

Thelma said, " What are you talking about, Poggi? "
then saw Douglas's face and realised something had happened.
There was the usual scene of excitement, affection and congratulations, capped by the general laugh when Thelma,
eternal woman, said: " Well I *do* think you might have told
me first."

Next morning, 14th September, the two extra squadrons
as promised flew into Duxford, and twice that day Bader led
the armed pack of sixty fighters into the air to patrol North
London. They saw no enemy; the Luftwaffe was coiling for
the next leap and only one bomber sneaked through the
cloud to bomb Buckingham Palace at the cost of its own
destruction. Eric Ball's D.F.C. came through, the first
decoration Bader had recommended.

In the still, cool, dawn of 15th September the five squadrons
of 12 Group Wing stood in groups about Duxford and its
satellite field, waiting. Broken cloud scattered thickly over the
sky offering good cover to attackers, and R.D.F. began reporting plots of enemy aircraft rising over the fields of Northern
France. In clumps the plots crept across the screens towards
England, and soon the shield of 11 Group squadrons round
London was savaging them over Kent. Then the first stage
was over; burning wrecks littered the fields, the remnants of
the bombers, some winged and smoking, were streaming
back to France and the Hurricanes and Spitfires, gun-ports
whistling where the patches had been shot off, were coming
in to refuel and re-load. At that moment R.D.F. showed
another wave of bombers heading for London.

Woodhall scrambled the 12 Group Wing five minutes
later.

In the air, the measured voice: " Hallo, Douglas. About
forty bandits heading for London. Will you patrol Canterbury-
Gravesend."

" O.K., Woodie."

Canterbury-Gravesend! That was fine. The morning sun still lay in the south-east, and if the bombers were going for London he knew where to look for them. The three Hurricane squadrons climbed steeply in vics line astern with the Spitfires a little to the left, a little above. To the right London lay under the cloud that had thickened. 12,000 feet . . . 16,000 . . . 20,000 . . . they kept climbing high over the cloud. Nearing angels 23 he saw black puffs staining the sky almost straight ahead, and somewhat below and ahead of the flak almost instantly saw the enemy, drilled black flies sliding towards the naked city. About five miles away . . . forty odd . . . JU. 88's and Dorniers.

Swinging right, he nosed down to come in diving. God, it was beautiful, the sun right behind them, the bombers below. He looked for the 109's behind and above and could hardly believe it . . . not a sign. Unescorted bombers. The heart leapt and the blood sang and the mind ran clear and sharp.

High out of a veil of cloud near the sun little grey sharks were darting. He called urgently:

" Sandy, watch those 109's."

" O.K., chum, I can see them." Sandy Lane, leader of 19 Squadron, was already wheeling the Spitfires up into the fighters.

" Break 'em up," yelled Bader and swept, firing, through the front rank of the bombers. He pulled up and veered behind a big Dornier turning away left, fired and fired again. A flash burst behind the Dornier's starboard engine, and flame and black smoke spewed from it. Suddenly he was nearly ramming it and broke off. Hell, aircraft of broken formations darting everywhere in the blurred and flashing confusion. In front—400 yards away—another Dornier seeking cloud cover between the 'cu-nims'; he was catching it rapidly when his eye caught a Spitfire diving steeply above and just ahead. It happened fast. The Spitfire pilot clearly did not see the bomber under the long cowling; he dived straight into the middle of it and the Dornier in a burst of flame split and wrapped its broken wings round the fighter.

Tumbling fragments glinted above the crumpled mass as the two aircraft fell in burning embrace.

Sweating, Bader looked for others. A Dornier was spinning down to one side, dragging a plume of flame and smoke, and as he watched a man jumped out of it. His parachute opened instantly—too soon—the canopy spread into the blaze and shrivelled to nothingness in a sheet of flame. The man dropped like a stone, trailing the cords like a tattered banner. Bader was snarling to himself: " Good show, you rat. Now you've got a little time to think about it and there isn't any answer."

After that only the miracle again of the empty sky.

Back at Duxford Eric Ball was missing.

They refuelled, re-loaded, and by 11.45 were on readiness again.

A phone call from Eric Ball. His Hurricane had been shot down in flames but he had baled out and would be back.

Two hours later the Wing was scrambled again to patrol North Weald, and Bader led them through a gap in the clouds. At 16,000 feet, flak bursts ahead, and in moments he saw the bombers; about forty of them, some 4,000 feet above the Hurricanes. Damn! Everything risked again because they were scrambled too late. Throttle hard on, the thundering Hurricane had her nose steeply lifted, nearly hanging on her propeller at about 100 m.p.h.

A voice screamed: " 109's behind."

Over his shoulder the yellow spinners were diving on them and he yelled as he steep-turned, " Break up!" Around him the sky was full of wheeling Hurricanes and 109's. A yellow spinner was sitting behind his tail, and as he yanked harder back on the stick an aeroplane shot by, feet away. Bader hit its slipstream and the Hurricane shuddered, stalled and spun off the turn. He let it spin a few turns to shake off the 109 and came out of it at 5,000 feet. All clear behind.

Far above a lone Dornier was heading for France, and he climbed and chased it a long way, hanging on his propeller nearly at stalling speed again. Near the coast he was just about in range and fired a three-second burst, but the recoil of the guns slowed the floundering Hurricane till she suddenly stalled and spun off again. He pulled out and searched the sky but the enemy had vanished.

Back at Duxford, Powell-Sheddon was missing.

That was the greatest day of the battle. Odd, looking back, that it seemed no different to any other day. None of the pilots thought much about it at the time; it was just another episode in the confused and wearying tension that had so recently and so completely enveloped them. No time to think, only to dress at dawn and sit waiting, hung in a limbo of queasy time, lazy small talk on the outside and taut nerves inside, waiting for the ring of the phone that sent them into battle again. They found, when they pieced that day's battle together, that the 12 Group Wing had fully justified itself, though in the second battle the roles had been reversed—the Spitfires had got among the bombers while the Hurricanes tangled with the 109's. But that was merely a quirk of the battle; the main point was that in the two mass fights that day the pilots of the five squadrons of the Wing claimed 52 enemy destroyed and a further eight probables.[1]

242 Squadron's share was twelve. At least they were consistent—it was usually either eleven or twelve. Cork, his face repaired, had got two Dorniers, one on each trip. Young Crowley-Milling, whose cut face was also nearly healed, had flown again for the first time since he was shot down, and avenged himself by chasing a 109 across Kent and sending it smoking into a field. McKnight, Turner, Bader, Stansfeld, Tamblyn had all scored. Even Powell-Sheddon, who rang up from somewhere near Epping. It had been going so well, he reported dolefully. He had shot a Dornier down and was chasing another when a 109 came out of cloud behind and he had had to bale out in a hurry as the flames spurted round his cockpit; in such a hurry that he had hit the tail plane and dislocated his shoulder. The doctor said he would be out of the battle for some weeks.[2]

---

[1] The R.A.F. claimed 185 German aircraft destroyed on September 15th. After the war Luftwaffe figures said that only 56 had been lost. R.A.F. pilots who fought in the battle flatly and vehemently disbelieve the German total. One might suspect that some of Goebbels's propaganda figures were discreetly promoted to official records status.

[2] Powell-Sheddon later went on to win a D.S.O. and D.F.C.

Bader went to Turner and said: " Stan, how d'you feel about taking over B Flight? "

" Swell, sir," said Turner.

Leigh-Mallory phoned that night:

" Douglas " (using his Christian name for the first time) . . . " What a wonderful show to-day! " The A.O.C.'s rather formal manner had completely melted. " It's absolutely clear your big formations are paying dividends."

Bader said: " Thank you very much, sir, but we had a sticky time on the second trip. They scrambled us too late again and the Germans were a long way above when we spotted them. It was a bad spot to attack. If we'd only been one squadron we'd probably have been chopped up by the 109's, but if they'd let us off ten minutes earlier we could have been just in the right spot to cope, and probably got a lot more of them.

" It doesn't make sense, sir " (warming to his theme). " As soon as they start building up their formations over Calais we should get into the air and go south. *We* should be the ones to attack them first while 11 Group get off and get height."

" Well, you know I feel somewhat the same as you on this point," Leigh-Mallory said. " At the same time don't forget we have to keep reserves available. It's 11 Group's job to make that decision and it isn't easy for them. I rather fancy they had every squadron they could call on committed to-day."

" Well, sir, reserves or no reserves, they called on us too late to-day."

" Quite," said the A.O.C. " But the wing score to-day won't go unnoticed—I'll see to that myself—and I fancy it will encourage them to call for you earlier."

" I hope they do, sir," Bader answered feelingly—then enthusiastic again: " D'you know, sir, what I'd really like to do is shoot down a complete raid so that not one of the Huns gets back."

The A.O.C. laughed. " Bloodthirsty, aren't you! If you chaps keep on the way you're going you'll probably get your chance."

The chance came on the 18th.

About 4.30 in the afternoon the five squadrons were scrambled, and over the R/T Woodhall said that forty plus bandits were heading for London from the south-east. Bader led the Wing through a thin layer of cloud at about 21,000 feet and levelled off in the clear at 23,000. Not far below, the soft feather-bed stretched flat and unbroken for miles, perfect backdrop for searching eyes. Nothing else in sight. But the invisible world under the cloud? In a shallow dive he took his fighters down through the thin layer and they cruised under the white ceiling, feeling comfortingly safe. No one could jump them blind through that curtain.

Once again the flak-bursts led them. First Bader saw the black puffs away to the south-east and in moments picked up the bombers. Two little swarms, about forty in all, were flying about 16,000 feet over a bend of the Thames near Gravesend. More British aeroplanes than enemy! It was unbelievable! As the fighters circled to close in behind he saw with fierce joy that they were all bombers—JU. 88's and Dorniers. Not a sign of any 109's. The bombers were 4,000 feet below, just where he would have wanted them. No question of coming out of the sun—the clouds hid the sun. He dived, aiming for the JU. 88's in the front rank of the bombers, and the ravenous pack streamed after him.

A Junkers filled his sights and as he fired from 100 yards astern its port engine gushed smoke and it fell away to the left. Pulling up into the thick of plunging, criss-crossing aeroplanes, he fired briefly at a couple that flashed across his sights and vanished again; then in quick succession nearly collided with two more bombers. A Hurricane screamed towards him at a crazy angle: he yanked the stick over to get out of the way, hit someone's slipstream and his Hurricane shuddered and flicked into a spin. He got her straight and level again after losing about 3,000 feet, and saw above that the split-up bombers had turned for home, hounded by the fighters. To the south-east, lower and away from the ruck, a Dornier was sneaking east and he chased it. No escape for the slower and cumbersome Dornier; he closed for the kill, holding his fire till he was barely fifty yards away, and then jabbed the button.

As the bullets still squirted, the enemy gunner lost his nerve and jumped. His awkward shape swept back out of the glasshouse and his parachute, streaming open at the same moment, hooked and tangled over one of the twin fins on the tail, pulling him up like a whipcrack. As he dangled helplessly on the shrouds the Dornier, obviously out of control, started "hurdling," soaring into steep zooms, hanging a moment at the top and then falling into dives, building speed and zooming again. Bader sheered off to one side, watching, amazed and fascinated. Two more men suddenly tumbled out of the glasshouse and the white silk of their parachutes blossomed below. The empty Dornier kept hurdling imaginary obstacles, losing more height, still trailing the wretched gunner. With sudden pity Bader dived and fired at him to put him out of his misery, but as far as he could see, missed. The Dornier fell into a deeper dive and he left it.

For once the sky above was not empty . . . many white flowers of parachutes were floating down. A little man in a strange brown flying suit fell past his Hurricane very fast with only a little remnant of silk left of his parachute. Bader thought whimsically he must be a Gestapo agent who had been sabotaged by the honest airmen.

At dispersals a mob of hilarious pilots clustered round the intelligence officer, most of them claiming victims. Turner was describing how he saw a German's opening parachute caught in the hatch as he jumped out of a burning JU. 88. The rest of the crew were trying to release it. . . . "I could damn' nearly hear the poor guy on the end howling 'For God's sake, don't tear it!'" They got him free and jumped out themselves just before the 88 went into the sea.

None of them had ever seen so many parachutes. McKnight had seen the gunner trailing on the cords behind Bader's Dornier and could not stop marvelling at it.

Bader summed it up prosaically in his log book: "London patrol. Contact." And alongside it a laconic note: "Wing destroyed 30 plus 6 probables plus 2 damaged. 242 got 11. Personal score: 1 JU. 88, 1 Do. 17. No casualties in squadron or wing."

In his formal combat report he wrote: "To every German

there seemed to be about three British fighters queueing up for a squirt, a little dangerous from the collision point of view but a most satisfactory state of affairs."

That time he rang Leigh-Mallory himself, described the fight like a fisherman telling his favourite story and mourned about the few that had got away.

Goering started to chop and change his tactics more, sometimes sending over squads of 109's in advance of the bombers to draw the fighters up and exhaust their petrol (something like the decoy idea that Leigh-Mallory had mentioned to Bader earlier). It was the beginning of the end of the daylight bombing, but no one knew that yet as the aura of ruthless power still clung to the Germans. At best it seemed a lull.

Bombers still occasionally battered through the defences to London, but the spearhead on that target was blunted: more and more they went for Kent, for the Estuary towns and, in particular, Southampton, all on the south-east fringes of England and away from the 12 Group area.

Once or twice nearly every day, especially at lunch or tea-time, the wing was scrambled to patrol an arc round London, and Bader had a new grievance—they never ran into the enemy any more. His personal score was eleven confirmed, but that only whetted his zest rather than satiated it. Besides, some others had twenty or more!

He was famous now, which would have been good for placating the little demon inside him if he had not been too busy to notice the publicity much. To stress " team spirit " the R.A.F. did not name its " aces," but every time there was some new epic about a fighter pilot with no legs, the Press knew well enough who it was. Bader himself lived in the little world of the Wing, the battle and the tactics. He was aware of the high morale of his pilots but hardly realised how much of it was due to himself: they looked on him as a super-man and would have followed him into the middle of a thousand 109's. He obviously knew what he was doing in the air better than anyone else, and there was a fire about him so much more than breezy confidence. He was a kind of machine genius of the new aerial art with an iron will exalted by the moment.

Every time the wing took off, the masterful voice started firing comments over the R/T with such assurance that pilots could not help feeling confident. His remarks, by design or accident, so often took the nervous sting out of the business ahead. On 20th August, for instance, a lanky, nineteen-year-old boy called Cockie Dundas flew with the wing for the first time. Exactly a month earlier Dundas had been with 616 Squadron at Kenley; they were waiting at readiness for an evening visit from Winston Churchill when they had been scrambled and run into a flock of 109's over Kent. It was Dundas's first fight and a 109 had " jumped " him, shot his controls to bits and put bullets in his engine and glycol tank. Smoke and glycol fumes filled the cockpit and he could not get his hood open. He spun out of control from 12,000 feet till finally he was able to jettison the hood and baled out at 800 feet, breaking his collar-bone at the same time. Now only two of the old pilots were left in the squadron, and Dundas, still shaken, shoulder still weak, was going back for more. They were scrambled in a great hurry and, being young and human, he had " the twitch," dry mouth, butterflies in the stomach and thumping heart. Then in his ears as they climbed, that odd, legless leader's voice:

" Hey, Woodie, I'm supposed to be playing squash with Peters in an hour's time. Ring him up, will you, and tell him I won't be back till later."

(Dear God. Legless! Playing squash!)

Woodhall's voice: " Never mind that now, Douglas, Vector one-nine-zero. Orbit North Weald. Angels twenty."

" Oh, go on, Woodie. Ring him up now."

" Haven't got time, Douglas. There's a plot on the board heading for the coast."

" Well, can't you make time? You're sitting in front of a row of phones. Pick up one and ring the chap."

" All right. All right," said the philosophical Woodhall. " For the sake of peace and quiet I will. Now would you mind getting on with the war."

Dundas flew on with lifted heart, like all the others.

Another squadron intercepted the plot on the board, and the wing landed an hour later and was released from readiness. Bader played squash and flew off to see Leigh-Mallory at

Hucknall. Dundas thought that evening he would never have the twitch flying behind Bader again. (He was wrong . . . but that came later.)

Some of the credit for the confidence also belonged to Woodhall. It is hard to say how much these absurd conversations were designed as confidence builders and how much was instinctive. Bader himself is not sure, though later he realised their value and used the technique a lot. Even then it remained at least as much unconscious as conscious. It was just part of him.

On 24th September a D.F.C. came through for Dickie Cork and Bader was as pleased as Cork, not only because he had recommended it but because it was, as far as he knew, the only D.F.C. ever awarded to a " Nautic " (the equivalent Naval decoration is the D.S.C.—Distinguished Service Cross). Cutting across the Navy's bows with a D.F.C. for Cork was a " jolly good giggle." He never stopped trying to lure Cork from the customs of the Navy and inject R.A.F. lore and outlook into him. That, too, was a " good frolic." He had Cork to the point now where he had naval buttons on the starboard side of his tunic, but down the port side, reading from top to bottom, an R.A.F. button, a Polish Air Force button (which was silver in colour, not even gilded), an R.C.A.F. button and a Czech button.

The abortive patrols went on till 27th September. About noon that day the wing was scrambled to patrol North London. Woodhall said " Angels fifteen." Bader knew that instruction came from 11 Group and climbed to 23,000 feet.

Woodhall on the air again: " There's a plot of thirty plus south-east of the Estuary. They don't seem to be coming in."

Bader led his pack over Canterbury. Nothing in sight. He carried on round Dover, headed west for Dungeness and swung back. Woodhall kept talking about bandits cruising about the south-east. Clumps of cloud littered the air below like papers blowing about a windswept park. Otherwise the sky was empty. Woodhall called again: " All right, Douglas, I think the lunch shift is over. You might as well come back."

" Just a minute, Woodie," Bader said. " I'll do one more swing round."

Turning back from Dungeness, his eye caught glints well below at about 17,000 feet, and soon he could make out an untidy gaggle of about thirty 109's milling round Dover.

18

"**O**.K., CHAPS," he called. "Take this quietly. Don't attack till I tell you." Rather like a huntsman who has sighted shy game, he began stalking them, turning the wing south over the sea so that they could dive out of the high sun. The 109's were so scattered it would have to be a shambles, every man for himself. Still the Germans weaved in a ragged undisciplined tangle like unwary rabbits at play. He yelled: "Right. Break up and attack!" and was diving steeply, turning in behind a 109. At the same speed it seemed to hang motionless in his sights. A two-second squirt and a pencil of white smoke trailed from it— abruptly the smoke gushed into a cloud spewing past its tail and the little fighter rolled slowly on its back, nose dropping until it plummeted vertically, scoring a long white scar through the clouds to the fields of Kent.

Another 109 crossed in front, rolled swiftly on its back and dived. Bader peeled off after him, but the 109 was faster and began to pull away. From four hundred yards Bader fired a forlorn long-range burst and a jet of smoke spurted from the 109. It seemed to be slowing. Bader fired again and again, seeing flashes of bullet strikes.

Something dark spurted from the 109 and a black shadow seemed to slap him nervelessly across the face. He felt nothing; only the eyes sensed it and then saw that his windscreen and hood were stained to black opaqueness by the enemy's oil that the slipstream was tearing in thin reluctant streaks across the glass. Dimly through it he saw the 109 veering aside and turned after it, seeing, amazed, that the Messerschmitt's propeller was slowing. The 109 was coming tail-first at him: he yanked the throttle back and the enemy floated close in front, the perfect shot. He jabbed the gun-button and heard the pssst of compressed air that hissed through empty breech-blocks. Hell! Out of bullets again.

He swore. The 109's propeller spun in shaky spasms and then it stopped dead, one blade held up like a stiff finger. They were over the sea at 10,000 feet, and the 109, still smoking, was gliding quietly down into the Channel. That was the last he saw of it.

The wing got twelve in that fight, half of them to 242 Squadron. One Spitfire and two Hurricanes did not come back, and one of them was Homer, of 242, who had already won a D.F.C. on bombers and was having his first fight in Hurricanes.

Bader hated losing pilots, taking it, illogically, as some sort of reflection on himself. He felt that every man was under *his* care. None of his emotions were half-hearted and under the aggressive exterior lay impulsive sentiment that could be deeply stirred. Yet the impact of a loss was always cushioned by the hope of a phone call. No call came from Homer, who was dead, but there was no time for grief. By tea-time the wing was patrolling London again. No incident, but waiting for the squadron at Coltishall that evening was an Air Ministry signal announcing the joyous news in prosaic official terms that Turner and Stansfeld were awarded D.F.C.s and Willie McKnight a bar to his D.F.C.

Leigh-Mallory phoned from Hucknall in what was becoming a sort of victory tradition and they had a long discussion about tactics. Bader said that the Hurricanes flew soggily at 23,000 feet. What about the new Hurricane II's?

Leigh-Mallory said: "Anything you want, I'll try my best to get for you, but 11 Group has priority for equipment."

From that day the tide of the battle clearly ebbed. Now the bombers rarely appeared, but in their place came packs of 109's darting for London and other targets with small bombs hanging on makeshift bomb-racks under their slim bellies. They came over fast and very high, dodging through cloud banks, and as autumn came the cloud clustered thicker and thicker. Compared to the sound and fury of a few weeks earlier, the new attacks were forlorn: they so often bombed blindly and the number of bombs was not much more than a trickle. The R.A.F. changed its tactics too. At 25,000 feet the Hurricanes found it harder than ever to catch the fleet 109's and the burden fell on the Spitfires, which were scrambled early now so that they were up there, waiting, when the 109's came. Not many Messerschmitts broke through the screen of Spitfires, and now in London, when the sirens wailed, people no longer bothered to stream out of the buildings into the cellars and shelters. It was the same in other cities. After the alarm sirens there was still a lot of noise, but now it was not the crashing symphony of bombs but the cracking of anti-aircraft guns. Apart from those one would not have known that the Luftwaffe was over except for the fantastic patterns of vapour trails high overhead where the fighters, sightless to the upturned faces, fought it out.

For another couple of weeks the 12 Group Wing kept assembling each day at Duxford and patrolling London, usually twice a day, always vainly now, still keyed up but with the tension easing like air leaking out of a bladder as the Luftwaffe faded from the scene. Even the 109 sneak raiders were dwindling and not till the second week in October did Bader get near one. Leading the wing over the Estuary, his radio died and he fiddled with it but it stayed mute, and at last angrily he slid the cockpit lid open, dropped back, signalled by hand to Eric Ball to take over the wing, and then peeled off for base. It was nearly dusk and as he dropped to about 7,000 feet near North Weald the land lay obscured under thick haze, with a low sun dazzling the eyes. Suddenly his radio popped and crackled to life again, and a few seconds later he heard Woodhall: " Douglas, are you receiving me? Are you receiving me, Douglas? Enemy fighters attacking North Weald with bombs. Do you hear? Do you hear, Douglas? Please acknowledge."

He called back: " Already there, Woodie " (which startled Woodhall considerably). " I'm alone, so tell the others."

At that moment a 109 shot out of the haze, climbing almost vertically and levelled off about four hundred yards in front, flying straight and level ahead. He was obviously not looking behind, and Bader, slamming the throttle on, practically licked his lips. It was a real squadron leader's shot, a piece of cake on a golden platter. He was overhauling the unwary 109 when another Hurricane shot out of the haze in front like a jack-in-the-box and levelled off about 100 yards behind the 109—right in Bader's path. Before he had time to be irritated the leading Hurricane fired one brisk burst; a great flash sparked on the cockpit of the 109, the perspex hood flew off and it turned on its back, and the pilot fell out as it dropped into its last dive. Bader flew up alongside the other Hurricane and recognised an old friend, " Butch " Barton. Barton turned and must have guessed what had happened because he lifted two rude fingers over the side of the cockpit.

The theatrical Goering provided no good " curtain " for the daylight battles. The Luftwaffe came in like a lion and went out like a lamb, accompanied by a few hesitant and diminishing squeaks from the muted brass. So slowly did it taper that for a while the awakening people on the ground did not fully realise the significance of what was happening. The Germans had been the slaves of time; they had to break Fighter Command to invade Britain before winter and they had failed. On 12th October Hitler postponed the invasion till the following spring. Some people in England still waited for the next assaults, and the fact that Hitler, the invincible, had suffered his first (and resounding) defeat did not make its full impact until Winston Churchill's phrase " The Battle of Britain " took firmer root along with those other famous words: " Never in the field of human conflict has so much been owed by so many to so few." Then the country rejoiced, but Fighter Command had lost 915 aircraft and 733 pilots killed or wounded.

Bader, perhaps alone, felt some sorrow that the brawling was over. The Duxford wing had shot down 152 enemy for the loss of thirty pilots and rather more aircraft. But now the dawn rendezvous of his five squadrons had petered out and the days were more predictable—back to normal readiness at Coltishall.

Among England's crumbled ruins other people were getting back to normal too—even the bureaucrats were catching up with their papers. A letter came to Sub-Lieutenant Cork from the Admiralty, pointing out with a great number of formal words that the D.F.C. was not awarded to naval officers and that Mr. Cork would therefore unstitch the ribbon of his D.F.C. and have the D.S.C. sewn in its place.

" By God, no you don't, Corkie," growled Bader. " The King has given you that D.F.C. and only the King can take it away from you—not my ruddy Lords of the Admiralty. When the King sends you another letter to say you've got to wear the D.S.C. instead of the D.F.C., then you can take it down. Not before. That's an order."

Now there was time for a little spit and polish and congratulations. 242 Squadron flew to Duxford again to be inspected and thanked by the Secretary of State for Air, Sir Archibald Sinclair. Bader made a point of introducing Cork and explaining about the medal trouble. Sir Archibald grinned and said: " I absolutely agree, Bader. Of course he must keep wearing the D.F.C. I won't let them change it." He leaned closer confidingly: " These Admiralty people are a bit funny, you know . . . sea complex and all that." He nodded meaningly.

Convoy patrols again! Life was dull. A few 109's still poked their yellow spinners over Kent, but they were reserved for the Spitfires. Bader felt aggrieved, though occasionally he persuaded Leigh-Mallory to let him take the Squadron down over the Estuary. No luck, though.

Now the worst crisis seemed over, the Lords of the Admiralty reclaimed Cork and Gardner and sent them to fly in Cornwall. The squadron farewelled them sadly. More pilots and aircraft came to fill the gaps of the dead, and the fire of the great days was dying. There were compensations. As ever when Mars leaves his arms on the field for home, other welcoming arms await with gratitude in the fire-warmed homes and pubs. Coltishall loved them. They were " our squadron," and if one or two parents had qualms, their daughters did not share them.

At The Bell, 242's favourite pub in Norwich, they were grieved to find that the landlord, a special friend, was in bed in a plaster casing. An incendiary had fallen on the pub and he had climbed on to the burning roof to fight it, had fallen through and broken his back. *En masse* the pilots stripped off his pyjama jacket and wrote messages and signed their names on the plaster.

One day a strange aircraft blipped on the radar screen off Harwich, but Bader was not on readiness at the time. A section took off and the handsome Neil Campbell found it, a Dornier, thirty miles to sea. They heard him over the R/T as he yelled that he was attacking, but that was the last they heard. The rear-gunner must have got him because he did not come back. Later the sea washed his body ashore.

A D.F.C. came through for John Latta.

Against the last, petulant stabs of the 109's Bader led his wing on one last flight: an emaciated wing of his own squadron and No. 19. Climbing over the Estuary, a lone startled shout came from Willie McKnight, and then a pack of 109's was spitting through them out of the sun. Only McKnight was quick enough to fire; he caught one as it darted in front and the 109 did not lift its nose like the others but went tumbling down the sky like a broken thing that had lost the grace of flight. Two Hurricanes were spinning down, too, one of them smoking. Later a phone call from one pilot, who had steadied his torn Hurricane and crash-landed. The other, Norrie Hart, was dead.

As autumn gusts whirled the last yellowed leaves across the aerodrome, the embattled nation realised that not even a madman could invade now. In a sturdy people danger deferred is more a stimulant than a cancer, and within the rampart of the sea confidence grew with the defences. For some time Thelma had been losing her fear for Douglas, and now inside her was an odd feeling that he was invincible. Quite illogical. Quite firm. In her pride lay no regret that he was back in the Air Force. Still, she was a practical young woman and therefore glad that the fighting was finished for a while.

Then the bombers struck again. At night!

19

OUT OF the black sky they rained bombs on London, the docks, the city, and the huddled houses around. Unable to invade, Hitler tried to destroy the will to resist. The nights glowed with acres of flame but the glow was never high enough to betray the bombers, and apart from anti-aircraft guns the people had almost no defences. Balloons were too low. Some Spitfires and Hurricanes went up, but it was like playing blind man's buff. They had no radar in aeroplanes then. Luck was the main chance and they found little of that. The bombers switched to Bristol, Liverpool, Hull . . . back to London.

242 Squadron was by-passed, the impotent patrols going to other squadrons, and his helplessness incensed Bader almost as much as the pity of the smoking ruins. In the daylight battle his feeling had been fierce but his emotion against Germans largely impersonal. He had been hot-blooded in the fight and the bombers were ordered pawns. He might have been born a German himself. . . . But the night bombing was different.

The phone rang in the mess one evening and the night controller from Duxford asked urgently: " How many of your chaps can night-fly Hurricanes? "

" Three," Bader answered. " Myself, Ball and Turner."

" Get 'em into the air as soon as you can," ordered the controller. " The Hun's going for Coventry."

A full moon shone in a cloudless sky as he climbed hard to 18,000 feet over Coventry and was emotionally shaken at the sea of flame below.

For an hour he swung grimly round the city, but a full moon was not enough and the bombers flitted unseen in the high darkness. Short of petrol, he turned back and could just see the flarepath 12,000 feet below when the engine suddenly coughed and then stopped dead.

Trying to force-land a fighter at night " deadstick " is too dangerous even to be sport. For a moment he was tempted to bale out, but the challenge of it caught him and he decided to try and land it. With the propeller windmilling, he dropped his nose and glided silently down in a series of S-turns, keeping his eye on the flarepath. They were lonely moments that picked at the nerves, but he straightened out finally for the last approach, dropped his wheels and did not even have to sideslip off the last few feet. She settled neatly and a lorry towed him in. The whole affair was a wretched anti-climax, except for one thing: he had begun to hate Germans more personally.

242 Squadron were changing their aeroplanes, becoming the second squadron to get Hurricane Mark II's, which had more power, were faster, could climb higher and all had the new and better V.H.F. radio. Now in the routine of unexciting readiness Bader sometimes swashbuckled about, jabbing his thumb nostalgically on an imaginary gun-button with an accompanying " raspberry " to signify the rattling guns. He took up squash again, clanking sweatily about the court and mortifying Crowley-Milling by beating him, though in fairness " Crow " scrupulously obeyed the convention of putting the ball barely within a reasonable distance. Bader fell noisily often but always rose and " pressed on." At a cinema in Norwich he tripped in the aisle one night and dented his right kneecap so that the leg hung crookedly. He merely dragged himself to the nearest seat, called an usherette to bring him a screwdriver from the projection room, pulled up his trouser leg, made a few adjustments and was mobile again.

Leigh-Mallory rang one day and said: " Douglas, we're having a fighter conference at Air Ministry to thrash out all we've learned from the recent daylight battles. I want you to come with me."

On the day, he went to London and met Leigh-Mallory, who said: " I don't know whether I can get you in. It's rather high-level stuff, but I'm going to try because you're the only chap who's led the really big formations."

At the Air Ministry building in King Charles Street, next to Downing Street, Bader followed the bulky figure into a quiet, carpeted conference room and felt a twinge of alarm when he saw the braided sleeves round the long table. Not a man below air vice-marshal. He recognised most of them: at the head the Chief of the Air Staff, Sir Charles Portal, "Stuffy Dowding" looking more craggy than ever, Keith Park, Sholto Douglas, John Slessor, Philip Joubert de la Ferté. And himself, a squadron leader. No other fighter pilots. Leigh-Mallory said to Portal: " I've brought Squadron Leader Bader along, sir." Portal nodded courteously.

Bader sat quietly, hands in lap, when the discussion started on the size of fighter formations and the idea of going to attack the enemy at the source when he was building up his formations over the Pas de Calais. Park pointed out very reasonably that if he sent squadrons over the Pas de Calais the Germans would quickly change their tactics, send up a bogus " build up " (probably of fighters) to draw the British fighters and then send off the real bombers, who would have a clear run while the British fighters were heavily engaged away from the targets they were to defend and short of petrol and ammunition. As for big formations—in a crisis 11 Group had no time to put up great wings of aircraft.

Leigh-Mallory said that the work of the Duxford wing showed that big formations paid handsomely if it were at all possible to organise them. He understood the difficulty of scrambling big formations in a hurry close to the enemy, but it could be done at a distance when the enemy build-up was first detected. That was the time to scramble a big formation at Duxford, for instance, which could then climb fast and dive into the German formations as they came in over the coast. Then the southern squadrons, which had taken off later, could set about the broken-up enemy.

Sholto Douglas cut in: " I'd like to hear what Squadron Leader Bader has to say about leading big formations."

The eyes were looking at him and he felt suddenly vulnerable. He pulled himself to his feet. Portal said: " You can stay seated if you like, Bader," and he cleared his throat

and said: " No thank you, sir, I'm quite all right." Pet ideas
were tumbling through his head, jostling each other into
confusion. Dowding seemed to be looking at him severely . . .
but Stuffy always looked like that. His mind cleared as it
focused on a new thought—" Whether I leave this room as a
flight lieutenant or not . . . I've got to put the fighter pilot's
point of view . . . it probably hasn't happened like this before."
. . . It all flashed across his mind very fast. He said clearly,
looking at Portal:

" We've been learning, sir, exactly what you gentlemen
learned in the last war " (that was a crafty start) . . . " Firstly,
that the chap who's got the height controls the battle, especially
if he comes out of the sun; secondly, that the chap who fires
very close is the chap who knocks them down; thirdly, and
most important, it is much more economical to put up a
hundred aircraft against a hundred than twelve against a
hundred.

" I know we can't always put equal numbers against the
Germans because their air force is bigger than ours—if
necessary we'll fight one against a thousand—but surely we
can manage to put sixty aircraft against a couple of hundred
instead of only one squadron of twelve."

He went on to develop his theories, and as he warmed to
them he forgot self-consciousness and the voice grew more
confident, more commanding. He delivered himself of a good,
terse homily to the effect that the chap in the air, not the
controller, should decide when, where and how to meet the
enemy. " In fact," he added, " it might be a good idea to
have the sun plotted on the operations board."[1] Making the
most of his chance, he covered every point he could think of,
all the things he had discussed with Leigh-Mallory, and then
suddenly ran dry—finished. There was an awkward silence.
He sat down abruptly. He must have said too much: everyone
was non-committal as the discussion continued. Some seemed
to favour the big wings, others did not. It went on for another
hour and a half before it broke up, and even then Bader felt
that nothing definite had been decided.

A week later he received a letter marked " Secret." It
said that Air Council had decided that wherever there were

[1] Later adopted.

two squadrons on one aerodrome they were to practise battle flying as a wing and be proficient as soon as possible. There followed details about recommended wing tactics—it was the stuff that Bader himself had found out and reported.

Fighter Command leadership was reshuffled. Dowding went, which upset Bader (and some others) deeply, and Sholto Douglas took over as C.-in-C. Park went to a new post and Leigh-Mallory took command of 11 Group. To Bader's joy, he immediately arranged that 242 squadron should go to 11 Group too, posting them to Martlesham, near Felixstowe.

For a while Bader was busy with the flurry of moving. He found a billet for Thelma in Martlesham village and sent Crow with the Humber shooting brake to drive her down; war or no war, Thelma was a woman and had tied up many odd little bundles without which she would not move. Martlesham brought back memories of the first time he had taken off for Dunkirk. How much had happened since then! And was still happening. The night skies over England were louder now with the rumbling of bombers dropping hideous loads. The scientists were working to fit radar into aeroplanes, and meantime the R.A.F. was nearly helpless. The fighters went up and roamed, and now and then they caught a bomber, but not often, and the news reports spoke more confidently than the men in private behind them.

242 Squadron still had no part in it. Bader flew convoy patrols with them but felt better the day a phone call came from 11 Group. "I wanted to be the first to congratulate you again," said Leigh-Mallory. "You've just been awarded the D.F.C. I'm afraid it's long overdue."

That time he made a point of telling Thelma first. She sewed the diagonally striped ribbon on his tunic after the D.S.O., and his exuberant exterior was awkward with the effort of hiding his pride when the others saw it. He could— and did—brag about things like squash and golf (often with his tongue in his cheek), but a decoration was different. Outside the heart one deprecated them. Privately he was gratified that they had given him the D.S.O. before the D.F.C.—the D.S.O. was for leadership and using his head for the common weal, the "team stuff" as against the solo effort. That was a smack in the eye for the little demon.

A D.F.C. also came through for Hugh Tamblyn.

Dickie Cork flew in one day for a Christmas visit and was delighted to see his old C.O.'s new ribbon. Bader was *not* delighted to observe that Cork's only ribbon was now the Distinguished Service Cross.

" Corkie," he bellowed, " where the hell is your D.F.C.? You turncoat! Didn't I give you an order? "

" Yes, sir," said Cork, " but it's a sad story."

One day on Bath Station, he said, an Admiral's eyes had suddenly focused on his D.F.C. ribbon.

" Young man, what's that? " barked the admiral crustily.

Cork explained.

" Distinguished Flying Cross? What's that? " snorted the sea dog (who knew perfectly well).

Rigidly at attention, Cork had explained the circumstances. The Admiral leaned closer to peer at the hybrid ribbon, and his eyes lit upon the silver of the Polish Air Force button, then travelled, bulging slightly, up and down the row, the R.A.F. button, the R.C.A.F. and the Czech Air Force buttons.

" There was an unparalleled scene, sir," Cork said feelingly. " You see, I've got new buttons too."

(Corkie grew up fast after that. Flying off the carrier *Indomitable* in a Malta convoy, he shot down six enemy in one day and was a lieutenant-commander with a D.S.O. as well when he was killed flying in Ceylon in 1944.)

On 1st January Bader neatly ruled off the year's flying in his logbook and under the line wrote:

" *So ends* 1940. *Since have had* 242 *Squadron* (*June*) *we have destroyed* 67 *enemy aircraft confirmed for the loss of five pilots killed in action and one killed diving out of cloud. The squadron has been awarded* 1 *D.S.O. and* 9 *D.F.C.s.*"

Leigh-Mallory sent for him one day and at his Uxbridge headquarters said: " I suppose life seems pretty dull lately."

" Yes, sir."

" What do you think about going over to France and giving them a smarten-up? "

Bader was glowing again.

" We thought we might send a few bombers over with a pack of fighters," the A.O.C. went on. " You're experienced in that sort of thing so I thought you might like to be in it."

The Operation Order labelled " First Offensive Sweep " came to Bader soon after in an envelope marked " Secret." Three Hurricane squadrons would escort six Blenheims to bomb suspected German ammunition dumps in the Forêt de Guisne near the Pas de Calais. From the Luftwaffe's bitter lesson the R.A.F. already knew that it did not pay to send swarms of bombers with a trickle of fighters. They had to find a new balance. It does not sound ambitious now, but then it was the first real probe into the unknown enemy and it was " offensive "—taking the fight to the enemy instead of waiting for him to come back. Much better for everyone's morale (except German).

On 10th January Bader, full of hopes for a fight, led 242 Squadron off and over North Weald joined two more Hurricane squadrons led by Wing Commander Victor Beamish. When Bader was thirteen Beamish had been one of the god-like athletic cadets at Cranwell who had inspired him. Now 38, the blocky, square-jawed Beamish had fought like a tiger in the Battle of Britain, even after Park had limited his battle flights to two a day on the grounds that, " I have to be able to talk to my station commanders *sometimes*." (Later Beamish was the man who spotted the *Scharnhorst* and *Gneisenau* leaving Brest.)

Over Hornchurch they tagged on to the Blenheims and flew out across the Channel. 242 Squadron was top cover at about 17,000 feet, and Bader felt bold and buccaneering. They nipped over the coast near Calais; France looked peaceful, lying softly under snow. In seconds they were over the Forêt de Guisne, only a couple of miles inland. Seconds later it was virtually over and they were darting out again. No time to look for bomb bursts; the wary eyes roamed the sky looking for 109's but none appeared. In the last moments before they crossed the coast the surprised Germans woke up and black puffs of flak stained the cold, crystal air. Odd to see the flak. It was a new enemy. In the Battle of Britain the bursts had been friendly pointers.

Then they were over the sea, and then they were landing at Martlesham. It was an anti-climax.

The next days were not so mild. Leigh-Mallory had another idea he called " Rhubarbs "—sending a pair of fighters darting across the Channel whenever layer cloud hung low over the land, to shoot at anything German aground or aloft. If they got into trouble they could climb and hide in the clouds. Some 11 Group squadrons had already tried them, and two days after the sweep Bader got his chance. He took Turner with him and conditions were perfect, a layer of ten-tenths cloud at about 800 feet.

They did not get as far as France. Just off the beach between Calais and Dunkirk, Bader spotted two trails of foam on the water, nosed down to look and saw they were German E-boats. Without a second's thought, he dived; the Germans must have thought they were friendly and been shocked when the bullets raked the first boat. At the last moment they started to fire, and Bader had a swift glimpse of two of the crew jumping overboard before he had swept past and was raking the second boat. He pulled up into the cloud, followed by Turner, then swept down again for another firing run. After that the bullets were gone and they flew back in high spirits.

At Martlesham when they told the story everyone wanted to jump into the Hurricanes and try the same lark. They could not *all* go, said Group, sounding slightly pained, so Bader fired off McKnight and Brown together, then a little later, Latta and Cryderman.

Brown was back an hour later. He and McKnight had been having a good time straffing a German battalion in a field near Calais, he said, when half a dozen 109's had " bounced " them and things had been pretty busy for several minutes until he had got back into the clouds.

McKnight did not return, which shattered everyone.

Then Cryderman landed, looking shaken after a running fight with Messerschmitts.

Latta did not return.

A week later Bader was leading Cryderman and Edmond in dull, protective circles round a cruiser and submarine heading north up the coast when the controller sent them haring east into the North Sea for a " suspected bandit." A few minutes later Bader saw a JU. 88 about a thousand feet above. Unseen by the German, he pulled steeply up and fired and a moment later the belly flapped open like a trap-door and half a dozen black bombs poured out. They just missed him as he wrenched the Hurricane over on a wingtip and recovered to see the JU. 88 a mile away, smoking from the port engine, vanish into a little cloud about the size of a man's hand.

Edmond leapt over the cloud and Cryderman dived underneath; unimaginatively the German went straight through and came out the other side, where Cryderman squirted into his starboard engine, which also started trailing a white stream. As the German turned away Edmond darted in and the same engine gushed black and orange smoke. Bader raced up to cut it off, fired, and both engines now were spewing black smoke. Edmond was in next and as his explosive bullets hit, the 88 sparked all over with flashes like a pintable machine. Bader was going in again but Cryderman cut in front with another burst. Douglas tried again but Edmond was darting in and, struck by a new emotion, Bader wheeled out to one side like a paternal old lion watching his two cubs eagerly trying to bring down their first meat. Itching for another burst, he stayed out of the way while the bullets of the other two kept clawing at the stubborn 88, which dragged the smoke of its wounds along its trail but would not fall.

At last Edmond's angry voice on the R/T said that he was out of ammunition. The smoke from the engines was thinning now but the 88 was flying in a peculiar way, hurdling like a car on a switchback railway. Cryderman went in; the 88 lit with flashes again but flew on, and Cryderman announced that his guns were empty. Amazed at the punishment the German had taken, Bader made a final pass and aimed at the cockpit; bits flew off it but the 88 flew on. Now the smoke had almost vanished. He thought in exasperation that the enemy would never go down when thick orange smoke poured out of the port wing. In a few moments tongues of flame licked through the smoke and slowly the 88 dropped her nose into a steepening dive till she went vertically into the sea in a welter of foam.

A few months ago it was so much part of the day to shoot

down an enemy; now there were columns in the papers and people rang up from all over the place with congratulations.

For a while the days drifted; they were busy but it was routine. Occasionally when the clouds were thick they tried a few " rhubarbs " but saw nothing. With up to four flights a day, Bader's logbook shows the routine: " Formation practice," " Convoy patrol," " Trying to find Huns " (that was a " rhubarb "), " Dusk and night landings," " Formation practice," " Engine test," " High flying," " Looking for Huns," " Testing rudder bias," and so on. Then they hit a bad patch. It started on 8th February, a cold day with ice cloud, when Laurie Cryderman sheered off from a convoy patrol to intercept a plotted " bandit." They heard him call half an hour later that his engine had cut. He was 600 feet up, far at sea, and never came back.

Only days later Ben Brown, pulling sharply out of a steep dive low down, spun off a high-speed stall into the ground.

With McKnight and Latta it made four dead in a very brief time and seemed so cruel and pointless after they had come so well through the battle. In flying death often seems to come in cycles.

Then Ian Smith, who had taught Douglas " Little Angeline," went out on a convoy patrol and did not come back.

Crowley-Milling caught a JU. 88 over the North Sea, and as he dived to attack his bullet-proof windscreen was smashed into a whitely opaque and splintered shield as a cannon shell hit it; he could not see to aim but went on chasing and firing until the 88 vanished into cloud. Crowley-Milling got back.

Then the steadfast, charming Hugh Tamblyn fought an intruder approaching a convoy. An hour or two later a ship found him floating in his Mae West, but he was dead.

Sergeant Brimble was posted to Malta and killed on the way.

Seven in a matter of weeks! At that rate a pilot could expect to live about three months. A squadron of twenty pilots would lose eighty a year, and there seemed no end to the war.

Early in March Leigh-Mallory sent for Bader. " We're

working out ideas to carry the attack across to France in the summer," he said. " Fighter sweeps, like that other one you did, but probably more ambitious. To do it we're building up our ' wing ' system and one of the items on that programme is to appoint wing commanders on certain stations to organise and lead the wings there.

" You," he went on, " are to be one of those wing commanders. Should be right down your alley. You'll probably be going to Tangmere."

There are times when words sound like music. In Army terms, wing commander meant a rise from lieutenant to lieutenant-colonel in a year. And Tangmere was in 11 Group —on the South Coast, just across from France.

When L.-M. had disposed of the congratulations, Bader said: " Will I be able to take 242 Squadron with me, sir ? "

" Afraid not," Leigh-Mallory regretted. " You'll already have three squadrons there. All Spitfires."

Bader suggested awkwardly that in that case he wasn't sure he wanted to be a wing commander.

Leigh-Mallory said firmly: " You'll do what you're told " . . . and then, because he knew his man: " Look at it this way. If you take 242 you won't be able to help favouring them a bit. I know you and how you regard them."

All he could do then was wait for the posting.

242 Squadron was not pleased. The whole squadron, from the lowest " erk " up, revolved round the C.O. as a tight and exclusive team that had been firmly knit even before the bloody comradeship of the battle. The greatest leaders in the field always have " colour " . . . a certain bravura. Bader certainly had it.

Still waiting, he drove with 242 to Debden to meet the King and Queen, and in the mess ante-room before the presentation, Turner jabbed his pipe into Leigh-Mallory's chest and said: " Look here, sir, you can't go and post our C.O. away because we won't work for anyone else."

It was enough to make an English officer's blood run cold.

" Turner," Bader bawled. " Stop prodding the A.O.C. with your pipe! "

Leigh-Mallory did not seem to mind at all.

On 18th March the bitter-sweet blow fell. A new man, "Treacle" Treacy, arrived to take over, and Thelma sewed the wing commander braid on Douglas's sleeves. The only man he was able to take with him from 242 was Stokoe, his conscientious and devoted batman.

20

TANGMERE, NOT far from Southampton, was a pre-war station built for two squadrons. Now three Spitfire squadrons, 145, 610, and 616, and a Beaufighter squadron lived there and the Spitfires were to fly as the wing. He was pleased about 616 because they had been in 12 Group Wing and knew his ways. All the Spitfires were Mark II's, still with eight machine-guns but a little better than the Battle of Britain types.

He arrived on the morning of the 19th, stowed his bags in a room in the station commander's house near the mess, and in half an hour was flying a Spitfire to get the feel again. Two hours later he was leading two of the squadrons over the Channel, having a " snoop " towards the French coast and trying wing formation. The squadrons had not flown as a wing before and in the next two weeks he trained them hard.

Unlike his early days with 242, there was no need to win their confidence. He was famous now, the R.A.F.'s first wing leader, and men and officers jumped to obey his brisk bellows. Most of the pilots (average age about twenty-two) had fought non-stop through the Battle of Britain and he saw that several, especially the leaders, were showing clear signs of overstrain. His impulsive, warm-hearted side became full of love for them, in a way rather like a vet with a hurt animal, and he felt he wanted to say to them: " Don't you worry, chaps. We'll get you right." He saw Leigh-Mallory and explained that some of the boys should have a rest. Could he have some good replacements and also have Stan Turner promoted to squadron leader to command 145 Squadron?

" By all means," said Leigh-Mallory courteously. " I'm glad you've asked for Turner because he's getting a bit of a nuisance not objecting to fly with anyone else."

Turner arrived a couple of days later with bad news. Treacy had been leading a 242 formation in a sharp turn when the man behind had collided with him. Bits of the smashed aeroplanes hit a third Hurricane and all three went into the sea, killing Treacy, Edmond and Lang. (The squadron was taken over then by Whitney Straight, pre-war racing motorist who had won an M.C. in Norway and is now deputy chairman of B.O.A.C.)

As 616 had the least battle experience, Bader attached himself to them and thereafter always flew at their head, leading the wing. It could have been uncomfortable for Billy Burton, ex-Cranwell Sword of Honour and C.O. of 616, but he and Bader got along well, though Burton [later D.S.O. and D.F.C.], short, eager and somewhat precise, was constantly appalled by Bader's uninhibited comments. Like Bader, he nearly always had a pipe in his mouth, and sometimes in the privacy of the pilots' room he would take it out and say: " D'you know what the wingco called me this morning? He called me a ——" He used to repeat these things in a voice of wonder as though they could not really have happened, and then break into a puzzled laugh.

Domineering, dogmatic and breezy, Bader saw everything in blacks and whites, never in doubtful greys, and in this new phase of welding an experimental wing together and evolving new tactics to carry the fight to the enemy he made decisions crisply and on the spot with a confidence that would have been dangerous in someone else. He startled Tangmere, whose men first regarded him as a noted curiosity, then were impressed and then, as at 242, became devoted (apart from a few, ruffled by his blunt toughness, who resented him. He left no one unmoved: they either half worshipped or detested him, and the little minority of the latter grumbled in their own wilderness). Fired by his new mission, he was far removed from the frustrated man of the peace. As the wing knit together he got the itch to fight again, but Leigh-Mallory would not let him cross to the French coast, so he took the wing " snooping " as near as a flexible interpretation of orders would let him, though they never saw a German aircraft.

They only heard them—at night. Tangmere had two long white runways, and on a moon-lit night raiders picked them out miles away, sometimes as a landmark and sometimes as a target. German bombers were over England every clear night, and now and then a low-flying enemy roared in the darkness over Tangmere and everyone hunched their shoulders and winced as the bombs crashed down, rattling the hangars and smashing windows. No one had been killed for some time, but some aeroplanes had been destroyed and it was not comfortable. Gangs of civilian workmen were camouflaging the runways by spraying them with green paint—or were supposed to be: they managed to do about fifty yards a week, working with the lethargy that many pilots noticed on aerodromes. It did not help to know that they were being paid more than the pilots, and Bader longed to have them under R.A.F. discipline.

At this time Woodhall, newly promoted to Group Captain, arrived at Tangmere to command the station and also to act as controller. Leigh-Mallory wanted his old team together again for the work ahead (and for a while Bader shared quarters near the mess with Woodhall). Other wings were training now at stations like Biggin Hill and Kenley under new wing commanders like " Sailor " Malan, who was top-scoring R.A.F. pilot. To be more easily recognised in the air during wing-flying, Bader had his initials " DB " painted on the side of his Spitfire, which prompted Woodhall to christen him " Dogsbody." He called him that in the mess and in the air, over the R/T, and the name stuck till it became Bader's official call-sign. He did not mind; it rather amused him.

Woodhall and Bader both plagued the workers on the runways to get a move on but it was like talking to a collection of deaf mutes; they sprayed a few more yards in the next week, and it looked as though next moon period Tangmere was going to catch it again (the workmen lived some miles from the airfield). Woodhall rang the Works Department, but the local officials seemed helpless and he could not locate any Olympian official who might have influence.

An ear-splitting crash woke Bader one night, and outside he heard shouts and saw flickering lights. Strapping his legs on, he crossed to the window and saw that a bomb had fallen on a corner of the mess, which was burning. Overhead came a sudden roar and rattle of machine-guns as the raider dived back to strafe the fire. As Bader stumbled out to it the fire-truck arrived and soon got it under control. Strangely, no one inside had been hurt; they had hurled themselves out of the windows into the nearest cover, and the hero of the night was the Roman Catholic padre who, tin hat firmly planted on his head, had walked into the burning mess looking for injured. The story went round that you could hear the German bullets pinging off his tin hat while all the brave fighter boys lay quaking in the air-raid ditches.

But it was the last straw. Bader sent his old golfing friend, Henry Longhurst, an invitation to visit Tangmere. It was just before Longhurst himself went into the Army; he was still a journalist and knew a story when he saw one.

The following week-end a caustic article appeared in the *Sunday Express* about squadrons on a " certain R.A.F. airfield " being endangered by the sloth of men engaged to camouflage runways.

It was serious for an officer to cut red tape binding the normal channels and tip off the Press about dirty official linen. Outraged officials demanded to know from the newspaper who had let the cat out of the bag, but the *Sunday Express* urbanely declined to say. Then they rang Longhurst, who also declined to say. At last the official asked: " Was it someone on an aerodrome near Oxford? "

Longhurst said craftily: " Oh, is it going on there too? "

The official hurriedly rang off. But eventually two and two were put together and the Under-Secretary of State for Air paid a visit to Tangmere, lunched amicably with Bader and Woodhall, and over coffee said, quite politely:

" Look, actually the reason I've come down here is to give you chaps a rocket over that article in the *Sunday Express*. The Air Ministry doesn't take a good view of it."

Bader, hackles rising, said: " Well, sir, you can take the rocket back to Air Ministry and tell 'em what they can do with it. Those runways have been glistening in the moonlight for months now, drawing German bombers like flies, so I asked Longhurst down here myself and damn' well told him to write it up."

The Under-Secretary looked startled at the truculent scorn for a high-level reprimand.

Woodhall put in: " And I absolutely agree with Bader. I knew Longhurst was coming down that week-end and I also asked him to have a look at the runways. I feel exactly the same as Bader about it."

Said the Under-Secretary resignedly, as though he were washing his hands like Pontius Pilate: " Well I was told to deliver the rocket and I've done it." He seemed glad to get it over.

The camouflaging of the runways was completed in a week, but by that time Bader had moved his aircraft to satellite fields nearby—610 and 616 to West Hampnett and 145 to Merston. He was also doing some reshuffling in his wing, getting Crowley-Milling and Ian Arthur from 242 Squadron as flight commanders in 610 and 145. Ken Holden, a big Yorkshire flight lieutenant in 616, was promoted to command 610 Squadron. The ruddy-faced Holden was about Bader's age, some years older than the other pilots, a resourceful and rather droll " old sweat," fond of adopting a Yorkshire accent and saying to his pilots: " Now coom on all you lads; trouble with you is you've got no expeerience. Ah'm older than thee."

Bader also found a house for himself and Thelma five miles from the mess, a pleasant little white place with a garden called the Bay House. Thelma came down with her baggage and bundles and her sister Jill, and was utterly delighted with it, the first house she had ever had. It became a social centre for some of Bader's pilots in the evenings, where everyone relaxed in a different atmosphere, though Douglas usually slept at the mess to keep in touch.

Still the tactical fanatic, he had begun to feel most dissatisfied with the vics of three which had been standard squadron formation for so long. A hangover from peacetime, they were clumsy to deploy in battle, and after a lot of thought he evolved a new basic unit, two aircraft abreast so that each pilot's eyes covered his comrade's tail and cut out the need for weaving. He began experimenting, building his wing round these small sections arranged in various patterns.

As his own Number Two he often picked the gangling

" Cocky " Dundas, who had been so cheered by his voice during a Battle of Britain take-off. He thought that Dundas, still in 616, still only twenty, was a likely lad, and also had his eye on another 616 pilot officer, Johnny Johnson, a muscular effervescent youngster, a " press-on " type, somewhat wild and in need of discipline but possessing a hawk-eyed talent for the game and no visible fear.[1]

The Luftwaffe's terrifying night raids were easing off a little and the war seemed to be static, though all 11 Group knew it was only a lull and wondered what it was going to be like on the other side. In mid-April Leigh-Mallory called Bader to H.Q. at Uxbridge, and there he found Malan, Harry Broadhurst, Beamish, Kellett and other leaders. They went into a plain room, sat on folding chairs round a table, and Leigh-Mallory, standing at the head of the table, said quietly:

" Gentlemen, we have stopped licking our wounds. We are now going over to the offensive. Last year our fighting was desperate. Now we're entitled to be cocky."

He talked a long time about tactics; the idea, briefly, being to send a few bombers over the Channel surrounded by hordes of fighters, and force the Germans to come up and fight.

On the morning of 17th April a screed about a yard long came over the Tangmere operations teleprinter headed " Secret. Operations Order. Circus No. 1." There followed a lot of details under headings like " Target," " Bomber Force," " Rendezvous," " Escort Wing," " Cover Wing," " Target Support Wing," " Rear Wing," with heights and speeds and map references.

That afternoon about 100 Spitfires escorted twelve Blenheims to bomb Cherbourg. Bader led his wing of thirty-six and did not see a single enemy. Far away a few puffs of German flak stained the sky, and then they were on the way home again. Leigh-Mallory said later: " We're just poking the bear in his pit, gentlemen. You'll get some reaction in due course."

---

[1] Bader's judgment and teaching seem to have been good. Two years later Turner, Crowley-Milling, Johnson and Dundas were all wing commanders with D.S.O.s and D.F.C.s. At twenty-three Dundas became the youngest group captain in the R.A.F., and Johnson was top-scorer at the end of the war with thirty-eight confirmed and a string of probables.

Over the next couple of weeks they did several more trips to Cherbourg, expecting any moment to be "jumped" by hordes of 109's, but never meeting one. Yet north-west France was said to be a hornet's nest that might swarm any day, an Unknown that must be invaded with more sense than Goering had shown. Rhubarbs were discouraged—two or four aircraft venturing across alone looked too close to suicide.

On the night of 7th May a spontaneous party developed in the mess (as it often did) with pilots talking shop and skylarking well into the night. Bader was surrounded as usual by his pilots (he always enjoyed that), sipping orangeade while they nuzzled cans of beer, and after a while Cocky Dundas said:

"Sir, let's have two of the new sections side by side— four aircraft line abreast so everyone can cover everyone else's tail and everyone can get an occasional squirt in."

The wing commander said it sounded fine. Everyone chattered about the new idea for a long time, working out, for instance, how to handle it in the air when "jumped" by enemy fighters. They decided that the "form" was for the two on the left at the critical moment to scream round in a full circle to the left and for the pair on the right to do likewise to the right, thus joining up again on the tails (it was hoped) of the foiled enemy. The debate lasted a long time.

In the morning Dundas came down to breakfast feeling not so gay as usual. His skull throbbed and the dry mouth had a taste of sump oil as his head nodded gently over a sausage, regretting that he had not gone to bed earlier. Bader stumped in and sat at the same table full of rude and ostentatious health. He boomed as he sat down: "That was a damn' good idea of yours last night, Cocky, about fours flying abreast."

Dundas smiled wanly and murmured: "Oh, thank you very much, sir. I'm glad you liked it."

"Damn' good," repeated Bader. "I've been thinking it over. We'll try it to-day."

Dundas thought without enthusiasm that he did not feel like practice flying.

"Just you and me and a couple of others," Bader went on

cheerfully. " We'll duck over to France and see if we can get some Huns to jump us."

For a moment it did not sink in, and then Dundas had a moment of lurching horror. He looked to see if Bader were joking. But he wasn't; he was turning to Woodhouse of 610 Squadron down the table and saying: " Paddy, get yourself a number two and come with us."

They took off at 11 a.m., Bader, Dundas (wondering why he hadn't kept his mouth shut the previous night), Woodhouse and a Sergeant Mains, and swept down the Channel at 25,000 feet between Dover and Calais in a slightly curving line abreast, as though one were looking at the nails of four fingers spread out; Dundas on the left, Bader fifty yards on his right and slightly in front, a hundred yards to Woodhouse level, and fifty yards again to Mains, slightly behind. Thus they flaunted themselves up and down off Calais for half an hour, seeing nothing. Dundas was thinking with longing that in a couple of minutes they would be turning on course for home again when above, five miles behind, slightly to the right and a thousand feet above, he saw five 109's turning on course after them. He called urgently: " Hallo, Dogsbody. Five 109's five o'clock above."

Bader's voice came delightedly: " Oh, good. I can see 'em, Cocky. I've got 'em." He throttled back a little and the Messerschmitts came up fast. Bader was keeping up a running commentary. . . . " Oh, this is just what we wanted. Wonderful, isn't it? "

Dundas refrained from answering. The 109's were boring in. Bader was going on exultantly: " Keep your eyes on 'em but don't break till I tell you. Let 'em come in. Let 'em come in. Don't break " . . . He was beside himself with enthusiasm. " Don't break yet. I'll tell you when . . ."

The 109's were slanting in for the kill when he snapped " Break now! " and abruptly four Spitfires spun round on their wingtips, Bader and Dundas fanning left, and Woodhouse and Mains right.

In one of the tightest turns Dundas could remember, Bader's tail-wheel bobbed above his windscreen, but his vision kept greying out as the mounting " g " kept loading his lanky, sagging frame, forcing the blood from the brain.

He'd heard some theory that Bader could turn sharper than anyone because he'd lost his legs and the blood could not sink that far. Better straighten a bit or ease the turn and see where the Huns were. Must be nearly round the circle. He eased pressure on the stick, and as sight returned the Spitfire flinched and shuddered under crashing explosions as cannon shells slammed into her. Sickeningly, he remembered the last time.

Bader, reefing his machine out of the turn, saw the leading 109 darting just in front, fired in the same moment, saw the flash of bullet strikes and the 109 keel over out of sight, shovelling out black smoke. He heard Dundas, tense and edgy, in his earphones: " Dogsbody, I've been hit." (They had actually turned inside the two rearmost 109's, which had opened fire as the last two Spitfires straightened. Sergeant Mains was also hit.)

With cannon shells in the wing roots and glycol pipes, Dundas was peeling off gushing white smoke. Bader nosed down after him to give cover, but the 109's had vanished and only one other Spitfire was in sight. With height to play with and some power still in the engine, Dundas nursed his aircraft back over the coast to Hawkinge Aerodrome, where it cut suddenly when he was too high to land properly and unable to go round again. Rather desperately he gingerly pushed his nose, wheels up, at about 150 m.p.h. on to the grass to try and break the speed, and she bounced and thumped rendingly, just missing a collection of brand-new Spitfires on 91 squadron's dispersal. Shaken, he climbed out and was met by a furious 91 Squadron C.O. demanding to know what the hell he thought he was doing.

Woodhouse got back to Tangmere all right, and Mains, tail damaged, but unhurt, landed at another field.

Holden flew a Magister two-seater to Hawkinge and took Dundas back to Tangmere, where Bader, seeing he was all right, boomed: " You're a silly clot, Cocky. What the hell did you go and do that for? Anyway, I'm damn'· glad to see you're back all right." Then, suddenly enthusiastic again: " I think I know what the trouble is. Instead of breaking outwards we should have all broken in one circle, all the same way, so we stick together and don't lose sight of the enemy. All it wants is some practice. We'll try again soon."

After that the desolate Dundas, oddly, was not so shaken; he felt it was just an incident in the search for knowledge and was proud to be on such terms with the C.O. Bader tried it again with another section the next day, but this time over Tangmere, with a friendly section of 616 Spitfires doing the attacking. Breaking the same way, he found that the " finger four " line abreast was ideal; flexible and good for both defence and attack. Inside a week the " finger four " became the backbone of the wing (and was later copied by other wings and used extensively throughout the war).

He tried it on Channel snoops and " circuses " to Cherbourg and Le Havre (they were not sent deeper than the coast at this trial stage), but had no chance to test it in action because the Messerschmitts stayed away, though at this time the wing had its first casualties. Coming back from France, 145 Squadron broke off over Tangmere to land in sections, and a flight commander, Pip Stevens, and Flying Officer Owen collided and crashed, locked together, just off the airfield. Both were killed.

Now and then over the French coast they began to see three or four Messerschmitts flirting well outside the fringes of the gaggle, obviously waiting for stragglers or trying to lure a section away, but Bader declined to snap at decoys; he wanted bigger game. So did Leigh-Mallory. Then the Hornchurch wing reported that a couple of Messerschmitts floating above had turned on their backs and dived through them firing. No one was hit but it was better than being ignored.

A couple of days later the Tangmere wing was returning from a snoop when Johnny Johnson's voice, high-pitched and excited, shouted: " Look out! Huns! " Every pilot thought it was a warning about a 109 on his tail, and the formation split like a lot of startled rabbits while a lone Messerschmitt dived through the middle spitting cannon shells, hitting no one, and vanished. When they landed, Bader tore a stinging strip off Johnson and lectured the wing on the importance of proper warnings. Enemy aircraft *must* be reported as to location and height and not (looking scathingly at the squirm-

ing Johnson) as " Look out! Huns! " Otherwise there would
be a shambles.

In June the Germans startled the world by marching on
Russia and it became imperative to force Hitler into diverting
more fighters back to France. Leigh-Mallory thought that
the Blenheims with a ton of bombs were too light to force the
issue, so he pestered Bomber Command till they reluctantly
let him have some four-engined Stirlings which, on the short
haul to France, could carry nearly six tons of bombs each.
He packed about 200 Spitfires round them and sent them
across the coast to an inland target, and with the swarm of
darting fighters about them Bader thought it looked like a
great bee-hive. He said so at the Group conference later,
and thereafter it was known as the " Beehive."

Leigh-Mallory sent the swarm inland again to blast the
rail yards at Lille, an important junction for the Germans.
Agents reported that the French rushed into the streets,
cheering and waving towels. Then the Beehive went and
wiped out a Messerschmitt repair factory at Albert.

Ah, this was better. The Germans were stung. A Staffel
of 109's savaged the Biggin Wing and some of each side were
shot down. Bader went off later to the usual wing leaders'
confab. with the A.O.C., and landed back storming: " Malan
got two to-day and his boys got a few more. It's damn' well
time we found some."

Leigh-Mallory's tactics began to pay: Goering was pulling
fighter squadrons out of Russia. Over France now they were
coming up in packs of thirty and forty. Oberstleutnant
(lieutenant-colonel) Galland, Germany's most distinguished
fighter leader, was reported in St. Omer with a full *Geschwader*[1]
of 109's. The R.A.F. estimated that their fighters were knocking down three Germans to every two Spitfires lost and that
was profitable. Rarely was a bomber lost, and then only to
flak. One bomber straggling with two engines burning was
brought back safely to Manston with about a hundred Spitfires
packed protectively round it.

On 21st June the Beehive went to St. Omer, and the
Tangmere Wing flew in ahead to de-louse. Several 109's
darted overhead, twisting back and forth waiting for a chance

[1] Group.

to strike at a straggler. Bader watched them intently. The Beehive came and bombed and left, and the Tangmere Wing was following across the coast when out of the sun two 109's dived in a port-quarter attack on Bader's section of four. He yelled " Break left! " wheeling fast.

The Germans must have been raw because they broke left, too, and Bader, turning faster than anyone, saw the belly of a 109 poised on its side fifty yards in front and fired. Bits splintered off the Messerschmitt and it pulled drunkenly up, stalled and spun.

Back at Tangmere, he marked an asterisk in his logbook with satisfaction and sat down to write his first combat report for some time. At the end he added: " I claim this as destroyed because (a) I *know* it was, (b) F/O Marples saw a 109 spinning down at the same time and place, (c) F/O Matchack of 145 saw a 109 dive into the sea, and (d) I am sure this 109 was mine."

After that things warmed up. Next day he led his wing with the Beehive to Hazebrouck, the day after to Béthune in the morning and to Béthune again in the afternoon; next day to Béthune again and the day after that to Commines. His romantic side was stirred to be flying fighters over towns with the names he had read in the books by McCudden, Bishop, Ball and company of the first war . . . Douai, Arras, Hazebrouck, Béthune.

Next morning to Béthune again at 26,000 feet, and this time he took a new sergeant pilot as his No. 2 to show him the ropes (not many leaders did that—they liked experienced No. 2's to guard their tails). Crossing the coast, packs of four or six Messerschmitts roamed about like scavengers, darting in now and then, and sheering off when challenged, pecking at the formations and trying to wing the outriders. Fed up with the nibbling, Bader dived 616 on six 109's about 500 feet below, and as they scattered he got a shot at one. Then the sergeant fired a long-range burst. Bader chased and caught it with another burst, seeing bullet strikes but no smoke or visible damage, yet suddenly a parachute blossomed as the pilot jumped and floated into the sea five miles off Gravelines. Bader thought scornfully he must have been frightened into jumping.

After lunch they were off again, this time to St. Omer, where perceptibly more Germans than before were waiting in the same scavenging packs. Eyes warily watched them behind, to the left and also below, then they were all round, moving dangerously into the sun. Someone yelled a warning as a pack lunged, and Bader sharply broke the wing for independent battle—it was the only way—and in seconds the sky was a milling whirlpool. He caught a trailing 109 at close range and it puffed orange and black smoke as it fell into a steep vertical dive. More 109's were diving on him. He got in a short head-on burst at one that flashed past, and as the battling aircraft sorted themselves out he joined up with Ken Holden's squadron, squirted at one more vagrant enemy, and came home bathed in sweat and exhilarated.

Two more asterisks in the logbook, and a score of two and a half destroyed in a week, plus some damaged. Things were getting better. From then on they averaged a sweep[1] a day, except when the weather was bad. Losses were comparatively low, but slowly mounted and an infinity of war stretched ahead. It was easier not to think of that—just to live for the present, but that was not easy either. It was worst when you woke before dawn, but in the air it was all right because the eyes and the mind were busy.

Bader was still immune from nerves, a rollicking figure in black flying suit and blue and white polka-dot silk scarf, stuffing his pipe into his pocket when he hoisted himself into the cockpit. In the air they assembled over " Diamond " (code name for Beachy Head) and set course for France, seeing far below the wash of air-sea rescue launches speeding out from the ports to take station where they might pick up the lucky ones who were shot down alive into " the drink " on the way back. Disconcerting but also comforting.

Always it was Bader leading 616 in a loose mass of three " finger fours," climbing to about 20,000 feet. A couple of thousand feet above, behind and to the right, Holden led 610, and far above them, perhaps climbing to 30,000, stretched right across the sky in a long crescent, Stan Turner covered them with 145, usually keeping up-sun. Often he lifted

---

[1] A " sweep " was nominally a raid without bombers but soon all the mass sorties into France, including the " circuses " (with bombers), were known as sweeps.

briefly into the floor of the vapour trail layer, then eased down just under it again and flew on at that level so that he and his squadron showed no trail but any aircraft above would immediately betray themselves by tails of white vapour. Sometimes the wing sallied into France alone, and sometimes they joined the Beehive round the bombers.

On the way across no one broke radio silence till they were nearly over the French coast where the Germans could see them. Then it was usually Bader:

" O.K., Green Line Bus.¹ Pull your corks out. You O.K., Ken? "

" O.K., D. B. In position." (Holden.)

" You O.K., Stan? Where the hell are you? I can't see you."

" O.K., D. B. Keep your cork in. I'm here."

" Hallo, Woodie, any trade in sight? "

" Hallo, Dogsbody. Beetle² answering. Seems to be a strong reaction building up over the Big Wood?³ About thirty or forty plus gaining altitude to the east of the objective. I am watching them. That's all for now."

And Bader:

" Did you get that, Ken? "

" O.K."

" Did you get that, Stan? "

Turner was more inclined to colour his answer, having a habit of saying in a quavering falsetto, like a startled chambermaid: " Oh dear! Oh dear! How terrifying. How simply terrifying," followed by a wild sound that was half laugh, half neigh.

As they crossed the coast by the " Golf Course,"⁴ Bader chatted amiably:

" That eighteenth green could do with mowing, Ken, couldn't it? " (From 20,000 feet the greens on Le Touquet golf course were the size of pinheads.)

After remarks like that the tension eased and Woodhall

¹ Code name for Tangmere Wing.
² Tangmere Ops. call-sign. Woodhall occasionally used it instead of his own name.
³ Code for St. Omer.
⁴ Code for Le Touquet.

knew exactly where they were; then Bader's voice lost its flippant tone and thereafter was crisp.

Woodhall's voice was unchanging, deep bass and clear, calmly matter-of-fact, sounding somehow as though he were beside you in the cockpit like a reassuring coach. The blend with Bader meant real leadership.

Soon Woodhall again: " Hallo, Dogsbody. The 109's over the Big Wood are climbing south. Looks as though they might be trying to come in down-sun on your right flank."

" O.K., Woody."

A few minutes silence and then:

" Hallo, Dogsbody. If you look about three o'clock above I think you'll see what you're looking for."

It was uncanny how accurate he was. Usually in a few moments someone saw them sliding into sun-ambush, looking against the sky like a stream of silver fish darting in a ragged straggle through a pool. They broke into small packs to come in from many angles, and Bader had his eyes everywhere, assessing, manœuvring the wing, warning, detaching sections, reorganising, picking the moment to lunge and start the roaring, whirling frenzy.

It used to go like this (taken from the actual radio log of a quiet day early in the season before the battle became savage):

" Fifty plus near two o'clock."

" I haven't got 'em, Johnny. What are they doing? "

" O.K., D.B. No immediate panic. They're going across us. I'm watching 'em."

" O.K., O.K., I see 'em."

(Silence for a while.)

Then:

" Aircraft behind."

" Aircraft three o'clock."

" Aircraft below."

" Turning right Bus Company."

" 109's overhead."

" O.K. I see 'em."

" Aircraft behind. Muck in, everybody." (Bader.)

" Tell me when to break. I can't see the bastards."

" Six bastards behind us."

" I can see 'em in my mirror."

" Two aircraft below."

Then some Messerschmitts must have attacked:

" Break right."

" He nearly had you, Cocky."

" Four right above."

" Right on top of you."

" Get organised."

" I'm —— if I can."

" Four behind and above."

" O.K. I'm looking after you."

" Look behind."

" It's only me. Don't get the wind up."

" All right, you ——! "

" Don't —— about. We'll have some collisions in a minute." (Apparently re-forming after an attack.)

" They're hell-cat boys." (Probably a Canadian.)

" Your R/T sounds bloody awful."

" Is mine O.K.? "

" Just like a lily."

That covered ten minutes when few German fighters made contact and no one was hurt on either side. It sounds garbled and disjointed, telling none of the visual drama and conveying little of the profane urgency of the voices.

Inside the blast walls of the Tangmere Ops. Room a loud-speaker purring with static clicked and spoke the metallic words of the pilots. Sitting at the radiophone, Woodhall had plenty to do, and so did the " Beauty Chorus," the team of W.A.A.F.s pushing the pawns of the radar plots across the Ops. table with long-handled paddles.

21

Now THE Messerschmitts were ever more numerous and bolder, every day savaging the flanks. More and more often Bader broke the wing to go for them, and for frantic minutes the sky was full of snarling, twisting, spitting aeroplanes. Several of the wing scored " kills " and three Spitfires did not come back.

The Messerschmitts—quite rightly—never stayed long to mix it with the more manœuvrable Spitfires as they could never hold their own in a round-about tail chase. Despite British propaganda, the 109's were slightly faster and their proper tactics were to dive, shoot and break off. Sometimes they pulled up again and sometimes they half-rolled on to their backs and dived steeply out of the fight in the reverse direction. Any Spitfire on its own after a fight was under standing orders to join up with the nearest friendly fighters so there would be at least two in line abreast to watch each other's tail. It was jungle law up there and the devil took the odd man out.

Coming back over the Channel one day, Dundas was startled to see Bader, flying alongside, flip back his cockpit top, unclip his oxygen mask, stuff his stub pipe in his mouth, strike a match (apparently holding the stick between his good knee and tin knee), light up and sit there like Pop-Eye puffing wisps of smoke that the slipstream snatched away. Dundas longed to light a cigarette himself, but desire was tempered by realisation that no normal man lit a naked flame in a Spitfire cockpit. Bader looked across, caught Dundas's wide eyes, beamed and made a rude gesture.

After that he always puffed his pipe in the cockpit on the way back, and pilots flying alongside used to sheer off, half in joke, half in earnest, in case Spitfire D.B. blew up. But it never did, adding to the growing and inspiring myth that Bader was bomb-proof, bullet-proof and fire-proof.

With virtually daily trips now, someone dubbed the wing " The Bader Bus Service. The Prompt and Regular Service. Return Tickets Only." That tickled everyone's fancy, and some of the pilots painted it on the side of their cowlings. It felt good to be one of the Tangmere Wing. Almost every night he took a few of his boys (and sometimes their girl friends) back to the Bay House, where Thelma and Jill made sandwiches and they sat yarning and quaffing beer. It began to be known affectionately as the " Bag House," which Thelma tolerated with her usual imperturbability.

Any new pilots he nursed carefully, yarning to them about tactics, air discipline (e.g. strict radio silence at the right times) and putting them in the middle of the pack for their first few trips. Once in mid-Channel on the way out a new boy in 145 called: " Hallo, Red Leader. Yellow Two calling. I can't turn my oxygen on."

A brooding silence followed.

The voice plaintively again: " Hallo, Red Leader. Can you hear me? I can't turn on my oxygen."

Then Turner's Canadian voice, ferociously sarcastic:

" What the hell do you want me to do? Get out and turn it on for you? *Go home!* "

No one made that mistake again.

On 2nd July they went to Lille, and Bader dived 616 on fifteen 109's. He fired a tone from almost dead behind, and as its hood flew off and the pilot jumped, another 109 plunged past and collected a burst. Smoke and oil spurted and he went down vertically. Bader left him and pulled up, obeying the dictum that it is suicide to follow an enemy down. Coming back over the Channel, he dived on another enemy, and as he started firing the 109 rolled on its back like lightning and streaked back into France. Bader was getting fed up with 109's diving out of a fight like that (though he respected the correctness of their tactics), and when he got back to claim one destroyed and one probable, he added as a flippant afterthought: " and the third one I claim as frightened."

He hoped for a bite from Intelligence at Group but they maintained a dignified silence. Instead he got a phone call from Leigh-Mallory, who said: "Douglas, I hear you got another 109 to-day."

"Yes, sir."

"Well," Leigh-Mallory went on in his deceptively pompous voice, "you've got something else too—a bar to your D.S.O."

Down at dispersals next day when he was congratulated, Bader said awkwardly: "All this blasted chest cabbage doesn't matter a damn. It's what the wing does that really counts." He meant it, too, and the pilots were surprised at the self-consciousness that lay under the boisterous exterior.

Coming away from Lille a couple of days later, little schools of Messerschmitts began pecking at them again. Bader fired at three but they half rolled and dived away. Two more dashed in and Bader shot one in the stomach from 100 yards. Explosive bullets must have slugged into the tank behind the cockpit because it blew a fiery jet like a blow-torch and fell out of the sky, dragging a plume of black smoke.

Remembering the three that got away, he claimed one destroyed and "three frightened," and this time got a bite from Group. A puzzled message arrived asking what he meant and he sent a signal back explaining. Group answered stiffly that they were not amused (though everyone else thought it was a "good giggle").

It takes an odd genius to handle a wing in the lightning of battle where it is so easy to become confused or excited or tempted by a decoy. There was a day a 109 flew in front and just below them, and Bader called: "That —— looks too obvious. Look up-sun, everyone, and see if you can see anything." No one could and at last Bader said: "Come on, Cocky. Let's take a pot. The rest stay up."

As he led Dundas down, the 109 half-rolled and dived, presumably transmitting, because seconds later his friends came out of the sun. Holden's squadron intercepted some and the rest came down on 616, which swung back into them. Turner's men plunged from above and the fight was on. Separated and set on by four 109's, Dundas fought them alone for five minutes, twisting and gyrating, unable to shake them off, until finally he took the last chance . . . stick hard back and hard rudder to flick into a spin. He let her go for 12,000 feet, came out at 5,000, dived for the coast, dodged several 109's, flashed over an airfield, squirted at a 109 coming in to land, and was chased by others for miles, seeing glowing little balls darting past his wingtip as they fired. Not till mid-Channel did he shake them off and landed with empty tanks, a dry mouth and sweaty brow.

Bader hailed him: " You stupid goat, Cocky. Serves you damn' well right. Teach you to get stuck out on your own."

A day or two later after a brisk " shambles," Bader found himself isolated and called Holden:

" Hallo, Ken. I'm on my own. Can you join me? "

" O.K., D.B. What's your position? "

" About fifteen miles north of Big Wood."

" Good show. I'm in the same area at 25,000 feet. What are your angels? "

" 8,000."

In his broadest Yorkshire, Holden said: " Eee, we'll be a bit conspicuous down there."

He heard Bader's domineering rasp:

" To hell with that. You come on down here."

A pregnant silence, and then Holden:

" Nay . . . you coom oop here."

Dreadful words came over the R/T, but Holden, grinning behind his mask, was already on his way down, and they all came home together.

After a while, to the regret of the Beauty Chorus, Woodhall disconnected the loud-speaker in the Ops. Room, feeling that some of the battle comments were too ripe even for the most sophisticated W.A.A.F.S. (" They laugh, you know," he said, " but dammit I get so embarrassed.") Bader was not exactly the least of the R/T offenders, but whenever his buccaneering presence lurched into the Ops. Room there was a lot of primping, giggling and rolling of eyes.

On 9th July, near Mazingarbe, he sent a 109 down streaming glycol and black smoke, and noted the flash on the ground where it presumably exploded. Another 109 lunged at him, and he turned quickly and got in a burst as it broke off. His combat report said:

" A glycol stream started. I did not follow him down and claimed a damaged. Several others were frightened and I claim one badly frightened, who did the quickest half-roll and dive I've ever seen when I fired at him."

No further bite from Group about the " frightened." They only allowed victories when the enemy was seen by witnesses in flames, or seen to crash, or the crew baled out.

Over Chocques next day he dived 616 on twenty Messerschmitts. More 109's swung in from one side and ran into Holden's squadron, then Turner's men came plunging down and the welkin shook to the roaring, swelling thunder of the dogfight. Bader sent one down shedding bits and pieces, pulled up behind another and fired into its belly. Under its cockpit burst a flash of flame, and suddenly the whole aeroplane blossomed with red fire as the tanks blew up and it fell like a torch. July was turning out a wonderful month. In eight days he had four destroyed, two probables and two damaged, but it only whetted his appetite.

For two days the weather was bad and he took Holden to a nearby links for golf, arranging first that if it cleared over France and a " show " was " on," they would fire Very lights from the airfield. Holden would then run to the car parked by the first tee, drive across the course, pick up Bader and have them both back at the airfield in ten minutes. Bader spent most of his time on the links watching for a Very light, on edge in case something happened and he missed it. He had led the wing on every sweep so far and obviously intended to keep on doing so. But he had little time to relax at golf; even when the wing was not flying, they were on stand-by or readiness in flying kit from dawn to dusk, waiting for a " show " or waiting in case the Luftwaffe attacked England again. There were no days off for the nerves to relax.

For Bader there was paper work, too, in his office, but he gave it little courtesy. Holden was with him one day when a flight-sergeant came in and dumped a pile of files in his " in " tray. Bader growled: "What the hell's this, Flight Sergeant?"

" Files for your attention, sir."

" I'll give 'em attention all right." He picked them up and threw the lot in his waste-paper basket.

He had time to write to a small boy, however. Norman Rowley, aged seven, had had both legs amputated after being run over by a bus in a Yorkshire mining village, and Bader wrote to tell him he would be all right and could be a pilot if he tried hard. (It helped the boy more than anything. He was proud to be Bader's friend.)

In some ways Bader overdid the personal leadership, leaving no one trained to follow him. He could not always lead the wing, and it was obvious what a gap his going would leave. But that did not seem in the realm of reality, and people were recognising now that he had more genius for fighter leadership than anyone else alive.

When there were no sweeps (rarely) he still liked to throw his Spitfire round the sky. His solid frame and square jaw would block Holden's doorway.

" Ken! Aerobatics! "

" O.K., sir. I'll be with you in a minute."

" What's the matter, you clot? " (rasping). " Don't you want to come? "

" Yes, sir, but I've got to finish this readiness roster."

" Damn that! You come with me! "

For the next hour Holden, Turner and Burton (press-ganged in the same way) would be careering round the sky following Bader in formation loops, rolls, stall-turns and the rest of the repertoire. It was forbidden to do them over the aerodrome, but Bader as often as not ignored that. Coming out of a formation loop one day, he saw other Spitfires doing the same thing over the airfield and snapped into his R/T: " Dogsbody calling. Stop messing about over the air-field."

Later, after he had reprimanded the offenders, Holden observed: " That was a bit tough, sir. Hardly fair to bawl 'em out when you do the same thing yourself."

With a deep laugh Bader said: " Ah, that's a very different thing, Ken."

But that was only cheerful bombast, not to be taken seriously. What he usually told aerobatic offenders was: " Don't do it. I lost my legs doing it and more experienced chaps than you have killed themselves doing it. If you're going to be killed let it be an enemy bullet, not bad flying. I know—you're thinking you've seen me do it. Well, when you're wing commanders you can do it too. Until then stick to the regulation height."

Aerobatics after battle was the worst offence. He had never forgotten a World War I picture in a hangar at Cranwell, " The Last Loop," showing a tail breaking off at the top of a loop after battle damage. He himself never in his life did one of the so-called " victory rolls " and threatened to " crucify " anyone else who did, adding: " Next time I'll have you posted."

In all important things he was meticulous. One heard muted criticism that he was too much of a " one-man-band," but all dynamic leaders get that. At least, ninety per cent of the feeling was devoted adulation. Even at dusk when they came off readiness, Bader had seldom had enough and kept pestering Tom Pike, C.O. of the night-fighter squadron, to take him up in a Beaufighter chasing night bombers, his excuse being: " I'd love to see one of these things come down in flames. It'd look so much better at night." But Pike could never take him because there was no room in the aircraft. An unusual friendship had sprung up between the two; they were such different types. Pike was tall and lean with a sensitive face and quiet manner. After he had knocked down several German bombers they had christened this gentle and modest man " Killer."

On 12th July, over Hazebrouck, Bader took 616 down on fifteen 109's, shot at one and saw a flash on its cockpit as he swept past, then fired head-on at another and saw pieces fly off as it swerved under him. A few seconds later he shot at a third, which spurted black smoke and glycol and wrenched into a violent dive. Then he chased a fourth through a cloud and fired from right behind. An orange, blow-torch flame squirted behind its cockpit and it fell blazing all over. One destroyed and three damaged, but he only put one asterisk in his logbook, no longer bothering to record " damaged."

A couple of days later, coming back with Dundas and Johnson, he streaked after a lone 109 below. Seeing him coming, the 109 dived and then climbed, and Bader, trying to cut him off, pulled up so sharply that he blacked out, hunched in the cockpit like an old man carrying a great weight, seeing nothing till he eased the stick forward and the grey film lifted. Then he still saw nothing—the 109 had vanished.

Back at Tangmere, when he landed Dundas and Johnson came charging over and Dundas said: " By god, sir, that was good shooting."

" What the hell are you talking about? " Bader grunted suspiciously, wary of sarcasm.

" Well," Dundas said, " you must have been 400 yards away when that Hun baled out."

" What! " (incredulously). " I never even fired."

None of them had fired. The patches were still over the gun-ports in the wings. Yet the German *had* baled out. Bader lurched over to get a combat report form and wrote it down quickly: " Claimed—one Me. 109 destroyed. Frightened. Confirmed. Seen by two pilots."

Group maintained a stony silence, in marked contrast to the mirth at Tangmere.

The wing was re-equipping with Spitfire Vb's instead of the II's. The Vb was faster, could climb higher and had a 20 mm. cannon planted outboard in each wing. Everyone was excited about them except Bader, who developed a sudden, dogmatic aversion, deciding that cannons were no good because they would tempt a pilot to shoot from too far away instead of getting up close. This time, for once, he was wrong, but nothing would budge him; he was like a choleric colonel barking out obstinately and luridly at Holden, Turner, Dundas, Johnson, Crowley-Milling and anyone else who dared oppose machine-guns. At Group conferences he grunted his vigorous views to Sailor Malan, Leigh-Mallory and even the C.-in-C., Sholto Douglas, but orders still said the wing had to fly Vb's.

As they arrived in ones and twos he gave them first to Turner's top-cover squadron, where their better performance was most needed. Then Holden's team got them, and lastly 616, with whom he led the wing. Stubbornly he himself refused to fly one. Allotting them in this order was ideally correct. A formation leader should fly the slowest aircraft because he sets the pace and people behind must be able to keep up without wasting fuel on constant high power. Not all wing leaders did that, though Bader would have done it the way he did even had he approved of cannon. Finally he got a Va—with machine-guns.

Bad weather set in again and the pilots had time off to

relax in surrounding towns. Bader always went with a group round him, demanding the presence of Holden, Turner, Dundas, Johnson, Crowley-Milling and others, even when they did not want to go. He hated being alone and liked to be the genial centre of a little Court Circle, ignoring their feelings in that respect. Not that they usually minded, being under the influence of his personality.

There was an evening dancing with Thelma at Sherry's in Brighton when the other dancers recognised him and queued up for his autograph. He loved it and no one minded that either, because he did not try to hide it but was like a small boy having a whale of a good time. In those moments the loss of his legs must have meant nothing at all. (It never seemed to worry girls either. His masculinity and audacity drew them in giggling clumps which Thelma eyed with a tolerant smile.)

Rugged mess parties known as " aerobatics " sometimes developed to let off steam. After one of them a group captain had his arm in a sling for days and others bore the marks of combat. There was a lot of " de-bagging," fire extinguishers were sprayed over the room and buckets of water thrown. At one party Cocky Dundas was drinking champagne out of a large water jug when the jug was dropped in a scuffle, and a scrum formed over the broken glass with Billy Burton underneath shouting " On, on, on! "

After another party a certain visiting wing commander whose name has already been mentioned wrote to the mess:

" Wing Commander —— desires to tender his sincere apologies for the usual black put up on the night of the 5th and 6th. He wishes to thank his many friends and admirers for the tender inquiries and floral tributes, and hopes by now you will have recovered from the shocking hangover from which, if there is a God above, you must undoubtedly have suffered."

And underneath: " Delete last sentence where applicable."

(A Cranwell man too!)

After the war Tom Pike, risen to Air Vice Marshal and Assistant Chief of the Air Staff, said this of Bader at the time: " I think he almost eliminated fear from his pilots. His semi-humorous, bloodthirsty outlook was exactly what is wanted in war and their morale soared. He was a tremendous tonic."

And the shrewd Holden, looking back: " I've never known a braver man. He was mad about getting at the Hun and couldn't talk about anything else. He was like a dynamo with terrific morale and a strange power over his men so that they all caught his spirit. After every show he got all the chaps together to yarn about it, though he didn't like people chipping in or putting him in second place. He could be pretty testy with his authority. He always had his own ideas and would take no opposition. It was just as well most of his ideas were sound. Now and then he got a wrong idea and nothing would shake him until he found out himself it was wrong, and then he'd suddenly switch right round the other way."

Everyone felt he was invincible, and that this power shielded those who flew with him. Thelma now literally *knew* that the enemy would never get him. Every time he came back from a sweep he swooped low over the Bay House to let her know he was safely back, but she had come to regard this more as an affectionate salute than a reassurance.

Some of the Messerschmitts had shrewdly taken to setting about the Beehive as it came home over the French coast when the fighters were short of petrol. It was suggested that a fresh wing should go out to meet the homing Beehive, and over the Channel on 19th July the Tangmere Wing came down like wolves on an unsuspecting pack of 109's. Bader's first burst sent a 109 spinning down in a sea of flame. His second shot pieces off another, and as the Messerschmitts split up in alarm his bullets flashed on the fuselage of a third. In seconds the fight was over, half a dozen Messerschmitts were going down and the rest hurrying back into France.

On 23rd July, when the weather prevented any sweep, he took Billy Burton on a " rhubarb," and near Dunkirk saw a Spitfire hurtling out of France, chased by a 109. He squirted into the Messerschmitt's belly and it cart-wheeled into the sea with a great splash.

The next weeks were frustrating. Under pressure, Bader at last tried a Vb, the last in his wing to do so, and only then because the Va was away for a check-up. He grumbled about it mightily because he got into the thick of a lot of fights, but never seemed able to knock anything down now, though Johnson, " Crow," Dundas, and the others kept scoring. He swore one day that his shells from each cannon passed each side of a 109 because he had gone up too close.[1]

He had done more sweeps now than anyone else in Fighter Command and still jealously insisted on leading the wing on every raid, urged by the inner devil, driving himself to the limit and driving others to keep pace.

In seven days he did ten sweeps—enough to knock out the strongest man, still more one who had to get around on two artificial legs. Now he was the last of the original wing leaders still operating—the rest were either dead or screened for a rest.

Peter Macdonald arrived at Tangmere on posting, and was disturbed to note that the skin round Bader's deep-set eyes was dark with fatigue. He and Woodhall began telling him that he must take a rest but Bader refused tersely. At last, at the end of July, Leigh-Mallory said to him:

" You'd better have a spell off operations, Douglas. You can't go on like this indefinitely."

" Not yet, sir," Bader said. " I'm quite fit and I'd rather carry on, sir."

He was so mulish that the A.O.C. at last grudgingly said: " Well, I'll let you go till September. Then you're coming off."

Thelma was increasingly worried about him but he would not listen to her, either. The *Daily Mirror* columnist Cassandra wrote that Bader had done enough, was too valuable to lose and should be taken off operations. He read it angrily.

He was not fighting on to build up a personal string of kills, though at this time he was fifth on the list of top-scoring R.A.F. pilots. He had 20½ enemy aircraft confirmed destroyed but, like other leading fighter pilots, his actual score was probably greater. In his logbook he had nearly thirty asterisks —the ones he himself was fairly sure he had got, though he never displayed them. Malan and Tuck had nearly thirty official victories each but Bader was not jealous, though he would have loved to have caught them. The wing was the

[1] Later he realised that he had been quite wrong in his dogmatic preference for machine guns.

thing and the battle an intoxicant that answered his search for a purpose and fulfilment.

No luck early in August. On the 4th he noted in his log-book: " High escort. Dull." Next day to Lille power station noted tersely: " Damn' good bombing. Blew 'em to hell."

On 8th August Peter Macdonald cornered him in the mess. " I'm going to insist you take a few days off," he said. " I'm taking you and Thelma up to Scotland for a week and you can relax with some golf at St. Andrews."

After an argument, Bader said: " I'll think about it," and that evening Macdonald forced the issue by ringing St. Andrews and booking rooms for the three of them from the 11th. That, he thought, would settle it.

Next day everything went wrong from the start.

22

FIRST THERE was a tangle on take-off and the top-cover squadron went astray. Climbing over the Channel, the others could see no sign of it, and Bader would not break radio silence to call them. Then, half-way across, his air-speed indicator broke, the needle sliding back to an inscrutable zero, which meant trouble timing his rendezvous with the Beehive over Lille, and after that a difficult landing at Tangmere, not knowing in the critical approach how near the aeroplane was to a stall. Time to worry about that later: more urgent things loomed. It looked a good day for a fight, patches of layer cloud at about 4,000 feet but a clear vaulting sky above with a high sun to veil the venom of attack. He climbed the squadrons to 28/30,000 feet so that they, not the Germans, would have the height and the sun.

The job that day was to go for German fighters where they found them, and they found them as they crossed the French coast, just south of Le Touquet—dead ahead and about 2,000 feet below, a dozen Messerschmitts were climbing the same way, spread in "finger fours" abreast (which they seemed to have copied lately). None of them seemed to be looking behind. They were sitters.

Bader said tersely into his mask: "Dogsbody attacking. Plenty for all. Take 'em as they come. Ken, stay up and cover us," and plunged down at the leading four, Dundas, Johnson and West beside him and the rest hounding behind. The Germans still climbed placidly ahead, and steeply in the dive he knew it was the perfect "bounce." Picking the second from the left, he closed startlingly fast; the 109 seemed to slam slantwise at him and, trying to lift the nose to aim, he knew suddenly he had badly misjudged. Too fast! No time! He was going to ram, and in the last moment brutally jerked stick and rudder so that the Spitfire careened and flashed past into the depths below, seeing nothing of the carnage among the enemy as the other Spitfires fired and pulled back up.

Angrily he flattened again about 24,000 feet, travelling fast, watching alertly behind and finding he was alone. Better climb up fast again to join the rest: deadly to be alone in this dangerous sky. He was suddenly surprised to see six more Messerschmitts ahead, splayed abreast in three parallel pairs line astern, noses pointing the other way. More sitters! He knew he should pull up and leave them; repeatedly he'd drummed it into his pilots never to try things on their own. But the temptation! They looked irresistible. A glance behind again. All clear. Greed swept discretion aside and he sneaked up behind the middle pair. None of them noticed. From a hundred yards he squirted at the trailing one and a thin blade of flame licked out behind it. Abruptly a flame flared like a huge match being struck and the aeroplane fell on one wing and dropped on fire all over. The other Germans flew placidly on. They must have been blind.

He aimed at the leader 150 yards in front and gave him a three-second burst. Bits flew off it and then it gushed volumes of white smoke as its nose dropped. The two fighters on the left were turning towards him, and crazily elated as though he had just pulled off a smash and grab raid, he wheeled violently right to break off, seeing the two on that side still flying ahead and that he would pass between them. In sheer bravado he held course to do so.

Something hit him. He felt the impact but the mind was curiously numb and could not assess it. No noise but something was holding his aeroplane by the tail, pulling it out of his hands and slewing it round. It lurched suddenly and then was pointing straight down, the cockpit floating with dust that had come up from the bottom. He pulled back on the stick but it fell inertly into his stomach like a broken neck. The aeroplane was diving in a steep spiral and confusedly he looked behind to see if anything were following.

First he was surprised, and then terrifyingly shocked to see that the whole of the Spitfire behind the cockpit was missing: fuselage, tail, fin—all gone. Sheared off, he thought vaguely. The second 109 must have run into him and sliced it off with its propeller.

He knew it had happened but hoped desperately and foolishly that he was wrong. Only the little radio mast stuck up just behind his head. A corner of his brain saw that the altimeter was unwinding fast from 24,000 feet.

Thoughts crowded in. How stupid to be nice and warm in the closed cockpit and have to start getting out. The floundering mind sought a grip and sharply a gush of panic spurted.

" Christ! Get out! "

" Wait! No oxygen up here! "

Get out! Get out!

Won't be able to soon! Must be doing over 400 already.

He tore his helmet and mask off and yanked the little rubber ball over his head—the hood ripped away and screaming noise battered at him. Out came the harness pin and he gripped the cockpit rim to lever himself up, wondering if he could get out without thrust from the helpless legs. He struggled madly to get his head above the windscreen and suddenly felt he was being sucked out as the tearing wind caught him.

Top half out. He was out! No, something had him by the leg holding him. (The rigid foot of the right leg hooked fast in some vise in the cockpit.) Then the nightmare took his exposed body and beat him and screamed and roared in his ears as the broken fighter dragging him by the leg plunged down and spun and battered him and the wind clawed at his flesh and the cringing sightless eyeballs. It went on and on into confusion, on and on, timeless, witless and helpless, with a little core of thought deep under the blind head fighting for life in the wilderness. It said he had a hand gripping the D-ring of the parachute and mustn't take it off, must grip it because the wind wouldn't let him get it back again, and he mustn't pull it or the wind would split his parachute because they must be doing 500 miles an hour. On and on . . . till the steel and leather snapped.

He was floating, in peace. The noise and buffeting had stopped. Floating upwards? He thought it is so quiet I must have a rest. I would like to go to sleep.

In a flash the brain cleared and he knew and pulled the D-ring, hearing a crack as the parachute opened. Then he was actually floating. High above the sky was still blue, and right at his feet lay a veil of cloud. He sank into it. That was the cloud at 4,000 feet. Cutting it fine! In seconds he dropped easily under it and saw the earth, green and dappled, where the sun struck through. Something flapped in his face and he saw it was his right trouser leg, split along the seam. High in the split gleamed indecently the white skin of his stump.

The right leg had gone.

How lucky, he thought, to lose one's legs and have detachable ones. Otherwise he would have died a few seconds ago. He looked, but saw no burning wreck below—probably not enough left to burn.

Lucky, too, not to be landing on the rigid metal leg like a post that would have split his loins. Odd it should happen like that. How convenient. But only half a leg was left to land on—he did not think of that.

He heard engine noises and turned in the harness. A Messerschmitt was flying straight at him, but the pilot did not shoot. He turned and roared by fifty yards away.

Grass and cornfields were lifting gently to meet him, stooks of corn and fences. A vivid picture, not quite static, moving. Two peasants in blue smocks leaned against a gate looking up and he felt absurdly self-conscious. A woman carrying a pail in each hand stopped in a lane and stared up, frozen like a still. He thought—I must look comic with only one leg.

The earth that was so remote suddenly rose fiercely. Hell! I'm landing on a gate! He fiddled with the shrouds to spill air and slip sideways and, still fumbling, hit, feeling nothing except vaguely some ribs buckle when a knee hit his chest as consciousness snapped.

Three German soldiers in grey uniforms were bending over him, taking off his harness and Mae West. No one spoke that he remembered. They picked him up and carried him to a car in a lane, feeling nothing, neither pain nor thought, only a dazed quiescence. The car moved off and he saw fields through the windows but did not think of anything.

After timeless miles there were houses and the car rumbled over the *pavé*, through the arch of a gateway to a grey stone building. The Germans lifted him out and carried him through a door up some steps and along a corridor . . . he smelt the familiar hospital smell . . . into a bare, aseptic room, and then they were laying him on a padded casualty table. Old memories stirred. A thinnish man in a white coat and rimless glasses walked up and looked down at him. A girl in nurse's uniform hovered behind.

The doctor frowned at the empty trouser leg, pulled the torn cloth aside and stared in amazement, then looked at Bader's face and at the wings and medal ribbons on his tunic. Puzzled he said: " You have lost your leg."

Bader spoke for the first time since the enemy had hit him. " Yes, it came off as I was getting out of my aeroplane."

The doctor looked at the stump again, trying to equate a one-legged man with a fighter pilot. " Ach, so! " he said obviously. " It is an old injury," and joked mildly. " You seem to have lost both your legs—your real one and your artificial one."

Bader thought: God, you haven't seen anything yet. He waited with a grim and passive curiosity for the real joke.

" You have cut your throat," the doctor said. He put his hand up and was surprised to feel a large gash under his chin, sticky with blood. It did not hurt.

The doctor peered at it, then stuck his fingers between the teeth and felt round the floor of the mouth. Light-headed, Bader felt a sudden horror that the cut might have gone right through. For some absurd reason that mattered terribly. But apparently it was all right.

" I must sew this up," the doctor murmured. He jabbed a syringe near the gash and the area went numb. No one spoke while he stitched the lips of the gash.

" Now we must have your trousers off and see your leg," he said.

Bader thought: This is going to be good, and raised his rump a little as the doctor unbuttoned the trousers and eased them down over the hips. The doctor froze, staring transfixed at the leather and metal that encased the stump of the left leg. There was a silence.

At last he noisily sucked in a breath, and said " Ach! "
He looked once more at Bader, back at the two stumps and
again at Bader, and said in a voice of sober discovery: " We
have heard about you."

Bader grunted vaguely.

" Are you all right? " asked the doctor.

" Fine," he said tiredly. " Whereabouts are we? "

" This is a hospital," said the doctor. " St. Omer."

St. Omer!

" That's funny," Bader said. " My father is buried here
somewhere."

The doctor must have thought his mind was wandering.
Two grey-uniformed orderlies came and picked him up,
carried him up two flights of stairs into a narrow room and
dumped him like a sack of potatoes, though not roughly, on
a white hospital bed. They took his clothes and left leg off,
wrapped him in a sort of white nightshirt, pulled the bed-
clothes over him, stood the left leg, still clipped to the broken
waistband, against the wall, and left him there.

He lay motionless, aching all over, feeling as though he
had been through a mangle, his head singing like a kettle.
Every time he stirred a piercing pain stabbed into the ribs
under his heart, cutting like a knife. Reaction drained him
and he knew only utter exhaustion and hurting all over the
body, so that for a while he did not think of England or the
wing or of captivity, nor even of Thelma.

A nurse came and held his head while she ladled some
spoonfuls of soup into his mouth. She went. His mind slowly
cleared and a thought came into focus: " I hope the boys
saw me bale out and tell Thelma."

Dusk gathered slowly in the room and he dozed fitfully.
Some time later he woke in darkness wondering where he was.
Then he knew and sank into misery, black, deep and full of
awareness. He remembered he was to go dancing with Thelma
that night and longed to see her, feeling lonely and helpless
without legs among enemies. There was the golf, too, at St.
Andrews. For the first time in his life he looked back over
his shoulder, rejecting the present and trying to hold on to
the past, but the clock would not go back and the night
moved slowly on.

No one had seen him go down. He had vanished after the first dive and did not answer when they called him. In the air they had been chilled by the absence of the familiar rasping banter. Back at Tangmere there was stunned disbelief when he did not return. They watched the sky and the clock until they knew he could have no petrol left, and a gloomy hush seemed to fall over the place.

Pike said to Woodhall: " You'd better tell his wife," and Woodhall stalled, saying: " No, give him time. He may have landed somewhere else with his R/T u/s. He'll turn up."

But John Hunt, a shy young Intelligence officer, thought Thelma had been told and drove over to cheer her up with a horoscope that a local woman had cast of Douglas, saying that he was in for a dreary time but had a magnificent career after that. He thought it would help her to think that Douglas might be a prisoner.

She was in a deck-chair in the sun, and only when she said: " Hallo, John. Come for tea?" he realised that she did not know. Somehow, in an agony of embarrassment, he talked of irrelevant things, trying to find an unbrutal way of breaking it, when a car drew up and Woodhall got out and walked straight up to them. Without preamble he said: " I'm afraid I've got some bad news for you, Thelma. Douglas did not come back from the morning sortie."

Thelma stood dumbly.

Woodhall went on: " We should get some news soon. I shouldn't worry too much. He's indestructible . . . probably a prisoner."

Too numb to ask what had happened, she stood very pale and said: " Thank you, Woody." Woodhall was saying something else and after a while she became aware that he had gone and that Jill was there. Hunt thrust a piece of paper into her hand and said: " This might be a comfort, Thelma. Read it later." Then he was gone. Jill was saying: " Darling, you *know* he'll pop up again. They can't get him." But Thelma had believed he was invincible and now the whole illusion had burst. She would not cry. A fortnight ago a young wife had cried for days when her husband in the wing had been shot down and Thelma stubbornly would not repeat the exhibition. As always with strong emotions, she covered them up.

Later Dundas came with flowers in one hand and a bottle of sherry in the other. He had been out twice alone that afternoon over the Channel as far as France looking for Bader's yellow rubber dinghy till Woodhall had ordered him back. He looked tired and felt guilty because he had not seen Douglas go down. He and Jill got Thelma to take a little sherry but she brought it up again. Stokoe, Douglas's batman, brought in some soup with tears rolling down his face.

Later, in bed when they left her, the tears came and she lay awake all night thinking: If they got Douglas, what chance have the other boys got? They haven't any chance. A thought rose and obsessed her all night: How can I warn them? How can I make them understand they will all be killed now.

In the morning the reporters came.

Dawn brought new strength to Bader. In the light he saw many things more clearly; knew where he was and what it meant and accepted it unwistfully. First things first and to hell with the rest. He must get legs and must get word to Thelma.

The door opened and in came two young Luftwaffe pilots, dark young men in tight short tunics pinned with badges, shapely breeches and black riding boots.

"Hallo," brightly said the leader, who was Count von Someone-or-other. "How are you?" His English was good.

"All right, thanks."

Bader was fairly monosyllabic but the Germans chatted amiably. Would he like some books? They'd just come over from St. Omer airfield to yarn as one pilot to another. Spitfires were jolly good aeroplanes.

"Yes," Bader said. "So are yours."

After a while the Count said politely: "I understand you have no legs?" He was looking at the fore-shortened form under the bedclothes.

"That's right."

They asked what it was like flying without legs. An elderly administrative officer came in and listened, looked at the left leg leaning against the wall and observed heavily: "Of course it would never be allowed in Germany."

Later they left and the next visitor was a baldheaded Luftwaffe engineering officer, who asked more boring questions about legs. Bader cut him short: "Look, can you radio England and ask them to send me another leg?" He did not know how they would do it, but if they did Thelma would know he was alive.

The German thought it a good idea.

"And while you're about it," Bader followed up, "could you send someone to look at the wreckage of my aeroplane. The other leg might still be in it."

The German promised to do what he could.

A nurse brought in a basin of water. She was German and not talkative, making signs that he was to wash himself. He did so, moving painfully, and when he got to his legs was shocked to find a great dark swelling high up on his right stump. It looked as big as a cricket ball and was terribly sore. For ten years since the agony at Greenlands Hospital he had flinched at the thought of anything going wrong with his stumps, and now it loomed large and ugly in his mind.

Later, yesterday's doctor came in, looking precise behind the rimless glasses. Bader showed him the swelling, and the doctor looked grave and prodded it. After a while he said hesitantly: "We will have to cut this."

Bader burst out, "By God, you don't," panicky at the thought of an experimental knife. They argued violently about it till the doctor grudgingly agreed to leave it for a while.

A dark, plump girl came in, put a tray on his bed, smiled and went out. He realised he was hungry till he tasted the bowl of potato water-soup, two thin slices of black bread smeared with margarine and the cup of tepid ersatz coffee. It left a sour taste in his mouth.

Later it was the doctor again, with orderlies. "We are going to put you in another room," he said. "With friends."

Friends?

The orderlies carried him along a corridor into a larger room with five beds and dumped him on one of them. A fresh-faced young man in another bed said cheerfully in an American accent: "Hallo, sir. Welcome. My name's Bill Hall. Eagle

Squadron. We heard you were here." He had a cradle over one leg which was in traction, the foot pulled by a weight on a rope. His kneecap had been shot off. In the next bed was a Pole with a burnt face, and beyond him Willie, a young Londoner who had been shot through the mouth. All Spitfire pilots. They chatted cheerfully till well after dusk. Willie and the Pole had been trying to think up some way of escaping, but the Germans had taken their clothes and they had only the nightshirts, which made it rather hopeless.

Bader asked: " Isn't there any way out of here? "

" Yes," Willie answered a little bitterly. " Soon as you can stagger they whip you off to Germany." Apparently he and the Pole were due to go at any moment.

" If you had clothes," Bader persisted, " how would you get out? "

" Out the bloody window on a rope," Willie said. " The gates are always open and no guards on them." He jerked his head at the door of the room. " They put the guards outside that door."

" How would you get a rope? "

Willie said there were French girls working in the hospital who might smuggle one in.

Bader slipped off to sleep thinking grimly about that, but he slept well and in the morning did not feel so stiff and sore.

The plump girl came in early with more black bread and acorn coffee, and Bill Hall introduced her to Bader as Lucille, a local French girl. He tried to joke with her but she barely understood his schoolboy French, though she coloured nicely and smiled at him again. She did not say anything: a German guard stood in the doorway.

The doctor came in to see his stump but the swelling was visibly less, which was an enormous relief. In his blunt way Bader told the doctor that the food was " bloody awful," and the doctor bridled. Bader waved a piece of black bread in his face and they had a shouting match till the doctor stormed out. Lucille came back with lunch—more potato water and black bread.

Later a tall, smart Luftwaffe officer of about forty came in. He wore the red tabs of the Flak, clicked his heels, saluted Bader and said: " Herr Ving Commander, ve haf found your leg." Like a star making his entrance, a jackbooted soldier marched through the door and jerked magnificently to attention by the bed, holding one arm stiffly out. Hanging from it was the missing right leg, covered in mud, the broken piece of leather belt still hanging from it. Bader, delighted, said, " I say, thanks," then saw that the foot still ludicrously clad in sock and shoe stuck up almost parallel to the shin.

" Hell, it's been smashed."

" Not so badly as your aeroplane," said the officer. " Ve found it in the area of the other pieces."

The soldier took two smart paces forward, clicked to a halt again, and Bader took the leg. He unpeeled the sock and saw, as he feared, that the instep had been stove in.

" I say," he said, turning on the charm. " D'you think your chaps at the aerodrome could repair this for me? "

The officer pondered. " Perhaps," he said. " Ve vill take it and see." After a mutual exchange of compliments the officer clicked his heels, saluted, swung smartly and disappeared.

Next it was a new girl, fair-haired and with glasses, carrying a tray. She was Hélène, and everyone goggled to see that she carried real tea on the tray and some greyish-white bread. Apparently the shouting match had been worth while.

In the morning the swelling on the stump had deflated with amazing speed and that was a great relief.

Later the officer with the red tabs marched crisply in, saluted, and as he said " Herr Ving Commander, ve haf brought back your leg," the jack-booted stooge made another dramatic entrance behind and came to a crashing halt by the bed, not flicking an eyelid, holding out a rigid arm with the leg suspended from it: a transformed leg, cleaned and polished and with the foot pointing firmly where a foot should be. Bader took it and saw they had done an amazing job on it; the body belt was beautifully repaired with a new section of intricately-worked, good quality leather and all the little straps that went with it. The dent in the shin had been carefully hammered out, so that apart from a patch bare of paint it looked normal. A dent in the knee had been hammered out, and even the rubbers correctly set in the ankle so there was resilient movement in the foot.

" It is O.K. ? " the officer asked anxiously.

Bader, impressed and rather touched, said: " It's really magnificent. It is very good of you to have done this. Will you please thank the men who did it very much indeed."

He strapped both legs on, eased off the bed, feeling unsteady for a moment, and went stumping round the room, a ludicrous figure in nightshirt with the shoe-clad metal legs underneath. Without a stump sock (lost in the parachute descent), the right leg felt strange, and it gave forth loud clanks and thumps as he swung it. The others looked on fascinated. Beaming with pleasure, the Germans finally left. Bader lurched over to the window and looked thoughtfully at the ground three floors and forty feet below. To the left of the grass courtyard he could see the open gates, unguarded.

They became aware of a drone that began to swell and fade and swell again. The Pole and Willie joined him at the window, and high above they saw the twisting, pale scribble of vapour trails against blue sky; obviously a sweep and some 109's were having a shambles over St. Omer. Tensely they watched but the battling aircraft were too high to see. Shortly a parachute floated down. A German, he hoped, and hoped there were more coming down without parachutes. He looked up at the con-trails, at the parachute and down at the court-yard and the gates, his mind a fierce maelstrom.

A Luftwaffe Feldwebel came in and told Willie and the Pole to be ready to leave for Germany after lunch. He would bring their clothes later.

When he had gone Willie, depressed, said: " Once they get you behind the wire you haven't got much chance." Bader began worrying that it would be his turn next. He *must* stay in France as long as possible.

Lucille came in with soup and bread for lunch. The guard looked morosely in the doorway, and then turned back into the corridor. Bader whispered to the Pole: " Ask her if she can help me get out or put me in touch with friends outside."

In a low voice the Pole started talking to Lucille in fluent French. She darted a look at Douglas and whispered an answer to the Pole. They went on talking in fast, urgent whispers, each with an eye watching the door. Bader listened eagerly but the words were too fast. They heard the guard's boots clump in the corridor, and Lucille, with a quick, nervous smile at Douglas, went out.

The Pole came across and sat on his bed. " She says you're ' *bien connu* ' and she admires you tremendously and will help if she can, but she can't get a rope because the Germans would guess how you got it. She doesn't know whether she can get clothes, but she has a day off next Sunday and will go to a village down the line called Aire, or something. She says there are ' *agents Anglais* ' there."

English agents? It sounded too good. But she was going to try, and hope welled strongly. Sunday! This was only Wednesday. Hell, they mustn't take him. The uncertainty of fear gnawed. Better try and act weak from now on.

They took Willie and the Pole that afternoon. Now he had to rely on his schoolboy French.

In the morning Lucille came in with the usual bread and acorn coffee. The sentry lounged in the doorway. She put the tray on Bader's bed, leaning over so that her plump body hid him from the sentry. He grinned a cheerful " *Bon jour* " at her as she squeezed his hand and then the grin nearly slipped as he felt her pressing a piece of paper into his palm. He closed his fingers round it and slid the clenched fist under the bedclothes. It was very quick. She said nothing, but her mouth lifted in a pale smile as she went out of the room. The door closed behind the sentry.

23

HALF UNDER the clothes, Bader unfolded the paper and
and read, written in French in a clear, child-like hand:
"*My son will be waiting outside the hospital gates every
night from midnight until 2 a.m. He will be smoking a cigarette.
We wish to help a friend of France.*"

It was signed "J. Hiècque."

Bill Hall looked curiously across the top of his suspended
leg and asked: "What's that?"

"Oh, just a message of good cheer," Bader spoke casually,
tingling inside with excitement. He tucked the note in the
breast pocket of the nightshirt and stuffed a handkerchief on
top. It was red hot. Somehow he must get rid of it. Destroy
it. He knew that the person who bravely signed a name to it
was liable to death. Lucille, too.

Now how the hell to get out of the hospital? And he *must*
get his clothes back! Couldn't walk round the town in a white
nightshirt. (And Bill Hall had said there was a curfew at ten
o'clock.) Pretend he was walking in his sleep! With tin legs
sticking out under his nightshirt! Silly thoughts chased their
tails in his head. *Must* get clothes and *must* destroy the note.

He had his pipe and matches.

Reaching out, he picked up his tin legs from the wall,
lifted his nightshirt, strapped them on and walked out of the
door. The sentry stood in his way. He pointed to the lavatory
and the sentry nodded.

Inside the lavatory he closed the door, struck a match and
burnt the note, holding it by one corner till it was all wrinkled
and charred, then dropped the ashes into the pan and
flushed it.

Walking back up the corridor, the sentry gaped at him
all the way and he knew angrily and self-consciously how
ridiculous he looked in the nightshirt with the legs under-

neath. It was then that the idea struck him. It was a chance.

When the doctor came in later to inspect the stump again, Bader said in a voice of sweet reason: " Look, I've got my legs back now but I just can't walk around in them with this nightshirt on. It's terribly embarrassing." He explained about the gaping sentry. " I'm sure you'll understand," he went on winningly. " I must have some clothes to wear. Even in bed this nightshirt's a damn' nuisance. It gets tangled up in my stumps."

The doctor looked professionally thoughtful and then smiled. " Oh, well, I suppose it is all right in your case. I will have your clothes brought to you."

Quite a moment! God, how easy.

Half an hour later a German nurse came in with his clothes, put them in a neat pile beside his bed, smiled briefly at him and went out.

Hall said wryly: " I wouldn't mind losing this damn' leg of mine just to get my pants back. I feel so stupid in this nightshirt."

How to get out of hospital! He lay there fiercely thinking about it. It was the last problem. The toughest! No good trying to walk down the corridors and stairs. The guards were on at midnight and all night. They'd frogmarch him back and he'd lose his clothes again, too. He walked over to the window and stood looking down into the courtyard. Perhaps Lucille's " *agents Anglais* " could help.

He was still there when the immaculate young count, the fighter pilot with the Knight's Cross, came in with his comrade. " Ha," he said, " it is good to see you on your legs again. Look, we haf brought you two bottles of champagne. Will you come and drink them with us? "

They took him down a flight of stairs to the doctor's room, but the doctor was not there, just the three of them. The first cork popped. It was the first time he had drunk champagne since his second wedding to Thelma, and it developed into a cheerful little party.

The Count had obviously shot down some British aircraft but was too polite to mention that or to ask how many Bader had shot down. In fact, neither he nor his comrade asked any dangerous questions, but both chatted gaily about their own tactics and aeroplanes. The Count said they always sat in their cockpits at readiness—he always read a book. Bader liked them both; they were " types " after his own heart and he would have liked to have had them in his wing. What a damn' silly war it was.

" Soon you may haf three legs," the Count said. " With the permission of Reichsmarshal Goering, the Luftwaffe has radioed to England on international waveband. They offer to give a British aeroplane unrestricted passage to fly your leg. We have given them a height and a course and a time to drop it over St. Omer." He shrugged, looking philosophical. " They have not answered. I think they will."

Bader gave a rich belly-chuckle. " I bet they drop it with bombs," he said. " They don't need any unrestricted passage."

The Count grinned amiably and raised his glass. " We will be ready," he promised. " Let us hope the next leg will not be shot down."

There was another thing he said. The Oberstleutnant Galland, who commanded at their airfield, Wissant, near St. Omer, sent his compliments to Oberstleutnant Bader and would like him to come and have tea with them.

" We do not try to get information from you," he added quite sincerely. " He would like to meet you. We are comrades, as you say, on the wrong sides."

Bader was intrigued. It would be churlish to refuse, and in any case he would love to meet Galland (probably they had already met in the air). It brought a breath of the chivalry lost from modern war. And it was a chance to spy out the country, to see the other side, life on an enemy fighter station, to weigh it up and compare it. Might get back home with a 109!

" I'd be delighted to come," he said.

" Good," beamed the Count. " A car will come for you."

Agreeably they finished the second bottle.

The car came bearing the bald little engineering officer, who sat by him all the fifteen miles to Wissant. It was a sunny day and it felt good to be out. They drew up in front of an attractive country farmhouse of red brick. German officers stood outside—it was the officers' mess. As Bader got out a good-looking man about his own age, dark-haired and with a little moustache, stepped forward. He had burn marks round the eyes and a lot of medals on his tunic. The Knight's Cross with Oak Leaves and Swords—almost Germany's highest decoration—hung round his neck. He put out his hand and said " Galland."

Bader put out his own hand. " Oh, how d'you do. My name is Douglas Bader." Galland did not speak English, and the engineering officer interpreted. A lot of others stepped forward in turn, clicking their heels as they were introduced. Galland led him off, trailed by the others, down a garden path lined with shrubs. Quiet and pleasant, Galland said: " I am glad to see you are all right and getting about again. How did you get on baling out? "

" Don't remember much about it."

" One never does," Galland said. " One of your pilots shot me down the other day and I had to jump out. I landed very hard. It must be unpleasant landing with only one leg."

Bader asked: " Is that when you burnt your eyes? " and Galland nodded.

He led the way into a long, low arbour, and Bader was surprised to see it filled with an elaborate model railway on a big raised platform. Galland pressed a button and little trains whirred past little stations, rattling over points, past signals, through tunnels and model cuttings. Eyes sparkling, Galland turned to Bader, looking like a small boy having fun. The interpreter said: " This is the Herr Oberstleutnant's favourite place when he is not flying. It is a replica of Reichsmarshal Goering's railway, but of course the Reichsmarshal's is much bigger."

After playing a little while with that, Galland led him and the others several hundred yards along hedge-lined paths, through a copse of trees to the low, three-sided blast walls of an aircraft pen. In it stood an Me. 109.

Bader looked at it fascinated, and Galland made a polite gesture for him to climb in. He surprised them by the way he hauled himself on to the wing-root, grabbed his right leg and swung it into the cockpit and climbed in unaided. As he cast a glinting professional eye over the cockpit lay-out Galland leaned in and pointed things out. Mad thoughts about starting up and slamming the throttle on for a reckless take-off surged through Bader's mind.[1]

Lifting his head, he could see no signs of the aerodrome. He turned to the interpreter. " Would you ask the Herr Oberstleutnant if I can take off and try a little trip in this thing? "

Galland chuckled and answered. The interpreter grinned at Bader. " He says that if you do he'll be taking off right after you."

" All right," Bader said, looking a little too eagerly at Galland. " Let's have a go."

Galland chuckled again and said that he was off duty at the moment.

As he stepped out of the 109, Bader looked across country and saw the sea. Far beyond he thought he could glimpse the white cliffs of Dover and for a moment felt quite sick. It brought it all home to him. And the future. England could be no more than forty miles away. Longingly he thought if only they'd leave him for a moment he could get off with the 109 and be back in the mess for tea.

They had tea in the farmhouse mess, waiters in white coats bringing sandwiches and real English tea (probably captured). It could have been an R.A.F. mess except that all the other uniforms were wrong. The atmosphere was wrong too, which was understandable. Everyone smiled, exuding goodwill, but it was a little strained and formal and the talk was stilted. With Galland there no one seemed to speak much. No one tried to pump him for information. The little interpreter told him that the day he was shot down the Luftwaffe had got twenty-six Spitfires for no loss, which was such obvious nonsense that it put Bader in a very cheerful mood, because it confirmed R.A.F. views on extravagant German claims.[2] He himself had got two that day, and

---

[1] After the war Galland sent Bader a snapshot of the scene, and only then did he discover that a German officer beside the cockpit had been pointing a heavy pistol at him all the time he sat there.

[2] In the Western Desert in 1942 the German " ace," Marseille, claimed personally to have shot down sixteen British aircraft in one day. That day the Desert Air Force lost two aeroplanes.

possibly three, counting the mysterious man who had hit him.[1]

Later they showed him some camera-gun films—a Blenheim which did not seem to be shot down, a Spitfire which shovelled out black smoke and obviously *was* shot down, and then an odd film of a 109 strafing a British ship and " sinking " it. The last few frames showed the half-submerged ship, but it was all too obviously a different ship.

Galland gave him a tin of English tobacco, and when he took him out to the car said: " It has been good to meet you. I'm afraid you will find it different in prison camp, but if there is ever anything I can do, please let me know."

He smiled warmly, shook hands, clicked his heels and bowed. At a discreet distance behind, everyone else clicked heels and bowed. Bader got into the car with the little engineer and they drove back to the hospital. He would have liked to have had Galland in his wing. Rumour said he had over seventy victories, but of course he had been fighting in the Spanish Civil War and in Poland too.

The engineer officer took him back up to the ward, shook hands, clicked his heels and bowed himself out. More black bread stood by his bed. Lucille had evidently been in with " dinner." After his tea with Galland he regarded it distastefully.

" How'd you get on? " Bill Hall asked.

" Fine," he said. " Jolly fine. They're a good bunch. Got some loot too." He held up the tobacco.

A comatose form lay in the bed by the window and the room stank disagreeably of ether. Bader looked across. " Who's that? "

" New boy came in while you were out," Hall said. " Sergeant pilot. Shot down yesterday. They've just taken his arm off. He's still under the dope."

The door opened and a German soldier wearing a coal-scuttle helmet came in. It was the first of the fabled helmets that Bader had seen. The soldier, who must have been awaiting his return, saluted and said in atrocious English: " Herr Ving Commander, to-morrow morning at eight o'clock you vill be pleased to be ready because you go to Chermany."

[1] Much later Bader found that his wing had got eight that day for two lost.

The words seemed to hit Bader right in the stomach. The German clicked his heels, saluted and clumped out. He sat on his bed, stunned. Then, with deep feeling, uttered an eloquent word.

Hall murmured: "Tough luck, sir. Looks like you've had it."

Bader roused and said crisply: "Well, I've got to get out to-night, that's all."

He lurched over to the window and pushed it open. It seemed a long way down, and immediately below were flag-stones. After the parachute affair he did not feel like jumping. He turned back and scowled round the room, austere with its board floor and five prim beds.

My god! Sheets! Knotted sheets!

One learned something from school!

Each bed had an undersheet and a double, bag-type sheet stuffed in the continental style. He stumbled over to his bed and ripped the sheets from under the blanket. Need a damn sight more than that! He clumped noisily to the two empty beds and stripped them the same way. With a sudden idea he began ripping the bag sheets along the seams to get two out of each one. The tearing seemed to scream a warning to the Germans.

"Make a noise," he hissed to Hall, and Hall started on a monologue in a loud American voice, talking nonsense, saying anything that came into his head and laughing loud and humourlessly. Both were acutely conscious of the guard just outside the door. Once they heard the rasp of a boot on the boards and then a couple of clumps. Bader looked up like an animal. Then a creak as the guard sat in the wicker-chair out there.

"Know anything about knots?" Bader whispered to Hall.

"Not a sausage."

He started knotting the corners together in an unskilled double " granny " with three hitches, jerking tightly to make them fast and hoping they would stay so when the test came.

"What about the curfew?" Hall asked.

He said: "—— the curfew! "

The knots took up a lot of length, and when he had finished the " rope " was clearly not long enough.

"Here, take mine," Hall said.

Gently he eased the sheet from under Hall and took off the top one. When he had added them the rope still did not look long enough.

"You'll be up the creek if you're left hanging," Hall warned. "Won't be able to climb back and won't be able to drop without bisecting yourself."

Bader went over to the bed of the sergeant pilot, who was breathing stertorously under the ether. Gently working the sheet from under him, he said: "This is frightful, but I've just got to."

"He won't mind," reassured Hall. "I'll tell him when he wakes up."

Soon he had fifteen sheets knotted together, littered around the room, and prayed that no one would come in. He pushed the sergeant pilot's bed to the window, wincing at the noise, knotted one end of the rope round the leg and stuffed the rest under the bed (it still looked pretty obvious). Then he straightened the white blankets on all the beds and climbed back into his own, sweating, heart thumping, praying that darkness would come before the guard.

Time dragged dreadfully while dusk slowly gathered in the room. He and Hall tried to talk in low tones, but his mind kept jumping away from the words. It was not quite dark when the door handle rattled, the door opened and a German soldier stuck his head in and looked round. Bader could not breathe. The guard muttered " *Gut Nacht,*" and the door closed behind him.

Three hours to go. As long as no nurse came to see the sergeant pilot!

That evening Thelma, who had eaten nothing for three days, braced herself and asked Stan Turner: "Well, what do you really think?"

Turner said with simple directness: "You'll have to face it. We should have heard something by this. I guess he's had it."

In London the Luftwaffe's radio message had arrived saying that a spare leg could be flown across in a Lysander

communications aircraft. Spitfires could escort it part of the
way and then Messerschmitts would take over. The Lysander
could land at St. Omer, hand over the leg and then it could
take off again.

From Leigh-Mallory and Sholto Douglas the reaction was
prompt, definite and identical. No free passage or German
escort (with its lump of propaganda plum cake for Goebbels).
They would send the spare leg in a Blenheim on a normal
bombing raid.

Dundas, Johnny Johnson and Crowley-Milling had gone
across to the Bay House to do what they could for Thelma.
She sat quietly, a sphinx-like stoic, and only roused when the
phone rang. It was Woodhall for her. The others could only
hear her saying: " Yes . . . yes . . . yes . . . yes, Woody."
She said " Thank you very much, Woody," hung up and
came back to the room. In the silence she sat down and lit a
cigarette, trembling a little. Then she blew out smoke and
said quietly: " D.B.'s a prisoner." Shouts of jubilation filled
the room but she hardly heard, feeling sick with astonishment
and delight and with emotions ploughing over her.

Weary æons of time seemed to have passed before a clock
somewhere in the darkness of St. Omer chimed midnight.
The night was breathlessly still. He eased on to the edge of
the bed, vainly trying to stop the creaks, and strapped his
legs on. Then his clothes. Praying that the guard was asleep
in his chair, he took a step towards the window; the boards
creaked and the right leg squeaked and thumped with a
terrifying noise. Hall started coughing to cover it up as, unable
to tiptoe, he stumbled blindly across the floor. One or the
other was bound to wake the guard. At the window he quietly
pushed it open and leaned out, but the night was coal black
and he could not see the ground. Picking up the sheet rope,
he lowered it out, hoping desperately that it was long enough,
but could not tell if it reached the ground. It must have
roused the sergeant pilot: coming out of the twilight of ether,
the boy was groaning.

Hall whispered: " We'll have a nurse here in a moment."

Holding the rope, Bader leaned his chest on the window-
sill and tried to winkle his legs out sideways. They seemed

fantastically clumsy, more than ever before, huge, disjointed
and swollen. Uncontrollable. Sweating, he took a hand off
the rope to grab his right shin and bend the knee. Then
somehow he was through, legs dangling, hands clutching the
rope on the sill. The terrible pain pierced his ribs again,
making him gasp.

Hall whispered: " Good luck! " It sounded like a pistol
shot.

He hissed: " Shut up." And then, " Thanks." Then he
started easing himself down.

It was simple. The legs rasping against the wall were
useless, but the arms that had developed such muscles since
the long-ago crash at Reading took his weight easily. He
lowered himself, hand under hand, under sure control. Holding the sheets was no trouble and the knots were holding—
so far. In a few seconds he came to a window and knew it
was the room where he had drunk champagne with the
Luftwaffe. He was horrified to feel that it was open, but
inside it was dark and he eased his rump on to the ledge for
a breather, hoping the doctor was not sleeping inside. Sitting
there, breathing quietly, he looked down but still could not
see the ground or whether the rope reached it. (Only later
he realised he should have counted the knots.) Too late to
go back now; he eased himself off the ledge and went on
down.

Very gently his feet touched the flagstones and he was
standing, dimly seeing that yards of sheet seemed to be lying
on the ground.

" Piece of cake," he thought, and moved a couple of
yards on to the grass, cursing the noise from his legs. Warily
he steered across the grass towards where the gates should be,
having no plan, only hoping the mysterious Frenchman
would be there.

Something loomed darker even than the night. The gates!
Good show. Then a shock—they were closed. He got his
fingers in the crack between and one gate opened easily a
foot. He squeezed through on to the cobbled *pavé* of the
road and instantly, immediately opposite, saw the glowing
end of a cigarette. He stumped diagonally across the road
and the cigarette moved, converging on him. It came to his

side with a dark shadow behind it that whispered urgently
" Dooglass! " in a strong French accent.

" *Oui*," he said, and the shape took his right arm and
they moved off along the *pavé*. The town was like a tomb
in which his legs were making an unholy clatter, echoing into
the darkness. He could not see, but the silent shape seemed
to know by instinct. A pressure on the arm and they turned
right and stumbled on.

The Frenchman began muttering to him: " *C'est bon.
C'est magnifique Ah, les sales Boches*."

After a while Bader thought how funny it was, walking
through the curfew in enemy-occupied St. Omer arm-in-arm
with a stranger he would not even recognise by day. He
began to giggle. The Frenchman said " Ssh! Ssh! " but that
only made him giggle more. He tried to stop but couldn't,
and the more he tried the more he giggled as the strained
nerves took control. The Frenchman started to giggle and
then it was so grotesque, the two of them giggling and clattering
down the street, that it grew into loud laughter mingled with
the terror inside him that the Germans would hear. Slowly
the pent-up emotion washed away and the laughter subsided
into suppressed sniggers that he was at last able to stop.

They walked on—and on—and on. Five minutes, ten—
twenty. His right stump without the stump-sock began to
chafe. Thirty minutes . . . it was sore and starting to hurt.
On and on they walked. He was limping badly and the
Frenchman made soothing noises that sounded in inflection
like " Not far now " in French. Forty minutes must have
passed. The steel leg had rubbed the skin off his groin and
every step was searing agony. Stumbling and exhausted, he
had both arms hanging on to the Frenchman's shoulders. At
last the man took his arms round his neck, picked him up,
dangling on his back, and staggered along. In a hundred
yards or so he stopped and put him down, breathing in a
rasping way. Bader leaned against a stone wall and the man
pushed open a gate in the wall beside him.

He led the way and Bader stumbled after him up a garden
path. A doorway showed ahead, framing soft light, and then
he was in a little, low-ceilinged room with flowered wallpaper,
and a tin oil-lamp on the table. An old man and a woman

in a black shawl got up from the chairs and the woman put her arms round him and kissed him. She was over sixty, Madame Hiècque, plump and with a lined, patient face. Her husband, spare and stooping, brushed his cheeks with a wisp of grey moustache. Fleetingly he saw his guide, remembering mostly the lamplight sheen on the glossy peak of a cap drawn low over the face and the glint of smiling teeth. The young man shook his hand and was off out of the door.

The old woman said gently: " *Vous êtes fatigué?* "

Holding on to the table, he said " *Oui* " and she led him with a candle up some cottage stairs into a room with a huge double bed. He flopped on it. She put the candle on the table, smiled and went out. He unstrapped his legs with enormous relief, stripped to his underclothes and slid under the bedclothes into a gloriously soft feather bed, thinking: " That's foxed the bloody Huns. I'll be seeing Thelma in a couple of days." Then he was asleep.

A hand on his shoulder woke him about 7 a.m. The old man was looking down, smiling with tobacco-stained teeth. He left a razor, hot water and towel. Bader freshened up and examined his stump, which was raw and bloodstained, terribly sore. No help for it. Just have to bear the pain. Done it before. He strapped his legs on and went wincingly down-stairs. Madame had coffee and bread and jam waiting, and while he ate she planted an old straw hat squarely on her head and went out. Bader sat for a couple of hours in a red plush chair trying to talk to the old man, a stilted, fumbling conversation of invincible goodwill.

Madame came back in great glee. " *Les Boches,*" it seemed, " *sont très stupides.*" He gathered she had walked to the hospital and stood watching mobs of Germans running around searching the area. Great joke! In halting French he tried to make her understand that his presence was very dangerous to them. If they found him he, himself, would only be put in cells and then sent to prison camp, but the Hiècques were liable to be shot. He should leave them and hide somewhere.

Madame said: " *Non, non, non, non* . . ." The Germans would never find him here. That evening her son-in-law, who spoke English, would come and they would discuss things and get him to the Underground. She examined his right stump and produced a pair of long woollen underpants. Cutting one of the legs off, she sewed up the end and there was a perfectly good stump-sock. After she powdered the stump he put the sock on under the leg and felt much better.

At noon the familiar drone came overhead and they took him out into the shelter of the walled back garden. Yearningly he watched the tangled con-trails and saw tiny glints as twisting aircraft caught the sun. Out from the windows of houses all round leaned the women waving mops and towels, and shrilling: " *Vive les Tommies. Vive les Tommies.*" It was moving and delightful. Soon he'd be back up there among the con-trails, thinking differently about the sweeps, knowing what they meant.

At 15,000 feet, just south of St. Omer, the Tangmere wing jockeyed round the Blenheim. Crowley-Milling, close escort, saw the bomb-bays open and the long thin box with the spare leg drop out. It looked like a little coffin. A parachute blossomed above it and it floated down, swaying gently, surrounded by the black stains of flak-bursts from the puzzled gunners far below.

The quiet, loyal and gallant Stokoe had asked to be dropped by parachute with it to look after the wing commander in prison, but permission had been refused. He had to content himself in helping Thelma stuff the leg with stump-socks, powder, tobacco and chocolate.

Madame gave Bader cold pork for lunch and went out again to the scene of the crime. She came back hugging herself with delight. Convinced that Bader could not walk far, the Germans had cordoned off an area round the hospital and were running about like ants, searching every house. But nowhere in this area.

He felt like twiddling his thumbs as the afternoon dragged. Madame went out again to see the fun. Sitting in shirt-sleeves in the plush chair, he thought: Roll on that English-speaking chap. About half-past five there came a sudden terrifying banging on the front door and a chill swept him. The old man jumped as though he had been shot, peered furtively through the curtain, turned and whispered " *Les Boches!* "

He grabbed Bader's arm and led him towards the back door. Only at the last moment Douglas thought to grab his battledress jacket. Together they stumbled into the garden, moving as fast as the legs would let him. Three yards from the back door, against a wall, stood a rough shed, galvanised iron nailed on posts, covering some baskets, garden tools and straw. The old man pulled the baskets and straw away, laid him on his stomach, cheek pillowed on his hands, against the corner of the wall and piled the straw and baskets on top. Lying there, he heard the old man's footsteps hurrying inside.

There was not long to wait. Within a minute he heard voices and then tramping feet by the back door. He knew the sound of jackboots. A vague kind of twilight filtered through the straw but he could not see anything. The boots clumped along the paved path to the shed. He heard baskets being kicked about. The straw over him started moving with a loud rustle. He lay still, thinking " Here we go! "

Miraculously the footsteps retreated, diminishing down the garden path. Elation filled him.

The boots were coming back up the path. Suddenly they clumped again into the shed, then stopped and rasped about a yard from his head. From his heart outwards ice seemed to freeze his nerves.

The baskets were being thrown around, the boots rasped on the paving, and then there was a metallic clang that mystified him. There was a movement in the hay just above and another clang. His eyes, turned sideways, saw a bayonet flash down an inch from his nose and stab through the wrist of his battledress jacket to hit the stone floor. He knew what the clang was and guessed that the next stroke would go into his neck or back.

24

IT WAS a lightning decision. He jerked up on his hands, heaving out of the hay like a monster rising from the sea, straw cascading off his back. A young German soldier, bayonet poised for the next jab, leapt back in shock and stared pop-eyed at him, holding rifle and bayonet on guard. He started yelling hoarsely in German. Boots pounded and three German soldiers clattered under the iron roof, all armed. They stood round him in a semi-circle, bayonet tips poised about four feet from him. Slowly he raised his hands.

A little Stabsfeldwebel (staff sergeant) with a dark, thin moustache ran up and covered him with a pistol as he stood there feeling like King Lear, or perhaps an escaped lunatic at bay, with straw in his hair and all over his battledress.

Looking pleased and quite friendly, the Stabsfeldwebel said in perfect, unaccented English: " Ah, Wing Commander, so we have caught you again."

" Yes," said Bader. " Would you mind asking these soldiers to put their rifles down. As you can see, I'm unarmed."

The Stabsfeldwebel rattled off some German, and the soldiers lowered the rifles.

Still with his hands up, Bader said: " You speak English very well."

" Thank you, Wing Commander," replied the German. " I lived at Streatham[1] for eleven years."

" Did you really," Bader said. " I used to live near Croydon myself."

(It struck him that the conversation was unreal.)

" Ah, I know Croydon well," the German answered. " Did you ever go to the Davis Cinema? "

" Yes. And I used to go to the Locarno at Streatham."

" Did you? " said the German. " Many Saturday evenings I have danced there."

---

[1] London suburb.

Bader never forgot a word of that dialogue. The German courteously invited him to follow, and he stumped out of the shed into the back door again feeling that the world might well be rid of politicians and that this was a perfect example of the fact that ordinary people never caused wars. He felt no rancour towards the soldiers who had winkled him out, and as far as he could see they felt no rancour for him. He was thinking it made Hitler and Mussolini look " pretty bloody stupid " when he saw the old man and woman standing in the room. They looked pale and he stiffly walked past, showing no sign of recognition.

At the front door he nodded his head back and said to the Stabsfeldwebel: " Those people did not know I was in their garden. I came in last night through that gate in the wall."

Quite pleasantly the German replied: " Yes, I understand that."

By the kerb stood the Germans' car, and as they led him to it the rear door opened and a blonde girl with glasses got out. Rather surprised, he recognised Hélène, from the hospital, and said automatically: " Hallo, Hélène," but she walked past him with her eyes down.

They drove him to Headquarters in St. Omer, where a German officer questioned him and got no answers. Then into a room where he was surprised and delighted to see the box containing his spare right leg. They explained, smiling, that it had been dropped that afternoon, and took his photograph standing by it. Then, to his annoyance, they refused to give it to him and prodded him instead into an upstairs room. There, for the first time, they really infuriated him; as he sat on a cot an officer and a soldier stood over him with a pistol and a bayonet, and made him take his trousers down and unstrap his legs: then they took the legs away.

He snarled at them, but the officer said stiffly it was orders from above. Two guards stayed and the rest went out, leaving him on the bed helpless, humiliated and seething. All night two men in full battle order, coal-scuttle helmets and loaded rifles stood over him. It was hot and he asked for the windows to be opened, but the officer came back and refused, saying that " orders from above " forbade that too. They were taking no chances!

He lay awake all night as the guards coughed and muttered ceaselessly. It was then he realised that Hélène had betrayed him and that the Germans must know about Madame and the old man, and he grew sick with worrying about what the Germans would do to them and to Lincille. Somehow he could not feel much resentment about Hélène. He supposed they had threatened her.

In Fighter Command Headquarters in England next morning the telephone rang in the office of Sholto Douglas. He picked it up and recognised the voice of Winston Churchill saying: " Douglas! "

" Yes, sir."

" I see from the newspapers you've been fraternising with the enemy, dropping a leg to a captured pilot."

" Well, sir," Sholto Douglas said, " you may call it fraternising, but we managed to shoot down eleven of the enemy for the loss of six or seven of our own, so I hope you might feel it was worth it."

There was a grunt, and then a click as the phone was hung up.

In St. Omer two guards were carrying Bader downstairs to an ambulance on a cradle of their hands, his arms unlovingly round their shoulders. Another carried his legs wrapped in a blanket. He gathered as the ambulance jolted along that they were going to Brussels for a train to Germany. It was the most depressing journey he had ever known, bouncing over the rutted roads and jostled against the wordless Germans while low cloud and pouring rain swept Northern France. He worried about the Hiècques and Lincille and wondered why the Germans looked so square-headed and stupid.

At last Brussels. An officer strutted in front, the two guards carried him and a third brought up the rear with the legs. People turned and stared as they bore him across a square into the railway station. Past embarrassment and humiliation now, he was seething with fury.

Thank God the carriage seats were soft. Sourly he watched the officer put his legs up on the rack. The train jolted off and clicketty-clicked through the rain. Once or twice the officer spoke to him, but in an evil mood he declined to answer. They passed Liège and then, without ceremony, were in Germany. He knew the first gesture he wanted to make. Hoping to get his legs back, he said he wanted to go to the lavatory. No legs! A guard carried him dangling helpless and angry round his neck, and sat him on the seat, then held the doorway open and covered him with a cocked pistol.

Bader snarled at him: " You stupid clot, how the hell d'you think I can get out of here? "

Guessing his meaning, the guard said woodenly: " *Befehl ist Befehl!* "[1]

That did it! It capped the humiliation, the stupidity, the bombing and killing, the whole misery of the war, and from that moment he loathed the Germans implacably.

High over St. Omer four 109's cut Crowley-Milling out of the wing and he roared and twisted all over the sky, no sooner shaking one off his tail than another was on him like a leech. A cannon-slug crashed through the side of his cockpit, sheared through glycol pipes and exploded into the supercharger. White smoke belched round him and the engine started shaking the little fighter like a grinding mill. The radiator needle spun off the clock, and a minute later the engine seized with a last violent spasm. He spun her on her back and pulled the nose straight down. Soon he crash-landed in a cornfield and was trying to set her alight when he saw Germans running for him half a mile away. Crawling off into the high corn, he tore off his flying overalls and jacket, muddied himself all over and walked south, hiding behind a dung-heap when German lorries went past. That afternoon he walked twenty miles, and at dusk knocked on a farmhouse door. They gave him eggs and a bed, and in the morning the farmer led him away on bicycles. In a couple of days he was hiding in St. Omer in the house of a shoemaker called Ditry, who was a leader of the growing Underground.

Ditry told him that Bader was being held in a local hospital and explained his audacious scheme to rescue him; an ambulance with two Frenchmen in Luftwaffe uniforms and a forged authority would drive to the hospital, the disguised

[1] " Orders are Orders."

Frenchmen would take a stretcher upstairs, put Bader on it and spirit him away. Then they would radio England and hope a Lysander would fly in at night-time to a secret field and take him back home. If caught it would probably mean a firing squad. Would Crowley-Milling like to set off "underground" to Spain, or stay and help? In his polite, shy way, Crowley-Milling said he would like to stay and help.

Next day word came that the Germans had already taken Bader to Germany, and a fortnight later Crowley-Milling was making the arduous trek over the Pyrenees. There Franco's men caught him and put him in the notorious Miranda Concentration Camp, where he nearly starved to death, then caught typhoid and went blind. Later his sight came back and he was evacuated to England, where he fought on for the rest of the war.

They came to Frankfurt at midnight and carried Bader to a car, which drove for half an hour through a crisp, clear night to Dulag Luft, the reception and interrogation centre for all Air Force prisoners. Two Luftwaffe men carried him into a stone building, down a corridor and dumped him on a wooden bunk in a little cell, stripped his battledress off and locked him in darkness and underclothes.

Tired, he slept well. About eight o'clock in the morning a dapper little man in a grey civilian suit came in, saying brightly: "Good morning." Sonderfuehrer Eberhardt spoke perfect English and was too friendly. He handed Bader a form to fill in, the usual fake form with the red cross at the top that the Germans always used. Bader looked down the headings:

"What base did you fly from?

"No. of squadron?

"What type of aeroplane?" and so on.

He scrawled his name, rank and number on it and handed it back.

"If you will fill in the rest," Eberhardt suggested winningly, "it will help the Red Cross inform your relatives and forward your letters. Just a formality, you know."

"That's all you're getting," Bader said. "I'm not half-witted. Now if you don't mind, I'd like a bath, a shave and my legs. Then I'd like some breakfast."

Eberhardt went out, saying he would call the Kommandant.

A tall, slim, good-looking man of about forty-five came in and said smoothly: " Oh, good morning, Wing Commander. I am the Kommandant. My name is Rumpel." He spread his hands sympathetically. " For you the war is over but we'll try and make you as comfortable as we can. I was a fighter pilot myself in the last war and we Germans want to try and keep alive the last war traditions of comradeship among pilots."

Bader answered shortly: " I don't know what you mean. We're enemies and that can't be overlooked."

" Well, we'll try anyhow," Rumpel said. " We're amused at your call sign. It's Dogsbody, isn't it? "

" If you know, why the hell ask me? "

Rumpel probed urbanely on, asking questions about aircraft. " Of course we know you're having a lot of trouble with the Rolls Royce Vulture engine, aren't you? "

" If you know," Bader repeated, " why the hell ask me? "

" We didn't want to fight this war," Rumpel went on earnestly, " but the Poles were determined to have Berlin, so we had to deal with them."

" Eighty million Germans scared of thirty million Poles," Bader growled acidly. " Why did you attack Belgium and Holland then? "

" What do these small countries matter? " Rumpel was bland. Bader, amazed, felt he was quite sincere.

" Why did you attack Russia then? " he demanded.

Rumpel spread his hands again. " We had to have the oil." He went on persuasively: " What makes us so sorry . . . it seems such a shame . . . but we Germans and British never seem to fight on the same side. . . . Of course we know you call us Jerries, but . . ."

" No we don't," Bader snapped. " We call you Huns! "

The charm fled from Rumpel and he shot up, face cold and rigid, and stalked out.

Bader yelled after him: " Send me my legs and some tea, damn you."

He was surprised a few minutes later when a Luftwaffe

orderly came in carrying his legs (including the new one, he was delighted to see), some soap and a towel, and took him along to the bathroom. When he got back to his cell he found a tray of English tea with milk and sugar, and some bread, butter and jam.

Usually one did a week or so " solitary " in a cell being softened up for questioning by mildly unnerving means before going to the adjacent barbed-wire transit cage to await " purging " to a permanent prison camp. Rumpel must have decided Bader was an improbable prospect because an hour after breakfast they took him out of the cell and thrust him into the cage.

The cage was not inspiring: three drab wooden barrack huts on a patch of trodden earth eighty yards square, fenced by double thickets of barbed wire eight feet high and buttressed at each corner by stilt-legged sentry boxes leaning over the wire with watchful eyes, searchlights and machine-guns. The sight of the gates closing him in that dismal patch was mellowed by the welcome from a few score grounded exiles of his own kind who clustered warmly round, making him feel, if not at home, at least among " chums." From the Red Cross store they gave him a toothbrush, razor and some rough aircrafts-man's clothes. Then quite a good meal—the cage had plenty of Red Cross parcels.

A big, wavy-haired Fleet Air Arm lieutenant called David Lubbock took him to his room, a wooden box with a dusty floor and double-decker bunks round the walls, each with paper palliasse stuffed with wood shavings and two grey blankets. There he found Pete Gardner, a dark young fighter pilot with eighteen victories, and other kindred spirits, and they gossiped, swapping stories for some time. He felt much better and with a sudden thought asked if they knew of Harry Day, who was a prisoner somewhere.

" Do we not," said Gardner. " He was here till a few days ago, but he was naughty and escaped through a tunnel with seventeen others."

Apparently they had all been caught and sent to a per-manent camp somewhere else.

At the mention of escape, Bader was practically on fire, leaning forward with his eyes intense and glowing, wanting to know all about it. Quite a short tunnel, Lubbock said, because the huts were near the wire. They burrowed from under a bed, and the night they went everyone else kicked up a racket to cover the noise.

" If they could do it," Bader demanded, " why can't we? "

Lubbock had apparently been thinking the same thing. Pete Gardner, shot down a couple of months ago, four days before his planned wedding, was almost hopping to get home. So were the others in the room.

A day or so later they started carving a hole in the floor under a bunk in an end room of the middle hut, and soon they were burrowing into the dark earth under the hut. With his legs, Bader was no good for the digging: he acted as stooge, watching for Germans outside the window while the others gouged out the dirt and lugged it up in a basin to hide under the hut floor. Like all tunnels, it went slowly, and he bubbled with impatience, obsessed with the idea of getting out and unable to think of other things. His ideas, once he had got out, were sketchy, typical of a new escaper. As usual, he refused to regard his legs as any inevitable barrier. The thing was, get out first and then, he thought vaguely, make for Switzerland . . . pinch a car, stow away on a barge or jump a train or something. The goal was infinitely alluring: he'd be back leading his wing, knowing what went on below in France, hitting back at the Germans instead of being humiliated by them. His mere getting back, a legless man, would mock the Germans in the eyes of the world. And perhaps (subconsciously) this unparalleled example would quell the entrenched demon[1] that said he had no legs and helped to drive him on?

Day by day, foot by foot, the tunnel lengthened. After a fortnight, when they thought they were nearly under the wire, Eberhardt came one day into the cage and sought Bader.

" Herr Wing Commander," he said, " you must be ready to leave to-morrow morning. You are being taken to Brussels to appear before a court-martial."

Bader stared at him, astounded, and demanded: " What the hell am I being court-martialled for? "

---

[1] Not so, I fear. The demon is part of Bader, as indestructible as the rest of him.

" I do not know," Eberhardt shrugged, " but you must go."

Outraged equally by the court-martial and the thought of missing the tunnel, he told the others, but rapidly cooled off when one of them, the Irish Paddy Byrne, gave him a bit of paper with a name and a Brussels address on it.

" Wonderful chance to crack off," said the crafty Byrne. " If you can duck the guards and get to these people, they'll hide you and pass you on to the escape chain."

Gratified, Bader looked forward eagerly to Brussels.

This time in the train they let him keep his legs, but a blond young Sonderfuehrer and two helmeted soldiers never left his side.

In Brussels, towards dark, they put him in a car and drove him through the streets—he hoped towards a ground-floor room in a lonely house. The car turned through a dirty stone arch and soon they were standing in a cold stone hall. Through a heavy barred grille, passages led gloomily away. A gaol!

He said angrily: " This is a civilian gaol. I'm not staying here."

" Oh, but you must, Wing Commander," said the Sonderfuehrer.

" But I damn' well won't." He was outraged again.

" Oh, please, please. You *must*, Wing Commander, because it would be very embarrassing to me. You must please stay here." The Sonderfuehrer looked perturbed.

" I won't. I'm an officer prisoner of war and you can't put me in a criminal prison." Feeling he was beginning to learn how to handle the Germans, he shouted: " I demand to see the general in charge of this district."

On the defensive, the Sonderfuehrer said uncertainly: " I do not think he is at home."

It sounded so fatuous that Bader nearly gave the game away by laughing.

" Well, go and get the clot," he said.

Despairingly, the Sonderfuehrer turned and talked to the stolid Army Feldwebel who seemed to be the gaol reception clerk. He turned back to Bader. " The Feldwebel says that perhaps if we could take you along and show you your room you might be willing to stay."

There was not much option really. Sooner or later they would force him, which would be humiliating, and perhaps they would take his legs too. Having had his fun and won some pride back, he grunted: " All right. I'll come and have a look."

Stumping at a leisurely pace, he went with them through the barred gate and along the passage, passing cell doors with little peep-holes in them. At one they stopped and pulled the door open. He looked into a tiny white-washed cell so narrow you could touch both walls by putting your arms out. A narrow bed nearly filled one side, and high up was a little barred window.

He snorted: " I'm damned if I'm going in there! "

" Oh, but *please*, Wing Commander," begged the Sonder-fuehrer. " You will find it quite comfortable and we will look after you."

" No! "

" But you *must*. I will be shot if you escape." He was genuinely distressed and frightened.

Bader eyed him amiably. " Will you really? "

" We will give you a servant here." Now he was per-spiring.

" What else? "

" We will leave the door open."

(That didn't mean much—the iron door at the end of the corridor would still be firmly locked.)

" I want a table, too. With a cloth. And some tea."

" Yes, Wing Commander. Now will you please go in."

" No. Bring me the servant and table first."

The Feldwebel went off and after a while came back with a little man in a white coat who carried a small table. Good show, a Belgian, Bader thought.

He stalked into the cell and the servant followed and put down the table. They left the door open and retreated, boots ringing on the stone floor down the corridor.

Alone at last, he moved quickly and shoved the table under the high window, then grabbed the stool, planted it on the table and climbed up till he was standing precariously on the stool. Hands clutching the bars, he tried to pull him-self up the extra few inches to see out: he got his eyes up to the bars but the thick wall stuck out beyond the bars and he could not quite see the ground that he was sure was just below. Using all the strength in his thick hands and wrists, he began shaking the bars violently, trying to loosen them.

A respectful cough sounded behind, and he swung and saw the servant standing looking impassively up.

" *Vous êtes Belge ?* " Bader asked eagerly.

" *Nein,* " said the little man, unwinking. " *Ich bin Deutsch.* "[1]

Deflated and with a foolish grin, Bader started climbing down. Impassively the servant helped him, removed the stool, put a tray of tea on the table, nodded a deferential head and glided out on rubber-soled shoes.

After that he found the bed as hard as a plank (which it **was**), and the night long and sleepless, giving time for discontent.

(Stung by humiliations and the frustration of captivity, Bader was now an unappeasable *enfant terrible*. Until he escaped, that was pride's only defence. Already with Rumpel and the timid Sonderfuehrer he had recaptured some *amour-propre* in scenes that were barely believable, but authentic. One might suppose that the Germans had made allowances and that had he possessed his own legs their tolerance would have frozen. Yet even with his legs, Bader would probably have behaved in much the same way because the demon was spurring him well before the Reading crash. And one doubts whether the Germans themselves would have reacted more firmly because his pulverising dynamism turned on full flood will daunt any civilised man. The Germans who bowed to rank and force were vulnerable targets . . . to a point, of course. But Bader's bull-like thrusts carry sensitive antennæ that feel precisely when the goad pricks too deep. Then, tactics somersaulting, he soothes the wound with disarming charm that baffles vengeance. With him it is no good pretending to be ruffled because he infallibly recognises a weak defence and is spurred to crisper aggression. Only when the goad is about to prick the nerve intolerably into frenzy is it suddenly withdrawn.)

About ten in the morning the Sonderfuehrer and guards drove him to a large house and led him into a big room. This

[1] German.

was it! At one end was a long table and sitting behind it six solemn officers. Three of them looked like generals (they were). He was not especially perturbed, insulated perhaps by the illogical English arrogance, bred by orderly decades of eminence, which assumed privileges and immunity from illegal international violence.[1]

Sitting on chairs at the other end he noticed the doctor and some soldiers and nurses from the St. Omer hospital. He grinned at them and said a cheerful " Hallo," but they only eyed him sourly. A young Luftwaffe officer motioned him to a lonely chair in front of the table, saying: " Will you please sit down? "

" No, I won't," he answered, conscious that if the officer had told him to stand up he would promptly have sat down.

The judges leaned towards each other and muttered among themselves. A bald, hatchet-faced general in the middle spoke to the Luftwaffe officer who acted as interpreter, and the officer turned to Bader: " Will you swear to tell the truth? "

" No," he answered. " Certainly not."

The officer looked as though he had not heard properly. " I beg your pardon," he said.

" I said certainly not. Go on. Tell the Court."

The officer turned nervously and spoke to the judges, and the bald general's eyebrows shot up.

The officer turned back. " The Herr General wishes to know why you will not tell the truth."

Bader said: " Well, if you're going to ask me questions about the French I will obviously lie."

Another muttered conference. The interpreter seemed to have trouble translating the replies politely. He turned again to Bader. " The Herr General says that the French have already been punished."

(" God," he thought. " What have they done to them! ")

" What the Herr General wishes to know is whether you think the hospital staff were careless when you escaped? "

It suddenly dawned on Bader that it was not he who was

[1] I once saw a noble lord (who snored abominably) throw his Italian captors into uncertain dismay by *demanding* marmalade for breakfast. He was of the Guards and not sensitive to atmosphere.

being court-martialled. He said: " Look, who is being court-martialled here? "

The interpreter looked surprised. " Why, the hospital staff, of course."

After that it was easy. He turned on the charm and explained that it was not reasonable to punish the hospital chaps because, of course, they couldn't guess he was going to climb out of the window. They had been very correct, posted a guard at his door and taken all proper precautions in the circumstances. Of course, it was easy to be wise after the event.

He felt he could almost hear the roars of applause from behind.

When he had finished and the Sonderfuehrer took him out, the hospital staff beamed at him. Thereafter the guards never left his side and there was no chance of bolting.

Back at Dulag, the first thing he asked was: " How's the tunnel getting on? "

Lubbock said it was plodding along quite nicely.

Hands in pockets, Bader was idly leaning in a doorway three days later when a Luftwaffe captain called Muller passed. Bader kept his hands in his pockets and his pipe in his mouth. Muller stopped, turned and said: " Ving Commander Bader, you should salute me."

" Why? "

" All prisoners of war should salute German officers."

Bader said shortly: " The Geneva Convention says I have to salute enemy officers of equal or senior rank. You're only a captain."

" I am the Kommandant's representative and you should salute me."

" I don't salute the Kommandant either," Bader remarked disagreeably. " He's only a major."

" Those are the Kommandant's orders ! " (angrily).

" I don't give a damn if they are. They're wrong and I'm damned if I'm going to salute you."

Half an hour later an orderly came in and told him to be ready to leave Dulag Luft in twenty minutes.

25

FOR TWO days he sat glowering on the hard boards of a third-class train that travelled through endless drizzle to Lübeck. Off-loading him there into a farm wagon they trundled him across bleak sandy flats to the lonely, barbed-wire compound of Oflag VIB, where they took his fingerprints, watch and signet ring (the last thing he had from his father) and turned him loose among some 400 thin and half-starved British officers behind the wire.

There the real misery started. Lübeck camp received no Red Cross parcels and was ruled by a gaunt, cropped Kommandant who had already achieved fame by saying that the Geneva Convention for the protection of prisoners of war had been drawn up by a lot of old women and he had no intention of observing it.

A few of the inmates were R.A.F. (most were Army), but he knew none of them. The huts were much the same as the ramshackle wooden affairs at Dulag Luft and there seemed nothing to do except talk and think about when the next meal was coming, though that gave little satisfaction when it did arrive. An entire day's food consisted of three slices of black bread with a scrape of margarine, a couple of potatoes and some soup. Now and then there was *Blutwurst* (blood sausage). There were supposed to be other rations but the guards stole them.

One of the guards shot a prisoner in the thigh for picking up a ball over the warning wire[1] and a Feldwebel rushed up to the guard and shook his hand. It was that kind of camp.

Two days after Bader arrived there Lubbock and Pete Gardner walked dolorously in.

[1] Ten yards inside the barbed wire ran the single strand of the warning wire. The No Man's Land in between was " *streng verboten.*"

" What the hell happened to the tunnel?" Bader demanded.

They looked disgusted and said that just after he had left, a posse of guards had trooped into the cage, gone straight to the trap-door under the bed and wrecked everything with patronising smiles. They even knew who the tunnellers were —hence their arrival.

In the next dreary month Bader adjusted to the new life. Surrendering no fraction of his passion to renew the Tangmere days he wasted little time in crying over spilt milk. As years before he had accepted the loss of his legs so he accepted now the loss of freedom, heartened by the thought this time that there was hope of a cure—escape. He talked about it a lot with men who had been a year or more behind the wire, absorbing what lore they had gathered on the subject and learning that getting out was only half the battle. The other half lay in getting beyond the reach of Germans, and that was the harder half.

Early in October the Germans bundled the whole camp into cattle trucks for transport to a new cage at Warburg, near Cassel, where they were concentrating all British officer prisoners. People were as excited as schoolboys going on holiday. It lifted the tedium and gave hope of better conditions. Also, there were ways of bolting from locked cattle-trucks; that is, ways for the nimble, not for the legless. During the night some of the Air Force officers sawed a hole in the floor of a truck with a jagged knife and during a brief halt several dropped out of it and ran into the darkness. Bader envied them until one man misjudged as the train started and it ran over him, cutting off both legs. He died soon after.

Warburg was a huge cage a quarter of a mile square holding 3,000 men in thirty of the same huts in the same dirt and squalor. But Warburg had Red Cross parcels, enough to give each man a good meal a day as well as the German food, plus chocolate and cigarettes. Print can hardly convey the effect of having real food every day: it killed something that gnawed at the mind as well as the stomach. The compound had a clear patch too where men played rugger and Bader found now that it no longer hurt to watch, unable to play. Unobtrusively the years had softened that blow and he was an eager and vocally critical spectator.

But confinement was a growing ordeal. Others could let off steam tunnelling for escape, by playing rugger, or by horse-play or walking mile after mile round the beaten circuit just inside the warning wire. Not Bader. The stumps had not taken kindly to captivity, having shrunken a little with hunger. They chafed more easily and there was little powder and no Elastoplast. There was no outlet for his brimming vigour. A lot of the time he spent on his bunk with a book in the tiny end room like a cubicle he shared with Lubbock and Gardner, who helped him with his chores.

At last a letter from Thelma. (Mail was very delayed.) She did not say much about the wing, of course, except that he was still badly missed, but she had had a letter from Woodhall which said: " I am delighted to be able to tell you that Douglas has been awarded a Bar to his D.F.C. As a matter of fact, the recommendation was in type the day he was posted as missing and so I had to hang on to it until I knew he was safe, and then it was forwarded and awarded."[1]

(That made him the third man in history to win Bars to both D.S.O. and D.F.C.)

A letter came too from the little Yorkshire boy, Norman Rowley. " I am sorry that they take your legs away so that you cannot escape. My mum says she will do that to me, too, if I don't be good and come home at the proper time. I have got one leg now and am getting on all right like you said. One day soon I will get the other one. With love from Norman."

Warburg had an escape committee headed by a tank major and Bader talked earnestly with them for hours on the subject of getting out, finding, a little grimly, that his legs barred him from most schemes. Unlike others he had little chance of walking out of the gates in disguise; his lurching roll was too familiar. He was game enough to try but not agile enough to succeed in other hare-brained ideas such as scaling ladders over the wires or stowing away, contorted, under a food wagon. Such chances had to go to those with more prospects of success. He could not tunnel, but he could at least crawl through one. The difficulty there was to find a tunnel that surfaced beyond the wire. His name was down for several. Eager syndicates

---

[1] Had Bader been killed when he was shot down the Bar to the D.F.C. could not have been awarded. Only V.C.s can be awarded posthumously.

were always digging them and at this time hawk-eyed Germans were always finding and wrecking them.

It was disillusioning, and even worse when the first snow fell and the escape committee had to bank the fires of their activities until next spring. No point wasting good ideas in getting out to be stranded in snow 500 miles from the nearest friendly frontier. One had to be able to sleep out. Bader found it getting harder to damp his unrest.

One outlet still remained—"Goon-baiting."[1] He found relief in the sport. With exuberance he tersely provoked all Germans except "Gremlin George," the Lageroffizier,[2] who had been a prisoner in the last war and was tolerant and sympathetic because he understood.

His chief butt was Hauptmann Harger, a large, red-faced, red-necked man known as "Horrible Harger, the —— of the Lager," with whom he had violent brushes which culminated in a day when Bader refused to stand out in the snow for half an hour on *appell*.[3] Harger found him in his room and angrily ordered him out and in a brief shouting match Bader flatly refused to budge, saying: "My feet would get cold in the snow. If you want to count me, come to my room and do it."

Harger shouted: "You . . . vill . . . go . . . on . . . *appell*," drew his pistol and levelled it.

The antennæ warned that the time had come and Bader suddenly turned on the glowing goodwill and beamed. "Well, of *course* I'll go on *appell* if you really want me to." He picked up a stool and stumped off to plant it on the snow and sit among his squad, leaving Harger seething.

Bader had found a new game, and on more than one occasion after that he goaded his captors into drawing their pistols and then disarmed them by pricking the strained bladder of their ire with maddening charm and last-minute surrender. It was a crafty technique that left a taste of moral defeat in the man who lost his temper.

Gremlin George was distressed at seeing the legless man sitting in the snow on *appell*. He said it was not correct or gentlemanly and it humiliated Germany. Thereafter he let

---

[1] To prisoners, Germans were always "Goons." It was a satisfying name.
[2] Officer in charge of the compound.
[3] Roll call by count.

Bader stay in his room for *appell*, which induced the man from time to time to go out and join the others in the snow, where soon he provoked Harger into drawing his pistol again. It was the only way left of fighting back.

Around Christmas time Lubbock and Gardner came to him, and said: " Look, we've got an idea for escape. Would you like to come with us? "

" What, in winter? "

" Yes. Why not? "

Bader said: " I'm in."

Lubbock explained the plot. Just outside the barbed-wire gate was a clothing store hut where occasionally prisoners were taken under guard to draw kit. Gardner, a born lock-breaker, had discovered how to open a spare room in the hut and the idea was for the three of them, together with a Commando captain, Keith Smith, to go on a clothing parade, lock themselves in the empty room till darkness, then climb out of the window, walk up a lighted road past some German huts (hoping no one came out) and then melt into the shadows beyond. Just down the road was Doessel railway station where they could catch a train down into occupied France and contact the Underground. Sounded easy, worked out like that. The escape committee had promised them several hundred smuggled marks, maps, a compass and forged passes, and Lubbock (son-in-law of the nutrition expert Lord Boyd-Orr) would bake an escape cake from hoarded food that would keep them going for days.

Everyone said they were mad to try in winter but on 9th January, when thin snow carpeted the frosty ground, they marched through the gate with a clothing parade to the hut. Someone started a loud-voiced diversion and under its cover Gardner picked the lock and the four crowded into the room.

Darkness fell early and the wait was long and cold. About eight o'clock they heard a tremendous clatter of tins by the wire, caused by an unruly young flight lieutenant, Peter Tunstall, giving the signal and creating another diversion. All the searchlights obligingly turned towards the noise and Gardner quietly opened the spare room window. Smith, a baldish six-footer, slipped out first and walked up the lighted path, followed by Lubbock and Bader and then Gardner.

Smith reached the shadows but the others were about fifteen yards short when a German soldier ran out of one of the huts right in front of them, apparently on his way to the latrine. He looked with shocked surprise at the three walking in British greatcoats and started bellowing for help. Germans came pouring out of huts for yards around and the three were seized by a jabbering crowd. Smith had vanished.

They started hustling the three over to the guardroom, and one of the Germans, not realising Bader had artificial legs, thumped him on the toe with a rifle butt to make him hurry. Bader started to laugh and the angry soldier banged harder and harder at his feet with his rifle until one of his comrades explained why it was painless and told him to stop making a fool of himself.

In the guardroom the Hauptmann security officer, a Party member, demanded to know how they had escaped, and Bader said flippantly that they had walked through the wire.

" Did you? " replied the Hauptmann, unamused. " Well, now you can try walking through the bars because you are going into the cells."

He went away to make arrangements and came back slightly flushed. Apparently the cells were already full and there was a waiting list. They would have to go back to the compound and await their turn.

Smith was back in five days, having nearly frozen to death in a cattle truck. He, too, had to wait for the cells.

It was about a month before the three were taken across to the wooden cooler[1] for their ten days' solitary. The cells were the usual things, about as wide as one's outstretched arms, but there were books and Red Cross food and prisoners of the rank of major and above were allowed to smoke (a not un-typical German rule). About the seventh night, after the guard had locked up and gone, Bader was lying on his bunk reading when the door opened. He looked up and was startled to see the face of Gardner.

" Hallo," Gardner grinned, holding up a piece of wire, " I've found out how to open these damn' doors."

Delighted, Bader got up and joined him in the corridor, and they unlocked Lubbock's cell. The three of them cautiously

[1] Cell block.

explored the place, but no Germans were about and only a couple of flimsy doors lay between them and freedom. Bader suggested they make a break for it then and there, but wiser voices prevailed. Snow still lay on the ground, thawing and slushy, and they had no food, maps, compass or money.

" I know," said Bader, " let's finish our time here and wait for the good weather. Then we can all kick that rat Harger in the tail and get sent back. We can smuggle some food and maps in and then make the break."

Brilliant, they all thought. The " Goons " would never expect an escape from the cooler and Harger's blood pressure would doubtless spray out of his ears. Cheerfully they went back to their cells.

Three days later they were released and immediately registered the scheme with the escape committee. The date was set for May.

And then, early in April, they got the chance of going out through a tunnel. It had been dug by Air Force men from a hut on the west side of the camp and was well over a hundred feet long. A week or two before, a digger had prodded a stick up at the end and watchers had seen it come up right under the barbed-wire fence. They had dug on a bit more and now with the weather mild everything seemed ready. One night thirty-five would-be escapers collected in the hut, Bader in a tunic roughly recut to look like a civilian jacket.

Lubbock said: " You'll never get through, Douglas. There's a right-angled turn at the bottom of the shaft and it's very small."

" Well, dammit," he said, " I'll take my legs off."

" Good idea," enthused Lubbock. " I'll come after you with your legs."

A Czech flight lieutenant crawled through to break out the far end and about 11 p.m. the tense watchers from the hut windows were appalled to see his head poke furtively out of the ground just outside the wire and almost in the middle of the sentry path. He bobbed back in alarm and for a while there was whispering confusion down in the tunnel. Then two other men poked their heads out, saw the sentries' backs were turned, nipped out and hared off into the darkness beyond the lights. Two more followed, then another one.

No more. The sentries were never walking away from each other again that night. Yet, strangely they did not stumble across the hole until dawn and by that time the rest of the would-be escapers had sneaked back to their own huts.

So it had to be the cooler scheme.

They were getting ready for it when a dismaying kitchen rumour buzzed round the compound that some Air Force officers were being moved to a new camp, Stalag Luft III, at Sagan, between Berlin and Breslau. That evening Germans confirmed it and before anything could be done they were shepherding an enraged Bader and fifty others on to the train. This time they moved them in carriages, under observation, and no one escaped.

Stalag Luft III was a little cage of six huts for officers and another one next door for N.C.O.s, all on barren grey Silesian sand, hedged from the world by spindly pine trees. The aspect did not charm. As they walked in, a lean, rangy figure walked up to Douglas with outstretched hand and the wry, twisted smile he so well remembered.

"Hallo, Douglas," said Harry Day, more hawk-faced than ever, "I thought you'd catch up some day."

Behind him appeared Bob Tuck, still debonair in silk scarf.

Being among old chums helped soothe him a little. The Warburg contingent took over one of the huts and Day and the compound "Big X",[1] Jimmy Buckley, came over to talk escape.

Almost before people in the hut had unpacked they had started tunnelling under a stove in the room opposite Bader. Other ambitious tunnels were already under way in the compound, but it was slow work because six inches under the grey topsoil lay bright yellow sand which came up in bucket-loads and was a devil to hide from German eyes. Also, Stabsfeldwebel Glemnitz, the leathery-faced chief German ferret,[2] was a shrewd man who had microphones buried round the wire so that tunnels had to be about thirty feet deep.

There was nothing Bader could do in the tunnels; he could only "stooge" outside as a sentry, feeling rather futile. Then

[1] Escape Committees were becoming known as the "X Organisation" and the leaders were known as "Big X." It was for security, not for drama.

[2] Ferrets were the blue-overalled German security guards who ceaselessly snooped round the compounds with torches and probes (for locating tunnels).

Glemnitz found two of the tunnels, including the one in Bader's hut.

His early hopes of getting away were shrinking further, the glorious days of the past receding under the grey present and probable future. Even if he did get out he was beginning to realise how conspicuous he would look; they would only have to take his trousers down to see who he was. He began to get a stiflingly trapped feeling.

Inevitably it inflamed his " Goon-baiting," and his scores of admirers, notably the Warburg contingent, followed his example. When German squads strode past singing their marching songs he organised bands to whistle opposition tunes and put them out of step. When Germans found a tunnel and started filling it in he had prisoners gathered round singing " Heigh-ho, heigh-ho, it's off to work we go." When the Germans ordered all shutters closed at dusk he wanted the camp to tear them all off and throw them into the middle of the compound, and had a violent argument about this with Harry Day, who was in an awkward position. Day himself had a streak of the fiery rebel and would have loved to have torn the shutters off, but he also had the job of keeping the Germans reasonably placated so the prisoners could retain privileges to help escape work. He put a firm foot down about the shutters but there were arguments on both sides (mostly favouring Day).

Camp opinion divided; there were the turbulent rebels devoted to Bader who believed in riling the Germans at every chance and others, some who wanted only peace and some, the wise cool heads, who wanted a judicial amount of Goon-baiting mixed with enough tact and co-operation to ensure peace for escape work.

Bader still desperately wanted to escape. He went to the " X Committee " with a scheme for a " blitz " tunnel to be dug in a night by himself, Lubbock and Gardner from a trench near the warning wire.

" How are you going to get away after that? " someone asked.

" The other two can get on each side and help me into the woods," Bader explained eagerly. " Then we go across country."

The Committee turned it down and Bader later growled to Day: " They say I'm no good for that scheme. It's a lot of ——s."

He went on with the Goon-baiting, backed loyally by many others, and life was a series of uproars. Now and then a German got him chatting in his room and on those occasions Bader was perfectly charming, just to show that he felt no personal grudge. But his pride was touchy. One day he was talking quite pleasantly with his arms folded to the Kommandant, Oberst Von Lindeiner, when the mild Lageroffizier, Hauptmann Pieber, came up, and said: " Wing Commander, you should stand at attention when you speak to the Kommandant."

Bader turned and snapped: " When I want you to teach me manners, I'll ask you. Until then, shut up! "

Von Lindeiner was an erect, elderly soldier of the old school, very fair and correct, but, as the baiting campaign worsened, inevitably the reprisals started and the compound lost privileges such as staying outside the huts after dusk, keeping Red Cross tins and others. There was a chance that this might affect escape work, but Bader dogmatically stuck to his view that maximum non-co-operation and baiting were the best ways of exasperating the enemy.

Something had to happen.

Pieber came in one day with Glemnitz and found him by the wire.

" Herr Wing Commander, you are leaving the camp. You must be ready to go in the morning."

" Oh, am I? Where am I going? " Bader demanded.

Pieber was vague. " We are taking you somewhere you will be more comfortable—it is not comfortable here "— tartly—" for anyone."

Bader grunted. " Well, I'd rather live in a pigsty with my friends than in a palace alone. I'm not going."

" The Kommandant says you must go."

" You take me to the Kommandant."

" He will see you on the way out to-morrow."

" No, he damn' well won't. Not unless he drags me out. I'm staying here."

Glemnitz angrily snapped an order and a guard cocked his rifle and aimed at Bader's chest. Abruptly the atmosphere was electric as the word to fire trembled on the German's lips and Bader knew he had gone too far. This time he would not give way but glared, defiant and stubborn, feeling bitterly he didn't give a damn if they fired. The seconds dragged and then Pieber snapped the tension, telling the guard to lower his rifle. He added: "We will see about this. You will go." And stalked out.

That evening the camp buzzed with crisis. There seemed no easy way out. Bader said he was not going and if necessary would jump into the compound firepool, throw his legs out and defy the Germans to get him. Somehow the Germans heard and knew they would be ridiculed floundering about in a pool after a legless man. What could they do? Von Lindeiner was too humane to shoot him in cold blood. In any case, that would lose the Germans far more than dignity throughout the world. They were nonplussed by a man who should have been in a wheel-chair, but even as a disarmed prisoner was an unmanageable and implacable enemy. They even feared that a man of his type might lead a mass rush on the guards.

In the morning you could feel the tension. Hours passed. Nothing happened. Then, towards evening, a company of guards in battle-order marched out of the Kommandantur[1] towards the barbed wire, fifty-seven of them in helmets and webbing, with rifles and fixed bayonets. Striding with them was Von Lindeiner, accompanied by nearly all his officers. Prisoners came running up to mass behind the wire. The Germans crashed to a halt outside. Bader stayed in his room. The new S.B.O., Group Captain Massey, went to the gate and talked to the Kommandant while an ominous hush hung over the place.

[1] German administrative compound.

26

MASSEY WENT back to Bader. "There's one thing we might consider," he said. "It only needs a spark to start an incident and someone may be shot."

After that there was only one thing to do. The watchers by the wire saw the legless man come out of his room and stump down the dusty path between the huts. In silence he went up to the gate, passed through and looked around like a man about to call a taxi, then strolled slowly along the ranks of the German squad. "My God," someone said behind the wire, "he's inspecting the bastards."[1]

Bader grinned at the squad and passed on. Von Lindeiner made an impatient gesture and followed with his officers. The tension burst like a bubble and suddenly there was something ludicrous about the sixty armed and armoured men who had come to quell a lone and legless man. A Feldwebel shouted an order. Fifty-six helmeted soldiers turned left and one fool in the front rank turned right. German faces crimsoned, a howl of laughter burst behind the wire and the squad tramped away tasting the ashes of ridicule.

They put Bader in a train and Glemnitz climbed into the compartment as escort. The prisoner turned on his charm and soon the two were chatting amiably.

He said after a while: "Look here, you weren't really going to shoot me yesterday, were you, Dimwits?"

"But of course, Wing Commander," said Glemnitz, who was respected by both sides as a first-class man and soldier.

"You *really* were?"

"Yes, Wing Commander. What else could I do?"

"But for heaven's sake," Bader exclaimed. "In England

---

[1] From Oliver Philpot's eye-witness account in his excellent "Stolen Journey." Philpot was the first of the three to reach safety in the famous "Wooden Horse" escape.

we wouldn't shoot the chap. We'd call a couple of guards and they'd each grab one arm and drag him out."

" Not in Germany," Glemnitz said comfortably. " It would be against an officer's honour to be touched by a soldier. He must be shot."

Bader put that in the back of his mind for the future, though he remembered soldiers at Oflag VIB upsetting officers' honour with rifle butts.

In an hour or so the train stopped at a little halt. Glemnitz motioned him out and they walked a mile along a dusty road to an enormous area of barbed-wire cages. It was Stalag VIIIB—Lamsdorf—where over 20,000 soldiers were imprisoned. Bader was put in a room in Sick Quarters, a hut in a separate cage near the main gate, with another new arrival, John Palmer, a rear-gunner flight lieutenant who needed special treatment for a damaged foot. Palmer was almost a caricature of an English officer, with a cavalry moustache, very blue eyes and a clipped accent.

Through a window a day or so later they watched a party of soldier prisoners march down the road from the big compound and out of the main gate. Bader turned to Duncan, one of the R.A.M.C. doctors, and asked where they were going.

" Oh, only a working party," Duncan said. " Off to some town a few miles away. There are thousands out on them."

" Mightn't be too hard to escape from one of those."

" Hard? " said Duncan. " It's a piece of cake."

Bader looked at Palmer and Palmer looked at Bader, who looked again at Duncan.

" Could *we* get on to one of those parties? "

" Not legally," Duncan said. " But I know of someone who might help."

That afternoon he presented three sergeants of the Lamsdorf " X Committee," and they started talking escape. First, Bader wanted to know, could he and Palmer get out on a working party? "

The leader, eyeing him, said: " You'll excuse me saying so, sir, but you might look a bit obvious going out. Still, I think we could fix something."

A blinding thought struck Bader like a revelation. Leaning

forward, eyes alight, he asked: " Sergeant, do these working parties ever go out to aerodromes? "

In his mind was a vision of the map with Sweden only 350 miles away. Stealing an aeroplane was the God-sent answer. Let the Germans take him to one. And then . . . No days of stumbling among the enemy, hopelessly conspicuous, waiting for the end. No trains with police checks or weary miles to walk. No food or language problems. Just sneak in and take off and—oh, the sweet triumph of landing on friendly ground with a piece of expensive loot and asking the Ambassador for a ticket home!

" Sometimes, sir," said the sergeant. " I see what you mean. Just leave it to us, sir."

Three weeks passed. The hospital was comfortable enough but ineffably boring. From the window Bader and Palmer saw many working parties straggle out of the big cage with their guards bound for the outside world. But before the main gate opened they were all stripped and searched in a hut next to the hospital. That was the catch. With his legs he would never pass a search stripped. Moodily he used to watch other prisoners sweeping the road right up to the main gates, and an idea began to dawn. He told the sergeant " Big X," who grinned approvingly.

The sergeant arrived one night with two tough-looking sergeant pilots—an Australian, Keith Chisholm, and an Englishman, Hickman (whom Bader had known in the Shell Company in London before the war).

" Now, look, sir," the army sergeant said, " there's a light working party going out to an aerodrome near Gleiwitz, up on the German-Polish- border. Just the sort of thing you want, simple stuff like cutting grass and so on. If you and Mr. Palmer would like to join . . ."

Bader and Palmer said that they would.

The sergeant indicated the two sergeant-pilots. " These two chaps are going and a Palestinian who is a Polish-Jew and speaks fluent Polish. They're all going to escape into Poland and they've all got false identities. We'll fix you up with the same."

Two days later he smuggled brooms and army battledress to them and that night Palmer shaved his moustache off.

The morning was warm and sunny, and they lounged on the front step of the hut, trying to look casual and brimming inside with excitement. The working party marched out of the big cage and the escort nudged them into the next door hut to be searched. Bader and Palmer grabbed their brooms, sauntered into the road and started sweeping. One by one the working party emerged from the hut and gathered in a loose knot by the verge. Bader and Palmer swept their way into them. The last man out of the hut dropped his kit which scattered over the ground. He started swearing loudly. The guards looked and laughed. Bader and Palmer handed their brooms to two of the working party who swept nonchalantly on through the others, back towards the big cage. The swearer gathered up the last of his kit, the guards yelled " Komm! Komm! " and the party marched up to the main gate. The escort showed passes, an Unteroffizier counted heads, swung open the gates and they walked through, breaking down the pace to a casual amble and clustering round the limping Private Fenton, alias Wing Commander Bader.

Someone took his kitbag and he whispered: " For God's sake none of you chaps call me ' sir.' I'm just one of you."

" Don't worry, mate," said Chisholm. " We're already a wake-up to that."

Into a train then at the little wayside halt, and as they rattled and swayed across the country for three hours he hugged the thought that the Germans were taking him to an aeroplane; in fact, were insisting on doing so. There came a sobering thought. It wouldn't take the Germans long to miss him and perhaps they'd put two and two together. He'd have to move fast.

On a blazing hot August afternoon they came to the grimy industrial town of Gleiwitz and started the two-mile uphill walk to the airfield. Within two minutes he was sweating freely and that started his leg chafing. A lanky New Zealand private called Lofty got alongside and helped him along, the others clustering round to hide them from the guards.

The leg was hurting him like that dreadful night in St. Omer and Lofty, pouring with sweat himself, was almost lifting and carrying him. Even so Bader was nearly finished when they came to two huts in a tiny barbed-wire cage isolated like a poor relation on the fringe of what looked like a military camp. No signs of an airfield anywhere. Other prisoners came out to greet them as he staggered through the gate, and sagging with fatigue he asked one of them: " Where's the aerodrome? "

The soldier nodded his head across a rise in the ground. " 'Bout a mile over there, mate."

" What sort of aeroplanes? "

" Gawd knows," shrugged the soldier. " They never let us anywhere near the airfield. We never even see it."

In disappointment, pain and exhaustion he found a room with Palmer, Chisholm and the other two.

An hour later, reviving fast, he said to Palmer: " We'll go with the other three when they nip off into Poland. If we can find some partisans we might get a wireless message back to England and maybe they'll send an aircraft over one night to pick us up."

A British sergeant had been in the cage some time as camp leader and he came into Bader's room. " We won't let the others know who you are, sir," he said. " It's safer that way. But it won't be so easy to hide it from the Germans. It's hard manual labour here, moving bricks, digging foundations, filling trucks and things like that."

Bader knew his limitations well enough. The work would be physically impossible.

" I know," said the sergeant, with joyful inspiration; " you can be lavatory man."

Bader stared at him.

" One chap's allowed to stay behind to clean the latrines and huts," the sergeant explained. " You can be him. We'll say you've been shot in the knee and can't walk properly.

Bader started laughing. How the mighty are fallen. " All right," he said.

Chisholm had been walking round spying out the land and came back to report. The wire was only a single fence instead of a double and just outside it at the back of the cage was a field of high corn. There was a wash-house window only a few feet from the wire and it would be easy at night to crawl out of the window and snake through the wire into the corn— except that two guards kept patrolling the cage.

During breakfast next morning the Palestinian went out

and started talking to one of the guards through the wire. He came back very excited. " He is a Pole, that guard," he said. " Several of the guard company are Poles, forced into uniform by the Germans. He says they will help us. A Polish guard at night will keep the German guard talking on the other side of the compound while we get out."

Bader said: " To-night! "

" No. Not to-night. Two Poles are on guard and it would look suspicious. He is frightened the Germans would shoot them."

" To-morrow? "

" No. There are two Germans on. But the night after will be a German and a Pole."

This was Monday. They set the date for Wednesday.

Germans arrived shouting: " Raus! Raus! " to muster the day's working party and as Bader watched them march out a grinning Cockney corporal thrust a bucket and mop into his hands. " 'Ere y'are, Mum," he said. " Get cracking."

He quite enjoyed himself sloshing out the latrines, not caring if he got his feet wet. It did not seem so odd in this camp for the noted wing commander to be washing lavatories —most of the prisoners had been captured at Dunkirk and had never even heard of him. The only thing that bothered him was whether the Germans would follow the trail from Lamsdorf before Wednesday night. Thinking about it only made it worse.

At evening the workers came back and he asked Palmer, who was sweaty and grimy: " Did you see any aeroplanes? "

" Didn't even see the ruddy aerodrome," Palmer said disgustedly.

The next day passed quietly enough. Same fears. Same routine. At sunset the Palestinian talked to the Polish guard who was going off duty and learned that the lone Pole who would be " on " with a German the following night would do what they wanted.

Morning dawned, warm and sunny, perfect weather for escaping, but the day dragged interminably. At last about five-thirty the working party came back and the five rested in their room with the familiar zero-hour feeling fluttering in their stomachs.

At six o'clock boots trampled in the wooden corridor and a German voice shouted: " Efferybody on parade! Efferybody on parade! "

Cursing, wondering what it was all about, the prisoners got to their feet and slowly shambled out. Raggedly they assembled on the trodden ground by the gate, where a Feldwebel stood watching and as they settled down he opened his mouth and shouted: " Everybody will take their trousers down."

The men who did not know burst into incredulous chorus, whistles, catcalls, rude remarks and giggles, but the order seemed to hit Bader in the pit of the stomach. He looked across at the sergeant camp leader who looked back and muttered: " Hold tight, sir. I'll order the men to refuse."

" And get yourself shot," Bader said wryly. " Thanks, sergeant, but it's no use. They still wouldn't take five minutes to pick me out."

He swung round but yards of open space separated him from the possible shelter of the hut. No chance of getting there. No escape at all. The mind buzzed furiously and he knew he could not stand the indignity. Heaving himself forward he stumped up to the Feldwebel and said: " I think I'm the chap you're looking for."

The Feldwebel stared as though he could not believe it and at that moment a Hauptmann from Lamsdorf and six guards tramped through the gate. The Hauptmann saw Bader, re-cognised him and his eyes lit up. " Ah, Ving Commander, I am *delighted* to see you again. Gootness, you *haf* caused troubles."

He was very friendly, even when he suddenly added: " Now perhaps Mr. Palmer vould come forvard as vell."

" Good Lord," said Bader. " Has Johnny Palmer escaped too? "

" No more troubles, please, Ving Commander," the Haupt-mann said tolerantly. " Otherwise we take you all back to Lamsdorf to check up."

It struck him instantly that that would wreck the escape plans of the other three.[1] A moment's furious thought. No

---

[1] That night the other three escaped as planned and soon made contact with Polish partisans. Later the Germans caught the Palestinian and Hickman and shot them. Chisholm, after two years of extraordinary adventures fighting with the Poles (including a gallant part in the deadly uprising in Warsaw), got back to England and was awarded the Military Medal.

way out. He turned to the men and called: " Come on, Johnny. It's all over."

Palmer shuffled disconsolately out of the ranks, the guards closed round and the two were led away.

The trip back to Lamsdorf was glum, though the Germans were friendly enough right up to the time they prodded them into the Lamsdorf guardroom and the Kommandant came in. Or rather, the Kommandant swept in like a tornado, in a towering anger, a tall, cropped, fine-looking man of about sixty, with cold deep eyes and a tight-lipped mouth that opened and started shouting in German the instant he saw them. He stood in front of them, the tirade pouring out till little flecks of foam flew off his lips. It went on and on, and on, and the interpreter standing beside him had no chance of getting in a word. Palmer still had a cigarette in his mouth and as the Kommandant shouted he drew on it, puffed smoke just past the Kommandant's cheek, turned rudely away to Bader, and said in an extremely British voice: " D'you know, I haven't the faintest idea what this fellow's saying."

Bader started to giggle and the Kommandant crimsoned. His voice rose in explosive fury. At last he stopped to draw breath, and the interpreter stepped forward and spoke a stern summary:

" The Kommandant says you have both disgraced the honour of an officer by dressing yourself up as common soldiers and that you have caused a great deal of trouble."

Bader said: " Well, will you tell the Kommandant that it's my job to cause him trouble."

The interpreter was tactless enough to do so and the Kommandant turned a rich red and loosed off another tirade until they thought he was going to have an apoplectic fit. At last he threw his arms in the air and shouted " *Arrestzellen! Arrestzellen!*" then spun round and strode off.

One of the few German words that Bader was familiar with was the expression for arrest cells.

Soon they were in familiar surroundings. An officer pulled open a cell door and Bader peered distastefully in at the familiar interior. With a sudden idea he said: " Just a minute. I'm not going in there. These are common soldiers' cells. It is most incorrect putting an officer in them."

The German security officer said politely: " Ve do not usually haf officer prisoners at Lamsdorf und therefore ve do not haf officers' cells."

" I can't help that," Bader said. " If I'm to have a cell I demand an officer's cell. I understand my honour has already been sufficiently disgraced."

" Look, Ving Commander," the German said wearily, " ve haf had a lot of troubles vith you and vith the Kommandant. He vas going to take your legs, but I haf talked to him und he has cooled down. If there are more troubles he vill take your legs."

" I can't help that either. Anyway, I demand a spring bed, not that damned plank."

" Please go in, Ving Commander, und ve vill deal vith it to-morrow."

" No, I won't. I want a spring bed, I want a table, I want proper food and a proper chair. And while we're on the subject I want a sentence. You haven't sentenced me yet and that is most incorrect. I demand to know how long I'm in here for."

The German, by some miracle keeping his temper, raised his eyes to the ceiling, muttering: " *Mein Gott!* " He said with resignation: " Vait here, Ving Commander. I go and get, not, I think, for your sake, the Kommandant, but the second in command." He strode out and Bader and Palmer waited with the guards.

Soon a dapper, red-faced German major came in and said fluently and heartily: " I'm sorry about this, Wing Commander, but I'll tell you what we'll do. You can have a spring bed, a chair and a table, proper food and a book to read and I'll send you a servant. A batman. And to-morrow morning we will also sentence you. How's that? "

" Good," Bader said. " I'll wait outside the cell till you get them."

Soon they brought spring mattress, table and chair, and he went in and the cell door locked.

Soon there came a thunderous knocking on it and he yelled: " Come in." He heard the bolts being withdrawn, the door opened and in the frame, filling it, was the rotund figure of a young man with a round, red face and glasses. He was in British battledress and said in strong Scots' accent: " Guid after-rnoon, sir. My name is Ross. I've been detailed to look after-r you. I've br-rought you some tea." He had a great mug of it in his hand.

That night, thinking it over, Bader felt some of his hate slipping. He had to admit that some of the Germans were incredibly decent and reasonable, and had a passable sense of humour.

In the morning he and Palmer were taken before the Kommandant who, cool and correct now, sentenced each to ten days' solitary. Bader again tried the gambit about the incorrectness of putting an officer in a soldiers' cell block and the Kommandant stiffly apologised. He did not have the correct cells so they would have to make do as they were. He hoped, a shade sardonically, that they would be comfortable.

The days in the cell seemed interminable, and remembering the Battle of Britain and with the old frustration rising in him again like a tide, the hate came back. The only bright factor was Ross, who was loyal, willing and unselfish, bringing tea and gossip and spreading a respectful but companionable cheerfulness.

On the ninth day the cell door opened and the Kommandant appeared. Bader got up from his bunk and they exchanged polite salutes. The Kommandant said: "I have some good news for you, Wing Commander. To-morrow you go to an *Offizierlager*."[1]

"Oh." Bader was interested. "Whereabouts, Herr Oberst?"

"The Offizierlager IVC. at Kolditz."

Bader knew that one.

"Oh, you mean the *Straflager?*"[2]

The Kommandant looked shocked. "*Nein, nein, Herr Oberstleutnant, Der Sonderlager.*"[3]

Bader started to laugh and then the Kommandant started laughing. Both knew well enough that Kolditz Castle, last stop for the naughty boys, was supposed to be escape proof. The Kommandant went out and Bader stopped laughing.

Next day he made one last effort to delay things by demanding an officer of equal rank as escort, but the Kommandant said curtly that the only such officer available was

[1] Officers' Camp.   [2] Punishment Camp.   [3] Special Camp.

himself, and he was the one who was *not* going to Kolditz. It was an elderly Hauptmann who got into the train with him and sat silently picking his teeth under cover of his hand. Ross was there too. When Bader had said he was bound for Kolditz, Ross said equably that it would be a nice change for them. Bader said: " No, Ross. Thank you very much, but it's the punishment camp, you know." Then Ross had argued and argued until Bader had sent a note to the Kommandant who said Ross could go.

The journey was long and dreary and the Hauptmann never seemed to stop picking his teeth. By the time they got to Kolditz it was dark and the station was blacked out. Then, struggling out of the gloom into the road, Bader looked up and got his first glimpse of the future. The fortress towered over the village, seeming to float in floodlight, enchantingly beautiful like a fairy castle. They moved off along a cobbled road which soon rose so steeply that Ross had to put out his hand and pull him along. He was exhausted when they came to the foot of the great wall that reared above, harsh and scarred in the glare of the floodlamps, giving no inch of cover to any would-be escaper. They trod across a drawbridge over a deep moat into the cavern of a stone archway, out of the light. Heavy doors closed behind with a clanking of iron bars and in the gloom a sense of chill pervaded him. Fortress guards, boots ringing on the stone, led them across a courtyard rimmed by stone, through a tunnel, along a cobbled path, through another gloomy archway into a smaller courtyard hemmed inside towering walls deep in the bowels of the castle, through a door, up stone steps. A German flung a door open and Bader looked into a small, stone cell. He thought: " Oh, God. Is this how we live? Is this the punishment camp? "

27

As a guard motioned him, in a voice behind hailed: "Douglas! There you are!"

He swung round. Geoffrey Stephenson in an old sweater and army trousers was grinning by the steps. An incredibly warming sight. He looked much the same, though not so dapper, and came bounding up the steps. "Heard you were shot down. Been expecting you. Knew you wouldn't behave."

They were shaking hands, grinning and talking. As a German started to separate them Bader nodded at the cell. "Is this how we live here?"

"Good God, no," Stephenson said. "You'll be out with us to-morrow."

He was hustled away and Bader, feeling better and wanting only to lie down, walked docilely into the cell and the door clanged behind.

In the morning they took him out, photographed, finger-printed and searched him, and handed him over to the hovering Stephenson, who took him upstairs into a large and quite pleasant room with a big window overlooking the inner courtyard.

"Your home," Stephenson announced. "Hope you like it."

In many ways it was the best he had known since becoming a prisoner. He shared it with three others, army officers, one of whom he already knew, George Young, who had been S.B.O. at Lübeck. The four single bunks had shelves over them; there were some wicker chairs and even a dirty brown wallpaper hiding the stone walls. The castle had a good supply of Red Cross food and downstairs one could even get a bath, a thing he had not had for over a year.

Stephenson took him on a conducted tour and the rest was

338

not so good. The grim old castle held then eighty British prisoners, 200 French and over a hundred Poles, Dutch and Belgians, and the only communal recreation space was the cobbled inner courtyard, forty yards long and twenty-two yards wide. All round it the walls towered seventy feet so that the cobbles in winter never saw the sun. He looked through a barred window on the castle's outer wall that was seven feet thick and dropped ninety feet to sheer cliff that dropped another hundred feet to a river. The stories about Kolditz being escape proof looked grimly true. Thirty miles south-east of Leipzig, it stood on a rocky peak that jutted into the river so that the only way out was the road up from the village, and to get to that one had to pass through the other half of the castle where the Germans lived. There were more guards than prisoners.

"Used to be a looney-bin before the war," Stephenson said. "It's quite a few hundred years old. Built by a chap called Augustus the Strong. We don't know much about him except that he was a pretty good performer. Was supposed to have 365 illegitimate children."

"Not surprised," Bader said. "Not much else to do here. What's it like for escape?"

"Damn' difficult. Everyone's trying like hell but only one or two have ever got out. Tunnels are pretty well out, and you have to be a gymnast to get over the roofs. Best trick is probably to try and walk out in disguise but of course your walk would give you away."

Within two days Bader had his first brush with the Germans, who then held two *appells* a day. He told the Lageroffizier, Hauptmann Püpcke, that he was damned if he was going to spend his days lurching up and down the stairs and was so determined that Püpcke finally said he could appear at the window till he was seen and counted. Püpcke was a good-looking elderly six-footer and later became one of the few Germans Bader liked.

He had a long and depressing talk with George Young and a resolute-looking tank captain, Dick Howe, who ran the " X Committee." Howe, a brilliant and unselfish escape organiser, pointed out that Kolditz was not like an ordinary camp. Every man was an intractable escape fiend and all sorts of schemes were constantly going on, but even the most acrobatic and the fluent German speakers were having no luck. After that Bader sat back a while to think things out.

Plenty of time for thinking! The days started early with *appell* and a slice of black bread. Then one could sit and look out of a window, or smoke and read, or sit, or walk round the little courtyard like an animal in a zoo. With escape hopes frustrated again he returned like an addict to his old sport and the repetitive theme of life at Kolditz was punctuated by a sort of trumpet *obbligato* of Goon-baiting. Bader was not alone in that; he was merely worse than the others. Nearly every man in Kolditz had his record-card marked " *Deutschfeindlich* "[1] and bands of prisoners known flippantly as " men of spirit " played noisy parts in the orchestrated discords of baiting, with the Maestro Bader making frequent appearances either as conductor or impresario.

Püpcke was not harried much; though alive, he was still regarded as a good German. The main butts were the security officer, a Hauptmann Eggers, and a little major, the second in command, who wore a cloak that gave him a musical comedy look.

For weeks Bader only acknowledged the major's existence by blowing smoke past his cheek when they passed and when the major at last demanded to be saluted Bader pointed out the difference in rank and suggested that if the major liked to wear the Kommandant's uniform into the camp he would salute him.

Often when sufficient sensitive Germans were in the court-yard prisoners in the windows bellowed an aggravating version of the German national anthem: " *Deutschland, Deutschland,* UNTER *alles.*" The taunting voice of Bader was usually identifiable, as it also was when the French started their favourite chorus: " *Où sont les Allemands?* "

A silence till the same voices answered: " *Les Allemands sont dans la merde.*"

" *Qu'on les y enfonce?* "

" *Jusqu'aux oreilles.*"

Bader also used to conduct his own leaflet raids, writing uncomplimentary messages in German on sheets of toilet paper and loosing them in a favourite wind from the Castle's outer windows to float down into the village.

---

[1] Definitely anti-German.

Finally, the little major asked him into his office and with a determined smile suggested that life would be easier for everyone if he would be more courteous and set a better example in future. Bader said he did not think it was exactly his job to influence the prisoners to make things easier for the Germans. He enjoyed the heated debate that followed, though the major did not.

The cheerful but unruly Peter Tunstall had arrived at Kolditz, having at this stage half-achieved his eventual record of six German courts-martial and 360 days in solitary confinement. He and Bader made a natural team. Tunstall had recently discovered an ingenious method of splitting a photograph so that a message could be written on the back, the photograph pasted together again and posted back to England. Bader wrote out a message for Tunstall to transfer to a photograph. It started: " Message from Wing Commander Bader," and included all he knew of conditions in Germany, the effects of bombing, the passage of troop trains and so on, and ended: " The bombing is doing a lot of good. Bomb the bastards to hell."

Tunstall put it in his wallet and a day or two later the Germans sprang a snap search in several rooms. When they tramped into Tunstall's room the wallet was lying loose by his bunk; he ran to grab it, but too conspicuously, and a German said: " Give that to me! " Tunstall flung it out of the window but it fell at the feet of Hauptmann Eggers and Eggers walked off with it.

It was all a little disconcerting, but nothing happened for three weeks, and Bader was beginning to think that nothing was going to happen when Eggers shook him awake at six o'clock one morning, saying: " Get up, Ving Commander. Ve are taking you to Leipzig."

" What the hell for? " Being woken early did not improve his temper.

" *Befehl ist Befehl*," Eggers said cryptically.

He was taken in a car with guards on each side, and it would have been good to be out of the grim old fortress but for the edge of uncertainty in him. In a room in Leipzig he faced a lean, severe German officer behind a desk, and the antennæ signalled that it was a moment for wariness. The officer stared at a paper on his desk, then looked up and fixed him with a cold eye.

" I have two charges against you, Wing Commander. The first is that since you have been at Oflag IVC. you have incited other officers to disobey and misbehave, and discipline has become very bad." His voice was impressively icy. " What do you say to a charge of inciting mutiny? "

" I don't know what you're talking about."

" Well, now, I have a much more serious charge against you." A pause. " The charge of espionage! "

Another silence.

" We have captured a message you were trying to send home with items of military value."

Leaning forward, Bader could just see on the desk the paper he had given Tunstall. The last line was heavily underscored and he remembered his provocative remark about the bombing.

" Military information! " the German repeated. " Trying to send that message back is espionage and this will have serious consequences for you. You can be shot for it."

With sudden inspiration Bader turned on a smile that he did not quite feel and said derisively, " Don't talk absolute nonsense. Here I am, a British officer, in your custody, where I've been for a long time, in uniform all the time. . . . How can you possibly charge a captured officer in uniform with espionage? "

The point did not seem to have occurred to the German and he looked momentarily uncertain, then returned to the attack. " Nevertheless, you tried to get information back."

" I *would* try," Bader said. " So would anyone. But it doesn't make me a spy. Here I am. You see me in uniform. You're holding me. How can you possibly charge me as a spy? "

They argued about it for some time until the prisoner became too domineering and the German stood up and snapped: " That is enough. You must be ready to go to a war court in Berlin on this matter."

Bader walked out buoyantly enough but on the way back to Kolditz in the car he was not so confident. Half-way back he was stirred by a thought. . . . It would be rather neat to escape and miss the whole unpleasant business.

During the next two days he was seen muttering to Geoffrey Stephenson and Peter Storie-Pugh, a young army lieutenant. Then they discussed the scheme with Dick Howe's escape committee. They would crawl out of an attic window on to the steep roof high over the courtyard and away from the searchlights, scramble somehow up on to the ridge and crawl from there till they could drop into the German part of the castle. Then, skulking through the shadows and climbing over more roofs they would reach a point where the cable of a lightning conductor stretched to the ground a hundred feet below. After sliding down this they would drop by rope forty feet into the dry bed of the moat, climb over a couple of barbed-wire fences and terraces sown with anti-personnel mines and then make for Switzerland. Would the escape committee be good enough to cough up some German marks, forged papers and other details?

" You can't do it," Howe tried to explain tactfully. " Two or three teams have had a go at somewhat similar schemes and damn' nearly broken their necks. They were athletes in good training. I'm sorry, but with your legs you just couldn't make it."

" Absolute tripe," Bader snorted. " Of course I could."

After a turbulent discussion the committee sensibly suggested that they could not cough up the marks and forged papers (which were in short supply).

A few days later Bader was involved with some Poles trying to find a way out of the fortress through the sewer pipes. One of the Poles, Ravinski, lowered himself through a grating into the sewers and snaked through the slimy pipes looking for an outlet. He was back in an hour, reporting that the pipe got narrower and narrower until he could squeeze no farther. However, there were other pipes and he would try again. Ravinski's surveys of the maze lasted several days but each new lead either narrowed or ended in concrete dead-ends, and they knew dolefully that they would find no way out through the sewers.

After that Bader realised the futility of banging his head against a barred window, and under the bravura his practical sense accepted that he was not likely to escape from Kolditz. Though it did not make him any pleasanter to the Germans, he stopped fretting about the Tangmere wing and the fighting. Now it all belonged to another world.

Once he had faced it there were compensations. Swinburne was one; an odd escape for a man of action who seemed such an extrovert, but the dormant crannies of reflection were sensitised by adversity. Thelma, knowing him, had sent volumes of poetry and he read them nearly every day, never tiring of the sardonic Swinburne mocking fate. That was the thing!

> For the glass of the years is brittle wherein we
> gaze for a span;
> A little soul for a little bears up this corpse
> which is man.

If a demon disguised as fame was the spur, there was also armour for the flank. And if the past called too hurtfully he found another answer from Robert W. Service:

> Have ever you stood where the silences brood
> And vast the horizons begin.
> At the dawn of the day to behold far away
> The goal you would strive for and win?
> Yet, ah, in the night when you gain to the height
> With the vast pool of heaven star-spawned,
> Afar and agleam like a valley of dream
> Still mocks you a land of beyond.

(Till the day he dies he will remember each word of those pages and more.)

Other things helped too. The prisoners' secret radio had told them of Alamein and Stalingrad and every day it was becoming clearer that the days of wondering if the war would ever end were over.

An army officer wrote in a letter home: " I had tea to-day with Douglas Bader and came away feeling as though I'd been having cocktails."

The thought of the Berlin court-martial still gnawed a little but there was nothing he could do about that either except put on a brazen face and keep asking Eggers tauntingly: " Well, how's the court-martial going, Eggers? " The Hauptmann kept assuring him meaningly that he would hear as soon as the Germans heard. Perhaps the Ving Commander would not be so happy then. Bader privately agreed.

Then came the day that Eggers, bracing himself to an unwelcome task, told him stiffly that the court-martial had been dropped (because the charge was " frivolous "). Bader, hiding his relief but not his glee, said wickedly: " *Hard* luck, Eggers. Frightfully hard luck! "

Stoolball was another diversion—a rough one; strictly a Kolditz game, devised to let off steam. In the cobbled courtyard two teams battled for a football, inhibited only by the flimsiest of rules which forbade actual slaying but approved of temporary throttling—or would have approved had there been such a refinement as a referee. There were no touchlines; one either bounced with dull thuds off the stone walls or was scraped off. Goals were scored by touching a stool with the ball at either end and the goalkeepers sat on the stools, thrusting vigorously with arms and legs till the avalanche of bodies threw them off on to the cobbles. Unable to join the mid-field mêlée Bader was an ardent goalkeeper and many plunging pates recoiled dizzily after contact with his metal legs. Eventually Dick Howe's intelligent but impregnable skull dented his right kneecap. Bader hammered the metal out again, but it kept getting dented, and at last he had to give the game up rather than be left with a permanently broken leg.

He was already having other trouble with his legs and the Germans escorted him to a village workshop for running repairs. As he later wrote to Thelma: " The leg crisis has passed. A little man has riveted a plate over that crack in the knee. You might tell the chaps who made the leg that I completely dismantled the knee, the brake and the freewheel and greased and reassembled the lot. It is a very well-made job, the freewheel is most ingenious, but I do want another right leg, sweetheart."

But in London the mould of his right thigh had been destroyed by bombing. The firm of J. E. Hanger and Co. (who now supplied his legs) tried tirelessly all sorts of ingenious methods of making another one (including telegraphed measurements through the Red Cross), but it just could not be done. They were, however, able to get a spare left leg to him through the Red Cross.

Bader began to suffer from the lack of exercise and outlet. It was partly mental. Even others found it bad enough walking round the sloping, uneven cobbles, but to him it was becoming intolerably irksome and bad for the legs. With the S.B.O.'s approval he asked the Germans if they would let him out for walks on parole, and after havering for a while the Germans, to their credit, sportingly overlooked his intransigence and agreed, even to letting him take another British officer for company. They did it probably partly out of kindness, certainly out of respect, and possibly because they thought it would make him a little less disconcerting.

As companion he chose Peter Dollar, a ruddy-faced lieutenant-colonel with whom he had become friends,[1] and they signed parole chits and were taken to the castle door where they found a German escort of a Feldwebel with a machine-pistol and two soldiers with rifles.

Bader instantly bridled.

" I've given my parole. I'm damned if I'll be insulted by an armed guard."

The Germans answered that *Befehl* was *Befehl*, and Bader snapped: " Well, I refuse to go. Come on, Peter, let's go back inside."

It was an odd scene that followed. The Germans who went to such trouble to lock everyone in Kolditz then insisted with the strange rigidity of their race that orders said that the Herr Wing Commander was to go for a walk; therefore the Herr Wing Commander must go for a walk. The Herr Wing Commander said he bloody well refused and there was uproar till the tolerant Püpcke arrived and, like Solomon giving judgment, decreed that the escort should leave the machine-pistol and rifles behind. That still left them with pistols in holsters on their belts, but Püpcke explained that they were part of the normal uniform. Would the Herr Wing Commander mind? No, said the wing commander, he wouldn't mind and, honour and *Befehl* both satisfied, he walked. They went down through the village and sauntered for a couple of soothing

[1] They had tastes in common. The Germans had already court-martialled Dollar for insulting them.

hours beside pleasant fields, the escort ambling discreetly behind.

After that he went for walks twice a week, usually with Dollar, and mellowed slightly towards the Germans, refraining in good-humoured moments from murmuring "*Deutschland kaput!*" as he passed Eggers and the little major.

The invasion was a relaxing influence too, and when the Allies broke out of the German ring in Normandy even the fervent escape activity at Kolditz eased a little (though not much). The end seemed very near then and prisoners endured a little more stoically the dreary repetition of life that ran on and on like a broken record of a Bach fugue.

Occasionally, however, the needle slipped into another groove and eccentric variations enlivened the theme. Most prisoners had the disturbing experience of seeing men among them slowly crack under the mental strain and start acting oddly. At Kolditz a good-looking young R.A.F. athlete took to playing a guitar in a washhouse with the guitar case on his head. He knocked at Bader's door one day, walked in carrying a bucket of water, came to attention before Bader, saluted, and said politely:

"Excuse me, sir, but I don't like the things you've been telling the king about me lately."

Then he threw the bucket of water in Bader's face, saluted and walked out again.

He was repatriated eventually, along with several others who were sick and maimed.

As Bader's legs had been giving trouble the S.B.O. suggested that he be repatriated too, a suggestion which Douglas emphatically refused, declaring that his legs had not been lost in battle and therefore he was no different as a result of captivity. The S.B.O., however, put his name on the list when the repatriation commission arrived, and then when the Germans called prisoners from *appell* to appear before the commission they left out the names of Bader and two very sick men. It was typical of the spirit of Kolditz that all the sick and maimed who were called—including some, like the Earl of Arundel, who were unlikely to recover—refused to see the commission until the three dropped names were restored.

Eggers called guards and tried to force them to appear, but

the sick men stood fast and an ugly scene developed until the Germans gave way. It was pure principle. Bader himself had no intention of being repatriated, but the other two needed it. When called before the doctors and asked how he felt, he answered: " Absolutely fit, thank you very much."

" But," said the chairman, " your wounds are giving you trouble? "

" Not a bit. They're fine."

" Are you sure you're all right? " The puzzled doctors had known plenty of prisoners who exaggerated their ills, but never one who did the reverse. One of them seemed to think that Bader should be repatriated on mental grounds, but he finally convinced them he wanted to stay and stick it out with the others. The other two, however, were passed for repatriation.

One day the Fortresses came. There had been a strange disembodied droning and then someone in the courtyard shouted and upturned faces saw the glinting shapes serenely dragging the thin, parallel lines of the con-trails like great rake-strokes across the blue patch over the high walls. Bader shouted: " *Wo ist die Luftwaffe?* "[1] and the rest took it up in chorus because there were no German fighters. It was an emotional moment seeing for the first time the Allied Arms reaching out unchallenged across Germany.

But the armies bogged down on the frontiers of a bravely fighting enemy and as the last leaves fell the prisoners who followed the war more acutely than anyone else guessed miserably that they were in for another winter.

Then the food parcels stopped coming and hunger came back.

---

[1] " Where is the Luftwaffe? "

28

O N THE twice-weekly walks Bader and Peter Dollar began
trading cigarettes with farmers for wheat, barley and
eggs (which Dollar put under his peaked cap) to bring
back to the communal food stores. It was strictly forbidden by
the Germans, but usually a few extra cigarettes were enough to
bribe the guards.

Little though it was, the food was such a help that Dollar
eventually hung a pillow-case round his neck under his greatcoat, stuffed it with grain and came back looking suspiciously
swollen. Everyone else was getting thinner and thinner, but
the Germans at the gate never thought to search the rotund
Dollar.

On the long walks back from the farms Bader was not able
to carry much for a while. He badly wanted to try and carry
a pillow-case like Dollar, but impervious as ever to cold he had
never worn a greatcoat and the food committee thought it
would look suspicious if he suddenly started. It only needed
a search at the gate to destroy the whole scheme. Then an
ingenious major, Andy Anderson, made him long, thin bags to
hang down inside his trousers and he went out armed with
those, banking on the fact that the Germans would always
expect him to look odd below the waist, anyhow. Twice a
week they went out looking gaunt and came back swollen like
Michelin tyre advertisements, but the forty or fifty pounds of
grain they brought were badly needed. That winter some
prisoners lost up to three stones in weight and some had to rest
half-way up the stairs.

It was the worst winter of all. For Bader it held some of
the joy of accomplishment in bringing back food for his friends,
but it took a lot out of him. His stumps were getting emaciated
and it was hellish struggling back with the grain bags across
the snow and up the slushy, slippery cobbles. As a matter of

pride he hid it from the others almost completely, but Dick Howe a couple of times caught him off guard, walking into his room and seeing him lying exhausted on his bunk.

One of the R.A.F. prisoners, Lorne Welch, a gliding expert, conceived the fantastic idea of building a glider and escaping in it by flying from the high castle walls. Two other cronies, Morison and Best, were helping him build it and Bader, as senior R.A.F. officer, was roped in as consultant. They were making a rough wooden frame from bedboards and planned to cover the wings with sheets, sticking the contraption together with glue made from potatoes. As the pieces were made they dispersed them, reckoning that if the Germans found them they would never dream what it was.

To launch the glider they planned to cut holes through all the floors, one under another, and from the roof drop an enormous stone on a rope through these holes to jerk the glider, perched on the battlements, into space. It was to be a two-seater and Bader hoped that he might have a chance of one of the seats. The fact that it would have to be night-flying as well (for secrecy) gave the scheme an added flavour. They hoped it would glide 400 yards, though, in fact, it would hardly be likely to travel more than a hundred feet, and that straight down at accumulating speed. (Luckily they were unable to finish it.)

Returning from a food-gathering walk one day, Bader's left foot seemed to disappear as he put it down and he fell forward on his hands. He looked down, surprised, and saw that his leg was broken by the ankle. As he tried to pull the sock down, the whole ankle and foot came away in his hand and he was staggered to see that the metal had corroded right through, apparently from perspiration which had gathered by the bottom of the ankle. There was nothing he could do except drag himself to the side of the road and send a guard back for his spare leg.

Dollar said unsympathetically: "This'll teach you to change your socks more often."

The guard came back with the faithful Ross carrying the leg and, unfortunately, a German officer too. As the officer solicitously bent down to help him change the leg it suddenly occurred to Bader that as soon as he took his trousers down the officer would see the full wheat bags underneath. That would be the end of the walks and the end of the extra food. He thought furiously, and then shook his head at the German, and said: "*Nein, nein,*" and tried to blush and pretend he was shy. Watched by the startled German, he dragged himself behind some bushes, coyly changed the leg there and the crisis was over.

Spring came at last and with it the Allies pouring across the Rhine. The secret radio followed their progress on the news, and within the old castle grew a tremulous tension of impatience. On 13th April they heard that an American spearhead was only a few miles down the road and that night they went to bed with febrile excitement, knowing that it was nearly over, and yet unable to grasp it. After some hours they slept.

Bader was woken early by a roaring noise. He strapped on his legs and through the window saw Thunderbolts shooting up a nearby target. They went after a while, but soon he heard the sound of engines again and thought it was the Thunderbolts returning until someone yelled: "Tanks!" Men rushed to the windows of the outer wall and two miles across the river, by a wood, saw gun-flashes and the crawling black beetles of armour. A fascinating and glorious sight! They were here!

The S.B.O., Willie Todd, appeared in the doorway and called soberly: "Listen a minute, everybody. The Kommandant has just ordered that we are to evacuate the castle by ten o'clock. He says we're to be marched back behind the German lines."

There was a stunned and icy silence. No one had dreamed that they would be marched away, though there had been rumours that Hitler was going to hold hostages.

Bader exploded: "We aren't going to move now."

"Don't worry," Todd said. "I'm going to tell him that, but I want you to be ready for anything if he brings up his Goons to winkle us out with guns."

They waited tensely while Todd argued with the Kommandant. Apparently an S.S. Division was going to make a stand behind a nearby ridge; the castle would be in the battleground, and the division commander thought that it and the men inside might impede his defence. Todd threatened that an evacuation would not endear the Kommandant to the Allies and the Kommandant retired to think about this and contact the division commander.

The prisoners were planning to barricade themselves in when the Kommandant sent in a message to say that they could stay at their own risk, provided that no one hung signals out of the windows.

That afternoon the men at the windows saw more flashes and smoke from fires, and shells started screaming over the castle. Bader was watching through the bars with Dollar and Howe when a blinding light flashed in his face with an ear-splitting explosion and he found himself dizzily on his back in the middle of the floor with plaster falling on him and his ears singing like a kettle. In the top corner of the window the stone had crumbled where the shell had exploded. A little later in the Kommandantur, a Feldwebel watching from a window caught a shell in the face and was killed.

No one seemed to know what was happening and at dusk the situation was still confused, though the dogged German guards still stood at their posts and the sentries marched up and down the wired terraces below. Looking at them with admiration, Bader said to Dollar: " Y'know, even if we tried to escape at this stage they'd still let fly at us."

That night nearly everyone, paradoxically, was querulous. Some had been in captivity over five years and the last few hours were unnerving. Bader himself had been down now three and a half years.

The castle was nakedly sandwiched in an artillery duel, and all night the shells screamed and whistled over and banged joltingly on each side. At last, towards dawn, it was quieter and a few slept.

Bader came drowsily up from sleep to hear tramping feet in the courtyard and shouting. In an instant he was fully awake and strapped on his legs while others less impeded ran down ahead. He heard shouts coming up and impatiently, with a fast and eager dot-and-carry motion, clumped down after them. In the courtyard, through milling cheering prisoners, he was staggered to see American soldiers, and nearby a line of stolid German guards stepping up one by one to hand over their rifles. He stumped across and joined the laughing noisy mob shaking hands with the Americans who, for once, were quieter than the British but seemed almost as pleased. The noise went on for a few minutes and then it died down.

It was all over. They were free. How confusing and nerveless it was. No one quite seemed to know what to do, or feel. The tension had snapped in a moment of joy that had flared like a roman candle, then left them groping in the afterglow.

Püpcke was there. Bader heard a British colonel say to him: " I want to say that you yourself have behaved very well the whole time we have been here."

Püpcke gave a little bow. " Thank you." And added quietly: " You know, this is the second time I have seen my country defeated."

Three American newspaper correspondents appeared and started firing questions at Bader. He was amazed to see that one of them was a girl, a real live girl, with red hair, in battledress, in the courtyard. After a while they said they were going back to First Army Headquarters at Naunberg in a jeep. Would he like to come?

He stuffed a few oddments and his books into a kitbag and then he was in the jeep driving out across the moat, down the cobbled hill and through the village where the white sheets and towels of surrender hung from nearly every window.

They drove fast and he did not feel like talking, but sat and watched the countryside, trying to let it soak in that he was free. But the cherished word had no meaning yet. He was drifting out of Limbo, the mists still round his head, and floating back over the Styx, cut off from the past and rootless in the present, unable to see the home shore, and oddly isolated from the Americans who were riding buoyantly across the everyday currents they knew. Behind he could still hear the guns.

Passing an airfield he recognised Me. 109's, all with broken bellies sagging on the ground. They looked different to the old ones—like tombstones.

" Krauts put grenades in 'em," one of the Americans said laconically.

They passed an American armoured division moving up, an endless thundering snake of steel that amazed him. In the villages the children waved at the tanks and at him in the jeep. It was unreal.

Around dusk they came to Naunberg, and officers in the school-turned-headquarters greeted him warmly, but they were busy coming and going, doing things, and for all the warmth he felt an odd man out again. Then a British major, a young liaison officer, greeted him and he found a little footing. They dined on army rations and he filled himself gloriously and guiltily. The army bread looked snow-white and tasted sweet, like cake. Feeling better, he asked the major: " Any Spitfires round here? "

No, the major said, they were all up north with the British forces.

" Can I get to them? " Bader asked. " I'd like to grab one and get another couple of trips in before this show folds up."

" Good god, man," said the shocked major. " Give it a miss and go home. Haven't you had enough? " He made it clear that it was futile.

Two officers took him through the blacked-out streets to sleep in a private house whose German family had retired quietly behind a blank door at the back. Browsing through the fruitily furnished living-room looking at the bric-à-brac of domestic civilisation, he stopped to look at an antique silver snuff-box.

" Hell, Doug," one of the others said; " take it. You don't have to be sorry for these bastards."

He left it there. The trouble was he *did* feel sorry for them. Now there was nothing to fight, some of the hate seemed to have withered, but he felt it unwise to try and explain it to the others because they were still living in the war and would not understand. Later, he crawled into a feather bed and lay wide awake all night, not disturbed, just thinking, feeling for a grip.

By dawn he had it. Kolditz was a year away and he was in the present, still a trifle insecurely, but looking forward to the future with the old, practical sense that seldom looked back over his shoulder.

They drove him to an airfield where the busy officer clerks said it was forbidden to fly prisoners back yet, so he thumbed a lift with a cheerful young American pilot who said insulting things about bureaucrats and put him in the co-pilot's seat of his pretty little silver Beechcraft bound for Paris. With the rising engine roar, the surge of take-off and the gentle sway as they lifted, a well-remembered thrill tingled in his blood.

The Beechcraft skimmed over bombed Coblenz and he looked at the decayed and stained teeth of the ruins with interest but no pleasure, thinking only how stupidly wasteful the war was. They landed on an airstrip in the Versailles woods and he found haven in a house where a dozen warm-hearted American officers offered him champagne to drink to his liberty, but unaccountably liberty did not seem to call for champagne and he drank Coca-Cola instead. Though they were tremendously kind and tactful he still felt awkward in his battledress, which was shabby. He was sitting, talking, when the commanding general tapped his shoulder and said: " Come on, Doug. I've got your wife on the phone."

It caught him off balance. He got to the phone and recognised Thelma's voice saying: " Douglas! Douglas! " Then there was so much to say that they could not say it for a while. A little later Thelma said: " When am I going to see you? "

" A few days, darling. I'm looking for a Spitfire. I want to have a last fling before it packs up."

" Oh, god," Thelma almost wailed. " Haven't you had enough yet? "

He talked a long time trying to make her understand, which was difficult because he did not quite know himself. He just wanted to be in it again where he knew reassuringly that he belonged.

That night he slept and in the morning they drove him to Paris. At R.A.F. Headquarters he started telling them about Lucille de Backer and the Hiècques, but they knew more than he did; the Germans had sentenced all three to death, an intelligence officer said, but there was a report that the sentence had been commuted to prison in Germany. They were trying to trace them and would let him know.

Lucille too! He went out hoping very, very hard that they would all be found safe—their fate was the only cloud on his liberty. He asked about old friends on the squadrons and heard that a dismaying number were dead. But Tubby

Mermagen was in France and they got him on the phone. He was at Rheims, an air commodore, and almost the first thing Bader said was: " Can you get me a Spitfire? I want to have another crack."

From the other end came a chuckle. " We thought you'd say that. I have strict orders from the C.-in-C. that you are not to have his Spitfire or mine or anyone else's, but I'm to stuff you straight into an aircraft for London."

That afternoon Mermagen flew to Paris and did so.

The humble Anson ambled over the fields that used to be Bader's hunting ground, but he could not recognise anything. Over the Channel he began looking for England, but half as a stranger, with too many tumbling emotions for anything so uncomplicated as simple joy. They crossed the coast at Littlehampton and out to the left he saw Tangmere, but only dimly through a veil of haze.

At Northolt Aerodrome, just outside London, the R.A.F. gave him sanctuary while the Great Machine sucked him in again, looking down his throat, planting stethoscopes on him, giving him clothes, forms to fill in, questions to answer and fending off the clamouring reporters.

On the third morning, with leave for two months, he drove down to Ascot and Thelma, free at last and for the first time tasting it fully. He pulled into the drive, walked up the flagged path and as Thelma ran out of the front door, two reporters stepped from behind a bush saying cheerfully: " Got you at last." And the moment was spoiled.

Next morning he and Thelma fled to a private hotel in a little Devon village and suddenly he could not face people, think coherently, make any plans, or even read the letters that came pouring in. The extrovert surface had cracked off and he was a raw-skinned creature wanting only to retire into an artificial shell of privacy with Thelma while he grew a new skin to live in a new world. His fame had not died but become a legend and people were clamouring to see him, which made it worse. Some old friends called one day and he climbed out of a window to avoid them.

After three weeks they went back to Ascot where he climbed out of a window again to avoid some visitors. Another time he was trapped in the street by a strange woman who gushed over him with goodwill and bad taste. He stuck it out till she twittered: " Now tell me . . . in all the wonderful things you do without legs, what do you find the most difficult? " Bluntly he answered: " Drying my bottom after a bath when I have to sit on a stool at the same time," and walked on, leaving her standing.

One night he *did* enjoy meeting people. Sailor Malan, Bob Tuck, Crowley-Milling, Johnny Johnson and a dozen or so others of the old 1940 team gave him a welcome-home dinner at the Belfry Club in Belgravia, and that night he felt at ease.

He got his old flying log-book back and entered up his last Tangmere flight of nearly four years before, with the laconic comment: " Good flight near Béthune. Shot down one 109 F. and collided with another. P.O.W. Two 109 F.s destroyed."

And underneath: " Total enemy aircraft destroyed—30."

That was his own private total which he never mentioned. All successful pilots had such totals, which included those they were sure had been destroyed, but which had been impossible to confirm under the stringent official rules. As it was, under those rules he had 22½ confirmed.

From Paris he learned with joy that the Hiècques and Lucille had been found alive in Germany and were now in an Allied hospital, recovering. He wrote asking to be informed when they returned to St. Omer. News came that the French had sentenced Hélène, who had betrayed him, to twenty years in prison. Still feeling no hate, only vaguely sorry for her, he wrote to the French Government suggesting they cut her sentence to five years and then send her back to live in St. Omer.

One day he drove to see Rupert Leigh at the Empire Flying School at Hullavington and Leigh gave him fifteen minutes dual in a Miles Master. Then he climbed into a Spitfire and twirled her round the air for half an hour, knowing with elation in the first minute that the touch was still the same. He landed with some of the old glow back in his eyes and a new confidence, and from that moment began to feel back in the swim again and to come resiliently out of his shell. Within two days he also began scheming for a posting to the Far East to fly fighters against the Japanese. The past might be past, but heady and consummating days might still lie within reach to make up for the life lost in the dead years in Germany. He put out feelers to the right quarters but the people at Air Ministry, though kind, were not in the least co-operative. He had done quite enough, they said, and in any case the doctors said his stumps would give trouble in the tropics. They might be all right for a fortnight, but the way he sweated with the effort of getting around would soon bring on the rashes and the chafing.

He knew privately that the latter part, at least, was correct and when the usually tolerant Thelma added a stubborn veto to the project he grudgingly shelved the idea.

His old 242 Squadron adjutant rang him at Ascot one night. Now *Sir* Peter Macdonald and still a busy Conservative M.P., he said: " Douglas, it's about the general election. We want you to stand and we've got a very nice safe seat for you at Blackpool."

" Sorry, Peter," Bader said; " but I'm not interested in being a politician."

Nonsense, Macdonald declared. It was the duty of chaps like him to go into the House.

Getting back to his old form, Bader said pugnaciously: " Look, I think all politicians are a lot of lousy so-and-so's, and I wouldn't be seen dead in the House."

Those were the opening shots of a patient campaign to persuade the inflexible to change his mind. He kept saying " No " with unmistakable vigour, but they persevered until he declaimed with some force: " Now, look, whenever you want me to be saying yes I'll probably be saying no, and when you want me to say no I'll probably be saying yes, depending on how I feel. I won't be following any party lines. After five years of that no party would put me up for re-election, would they? "

Peace again.

Then in the R.A.F. Club he met Air Commodore Dick Atcherley, the former Schneider Trophy pilot, who said: " Douglas, I want a man to run the Fighter Leader School at Tangmere. It's a group captain's job. Would you like it? "

He answered with feeling: " Yes, please."

Eager for the comfort of harness again, he cancelled the

rest of his leave and early in June drove nostalgically to the well-remembered Tangmere. He should have known better. The place looked the same, but that was all that remained of the old days. The tactics were new, the faces were new; above all, the atmosphere was new. It seemed to have turned upside down. Now there was none of the urgency or the inspiration of war, only a team of battle-weary men who wanted to shed the medal ribbons and be civilians again. He tried to revive some of the spirit but there was no spark left in the embers, and it brought only unhappiness, so when he was offered command of the North Weald Fighter Sector he took it.

It brought him control over twelve fighter squadrons spread over six aerodromes, but there was little joy in that either because there was no dynamic purpose any more: he was presiding over their disintegration. The great war machine of the R.A.F. was breaking up as the bolts holding it together were withdrawn and great chunks chopped off and channelled back to civil life. He tried to preserve a hard core, but the best men would not stay because the R.A.F.'s future did not look encouraging. It was dispiriting, though at least without the hurt of memories at Tangmere. For miles around he could find no house for Thelma and had to fly disconsolately to see her at week-ends. At least he had his own Spitfire again, and had his old " D.B." painted on it.

A letter from Paris told him that Lucille and the Hiècques were back in St. Omer and he immediately got into " D.B." and flew over there. When he knocked and the door opened, recognition was mutual and there was a tremendously emotional scene, everyone crying and laughing and kissing each other. The Hiècques had not changed as much as he had feared. Madame, a little more wrinkled, was still the same resourceful and compassionate soul, and Monsieur still brushed his cheek with the wisp of moustache. The brave Lucille was thinner and shy, and he could find no way of thanking them properly. The young man who had led him through the dark streets was not there: he had been missing for two years.

In the North Weald Sector one of his squadrons had Meteor jets and as a matter of both desire and duty he flew one. Oddly, the Meteor, which was soon to win the world's speed record at over 600 m.p.h.,[1] was the first twin-engined aircraft he had ever flown; also oddly he found that without legs it was easier for him to handle than any other aeroplane because there was no torque and therefore no need to prod the rudder much to correct swing on take-off or in the dive. Comforted by this it occurred to him that when the Far East war moved north to invade Japan the climate would not affect his legs. He was scheming a way of getting out to it when the atom bomb fell and the whole shooting match was over.

For the world, Bader rejoiced as much as anyone; for himself a little less. A tinge of regret itched for a few days but common sense soon dismissed the past, as it had dismissed his legs. Now it was the future that occupied him, like so many others, but he knew his own problem was different to theirs; it could be materially easier if he chose to stay with the R.A.F., but mentally and physically harder whatever he did. He had enjoyed the glory but you couldn't live on that. Anyway, there was no hurry. Get some of the mess cleared away first and then one could see.

On 1st September he found a letter from Group in his " In " tray. It said there was to be a victory fly-past over London on 15th September to celebrate peace, and the fifth anniversary of the greatest day in the Battle of Britain. Three hundred aircraft were to take part, with twelve survivors of the battle in the van. Group Captain Bader was to organise the fly-past and lead it.

Stuffy Dowding arrived at North Weald early on the 15th and stood talking to the chosen twelve, looking much the same as five years earlier. The others looked a little different. Crowley-Milling, who had been a pilot officer in the battle, wore wing-commander braid and a D.S.O. and D.F.C. on his chest. So did Stan Turner. So also Bob Tuck and nearly all the others. The atmosphere was different too; they spoke more soberly and hardly mentioned the battle. Bader wound a blue polka-dot scarf round his neck, called: " Let's go," picked up his right leg and swung it into " D.B.'s " cockpit.

Cloud was drooping over London and down in the grey streets the city gathered in stillness, some in tears, watching the

[1] Flown by Thelma's cousin, Teddy Donaldson.

cavalcade of three hundred sweep thunderously over the roof-
tops. Bader hardly saw them—Turner on one side, Crowley-
Milling on the other, he was too busy picking his course through
the haze. Once, over the city, he remembered the battle and
for a moment, nostalgically, wanted to fight it again.

Interim Epilogue

Now THE problem of what to do with life began to concern him urgently. The old dream had come true; the Air Force wanted him back permanently. Though still there was nothing in King's Regulations to cover his case, they offered to wipe out all the wasted years and give him the seniority he would have had if he had never crashed in 1931. He could keep his hundred per cent disability pension, and if he ever crashed badly again he could have another hundred per cent disability pension on top of that. It was more than he had ever dreamed possible—and yet . . . the legs would still not let him serve overseas in the heat, which would limit his experience and therefore his value and promotion. And this strange, post-war Air Force with its sinews cut was different to the dream, holding neither the proud purpose of war nor the old club warmth of 1931. He had achieved the peak and justified himself and the valley on the other side looked barren. Only the distant fields behind were green and he would never see them again except in memory.

The Shell Company wrote pleasantly to him and he dined with his old boss, who was affable and said: " We've got just the job for you if you'd like to come back." Douglas, he went on, could have his own aeroplane and fly all round the world on aviation business.

His own aeroplane! Virtually. And what a grand job! A week or two at a time in the tropics would not upset the legs much. It would give him the chance of world travel that otherwise would be lost for ever. They named a salary that was tempting, and said: " Take your time. No need to make up your mind in a hurry."

He took four months to think about it, and at the end of February decided. Writing out his resignation from the Air Force, he felt how odd it was that he should choose to turn his back on the old heaven to return to the old hell. Though this time a somewhat transformed hell!

The most heart-warming messages came to him—summed up in a sentence from the Chief of Fighter Command, Sir James Robb. " All I can say is that you are leaving behind an example which as the years roll by will become a legend."

In March when the time came to leave he did not feel so badly about it. The job was done and now he knew he would feel a part of the Air Force for the rest of his life. It was on a Saturday after breakfast that he took off his uniform, dressed in civilian clothes, and drove away from North Weald towards Ascot in the M.G. (a saloon car this time, obtained during his captivity by Thelma, who liked fresh air but in controllable quantities). There was no need to start work yet; officially, he was still on leave from the R.A.F. for three months.

Most of that time he spent working on his golf. Before the war he had never taken a single lesson, partly because he could not afford it and partly because he thought that being without legs would call for a peculiar style so different from normal golf so that a professional could not help. Practising ardently at the Wentworth Golf Club with Archie Compston he soon found he had been wrong, and within three months he had reduced his handicap from nine to four, which is not likely ever to be approached by a legless man again and, in fact, is equalled only by about one golfer in a hundred. Dessoutter once told him he would never walk without a stick. He played Dessoutter, and beat him seven and six. If the little demon became restive in the doldrums of peace it already had something to ponder over. During these months he became increasingly involved in encouraging amputees and cripples. His very existence as much as his bearing and example was a tonic to them.

Late in June he and Thelma moved back to their old flat in Kensington and on the first Monday in July Bader went back to the office for the first time in six and a half years. This time he had an office of his own and the manager tossed him a letter. " This'll interest you, old boy. We've ordered a Percival Proctor for you. It'll be ready in a couple of weeks." He went along to the Ministry of Civil Aviation to get his first private pilot's licence and the clerk when he gave it to him said apologetically, without mentioning the legs: " Just for the records, sir, would you mind getting us a letter from some competent authority to say you are fully capable of flying."

A few days later he collected the Proctor, a neat little single-engined cabin monoplane. She was a four-seater, silver with a blue flash down the side, and cruised at 130 m.p.h. He was like a small boy with a new toy. As she was registered " G-AHWU " (in alphabetical code " George Able How Willie Uncle ") he christened her " Willie Uncle."

In August he started his first trip, accompanied by Lieutenant-General Jimmy Doolittle, a Shell Company vice-president in U.S.A. They were a good pair. Doolittle was another dynamic type, chunky and good natured, able to be as friendly with office clerks as with directors. A former Schneider Trophy winner (1926), he was America's most noted pilot and had led the famous carrier-borne raid on Tokyo in 1942, one of the bravest feats of the war.

First stop was Oslo, where they had an audience with King Haakon, who was delightfully informal. (" That silly man Quisling came and stayed at the palace here during the war," he said. " A very foolish thing to do. The people disliked it intensely.")

In Stockholm a radio announcer asked him what his greatest thrill had been, and Bader said: " Going round Hoylake golf course in seventy-seven a few weeks ago."

Then to Copenhagen, The Hague and Paris and receptions in every spot. Doolittle beside him in the Proctor, he flew to Marseilles, Nice and Rome, across the Mediterranean to Tunis, Algiers, Tangier and Casablanca. With only a day or two in each spot and champagne and goodwill flowing all round, the pace began to tell, though Bader never touched the champagne. It was cumulative weariness that caught up with him in Casablanca where he sat next to a French general at a welcome dinner on a very hot night. His head was drooping on his chest as he tried to do his duty, saying: " *Oui mon générale, oui mon générale*," until he actually fell asleep sitting there, toppling sideways until his forehead squashed into the remains of the fish course on the general's plate. He jerked upright with a " *Pardon, mon générale, je suis un peu malade*," and they whisked him off to bed where he slept for eleven hours.

Back to London via Lisbon, Madrid and Paris, then off

again in the Proctor for West Africa, " White Man's Grave," where he could test his legs in the tropics for the first time. Down through Bordeaux, Perpignan, Barcelona, Tangier and Agadir into the steamy heat of Dakar, Lagos, to Leopoldville in the Belgian Congo. Most of the time he flew over jungle that stretched as far as the eye could see and looked like parsley from 7,000 feet, but was quite as dangerous as flying over oceans in a single-engined aircraft. Had the engine failed Bader would have had no chance. Once, in fact, the engine did stop and he was gliding down in a highly disconcerting silence with the propeller windmilling when at about a thousand feet as he was tightening his belt and getting ready to hang on to the crash-pad, the engine suddenly coughed and started again.

Sweat from steamy West African heat soon made the stumps uncomfortable but talcum powder kept the heat rashes under control for three weeks until he was on the way back.

In 1947, on Doolittle's invitation, he went on Shell business to the U.S.A which had 17,000 amputation cases from the war, and visited several veterans' hospitals to help men learn to walk again. He found one who had lost both legs below the knee and was struggling between the kind of low parallel bars that Bader had first seen at Roehampton. Without an introduction he stumped over, and said: " Why don't you come out from those bars and try walking without 'em."

Not unnaturally the man growled: " Who the hell are you? "

" Just a Limey travelling through, but I've lost 'em both too, and I've only got one knee, not two like you."

" Let's see you walk."

Bader stumped up and down the room.

" I don't believe you," the man said.

Bader pulled up his trouser legs and showed him, and the man said: " Well, goddam."

He lurched out, and Bader got on one side and helped him to struggle up and down the room. After a while the man was able to take his first couple of steps unaided and his whole manner had changed.

" You figure I'll be able to dance? " he asked.

" Don't see why not. I do."

" Hell," the man said. " I nearly shot myself when I woke up this morning, but I reckon now it's all right again."

In Chicago Bader read of a small boy of ten who had spilled burning petrol over himself and had both legs cut off below the knee. Douglas, who would do almost anything for children, spent an hour and a half by his bed, showing him that legs did not matter so much. Later the boy's father said worriedly: " The boy just doesn't realise how serious it is yet."

Bader said passionately: " That's the one thing he must *never* realise. You've got to make him feel this is another game he's got to learn, not something that will cripple him. Once you frighten him with it he's beaten."

That in a nutshell was the Bader philosophy, concerning not only legs but life itself. He spoke to the boy's father for twenty minutes impressing it on him.

In San Francisco he met Harold Russell, the American soldier who had had both hands blown off and been fitted with a pair of mechanical hooks that worked like hands. At that time Russell had just finished his part in the Oscar-winning film, *The Best Years of Our Lives*. Bader found him having dinner with Walter McGonigal, a World War I veteran who had lost both hands and used the same kind of hooks. As Bader lurched in Russell got up with a mouthful of steak and put out his hook to shake hands. Laughing, Bader watched the two of them handling their knives and forks with amazing dexterity. " Have some coffee," Russell said, picked up a coffee pot in one hook and a cup and saucer in the other and poured. McGonigal flipped a cigarette out of a packet into his mouth, pulled out a box of matches, picked one out with a hook, struck it and lit his cigarette. It was amazing to watch the two of them enjoying life, unbothered by the hooks, spreading their own bread, stirring their coffee, flicking ash off cigarettes and stubbing them out, all with the hooks.

" I don't know how you do it," Bader said admiringly.

" Well, I dunno how *you* do it either," said Russell. " I'm glad I lost my hands and not my legs."

In Los Angeles a telegram was waiting. " Welcome, chum. Ring me at the studios up to six o'clock. David Niven." He did so, and next day was playing golf with Niven, Clark Gable and James Stewart

Back in London he took Thelma with him in the Proctor on his next trip, a tour of Scandinavia, and at Tylosand he entered for the Swedish golf championship and delighted everyone by winning his first round match, then was beaten in the second.

Next journey was down to West Africa again and this time he flew on to Pretoria to meet Field Marshal Smuts, and for a gay reunion with Sailor Malan in Johannesburg, where he also caught malaria and lost two stone in weight in five days. That bout emaciated the stumps so that it was days before he could walk properly again. Later came a trip to the Middle East, Tripoli, Benghazi, Tobruk, Cairo, Cyprus and Athens. In time left over from work he visited several limbless people and the warmth he showed them was in inverse ratio to the pulverising vigour he still turned on tiresome people such as bureaucrats. One day he landed at Tangier, tired after nearly seven hours in the air from Las Palmas, and when he opened his bag in the Customs shed an unshaven official dug grubby hands into it and began pulling the clothes about. Bader grabbed the bag, up-ended it and shook everything out on the table.

" There, you clod," he said wrathfully. " *Now* look at it! "

The Customs man did not understand English, but the gist was unmistakable. Red-faced, he said in French, his voice rising: " I have examined the baggage of Englishmen, Americans, Frenchmen, Spaniards, Italians, Greeks, Swedes, Danes . . . and they are all gentlemen except you."

In the violent debate that followed Bader gave the game away by starting to laugh.

In 1948 he took Thelma with him in the Proctor out to the Far East, and on the way out an Athens newspaper ran his photograph with limbless Greek veterans, referring to him as the " famous cripple." Cripple! Servicing his own aircraft in all weathers he flew by way of Turkey, Damascus, Baghdad, Basra, Bahrein, Sharjah, Baluchistan, Karachi, Delhi, Allahabad, Calcutta, Akyab, Rangoon, Mergui and Penang to Singapore. From there they went by air to Borneo, Celebes, Java, Bali and New Guinea, covering over 20,000 miles. Only a few years before men with legs had their names blazoned to the world for doing trips like that in single-engined aircraft. In the two months they were away Douglas sweated off many pounds and Thelma put on a stone, earning the new nickname of " Chubby." She lost the weight when she got back, but lost only two letters from the nickname, which is now permanently " Chub."

Bader was always sorry he could not take the third member of the family on his overseas trips. Shaun was a handsome and intelligent golden retriever and Douglas was utterly devoted to him. He seldom played golf without Shaun loping along beside, and on flights within Britain Shaun usually climbed nonchalantly into the aircraft and flew with him.

In 1949 he took to flying twin-engined aircraft and delivered a Percival Prince to Singapore (taking Thelma again). In 1951 the company thought he should have two engines on his long trips so he changed the Proctor for a twin-engined Miles Gemini which he immediately flew to the Congo.

After a time in London he is off again, sometimes flying himself by Gemini sometimes delivering a new aircraft to out-of-the-way places, sometimes by airliner. For a man who might be excused for living in a wheel-chair he is fantastically peripatetic, liable to pop up in almost any corner of the globe at any time. Often his golf clubs go with him, and often Thelma too. If you told him to go to Timbuktu he could answer truthfully: " I've been there." He has flown forty-seven different types of aircraft now and some fifty or more countries have known memorable and often repeated contact with his exuberance.

Probably no one has done as much for the limbless as Bader's example, which inspires them in a way no doctor can emulate. Tinny Dean, for instance, his old pre-war rugger and golfing partner, had a leg blown off in a Western Desert tank battle and wrote afterwards to Bader, truthfully, that he was not at all concerned about it.

In 1939 a young naval pupil-pilot, Colin Hodgkinson, lost both legs just like Bader in a collision. After Bader's example he was able to talk his way into the R.A.F. and flew Spitfires on operations (later, by a coincidence, being shot down and captured, badly injured, by the Germans, though he never met Bader in prison camp). Hodgkinson, too, plays golf and squash and dances on his artificial legs.

There was Richard Wood, Lord Halifax's son, who had

both legs blown off when he trod on a mine in the Western Desert. Oddly enough, he was nursed in hospital by Geoffrey Stephenson's fiancée and after hearing about Bader from her, wrote to Thelma (Douglas was then in prison camp): " When I woke up from the operation I asked if I would ever be able to walk again and they said, ' Of course, look at Douglas Bader.' Ever since then I have been determined to do whatever he has done and be to others without legs what he has been to me. I should love to meet him some time and thank him myself. I have just got my legs and started walking."

[Wood's legs are both off above the knees but he walks with only one stick and is also an M.P.]

It seldom occurs to me when with Bader that he has no legs, a common experience with those who know him. Bader himself has forgotten the feeling of ever having his own legs, except sometimes, weirdly, when he still gets the phantom feeling of his feet. Some of the nerves and muscles are still in his stumps so that he can wiggle them and feel that he is wiggling his toes. He puts on his legs in the morning as casually as I put on my shoes and this casual acceptance is deceptive. The legs are never entirely comfortable and often are hurting him though he will not confess it. Rarely, in the most intimate circle, there may be a fleeting sign: that is all.

Playing golf with him once in Cornwall he gave no sign of pain but suggested at lunch that the afternoon round might be deferred. I said flippantly: " You're getting soft," but when he took his right leg off the thigh was raw and purple all round the top because the metal socket had been dented slightly. It must have hurt wickedly struggling round the course. Next morning a spare leg arrived in a cricket-bag on the train, and with the raw patch taped over, he was playing again. His secret is simple and sounds trite; it is merely that he will not yield.

In 1948 he won the Nineteenth Club's Challenge Cup, playing thirty-six holes (medal) in one day over the hilly Camberley course whose narrow fairways are flanked by thick heather. A full day on that course would tire any man. Bader's off-the-stick card was a 79 and an 82. He was as fit as most athletes of twenty-five, and Rupert Leigh was convinced he would still be playing fly-half for England if he had not lost his legs. At Cranwell they hung an oil painting of him by Cuthbert Orde in the gallery over the main hall, and that stirred him considerably.

He is still a mixture of modesty and ego. In a swash-buckling way he is given to bragging about his golf scores as blatantly as a fisherman describing the one that got away. People who do not know him well have resented that, but they have never heard him brag about important things. It was not from Bader I learned that he would have played rugby for England, and the research for this book was nearly completed before I discovered by seeing one of his old uniform tunics that as well as two D.S.O.s and two D.F.C.s he also holds the Légion d'Honneur and the Croix de Guerre. They were awarded for his fighting over Dunkirk in 1940 and over Northern France in 1941, but that I had to learn elsewhere too. All Bader would say was that the French Ambassador kissed him on both cheeks after pinning the medals on him.

He rarely, if ever, wears his uniform now. Once he did at a Battle of Britain Day at North Weald in 1949 with other famous pilots. Richard Dimbleby, noted BBC commentator, held a microphone in front of their faces and they spoke a few self-conscious words. A boy of about twelve who could hardly have remembered the battle slipped through the police barrier and walked up to them with an autograph book. He gave it to Dimbleby who signed it and the boy took the book again, innocently turned away from the pilots and walked back to the barrier. The war was really over.

People are too easily deceived by Bader's swashbuckling. Underneath is a generosity easily touched by other people's adversity so that he finds it difficult to walk past a beggar without wanting to help him. He lost a lot of money lending to old associates after the war. Now he prefers to give rather than to lend. He is still as much a man of extremes as ever, blowing hot or cold in enthusiasms, an intensely loyal friend, an uncompromising foe.

I once heard someone suggest that Thelma must have a difficult time with such a man. She doesn't. I have seldom seen a more devoted couple and Thelma is no door-mat. When she decides that enough is enough she waits with unerring timing for the right moment, and then when she sticks her toes in Douglas cannot budge her. Neither is afraid of crashing when they fly in the same aircraft because then they would go together. He will not let her fly without him because, though he does not fear death himself, he cannot bear the thought of those close to him dying. The one thing he fears is loneliness. He has beaten everything else, but that he will never conquer.

I agree with all those who class him as the best fighter leader and tactician of World War II (and one of the best pilots). Also, I know of no other fighter tactician so outstanding in other wars. But his main triumph is not his air fighting: that was only an episode that focused a world's attention on the greater victory he was achieving in showing humanity new horizons of courage, not in war, not only for the limbless, but in life. Sometimes I know he looks back at the war days with nostalgia though not with faint longing. One's life can carry memories without succumbing to them. At times I know he feels lurking regret that his great days are over, not realising that they will never leave him. I do not mean the aura of the past. Bader's war goes on unsung and unceasing to be won anew each day. He has been honoured for courage and skill in the air against the enemy, but no one yet has thought to honour him formally for his continuing fight which profits Man more than his battle deeds. He himself has not considered that as he should; his nature would welcome a more urgent and spectacular battle than the repetitive daily one.

I am no churchman, being unable to imagine God as the rigid Victorian patriarch that some dogmas suggest, but sometimes a vagrant thought intrudes that some hand not of this world may be using Bader as a vessel bearing another lesson for Man in his struggle. Otherwise, it seems odd that the man most fitted to lose his legs and rise above it should do so and reveal the new horizons by means of a war that tested the old ones. Or it may be coincidence, if a long one.

There was the strange intervention of Dingwall, helping him get through school to Cranwell. There was the meeting with Halahan at Air Ministry in 1939 that led to his being accepted for flying again. (That was an odd coincidence—he was summoned by mistake for a ground job.) There was the weird affair of having his right leg ripped away when he baled out. Had the artificial leg not torn away he would have landed on it and very likely been cruelly maimed. And had a real leg been caught he would have been dragged down to death.

How, then, to end this story of a man whose life is not ended. With its meaning? That is a task for a Shakespeare:

" There's nothing either good or bad but thinking makes it so."

THE END

INDEX

In this index B = Bader